23 Schriften aus der Fakultät Wirtschaftsinformatik
und Angewandte Informatik der Otto-Friedrich-
Universität Bamberg

Contributions of the Faculty Information Systems
and Applied Computer Sciences of the
Otto-Friedrich-University Bamberg

Schriften aus der Fakultät Wirtschaftsinformatik und Angewandte Informatik der Otto-Friedrich-Universität Bamberg

Contributions of the Faculty Information Systems and Applied Computer Sciences of the Otto-Friedrich-University Bamberg

Band 23

University
of Bamberg
Press
2016

Portability of Process-Aware and Service-Oriented Software

Evidence and Metrics

von Jörg Lenhard

University of Bamberg Press 2016

Bibliographische Information der Deutschen Nationalbibliothek
Die Deutsche Nationalbibliothek verzeichnet diese Publikation in der
Deutschen Nationalbibliographie; detaillierte bibliographische Informationen sind im In-
ternet über http://dnb.d-nb.de/ abrufbar.

Diese Arbeit hat der Fakultät Wirtschaftsinformatik und Angewandte Informatik
der Otto-Friedrich-Universität Bamberg als Dissertation vorgelegen.
Gutachter:
Prof. Dr. Schahram Dustdar, Technische Universität Wien
Prof. Dr. Guido Wirtz, Otto-Friedrich-Universität Bamberg
Tag der mündlichen Prüfung: 21. Januar 2016

Herstellung und Druck: docupoint, Magdeburg
Umschlaggestaltung: University of Bamberg Press, Anna Hitthaler

ISSN: 1867-7401
ISBN: 978-3-86309-399-0 (Druckausgabe)
eISBN: 978-3-86309-400-3 (Online-Ausgabe)
URN: urn:nbn:de:bvb:473-opus4-462521

Acknowledgments

First and foremost, I want to thank my supervisor, Prof Dr. Guido Wirtz, for giving me far-reaching freedom in the pursuit of my research interests. I deeply thank him for integrating me into the research work of his group already at times when I was still a Bachelor student. This gave me the opportunity to experience academic life and to learn how to do research early on. I am very grateful to Prof. Dr. Schahram Dustdar for reviewing my thesis as external examiner. Moreover, I am thankful to Prof. Dr. Sven Overhage and Prof. Dr. Gerald Lüttgen for critical feedback as members of my dissertation committee.

I am indebted to my Ph.D. colleagues Matthias Geiger, Simon Harrer, and Stefan Kolb. Not only have they provided an enjoyable working atmosphere, but also countless helpful discussions on all aspects of work. Moreover, we started several joint projects, which have influenced my dissertation. I want to thank Simon Harrer for his cooperation in the development of our conformance benchmarking tool betsy. Matthias Geiger helped sharpen my approach with his knowledge on BPMN and has also contributed to betsy. I am thankful to Stefan Kolb for his work on adapter synthesis in his master thesis, which I supervised, and for our cooperation in adapting my framework for measuring installability to Platform-as-a-Service environments. I owe thanks to many more Ph.D. students and friends of different subject areas of the faculty. Special appreciation goes to Cornelia Schecher. Being the intermediary between me and the travel expenses department, her support has been of tremendous help. Furthermore, I am obliged to all students of the University of Bamberg who have contributed to my work through software projects or theses, including Andreas Vorndran, Mathias Casar, Adrian Bazyli, Annalena Bentele, Christian Kremitzl, Lea-Louisa Maaß, Frederick Müller, Severin Sobetzko, and Matthias Weiß.

I am highly grateful to Prof. Dr. Claes Wohlin and the team of the Software Engineering Research Lab at the Blekinge Institute of Technology for welcoming me in their group during my Ph.D. studies. The impressions I got during my stay and the discussions with the members of the group have helped to shape my view on my research topic.

Last but not least, I am thankful to my family, specifically to my brother Wolfgang without whose guidance I might never have attended higher education and reached this level of expertise, and to my parents, who raised me to be an independent person. But most of all, I want to thank my beloved wife Regina. Her moral support during the dire parts of the thesis project, her minute help in my travel organization, and her ability to free my mind after long hours of work have been invaluable. Finally, while I am at it, I want to take this opportunity to thank Radiohead for the beautiful music they keep making.

Kurzfassung

Moderne Softwaresysteme werden zunehmend vernetzter und sind gezwungen durch Netzwerke über die Grenzen von Organisationen hinweg zusammenzuarbeiten. Die Entwicklung solcher verteilter Softwaresysteme wurde in den letzten Jahren durch die orthogonalen Trends der Dienstorientierung und des Prozessbewusstseins geformt. Diese Strömungen legen Wert auf technologische Neutralität, lose Kopplung, Unabhängigkeit von der Ausführungsplattform und Standorttransparenz. Ausführungsplatt-formen, die diese Trends unterstützen sowie Kontext und Querschnittsfunktionen für Anwendungen bereitstellen, werden *Engines* genannt.

Anwendungen und Engines werden durch Sprachstandards miteinander verknüpft. Eine Engine *implementiert* einen Standard. Wenn eine Anwendung konform zu einem Standard *implementiert ist*, kann sie auf der Engine ausgeführt werden. Ein wesentlicher Aspekt der Verwendung von Standards ist die *Portabilität* von Anwendungen. Portabilität, die Fähigkeit Software zwischen verschiedenen Ausführungsplattformen hin- und herbewegen zu können, ohne dass eine partielle oder völlige Neugestaltung notwendig wird, schützt vor der Abhängigkeit von Softwarelieferanten und ermöglicht es, eine Anwendung auf neuere Engines zu migrieren.

Das Aufkommen des Cloud Computings vereinfachte die Bereitstellung neuer und skalierbarer Ausführungsplattformen. Bereits existierende internationale Standards zur Implementierung dienstorientierter und prozessbewusster Software bezeichnen die Portabilität von standardisierten Artefakten als wichtiges Ziel, um einfache Plattformänderungen zu ermöglichen. Des Weiteren stellen sie plattformunabhängige Serialisierungsformate bereit, die die portable Implementierung von Anwendungen ermöglichen. Dennoch zeigt die Praxis, dass dienstorientierte und prozessbewusste Anwendungen heute in ihrer Portabilität begrenzt sind. Ein Grund dafür ist, dass Engines selten einen kompletten Sprachstandard implementieren und stattdessen Teile auslassen oder sich in ihrer Interpretation des Standards unterscheiden. Daraus folgt, dass sogar Anwendungen, die Portabilität für sich beanspruchen, da sie konform zu einem Standard sind, dies nicht erfüllen.

Die vorliegende Arbeit trägt auf zwei Ebenen zur Entwicklung von portabler dienstorientierter und prozessbewusster Software bei: Erstens liefert sie Belege für existierende Portabilitätsprobleme und die Unzulänglichkeit von Standards zur Sicherstellung von Softwareportabilität. Zweitens leitet sie einen neuartigen Bewertungsrahmen zur Quantifizierung von Portabilität ab und validiert diesen. Es wird eine Methodik zur Bewertung der Standardkonformität von Engines in Bezug auf einen Sprachstandard präsentiert und in einem vollautomatisierten Bewertungswerkzeug implementiert. Mehrere Testsuiten von Konformitätstests für zwei verschiedene Sprachen, die *Web Services Business Process Execution Language 2.0* und die *Business Process Model and Notation 2.0*, ermöglichen es, eine Vielfalt von Standardkonformitätsproblemen in gegenwärtigen Engines aufzudecken. So wird belegt, dass standardbasierte Anwendungsportabilität problematisch ist. Basierend auf diesen Ergebnissen leitet die Arbeit einen Bewertungsrahmen ab. Dieser Rahmen ist an die Methodik des *ISO/IEC Systems and software Quality Requirements and Evaluation* Standards, der neuesten Version des renommierten ISO/IEC Softwarequalitätsmodells und der dazugehörigen Messmethodik, angepasst. Das Qualitätsmodell unterteilt die Softwarequalitätscharakteristik *Portabilität* in die Subcharakteristiken *Installierbarkeit*, *Adaptierbarkeit* und *Ersetzbarkeit*. Jede dieser Charakteristiken stellt einen Teil des Bewertungsrahmens dar. Die vorliegende Arbeit behandelt jede Charakteristik mit einer separaten Analyse, der Ableitung von Metriken, einer Evaluation und Validierung. Es werden bestehende Metriken aus der Literatur diskutiert und neue Erweiterungen, spezifisch abgestimmt auf die Evaluation von dienstorientierter und prozessbewusster Software, abgeleitet. Vorgeschlagene Metriken werden formal definiert und durch einen informalen sowie einen formalen Validierungsrahmen validiert. Des Weiteren wird die Berechnung der Metriken prototypisch implementiert. Diese Implementierung wird genutzt um die Leistungsfähigkeit der Metriken in Experimenten auf Basis großer Softwarebibliotheken, die von öffentlichen und quelloffenen Softwarearchiven erworben wurden, zu evaluieren.

Zusammenfassend liefert die vorliegende Dissertation Belege dafür, dass gegenwärtige Standards und deren Implementierungen nicht ausreichen um die Portabilität von dienstorientierter und prozessbewusster Software sicherzustellen. Darüber hinaus schlägt sie einen Bewertungsrahmen zur Messung von Portabilität vor und validiert sowie evaluiert diesen praktisch.

Abstract

Modern software systems are becoming increasingly integrated and are required to operate over organizational boundaries through networks. The development of such distributed software systems has been shaped by the orthogonal trends of service-orientation and process-awareness. These trends put an emphasis on technological neutrality, loose coupling, independence from the execution platform, and location transparency. Execution platforms supporting these trends provide context and cross-cutting functionality to applications and are referred to as *engines*.

Applications and engines interface via language standards. The engine *implements* a standard. If an application *is implemented* in conformance to this standard, it can be executed on the engine. A primary motivation for the usage of standards is the *portability* of applications. Portability, the ability to move software among different execution platforms without the necessity for full or partial reengineering, protects from vendor lock-in and enables application migration to newer engines.

The arrival of cloud computing has made it easy to provision new and scalable execution platforms. To enable easy platform changes, existing international standards for implementing service-oriented and process-aware software name the portability of standardized artifacts as an important goal. Moreover, they provide platform-independent serialization formats that enable the portable implementation of applications. Nevertheless, practice shows that service-oriented and process-aware applications today are limited with respect to their portability. The reason for this is that engines rarely implement a complete standard, but leave out parts or differ in the interpretation of the standard. As a consequence, even applications that claim to be portable by conforming to a standard might not be so.

This thesis contributes to the development of portable service-oriented and process-aware software in two ways: Firstly, it provides evidence for the existence of portability issues and the insufficiency of standards for guaranteeing software portability. Secondly, it derives and validates a novel measurement framework for quantifying portability. We present a methodology for benchmarking the conformance of engines to a language standard and implement it in a fully automated benchmarking tool. Several test suites of conformance tests for two different languages, the *Web Services Business Process Execution Language 2.0* and the *Business Process Model and Notation 2.0*, allow to uncover a variety of standard conformance issues in existing engines. This provides evidence that the standard-based portability of applications is a real issue. Based on these results, this thesis derives a measurement framework for portability. The framework is aligned to the *ISO/IEC Systems and software Quality Requirements and Evaluation* method, the recent revision of the renowned ISO/IEC software quality model and measurement methodology. This quality model separates the software quality characteristic of *portability* into the subcharacteristics of *installability*, *adaptability*, and *replaceability*. Each of these characteristics forms one part of the measurement framework. This thesis targets each characteristic with a separate analysis, metrics derivation, evaluation, and validation. We discuss existing metrics from the body of literature and derive new extensions specifically tailored to the evaluation of service-oriented and process-aware software. Proposed metrics are defined formally and validated theoretically using an informal and a formal validation framework. Furthermore, the computation of the metrics has been prototypically implemented. This implementation is used to evaluate metrics performance in experiments based on large scale software libraries obtained from public open source software repositories.

In summary, this thesis provides evidence that contemporary standards and their implementations are not sufficient for enabling the portability of process-aware and service-oriented applications. Furthermore, it proposes, validates, and practically evaluates a framework for measuring portability.

Contents

Contents

List of Figures

List of Figures

List of Tables

List of Tables

List of Listings

List of Abbreviations

API   Application Programming Interface

B2Bi   Business-to-Business integration

BPEL   Web Services Business Process Execution Language

BPM   Business Process Management

BPMN   Business Process Model and Notation

BPMS   Business Process Management System

CDDL   Common Development and Distribution License

CI   Continuous Integration

CSS   Cascading Style Sheets

ESB   Enterprise Service Bus

GPL   GNU General Public License

GUI   Graphical User Interface

HATEOAS   Hypermedia as the engine of application state

HTML   Hypertext Markup Language

HTTP   Hypertext Transfer Protocol

HTTPS   Hypertext Transfer Protocol Secure

IEC   International Electrotechnical Commission

IoT   Internet of Things

ISO   International Organization for Standardization

JSON   JavaScript Object Notation

LGPL   GNU Lesser General Public License

OASIS   Organization for the Advancement of Structured Information Standards

OMG   Object Management Group

List of Abbreviations

PaaS	Platform-as-a-Service
PAIS	Process-Aware Information Systems
REST	Representational State Transfer
SMTP	Simple Mail Transfer Protocol
SOA	Service-Oriented Architecture
SOAP	SOAP
SOC	Service-Oriented Computing
SQuaRE	Systems and software Quality Requirements and Evaluation
TAR	Transition Adjacency Relation
TOSCA	Topology and Orchestration Specification for Cloud Applications
URI	Uniform Resource Identifier
W3C	World Wide Web Consortium
WADL	Web Application Description Language
WCP	Workflow Control-Flow Pattern
WF	Windows Workflow Foundation
WSDL	Web Service Description Language
WS-I	Web Services Interoperability Organization
XML	Extensible Markup Language
XPDL	XML Process Definition Language
XSD	XML Schema Definition
XSL	Extensible Stylesheet Language
XSLT	Extensible Stylesheet Language Transformation
YAWL	Yet Another Workflow Language

Part I.

Background and Problem Identification

1. Introduction

In today's networked society, basically any computing system is a distributed one. The advantages of distribution are well-understood and covered in established text books, e.g., [1,2]. However, distributed systems face a multitude of challenges in practice and have to cope with ever changing hardware and software environments. System size and the level of system interconnection increase [3]. At the same time, systems are being revolutionized by new technological trends and devices at an accelerating rate. Examples of such trends are process-awareness [4], service-orientation [5], cloud computing [6], or the internet of things (IoT) [7]. Not only these paradigm shifts, but also fierce market competition, force enterprises to evolve their computing systems with respect to their hard- and software.

On the architectural level, distributed software systems are separated into custom-purpose application software and general-purpose middleware, such as application servers or execution engines. The middleware provides cross-cutting functionality based on which custom applications are executed [8]. Additionally, it offers standardized interfaces to application software, which enables the transparent replacement of specific middleware products with newer and more powerful versions. Especially the arrival of cloud platforms has opened up new opportunities for gaining performance or scalability improvements by switching the platform or middleware on which an application is executed [6]. Put differently, application software can be *ported* or *migrated* between different middleware products and platforms that offer the same standardized interfaces to leverage a plenitude of advantages [9]. This application *portability* is an enabler for software evolution and the focus of this work.

One set of architectural and technological trends that favor simpler migration of distributed application software is formed by *Service-Oriented Computing* (SOC) and *Service-Oriented Architecture* (SOA). SOC is a computing paradigm that calls for the construction of distributed software as sets of services instead of monolithic applications [5]. Services are basic units of computation that support rapid and low-cost development of heterogeneous distributed systems. They put an emphasis on technological neutrality, interfaces, and loosely-coupled message-based interaction [10,11]. Alongside other benefits, these principles facilitate the exchange of underlying middleware infrastructure. SOA denotes the architectural paradigm with which service-oriented systems are developed. Service-oriented systems have become ubiquitous today. SOC is an enabler for the current top technology trend of cloud computing [12,13] and the paradigms can be combined to much benefit [14]. Initially being closely tied to *Web Services* technologies [15], SOC is evolving towards different architectural styles, such as *Representational State Transfer* (REST) [16], or *microservices* [17]. The emphasis on technological neutrality, interfaces, and loose coupling not only improves portability, but also enables the *composition* of services [5, 18]. Higher-level services with an added value can be built on the basis of other services, by defining data- and control-dependencies between their invocation in a process-driven manner [19]. The task of service composition introduces another set of trends marked by *Process-Aware Information Systems* (PAIS) [4, 20, 21]. The combination of the principles of service-orientation and process-awareness in executable software artifacts is the object of study in this thesis.

Process-aware information systems utilize explicit notions of processes, often captured by representations of processes in *process models*, for designing, implementing, and executing software [4, 20, 21]. Put differently, PAIS represent software systems that are *aware* of the processes that underlie the software execution. The use of PAIS introduces a variety of advantages for system development [4, pp. 7 f.]. Examples are i) easier communication among the different stakeholders of the system, due to the explicit representation of a process, ii) easier changes to the execution logic of a system, by adapting the positioning of activities, instead of having to recode parts of the system, or iii) a better integration with verification and validation tools that can work with explicit process representations instead of code. Moreover, process-awareness has frequently been found to reduce cost and improve product quality [22]. The utilization of PAIS is not limited to service composition, but extends to a variety of subject areas [23]. Basically, the term can be seen as an umbrella for *Business Process Management* (BPM) systems [20] and workflow management systems [24]. The explicit notion of a process is fundamental to PAIS and has led to the definition of numerous notations, standards, and languages for representing processes [25]. A subset of these notations and languages, e.g., [26–28], provide built-in facilities for supporting service composition and aim at the direct execution of process models on dedicated *process engines* [20, Sect. 3.1.1]. Engines serve as a layer of abstraction for process execution and, in the terms of a distributed system, an engine represents the middleware, whereas a process model is the application. Referring to the migration scenario described in the first paragraph, process models can be ported among engines to leverage the benefits of newer and better engines.

Application portability depends on standardization and standard conformance [29]. In theory, if processes are implemented in conformance to a standardized notation, which corresponds to the interface offered by different process engines, they should be portable to any of those engines. This independence of format and execution environment protects from vendor lock-in and is a major design principle for process languages [30]. Notable international process standards, such as the *Business Process Model and Notation* (BPMN) [26], the *Web Services Business Process Execution Language* (BPEL) [27], or the *XML Process Definition Language* (XPDL) [31], name the portability of process models as an important goal. For instance, BPEL claims to define *"a portable execution format for business processes"* [27, p. 7] and BPMN states that its goal *"is to enable portability of Process definitions"* [26, p. 20]. Since the provisioning of new execution environments is becoming increasingly easy and cheap with the help of cloud platforms, leveraging the benefits of quick environmental changes is becoming more and more realistic. This is emphasized by recent work on application portability in cloud environments, e.g., [32–34], or the advent of cloud-based process management systems [35]. Standardization initiatives for cloud application portability, such as the *Topology and Orchestration Specification for Cloud Applications* (TOSCA) [36], make use of process standards such as BPEL or BPMN for parts of their specification, precisely because these standards are assumed to provide portability. TOSCA states that "*the specification relies on existing languages like BPMN or BPEL. Relying on existing standards in this space facilitates portability*" [36, Sect. 3.1]. In the case of TOSCA "*portability is inherited from the workflow language and engines used*" [37, p. 83].

Despite the assumption that contemporary standards provide portability, the porting of process-aware applications based on language standards faces severe limitations in practice. The engines that implement international standards rarely support the complete standard specification, but omit parts or differ in the interpretation of the standard, which hampers porting in practice [38, 39]. For instance, a recent survey by DZone research [40] identified *standards interpretation differences* as the highest rating obstacle to cloud integration. An analogy, which many Internet users experience occasionally, can be observed for the Hypertext Markup Language (HTML) standard [41], Cascading Style Sheets (CSS) [42], and web browsers. HTML and CSS are used to define the structure and layout of web pages that should be rendered identically with any web browser. However, browsers do not necessarily support all parts of HTML and CSS and may even support custom extensions. As a result, web pages might be rendered differently in different browsers and also web applications might behave differently [43, 44]. The same problem applies to the software in focus here. Standard-compliant process models that can be executed on one engine might work only partly on another one. In summary, it is not possible to solely depend on a standard for achieving application portability, the implementation conformance of engines is also critical [45].

As a result of standard conformance issues, the direct porting of process-aware and service-oriented software, i.e., software implemented in dedicated languages [26–28, 31], currently faces many challenges. Consequently, many of the advantages and benefits of platform and engine migration cannot be leveraged and users are frequently locked into the engines they operate. This situation calls for research on the portability of process-aware and service-oriented application software. Work on application portability that takes current software environments into account is only in its beginning [32, 33, 46]. For instance, in the area of cloud platforms, standards are lacking and approaches for improving portability mainly aim to streamline different cloud platforms through the definition of new standards, open libraries or services, or model-driven mappings to specific platforms [46]. In the area of process-aware and service-oriented software, standards are already in existence. These standards can be used as-is to approach the problem of portability, instead of defining a new standard or model.

From a software engineering point of view, portability is a quality characteristic of software. Hence, software quality improvement techniques can be applied to enhance the portability of service-oriented and process-aware software. A classic quality improvement technique, and a prerequisite for many others, is *software measurement* [47, Chap. 1]. This technique deals with the quantification of software characteristics, such as portability, through software metrics. When applied in the context of agile techniques for software quality improvement, such as continuous inspection [48, 49], software measurement can lead to quality improvement [48, 50–52]. Software portability has long been recognized as a central characteristic of software quality and is part of many software quality models, e.g., [53–60]. Nevertheless, only little work on measuring and quantifying portability is available. One of the most renowned software quality models is defined by the International Organization for Standardization (ISO)/International Electrotechnical Commission (IEC) series of standards [53, 57, 58]. The quality model is currently being revised in the context of the ISO/IEC *Systems and software Quality Requirements and Evaluation* (SQuaRE) method [53] for software quality measurement. This framework subdivides portability into several further quality characteristics, namely *installability*, *adaptability*, and *replaceability*. The reasoning behind this classification is that for porting an application, first a new execution environment has to be installed. Thereafter, the application can either be ported directly without modification or might need to be adapted or replaced in part or whole.

This thesis addresses the portability of service-oriented and process-aware software by analyzing the implementation conformance of process engines and developing a measurement framework for portability aligned to the ISO/IEC SQuaRE method. The following sections describe the research questions addressed in this work, outline its structure, and provide an overview of the contributions made.

1.1. Outline of the Thesis

The research objective of this work is:

i) *to investigate and gather evidence for standard-conformance induced portability issues that exist in service-oriented and process-aware software,* and

ii) *to design and evaluate a software measurement framework for quantifying portability as a means of coping with portability issues.*

On the one hand, this poses a number of research challenges, in terms of concept and model development and formalization. On the other hand, it presents a number of engineering challenges, in terms of prototype implementation and practical evaluation. We address the research objectives in a number of research questions, which are detailed in the following Sect. 1.1.1. Thereafter, Sect. 1.1.2 describes the methodology used to answer these questions and relates the methodology and questions to the structure of the thesis.

1.1.1. Research Questions

Although application portability is of high concern in the area of process-aware and service-oriented software, and a design principle of process languages [30], practical obstacles to porting applications are uncataloged. A number of studies, e.g., [38, 39, 61], report on standard-conformance induced portability issues, but focus on singular language aspects or provide no comprehensive evaluation of several standard implementations. Such a systematic study or benchmark that provides a comprehensive evaluation of the support for the feature set of a standard provided by several standard implementations is still lacking. Therefore, the first step in this thesis is to investigate the current state of portability of process-aware and service-oriented software. This is captured in the first research question:

> **Research Question 1:**
>
> *What is the current state of portability of service-oriented and process-aware software?*

It is a popular conception that all that is necessary to build portable software is to implement an application in conformance to an international standard. If an application conforms to a standard, it can be executed on any conforming implementation of that standard. As a result, the availability of a standardized serialization format for an application is often sufficient to silence a debate regarding its portability. This forms a clear advantage for the implementers of a standard over the users of an implementation. Support for a standard can be easily claimed due to a lack of certification authorities.

As a consequence, to investigate the portability of service-oriented and process-aware software, it is necessary to look at the implementation conformance of existing execution environments [45]. Only if these environments conform to the standards they claim to implement, the porting of applications is feasible. For this reason, we divide the first research question into two subquestions. The first subquestion challenges the assumption that the existence of standards is sufficient:

> **Research Question 1.1:**
>
> *Are current standards and their implementations sufficient for enabling portability?*

We address this question by benchmarking the implementation conformance of a range of engines for service-oriented and process-aware applications. The results of the benchmark demonstrate that huge differences in standard conformance are the norm. Hence, the change of an engine is problematic.

Since application portability is not given per se, it becomes necessary to examine what features typically hinder or reduce it. It can be expected that certain programming concepts or constructs are more problematic with respect to portability than others. For instance, constructs related to parallel execution might be less portable than constructs related to sequential execution. We address this in the second subquestion:

Research Question 1.2:

What are existing portability issues and their implications?

If portability is problematic, the advantages of quick environmental changes cannot be leveraged and system evolution is complicated. Therefore, the improvement of the portability of service-oriented and process-aware software becomes a relevant research goal. As a first step in this direction, we propose to apply techniques of software quality improvement, in particular software measurement and continuous inspection [49]. We discuss how such techniques work and why they have the potential to improve software quality, or, with respect to this thesis, to improve software portability. This leads to the question if and how portability can be measured, the second main research question:

Research Question 2:

Is it feasible to measure the portability of service-oriented and process-aware software?

A large body of work on software quality frameworks and models exists, e.g., [53–59, 62]. However, portability is not typically the focus of software quality evaluations, in particular for service-oriented and process-aware software. More frequently, performance-related quality characteristics, such as throughput or latency [63, 64], or application complexity, cohesion, and coupling [65, 66] are the target of evaluation. As a result, little work exists on measuring and assessing the portability of software in general, and of service-oriented and process-aware software in particular.

To evaluate the feasibility of measuring portability, we select a software quality model, based on a survey of several quality models, as foundational model for the design of a measurement framework. The model selected is the ISO/IEC SQuaRE model [53]. This model provides the common thread for the second part of this thesis. In this model, the quality characteristic of portability is not defined as a stand-alone and isolated characteristic of software quality, but as a conjunction of a number of quality characteristics, notably *installability*, *replaceability*, and *adaptability*. The model calls for the quantification of each of these characteristics when measuring portability. A weighting of the characteristics is not part of the model and they are considered as equally important. As a result, we address each one by a set of dedicated software metrics, which, in combination, form the measurement framework. The derivation, validation, and evaluation of these metrics forms a separate research question for each quality characteristic, each of which is dealt with in a separate chapter of the thesis.

The starting point is the *direct portability* of an application, without the need for adaptation or replacement. This aspect is addressed in research question 2.1:

Research Question 2.1:

What are suitable metrics for measuring portability?

Regardless of whether software can be ported directly, or has to be adapted or replaced, it has to be installed into the new target execution environment. Therefore, research question 2.2 focuses on the measurement of installability.

Research Question 2.2:

What are suitable metrics for measuring installability?

Although desirable, it can hardly be expected that software can always be ported without any modification. Instead, nonportable parts of an application must be adapted for the new target environment. The ease of this depends on the adaptability of the software and should also be quantified. Adaptability is addressed by research question 2.3.

Research Question 2.3:

What are suitable metrics for measuring adaptability?

Finally, if an application cannot be ported directly and it is hard to adapt, the remaining option is to replace it as a whole. However, this can only be done if it is replaceable by another piece of software. This can be determined by evaluating its replaceability, which is the focus of research question 2.4.

Research Question 2.4:

What are suitable metrics for measuring replaceability?

To maintain scientific rigour when answering the research questions we use a structured methodology and top-down approach to metrics definition and evaluation. As indicated above, this leads to the structuring of the remainder of this work. The methodology and structuring are the topic of the following subsection.

1.1.2. Research Methodology and Structure

The research methodology used to answer the research questions and the structure of the thesis is depicted in Fig. 1.1. The center of the figure shows the methodology

9

1. Introduction

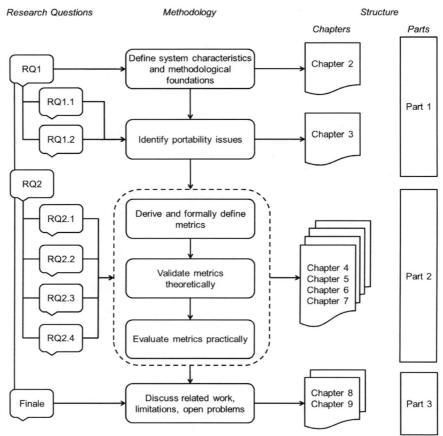

Figure 1.1.: Map of the Thesis

applied and the different steps of the work. Furthermore, it describes how the different steps of the methodology relate to the research questions posed in the previous section, i.e., it explains through which activities the questions are answered. Finally, the figure also shows the relation of the steps in the methodology to chapters of this thesis and explains where the answers to the different research questions can be found. In the following, we explain each of the different methodological steps and their relation to the research questions and thesis structure.

To enhance the readability of the thesis, we streamlined the structure of the different chapters, in particular of Part II. There, all chapters follow a certain template when it comes to metrics definition and validation. The application of the same template for every chapter is intended to facilitate reading comprehension. Moreover, we added margin notes to this section and the remaining parts of the work to guide the reader throughout the document.

System character-istics We begin by defining the characteristics of the systems that are the objects of study and lay the methodological foundations. The central characteristics of service-oriented and process-aware software that are relevant to the topic of this work are identified through a discussion of the literature. This includes the foundational theory and technological background of, both, process-aware and service-oriented systems, as well as a closer description of their synthesis. We explain prevalent architectural styles of service-oriented systems in Sect. 2.1, i.e., Web Services [15], REST [16], and microservices [17]. The characteristics of process-aware information systems are described in Sect. 2.2, along with a summary of the languages used in the practical part of this work, i.e., BPEL 2.0 [27] and BPMN 2.0 [26]. Sect. 2.2 also explains how process-awareness and service-orientation can be combined for the task of service composition. This forms the content of the first part of Chap. 2. Thereafter, Sect. 2.3 provides an overview over several software quality models, which is the basis for the selection of the ISO/IEC SQuaRE model [53]. We take a closer look at the relation between portability and standard conformance, and motivate the necessity of evaluating it. Furthermore, we describe the advantages and potentials of software quality measurement, i.e., the reason why we design a measurement framework for portability. Finally, we discuss the theoretical foundations for defining, validating, and evaluating software metrics in Sect. 2.4 and outline the architecture of our prototypic implementation of a software metrics suite. In summary, Chap. 2 lays the theory for answering research question 1 and its subquestions and presents the approach for answering research question 2 and related subquestions.

Research questions 1, 1.1, and 1.2, regarding the current state of application *Portabil-ity issue identifica-tion* portability and the sufficiency of standards, are conclusively addressed in Chap. 3. This chapter demonstrates that the portability of process-aware and service-oriented software is a real practical problem and provides evidence for it. We begin by listing requirements for a standard conformance benchmark in Sect. 3.1. Following this, we describe the design of the benchmark, including the systems under test, the benchmarking tool and the benchmarking test suites in Sect. 3.2. Through the benchmark, a variety of problems can be identified and an overview of the current state of the art can be given, thereby advancing the state of knowledge. These results are discussed in Sect. 3.3.

Each of the chapters of Part II, Chap. 4 to 7, focuses on a particular part of *Metrics deriva-tion and evalua-tion* the measurement framework, as prescribed by the software quality model defined in the ISO/IEC SQuaRE methodology [53], and derives, defines, validates, and evaluates a set of metrics. Each of the chapters uses a similar structure for defining and validating the metrics, following common metrics derivation processes, like proposed in, e.g., [67,68]:

1. Define the goal of the measurement, by specifying its purpose, the objects of study, the quality focus and context, and the viewpoint taken.

2. Specify the questions to be answered by the metrics and experimental hypotheses.

3. Define and validate the metrics.

In each of these chapters, we first state and motivate the measurement goal as defined above and the question the metrics should answer. Thereafter, we derive and formally define a number of metrics based on the existing literature and the problem domain and state their type and scale. This is followed by their validation according to the validation approach described in Sect. 2.4. In particular, this includes their theoretical validation, formally and informally, with respect to measurement theory [69] and construct validity [70]. Thereafter, we perform a practical evaluation, as described in Sect. 2.4.3. Alongside the practical evaluation, we also state and evaluate a number of hypotheses. Chap. 4 focuses on portability, Chap. 5 on installability, and Chap. 6 on adaptability. For replaceability, dealt with in Chap. 7, we deviate slightly from this methodology. The reason for this is that a plethora of metrics for measuring replaceability is already available and has been validated theoretically and practically. To avoid the duplication of this work, we first perform a review of and a selection from the body of existing metrics. Thereafter, we propose an extension to their computation tailored to the focus of this thesis, and evaluate this extension.

Discus-sion of limita-tions The thesis is concluded by a discussion of related work in Chap. 8 and a summary of contributions in Chap. 9. The final chapter also points out limitations of our approach and open problems that offer areas of future work.

1.2. Contribution

The contribution of this thesis is twofold. On the one hand, it substantiates evidence for portability issues that do exist in service-oriented and process-aware software and the insufficiency of standardization for guaranteeing application portability. On the other hand, it provides a novel approach for evaluating portability that has been validated, both theoretically and practically:

1. *Evidence for Portability Issues:* We provide a detailed evaluation of the standard conformance of a total of eleven process engines. This includes open source and proprietary engines for the two languages, BPEL 2.0 [27] and BPMN 2.0 [26]. The evaluation uncovers a variety of standard conformance issues, which result in portability issues. This advances the state of knowledge. We identify areas of functionality that are particularly problematic with respect to portability. Moreover, we investigate the impact that standard conformance issues have on the expressiveness of the language dialects supported by the engines with the means of workflow control-flow patterns [71]. The benchmarking methodology we propose and implement is independent of the respective process languages and engines and, hence, can be extended easily. The benchmark is also fully repeatable and the data we discuss can be reproduced by other scientists.

2. *Measurement Framework:* The measurement framework we propose is comprehensive with respect to the ISO/IEC SQuaRE method [53] and specifically tailored to the evaluation of process-aware and service-oriented software. The framework is new and has been validated theoretically with respect to measurement theory [69] and construct validity [70]. The feasibility of

the application of the framework is demonstrated by a prototypic implementation. This implementation is used for the evaluation of a large set of realistic applications gathered from public software repositories in three separate experiments.

Parts of these contributions have been submitted to scientific forums at different stages throughout the dissertation project. This resulted in the publication of a number of peer-reviewed workshop and conference papers, a book chapter, and a number of non-peer-reviewed technical reports. The thesis is partly based on these publications and we state at the beginning of a chapter or section, if this is the case. In the context of this work, the following papers have been published or have been accepted for publication:

1. Lenhard J., Wirtz G.: *Building Orchestrations in B2Bi – The Case of BPEL 2.0 and BPMN 2.0*, Proceedings of the 4th Central-European Workshop on Services and their Composition (ZEUS), Bamberg, Germany, February 23 –24, 2012, [72]

2. Harrer S., Lenhard J.: *Betsy – A BPEL Engine Test System*, Bamberger Beiträge zur Wirtschaftsinformatik und Angewandten Informatik Nr. 90, Bamberg University, July 2012. ISSN 0937-3349, [73]

3. Harrer S., Lenhard J., Wirtz G.: *BPEL Conformance in Open Source Engines*, Proceedings of the 5th IEEE International Conference on Service-Oriented Computing and Applications (SOCA), Taipei, Taiwan, December 17-19, 2012, [74]

4. Kolb S., Lenhard J., Wirtz G.: *Bridging the Heterogeneity of Orchestrations – A Petri Net-based Integration of BPEL and Windows Workflow*, Proceedings of the 5th IEEE International Conference on Service-Oriented Computing and Applications (SOCA), Taipei, Taiwan, December 17-19, 2012, [75]

5. Lenhard J., Wirtz G.: *Detecting Portability Issues in Model-Driven BPEL Mappings*, Proceedings of the 25th International Conference on Software Engineering and Knowledge Engineering (SEKE), Boston, Massachusetts, USA, Knowledge Systems Institute, June 27 - 29, 2013, [76]

6. Lenhard J., Wirtz G.: *Measuring the Portability of Executable Service-Oriented Processes*, Proceedings of the 17th IEEE International EDOC Conference, Vancouver, Canada, September 9 - 13, 2013, *Awarded Best Student Conference Paper in Service Science*, [77]

7. Harrer S., Lenhard J., Wirtz G.: *Open Source versus Proprietary Software in Service-Orientation: The Case of BPEL Engines*, Proceedings of the 11th International Conference on Service Oriented Computing (ICSOC), Berlin, Germany, December 2 - 5, 2013, [78]

8. Lenhard J., Harrer S., Wirtz G.: *Measuring the Installability of Service Orchestrations Using the SQuaRE Method*, Proceedings of the 6th IEEE

International Conference on Service-Oriented Computing and Applications (SOCA), Kauai, Hawaii, USA, December 16 - 18, 2013, *Awarded Best Conference Paper*, [79]

9. Lenhard J.: *Towards Quantifying the Adaptability of Executable BPMN Processes*, Proceedings of the 6th Central-European Workshop on Services and their Composition (ZEUS), Potsdam, Germany, February 20 - 21, 2014, [80]

10. Harrer S., Lenhard J., Wirtz G., van Lessen T.: *Towards Uniform BPEL Engine Management in the Cloud*, Proceedings of the CloudCycle14 Workshop, Stuttgart, Germany, September 22, 2014, [81]

11. Geiger M., Harrer S., Lenhard J., Casar M., Vordran A., Wirtz G.: *BPMN Conformance in Open Source Engines*, Proceedings of the 9th International IEEE Symposium on Service-Oriented System Engineering (SOSE), San Francisco Bay, USA, March 30 - April 3, 2015, [82].

12. Lenhard J., Geiger M., Wirtz G.: *On the Measurement of Design-Time Adaptability for Process-Based Systems*, Proceedings of the 9th International IEEE Symposium on Service-Oriented System Engineering (SOSE), San Francisco Bay, USA, March 30 - April 3, 2015, [83]

13. Kolb S., Lenhard J., Wirtz G.: *Application Migration Effort in the Cloud – The Case of Cloud Platforms*, Proceedings of the 8th IEEE International Conference on Cloud Computing (CLOUD), New York, USA, June 27 - July 2, 2015, [84]

14. Lenhard J.: *Improving Process Portability through Metrics and Continuous Inspection*, in Advances in Intelligent Process-Aware Information Systems, M. Reichert, R. Oberhauser, and G. Grambow, Eds., Springer-Verlag, Germany, to appear, [85]

The experimental parts of the work resulted in several software tools and proof-of-concept prototypes. The tools which the author built in the context of this work, or significantly contributed to as a core developer, are:

betsy: *The BPEL/BPMN Engine Test System* is a conformance benchmarking tool for BPEL and BPMN engines. It implements the benchmark for standard conformance assessment discussed in Chap. 3 and is used to uncover contemporary portability issues. It is available at `https://github.com/uniba-dsg/betsy`[1].

bpp: *The BPEL Portability Profile* is a tool for detecting portability issues in the code of BPEL process definitions. It is used in the computation of portability metrics and to provide a classification of model-driven mappings of several specification languages to BPEL. It is available at `https://github.com/uniba-dsg/bpp`.

---

[1]All links in this thesis have been last accessed on February 24, 2016.

prope: *The **PRO**cess-aware information systems **P**ortability m**E**trics suite* is the proof-of-concept metrics suite that bundles the computation of the metrics defined in this thesis. It is a static analyzer that *probes* for portability issues in application code and highlights these issues by computing metrics. The tool also includes the bpp tool described above as a library, which nevertheless is also maintained as a separate project, because it is referenced and used in several research papers. Prope is available at `https://uniba-dsg.github.io/prope/`.

All tool development was performed as open source and, therefore, all pieces of software that are used for the experimentation in this thesis are publicly available. All are free to use and are licensed with either LGPL or MIT license. These tools can be used to reproduce the results presented in this thesis. In parts, the tools also include the scripts used to perform the statistical computations and significance tests presented in this work.

2. Theoretical and Technological Foundations

The design, implementation, and usage of service-oriented and process-aware software has received considerable attention by the software industry and academics alike. Due to the diversity and interests of these groups, there is a lack of common consensus with respect to the meaning of many terms in the area. In this preliminary chapter, we synthesize these views and define the terms used throughout this work. To begin, we define the term *process-aware and service-oriented software* as follows:

> ### Definition 1: Process-Aware and Service-Oriented Software
>
> *Process-aware and service-oriented software* is software that combines service-oriented and process-aware design principles and programming concepts, for the implementation of executable programs.
>
> It manifests itself in software applications that are written in languages dedicated to the combination of service-orientation and process-awareness, i. e., languages for implementing service compositions based on process models that are executed on process engines.

This term is not commonly used in the literature. We introduce it in this work to stress that our focus lies on *executable software artifacts* and not on conceptual models or formal abstractions. Emphasizing the term *software* is supposed to eliminate the overloading of the term *process model*, which is used to describe many artifacts in the diverse literature of service-oriented and process-aware systems, including executable applications and abstract models [23]. To make sure that our notion can be properly positioned in the existing literature, we explain its relation to other common notions in the area, such as service compositions [19], orchestrations, or choreographies [86], in the respective parts of this chapter.

Structure of the chapter We begin by explaining the nature and technological foundations of service-oriented software and systems in Sect. 2.1 and of process-aware information systems and applications in Sect. 2.2. We describe why process languages are particularly useful for combining service-orientation and process-awareness and briefly discuss predominant languages. Software applications implemented in these languages are used in the practical parts of this work. This leads to the definition of software portability in Sect. 2.3, including a discussion of contemporary software quality models. There, we also describe how software quality measurement, the approach taken here, can help to improve portability. Finally, we explain the theoretical foundations of developing, validating, and evaluating a metrics framework, and outline the functioning of our prototypic implementation of this framework. Taken together, this chapter lays the theoretical and methodological foundations for answering the research questions specified in the introduction.

2.1. Service-Oriented Systems

Service-oriented systems are systems that use services as the fundamental primitive of computing [5]. On a conceptual level, services are platform-independent and self-contained applications that offer self-describing and composable parts of functionality via uniform and technologically neutral interfaces and interact in a loosely-coupled fashion via message exchanges [87–89]. Initially being closely tied to Web Services technologies [90], services can be seen as the next evolutionary step in distributed computing originating from component-based systems [91, 92]. In the following sections, we discuss the central characteristics of services and service-oriented applications, and the different architectural styles and technologies that are used for their implementation.

2.1.1. Characteristics of Service-Oriented Systems

The rise of service-oriented systems and SOAs began at the turn of the millennium. Though our focus in this work lies on technical reasons for their usage, SOAs have also been found to provide economic benefits [93–95].

Since the conception of SOC a lot of technological advances have been made and different styles, paradigms, and approaches for implementing service-oriented software have emerged, i. e., Web Services [15], REST [16], and microservices [17]. SOA and the respective paradigms and styles have triggered industry hypes [96]. As a result, their boundaries are somewhat blurred [97] and it is hard to give a uniform definition of the term *service*. Nevertheless, foundational articles [5, 87, 89, 98], formalizations of the concept [88], agreements among experts [11], and industry reference models [99] share a number of characteristics. Here, we build on these works and define the term service as follows:

> **Definition 2: Service**
>
> A *service* is a platform-independent and interface-based computing facility that:
> - is described in a uniform, technology-neutral manner,
> - allows for loosely-coupled message-based interaction,
> - is transparent with respect to its location, and
> - encapsulates an atomic unit of functionality.

Technical benefits of services The emphasis on these properties offer a variety of benefits for the implementation of distributed computing systems [89, 98, 100, 101]. The focus on technological neutrality and platform independence leads to a higher level of intrinsic interoperability of software components and a higher degree of independence from vendor lock-in and portability of software artifacts. In [10], portability of service implementations is also considered as an architectural principle. Loose coupling and message-based interaction enables easier software reuse and allows for a quicker adaption of single services, whereas location transparency makes it easier to replace services in the face of failures. Finally, the focus on atomic units of functionality ensures the single responsibility principle [102].

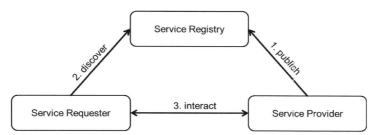

Figure 2.1.: Service Interaction Framework – adapted from [90, p. 69]

The term SOA denotes the architectural paradigm for structuring systems of services [5]. In its core, a SOA is a form of client server architecture. The general interaction framework is depicted in Fig. 2.1. This scenario includes three parties: the *service provider*, the *service requester*, and the *service registry*. The service provider offers the service functionality, described in a uniform, platform-independent, and technology-neutral manner. The functionality is accessible via loosely-coupled message-based interaction and the service provider publishes the description of this functionality to a service registry. This registry provides search engine functionality and enables a service requester to discover the service description and the location of the service provider. Based on this information, requester and provider can interact with each other via message passing. This principle underlies any service-oriented system, although in practice the functionality of service provider and service registry often coincide. A SOA is implemented through a variety of service providers and requesters that interact with each other. To maintain loose-coupling among service providers and requesters, their private inner structure is not considered from an architectural point of view. In a SOA, the interest lies on publicly visible behavior, i.e., communication relationships and sequences of message exchanges among providers and requesters. This *observable behavior* of services is the decisive driver for the architectural properties of a SOA, such as coupling or complexity [65,66].

More advanced service-oriented systems can be formed by composing the functionality of several service providers by means of message exchanges with these providers to construct value-added compound services [19]. This forms the second layer of a SOA, as depicted in the so-called SOA pyramid in Fig. 2.2. This kind of loosely-coupled composition allows for a high degree of flexibility, since services can be replaced simply by directing messages to another provider. Oftentimes, such composite services are implemented through explicit process representations [19,86]. A service composition that is controlled by a single entity is called a service *orchestration*.

Service interaction framework

Layers of a SOA

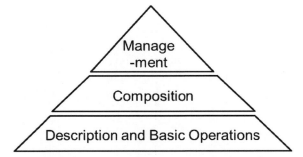

Figure 2.2.: Layers of a SOA, adapted from [5, p. 26]

Today, there exist three primary styles or paradigms, with which service-oriented software is implemented, Web Services technologies [90], REST [16], and microservices [17]. The software artifacts that are the target of this work utilize these styles and technologies and portability issues also originate from their usage, e.g., if a particular technological feature is supposed to be supported, but is not. For this reason, we give a brief overview of the different styles in the following section and describe notable technological features necessary for understanding this work.

2.1.2. Architectural Styles and Technologies

Despite heated debates on the technical merits of the different styles for implementing service-oriented software, there is no consensus on a one-size-fits-all style. Instead, it can be said that the different technologies are suited for different kinds of application scenarios [97]. Initially, the concepts of SOC and SOA were strongly related to their by then primary implementation technology: Web Services [15]. The importance of Web Services technologies is reclining today in favor of RESTful services [16]. Recently, also microservices [17, 103] have been coined as the next evolutionary step in SOC. Any of these styles can be used to implement applications that are described in a uniform, platform-independent, and technology-neutral manner, that interact via message exchanges, and that are transparent with respect to their location, i.e., services. Furthermore, all styles are meant to build services that can easily be composed [103, p. 7]. In a SOA, services implemented in different styles can also be combined with each other.

The software applications we analyze in this thesis use at least one of the different styles as the primary means for implementing distributed interactions. In some cases, in particular for BPEL [27], the usage of Web Service technologies [15] is required. In other cases, in particular for BPMN [26], the choice of the service-oriented style is left open. We give an overview over the technologies and principles underlying the different prevalent styles in the following subsections.

2.1.2.1. Web Services

Web Services advertise the utilization of Internet-related standards for the implementation of a SOA [90]. The primary use case for Web Services are integration scenarios that require the interoperation of heterogeneous systems [97]. Such scenarios are common in the Business-to-Business integration (B2Bi) domain [104].

Web Services are promoted by the World Wide Web Consortium (W3C) and *WSDL and* are based on a vast set of international standards. The Web Services architecture *SOAP* white paper defines a Web service as a *"software system designed to support interoperable machine-to-machine interaction over a network"* [90, p. 7]. This definition reflects the target application scenario of integrating heterogeneous systems. The core standards for implementing Web Services are the Web Service Description Language (WSDL) [105, 106] and SOAP [107, 108]. WSDL is the language in which interface definitions for services are written and SOAP defines the message format used for interaction. The newest revision of WSDL, version 2.0 [106], is rarely used in practice and the older version 1.1 [105] is much more common. The systems we use here utilize version 1.1 and it is unclear whether version 2.0 will ever receive widespread adoption. All Web Services standards make heavy use of Extensible Markup Language (XML) [109] to guarantee technological neutrality and platform independence. Even interface definitions in WSDL are written in XML.

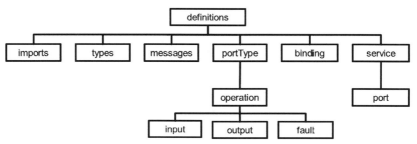

Figure 2.3.: Structure of a Web Service Definition

The uniform structure of a Web service definition [105] is depicted in Fig. 2.3. *Structure* A WSDL interface definition starts with a *definitions* element. It first lists *of interfaces* *imports* of necessary files such as XML Schema Definition (XSD) [110] types that serve as parts of messages, which the Web service sends and receives. The actual messages are defined in the *types* and *messages* elements. The central interface definition part is the *portType* which corresponds to a cohesive set of the *operations* a service offers. Each *operation* may define *input, output,* and *fault* messages as parameters and return values of an invocation of the service operation. Thereafter, a *binding* element maps each *operation* to a transport protocol and message format, i. e., a particular version of SOAP, with which messages are transmitted. Finally, a *service* element lists one or more *ports*, which are endpoints with a concrete address under which a service provider can be reached. The distinction between the *portType* of a service and its *port* ensures location transparency. To communicate with a service provider, a requester has to build a SOAP message, consisting of a header and body. The body contains one of the *messages* specified in the WSDL definition that is referenced as the *input* of one of the *operations* of the service. The transport protocol with which the message is transmitted depends on the *binding* of the service. Most frequently, the Hypertext Transfer Protocol (HTTP) [111] is used for message transmission. If it is specified in the service *operation*, the service provider may reply with a SOAP message that contains on *output* message in its body or a *fault*.

WS- standards*   The Web Services ecosystem encompasses many more standards that are used to specify and implement various quality of service attributes for the provided functionality or interaction. These standards are called *WS-* standards*. Examples of such standards are WS-Security [112] for specifying message encryption, WS-ReliableMessaging [113] for implementing reliable interactions, or WS-Agreement [114] for enabling agreement negotiation among services. The usage of WS-* standards can be enabled by attaching policy specifications [115] to a WSDL definition. WS-* standards have been criticized for their complexity [97], but many of the features enabled through these standards are mandatory in enterprise-level interactions. A prerequisite for the usage of WS-* standards is mutual support for these standards by the execution environments of a service provider and requester. However, studies show that interoperability among different WS-* implementations is poor [116]. In this work, we concentrate on the functional portability of an application and abstract from the portability of additional quality of service requirements. Hence, we refrain from the usage or evaluation of WS-* standards, as far as this is possible.

2.1.2.2. RESTful Services

The perceived complexity of Web Services technologies has lead to a focus on more simplistic types of interaction and to the rise of RESTful services[2] [117]. RESTful services are services that follow the REST architectural style [16, Chap. 5]. Similar to Web Services, RESTful services utilize common Internet technologies, in particular HTTP, to enable interoperable machine-to-machine communication over a network, albeit in a more minimalistic fashion [118]. The REST architectural style tries to mimic the design principles of the Internet for constructing the architecture of a distributed application based on interacting services. Due to their perceived simplicity, RESTful services are predominantly used for building service-oriented software today, to the disadvantage of Web Services technologies.

REST principles   RESTful services are centered around a uniform, technology-neutral interface [16, Chap. 5]. The constitutional constraints for such an interface are [117]:

1. the identification of resources,
2. their manipulation through resource representations,
3. self-descriptive messages, and
4. Hypermedia as the engine of application state (HATEOAS).

---

[2]The terms REST service and RESTful service are both common in practice to denote the same entity. In this thesis, we use the term RESTful service.

These constraints are typically implemented with standard Internet technologies: Resources are identified through Uniform Resource Identifiers (URIs) and represented in a technology-neutral format, such as XML, HTML, or the JavaScript Object Notation (JSON) [118]. Especially the latter one is preferred today. Resources can be manipulated by transmitting messages in the required representation to the service provider. The universally accepted transport protocol for performing this transmission is HTTP. In contrast to Web Services technologies, different protocols, such as the Simple Mail Transfer Protocol (SMTP) [119] are not considered. Due to the strong ties to HTTP, certain HTTP verbs, in particular *GET*, *PUT*, *POST*, and *DELETE*, are used to transmit resource representations [118]. *POST* is used to create a resource, *GET* to read its representation, *PUT* to update the state of the resource, and *DELETE* to remove it. The verbs, in combination with URIs and resource representations, constitute the uniform, technologically-neutral interface of a RESTful service. The last constraint, HATEOAS, requires that state transitions for resources, i. e., operations available for a resource, are determined dynamically by the provider in the form of hyperlinks encoded in resource representations. This means that the state of a resource is not explicitly maintained by the provider or requester, but encoded into the representation of a resource.

Based on these constraints, a RESTful service is identified by a base URI, which *RESTful* marks the initial access point for a service requester to the service provider [118]. *service* A service requester can invoke operations on the service via standard HTTP verbs *interac-* and transfer resource representations via formats such as JSON. By following *tion* hyperlinks from the base URI, the requester can discover further resources provided by the service and can invoke state transitions on these resources, i. e., it can trigger the execution of operations by the service provider. Note that an explicit interface description for a RESTful service, similar to a WSDL definition, is uncommon in practice. Nevertheless, specific languages for this task do exist, such as the Web Application Description Language (WADL) [120]. Also WSDL 2.0 [106] could be used for this purpose.

The profound success and industry adoption of RESTful services can be *REST* attributed to the fact that the technologies used for their implementation are *and* well-known, ubiquitous, and largely interoperable in heterogeneous systems [117]. *quality of* However, RESTful services lack most of the advanced features provided by WS-* *service* standards. For example, point-to-point encryption can be achieved by using the Hypertext Transfer Protocol Secure (HTTPS) [121], but there is no standard way of achieving end-to-end encryption as for WS-Security [97]. Due to such functional limitations, RESTful services are necessarily more simplistic, but also more interoperable. As before, the focus of this thesis resides on the portability of application functionality, therefore more advanced quality of service features are not discussed further.

2.1.2.3. Microservices

The most recent evolutionary step of SOC are *microservices* [17, 103]. Currently, the microservices architecture is still in the definition phase and not all aspects are fully specified. Lewis and Fowler [17] advocate the microservice architecture as a form of *fine grained SOA*. Also other sources state that microservices can be seen *"as a specific approach for SOA"* [103, p. 9]. As discussed in the previous sections, the main difference between Web Services and RESTful services is the way in which service interfaces are defined and messages are exchanged between provider and requester. The microservices architecture does not propose yet another way for addressing these aspects, but reuses the concepts of REST for providing uniform and technology-neutral interfaces and exchanging messages. Instead, it puts more emphasis on the isolated deployment, autonomy, and self-containedness of services [103, Chap. 1]. As a result, technological heterogeneity, platform independence, composability, and easier replacement are crucial benefits of microservices.

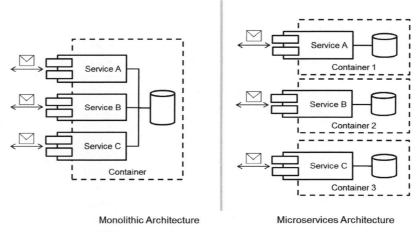

Monolithic Architecture   Microservices Architecture

Figure 2.4.: Monolithic Architecture versus Microservices Architecture

Container isolation The key differences brought by a microservice architecture [17] are depicted in Fig. 2.4. The figure contrasts two different architectures consisting of three services, A, B, and C, and their execution environments. In both of the architectures in Fig. 2.4, the different services look independent from the service requester point of view. In the left-hand case, these services are hosted in a single container and are linked to each other via shared dependencies, which is not visible from the outside. They might even be provided by the same operating system process. This forms a monolithic architecture, due to the shared environment. In contrast, in the right-hand case, each service is hosted in a separate container. Each container might also be a completely different software product. As a result, there is a higher degree of isolation and location transparency among the different services. The failure of one of the services has no influence on the behavior of the others, which can occur in the case of a monolithic architecture. This strong focus on deployment-related aspects and restrictions on private inter-service relationships is what makes microservices different when compared with Web Services or REST.

The advent of microservices can be attributed to the arrival of techniques for *Drivers for micro-service adoption* easier management and provisioning of scalable execution environments, i. e., cloud computing platforms [103, Chap. 1]. Container technologies, such as *Docker*, enable the relatively simple and fast construction of isolated containers for a single service [122, 123]. Another principle mandated by the microservices architecture is of organisational nature: All lifecycle aspects of a single service, including development and operations, should be performed by a single small-scale team [17]. This is in line with a common agile software development practice, the DevOps movement [124], and also the practices of continuous integration [103, Chap. 6]. In summary, it can be said that the microservices architecture is a form of SOA that is orthogonal to the Web Services or REST architectural paradigms.

2.2. Process-Aware Information Systems

Process-Aware Information Systems are systems that use explicit notions of processes, in the form of process representations, definitions, or models, for information systems design, implementation, and execution [4, 20, 21]. PAIS have been the target of extensive research in recent years [23] and comprise a vast area of systems and management-related tasks. Their origins lie in the fields of workflow management [125] and business process management (BPM) [20, 126]. As is the case for SOC and SOA, commonly accepted, clear, and distinctive definitions of these fields are hard to find and their borders are blurred in practice. Here, we *Delin-eation of PAIS* adopt the view taken by leading researchers and industry standards [20, 21, 127–129]. BPM includes all lifecycle aspects, the design, monitoring, optimization, and execution of processes in an enterprise environment [128]. Workflow systems focus on process execution through computer systems, in particular workflow engines [129]. Clearly, there is an overlap in these areas. PAIS synthesize these fields and the term can be defined as follows:

Definition 3: Process-Aware Information System

A process-aware information system is *"a software system that manages and executes operational processes involving people, applications, and/or information sources on the basis of process models"* [4, p. 7].

According to this definition, a system that uses a workflow engine is also process-aware. However, process-aware systems are not limited to workflow technology, because not every software system that executes process models, i. e., a process engine, necessarily fits into the requirements for a workflow engine. In particular, certain functions such as worklist and workitem handling [129, p. 34] are often not part of contemporary process engines. Instead, process engines can be seen as a superset of workflow engines. Furthermore, it has to be noted that the term process-*aware* is not unanimous. In particular, the terms process-*driven* [127], process-*oriented* [130], or process-*based* [131], are more or less synonymous.

Today, more and more applications are implemented in a process-aware way and more and more tooling for PAIS becomes available [23] Studies that analyze

Benefits of process-awareness the effects of process-awareness have found that the application of associated principles improves organizational performance [22]. In particular, speed and quality improvements, cost reduction and an improved financial performance have been observed. Process definition standards are constantly being revised and new process engines are being built. This influx leads to the necessity to migrate applications, a motivating factor for this work.

This section explains the theoretical foundations of PAIS that are needed to understand the main part of the thesis, including the structure and functioning of process models and engines. We first give an overview of the conceptual aspects of PAIS, and thereafter discuss the standards and languages used in the practical parts of this work.

2.2.1. Lifecycle and Architecture of Process-Aware Information Systems

PAIS lifecycle The lifecycle of a process-aware information system is depicted in Fig. 2.5 [4]. A process is designed and implemented, i.e., modeled and programmed in a *process language*. For process enactment, this model is deployed to a *process engine*. At run-time, *process instances* are created and executed as specified in the process model. A process instance is a concrete run of the execution logic defined in a process model [20, Sect. 3.5.2]. These instance executions are independent of each other and may occur in parallel. After execution, diagnosis tools are used to verify that process instance execution was correct. Furthermore, areas of improvement are identified, possibly leading to a redesign of the process model.

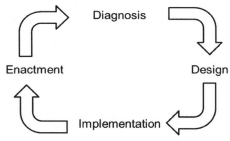

Figure 2.5.: Lifecycle of a PAIS adapted from [4, p. 12]

The focus of this thesis lies not on the design or diagnosis phase, but on the implementation and enactment phase. Therefore, aspects such as modeling support for creating process models, the suitability and appropriateness of process modeling languages for humans [132], or the understandability of process models [133] are explicitly out of scope. Instead, we focus on the portability of executable process models among different process engines.

Architecture of PAIS The architecture of such engine-based software systems, which is inspired by the workflow reference model [129, p. 20], is depicted in Fig. 2.6. As discussed earlier, process models are defined at design-time and implemented in a process language, e.g., in BPMN [26], BPEL [27], or the XML Process Definition

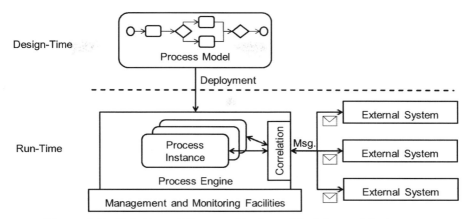

Design-Time

Run-Time

Figure 2.6.: Relation of Process Engines, Models, and Instances

Language (XPDL) [31]. This task is often assisted by visual editors and several languages provide a visual notation, next to a serialization format. Executable process models correspond to software artifacts that adhere to a specific structure defined in a process language (cf. Sect. 2.2.2). Therefore, the modeling of executable processes is a form of visual programming [134]. After their definition, process models can be deployed to an engine that implements the language the model is written in. Akin to the definition of a workflow engine in [129, p. 22], we define a process engine as follows:

Definition 4: Process Engine

A *process engine* is a software service that provides the run-time execution environment for a process instance.

Note that the term Business Process Management System (BPMS) is also frequently used to describe a process engine. For instance, Weske defines a BPMS as *"a generic software system that is driven by explicit process representations to coordinate the enactment of business processes"* [20, Def. 1.3, p. 6]. In this thesis, we use the term *process engine* when referring to the software execution environment for process models and instances. Typically, the engine parses the process model and constructs an internal model that is executed in conformance to the process model [135]. An executable process model needs to specify the conditions under which process instances should be created and executed. The engine takes care of cataloging if these conditions are met and, if so, creates new instances. During execution, process instances may communicate with external services or humans and may require external input. The process engine takes care of routing messages to particular instances and directs incoming input to the desired process instance. This feature is called *correlation*. All the while, the engine offers management and monitoring functionality to supervise the execution of process instances. Taken together, process engines and executable process models form a service-oriented and process-aware software system in the sense of this thesis. The process engine is the middleware and the executable process model is the application software.

Technical benefits of process-awareness The separation of the execution logic (the process model) from the execution environment (the process engine) offers a variety of technical benefits. For instance, different parts of a process instance can be scheduled for execution on different machines by the process engine, thereby improving the scalability of the application. This is the focus of cloud based process engines [136]. Further benefits include an easier coordination of parallel work and the possibility to unload application state from memory and resume it later, which is necessary to support long-running process instances [137].

2.2.2. Process Languages and Models

Structure of process models As clarified in the previous section, process models form a central part of PAIS. They are typically not developed in general purpose high-level programming languages, but in specific process languages, e.g., BPMN [26], BPEL [27], or XPDL [31]. The most basic building block of process models are *activities*. Activities are atomic steps of work, such as the execution of a program or the sending of a message to an external service. The execution of activities can be fully automated, involve user interaction, or even refer to a purely manual action [20, Chap. 3]. The concrete types of activities available for a process model and their semantics are defined by a process language. During the execution of a process instance, activity instances are created from the process model, similar to the creation of process instances from the model. Like a process instance, activity instances follow a certain lifecycle, which is depicted in the state machine in Fig. 2.7. After creation, an activity instance is initially inactive until all preconditions to its execution, such as the availability of data elements, are fulfilled. When all preconditions are met, the activity instance changes to the *active* state and its execution logic is being run. During execution, the instance may change back to the *inactive* state, because it needs to wait on the fulfillment of certain conditions, such as the arrival of a message from an external service. While being inactive, an activity may also be suspended by the engine. Ultimately, the activity instance reaches the *completed* state and terminates. Completion can refer to an ordered termination, but also to a failure of the execution logic defined in the activity. In any case, the execution of the activity is finished.

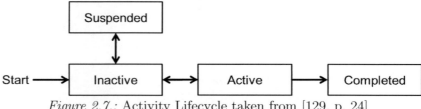

Figure 2.7.: Activity Lifecycle taken from [129, p. 24]

Further elements of process models are *gateways* and *events* [20, Chap. 3]. Gateways are constructs for control-flow routing and are used to schedule the order of activity execution. Events mark states in a process model, such as its start or end, or the occurrence of certain actions, such as the expiration of a timeout or the arrival of a message. The activities, gateways, and events of a process model are connected via directed edges that describe their execution dependencies. Based on these language elements, a process model can be characterized as a program written in a process language that coordinates the execution of a set of activities and the occurrence of a set of events and using gateways. These elements are typically depicted in a graphical visualization of a process model. They are the sole elements of nonexecutable and abstract process models. Formally, such a process model is commonly defined as follows [20, Def. 3.3, Sect. 3.5]:

Definition 5: Process Model

A *process model* $PM = <N, C>$ is a tuple of a *set of nodes* N and a *set of connectors* C, where
- $N = A \cup E \cup G$: the set of nodes N consists of the set of activities A, the set of events E, and the set of gateways G. These sets are mutually disjoint.
- $C = N \times N$: the set of connectors C consists of directed edges between elements of N that describe execution order dependencies.

Implementing executable process models, the core part of service-oriented and process-aware software, requires the usage of additional process elements. These elements are details of technical nature that are needed to execute the *Executable process models* process model and transfer the model into the realm of application software. Such technical details are often not visible in a visualization of the process model and not needed in abstract and nonexecutable models. Hence, they are often ignored in such models. Examples of such elements are variable definitions, correlation definitions, import definitions, and more, depending on the vocabulary of a process language. Since this thesis targets executable process models, i. e., application software, we need to take every language element into account, regardless of its level of technical detail. As a result, the common definition of a process model in Def. 5 is not sufficient for defining software metrics and we extend it for a formal definition of executable process models:

Definition 6: Executable Process Model

An *executable process model* $EPM = <N, C>$ corresponds to a tuple of a *set of nodes* N and a *set of connectors* C, where

- $N = A \cup E \cup G \cup B$: the set of nodes N consists of the set of activities A, the set of events E, the set of gateways G, and the set of basic language elements B. These sets are mutually disjoint.
- $C = N \times N$: the set of connectors consists of directed edges between elements of N that describe execution order dependencies. The mapping in C is not necessarily total, i. e., not all elements of N need to be embedded into the control-flow graph. Particularly, this applies to the elements of B.
- $V = N \cup C$: every element of the process model is part of the vocabulary of the process language, V. In particular, B includes all elements of the vocabulary, V, not found in the other sets, i. e., $B = V \setminus (A \cup G \cup E \cup C)$.
- Additionally, $S \subset A \cup E$ is the set of elements for service communication. It includes all activities and events that are used for sending or receiving messages. This specialization is necessary for defining metrics that have a particular focus on service-oriented characteristics.

Since this thesis deals only with executable process models, for reasons of brevity, we will use the two terms process model and executable process model interchangeably in the following. We have to emphasize that, in this work, an executable process model solely corresponds to a program written in the vocabulary of a process language. Apart from syntactical correctness, we make no assumptions about such a model. This means that an executable process model need not be deadlock free or guaranteed to terminate, *as long as it conforms to the syntactical rules of the language standard.* An executable process model can be deployed onto a process engine, which compiles or interprets it. This often requires the definition of additional files, such as deployment descriptors, and the packaging of the process model. In conjunction, these artifacts form a piece of service-oriented and process-aware application software.

2.2.2.1. Graph-Orientation and Block-Structure

As discussed, the purpose of a process model is to coordinate the execution of a set of activities and events. This coordination is achieved through the definition of control- and data-dependencies among these elements with the help of gateways. The way in which these dependencies are defined is a central point of focus and a discriminating factor for process languages. There are two styles in which dependencies are expressed [138]. These are either a *graph-oriented* or a *block-structured* style. In a graph-oriented style, directed connectors are used to link nodes. This resembles a flow chart. The activation of connectors is conditional and depends on the type of preceding gateways. In a block-structured notation, nodes are nested into each other and connectors are not represented explicitly [138]. Instead, control-dependencies are implied by the nesting. For instance, a parent node *sequence* with enclosed nodes n_1 and n_2 signals that the nodes are to be executed sequentially in the order of their definition. Process languages may support either or both of these styles and process models can be transformed from a block-structured to a graph-oriented style and the other way round [139].

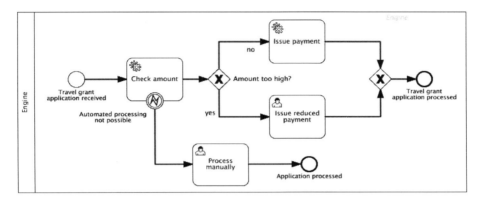

Figure 2.8.: The Travel Grant Process taken from [80] in Graph-Oriented Notation

Fig. 2.8 depicts a fictional exemplary process model, taken from [80], in a graph-oriented style in the BPMN notation. This process model implements the handling of a travel grant application at a university department. First, a travel grant application must be made and this triggers the creation of a new process instance via a start event (circle). An initial activity (rounded rectangle) first checks the amount of the application. An exclusive gateway (diamond) controls the activation of different control-flow branches depending on the result of this check. If the amount exceeds a certain threshold, the application must be handled manually, otherwise automatic handling is possible. Both of these actions are implemented as specific activities. Another exclusive gateway merges the two branches and, thereafter, the process model is terminated with an end event. If an error is thrown during the checking of the amount, represented by an error event, the application must also be handled manually. Fig. 2.9 depicts the same process in a block-structured notation[3]. Here, all nodes are represented as rectangles and nested into each other. The activation and execution of each node is controlled by its parent. If a node has multiple children, these are executed either sequentially or as alternatives. The execution logic depicted in both process models is identical, albeit the difference in representation.

Underlying the graphical representation, a machine-readable serialization format of a process model is required for the execution by an engine. Contemporary process languages provide an XML serialization format. The usage of XML is primarily motivated by the platform-independent nature of XML, which is ex-

Visualization

Serialization

---

[3]This is an ad-hoc notation used solely for visualization here.

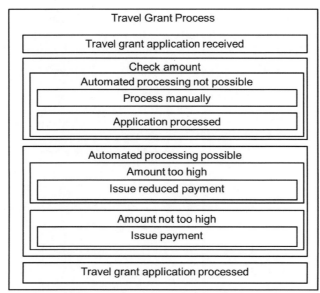

Travel Grant Process

Travel grant application received

Check amount

Automated processing not possible

Process manually

Application processed

Automated processing possible

Amount too high

Issue reduced payment

Amount not too high

Issue payment

Travel grant application processed

Figure 2.9.: The Travel Grant Process taken from [80] in Block-Structured Notation

pected to enhance the portability of process models among engines [30]. List. 2.1 shows a simplified outline that omits parts of the process model[4] of the XML code of the travel grant process model.

Listing 2.1: Outline of the XML Serialization of the Travel Grant Process

```
<?xml version="1.0" encoding="UTF-8"?>
<definitions ...>
  <process name="Travel Grant Application Process"
    isExecutable="true">

    <startEvent name="Travel grant application received">
      <outgoing>SequenceFlow_1</bpmn2:outgoing>
    </startEvent>

    <serviceTask name="Check amount">
      <incoming>SequenceFlow_1</incoming>
      <outgoing>SequenceFlow_2</outgoing>
    </serviceTask>

    <exclusiveGateway name="Amount too high?" >
      <incoming>SequenceFlow_2</incoming>
      <outgoing>SequenceFlow_5</outgoing>
```

---

[4]The complete serialization would cover many pages, but can be accessed at https://github. com/uniba-dsg/zeus2014.

```
    <outgoing>SequenceFlow_12</outgoing>
  </exclusiveGateway>
  ...
  <endEvent name="Travel grant application processed">
    <incoming>SequenceFlow_9</incoming>
  </endEvent>

  <endEvent name="Application processed">
    <incoming>SequenceFlow_11</incoming>
  </endEvent>

</process>
...
</definitions>
```

2.2.2.2. Service Composition

As discussed in Sect. 2.1.1 and depicted in Fig. 2.2, the second layer of a SOA is the service composition layer [5]. In this layer, higher-level and value-added services are constructed on the basis of other services. The service composition layer is seen as a significant part of a SOA and as a prerequisite for achieving its full potential [19, 87]. It is as important in a microservices-based SOA, as it is in a Web Services-based SOA [103, Chap. 4]. Service composition is achieved by coordinating interactions with multiple services in a single program. These programs are predominantly implemented in a process-aware fashion. Therefore, processes that build on services are also called service compositions [20, Sect. 2.5.4].

Service-oriented and process-aware systems intersect at the level of an activity *Service* or event. Contemporary process languages specify activities that can be used for *composi-tion* interacting with a service, i. e., for sending messages to and receiving messages *through* from a service provider. For instance, BPEL 2.0 [27] provides *receive, reply,* *invoke,* and *onMessage* activities that can be used to communicate with a Web service endpoint. An example of a process-aware service composition is depicted in Fig. 2.10. The figure shows a simple inventory planning process that consists of three activities. Each of the activities sends a message to and receives a message from an external service. As a result, the purpose of the inventory planning process is the coordination and composition of the invocation of the three external services in a common context. In a realistic application, the invocation of services may be mixed with arbitrary further activities and the process model may also involve human interaction.

A process-aware way of service composition provides a variety of advantages *Advan-tages of* over alternative approaches for composition [19, 86]. Basically, it combines the *process-* benefits of service-oriented systems and process-aware systems and can be used *aware* to leverage the advantages of both paradigms. On the one hand, this is the *service* technological neutrality, platform-independence, loose-coupling, and location *tion* transparency coming from service-oriented systems (cf. Sect. 2.1.1). Added to

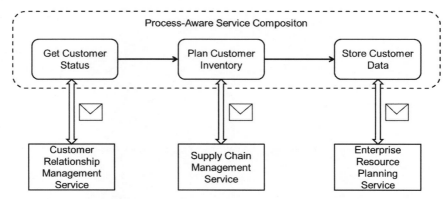

Figure 2.10.: Process-Aware Service Composition adapted from [20, Sect. 2.5.4]

this, a process-aware service composition provides an improved separation of concerns in the overall application. More precisely, the business logic that is executed can be encapsulated in the services, whereas their coordination can be captured in the process model. This enhances the flexibility of the system, because the coordination can be modified without influencing the actual business logic. Moreover, process languages, such as BPEL [27] or BPMN [26], and respective engines come with built-in support for long-running interactions among services, message correlation, and provide sophisticated facilities for fault handling and compensation that are not typically found in higher level programming languages. Last but not least, the implementation of a service composition in a process language is supposed to be portable among different engines and should defend from vendor lock-in.

Orchestration and choreography   If service execution is coordinated by a single entity, for instance by a single process instance, service compositions are also called *service orchestrations* [86]. As opposed to this, a *service choreography* describes a compound interaction among multiple independent coordinators from a global point of view. This is the case if multiple process instances interact with each other by sending messages. The distributed interaction among the different instances forms the implementation of the choreography [140]. In this thesis, we focus on process-aware applications that can be directly executed on a process engine, i. e., singular process models. Therefore, applications that are formed by the distributed interaction of multiple process instances, i. e., service choreographies, are not considered. Service orchestrations come quite close to our notion of process-aware and service-oriented software. However, service orchestrations are considered to consist of activities for service interaction exclusively [86]. Our target is the complete vocabulary of a process language, which is not necessarily limited to service interaction. For instance, the vocabulary of BPMN as outlined in the following section, includes language elements that cover non-service related aspects, such as user interaction or business rule execution. Hence, we target applications that involve service interaction *and* all further aspects defined by a process language. For this reason, we use the term process-aware and service-oriented software as a delimitation from service choreographies, orchestrations, and compositions.

In the following sections, we discuss the two languages that we consider most important for building service-oriented and process-aware software today. Applications implemented in these languages are used in the practical parts of this thesis.

2.2.2.3. The Business Process Model and Notation

The Business Process Model and Notation [26] is an international standard that specifies a framework for the modeling of a variety of different types of processes, including processes intended for execution on process engines. For BPMN, a special emphasis is put on the visual notation for depicting process models. The standard is maintained by the Object Management Group (OMG) and its goal *"is to enable portability of Process definitions"* [26, p. 20]. In its most recent revision, version 2.0.2, it has been accepted as an ISO/IEC standard. This revision is a minor update, involving no significant semantic changes, of version 2.0, published in 2011. Already since the publication of this version, BPMN has received much attention in practice and more and more engines that claim to implement the standard are made available. As such, BPMN is expected to supersede related languages when it comes to the direct execution of process models.

The specification document [26] defines a common grammar and set of basic *Process types in* language elements for different types of processes. These are not only executable *BPMN* *processes*, but also process *choreographies* or *collaborations* [26, Sect. 7]. The latter two refer to sets of interacting processes, which are typically distributed over several parties and not executed in a single environment. As discussed in the previous section, such types of processes are out of the scope of this thesis. Hence, we do not consider BPMN choreographies or collaborations. Also when it comes to *processes* with a single execution context, BPMN allows to specify private non-executable, private executable and public processes. Since our focus lies on executable software, only executable processes are of interest. The elements of such executable processes are specified in [26, Sect. 10], and execution semantics in [26, Sect. 13].

The standard defines an XML serialization format in which process models *Structure of a* are implemented. Every BPMN file starts with a *definitions* root element that *BPMN* serves as a container for several top-level elements, such as a process model. *process* BPMN process models predominantly use a graph-oriented style for control-flow *model* definition. The core elements of a process model are *activities*, *events*, and *gateways*. These elements are connected by directed edges, called *SequenceFlows*. Every BPMN element specifies incoming and outgoing *SequenceFlows*, thereby building the process graph. When it comes to the definition of data, BPMN *"does not itself provide a built-in model for describing structure of data or an Expression language for querying that data"* [26, p. 202]. The standard designates XSD and XPath as default technologies for defining data, but states that vendors are free to substitute these technologies. For this reason, data handling aspects of BPMN are not considered further here.

2. Theoretical and Technological Foundations

Activities   *Activities* [26, Sect. 10.2] can refer to atomic steps of work, in BPMN called *Tasks*, but also to *SubProcesses*, which are used to implement hierarchical decomposition, and to references to globally defined tasks or processes. Different types of tasks with a different purpose and structure are defined by the specification [26, Sect. 10.3.3]:

Service Tasks are used to invoke an operation on a service. BPMN is not tailored to a specific service-oriented technology, but Web Services are specified as default implementation technology.

Send Tasks transmit a message to an external party. Similar to a *Service Task*, the default implementation technology are Web Services and the operation invoked needs to be specified. Additionally, the message sent may be defined as a top-level element of the process model and can be referenced in the *Send Task*.

Receive Tasks can be used to wait for the arrival of a message from an external party. As such, a *Receive Task* is the counterpart to a *Send Task* and can be configured in the same fashion. Additionally, a *Receive Task* can trigger the creation of a new process instance.

User Tasks represent tasks that are semi-automated and require human input. A process engine is expected to provide assistance in processing the execution of the task and it may be implemented using a specification for managing human interactions in a process model, such as WS-HumanTask [141].

Manual Tasks serve as placeholders for non-automated actions in the process model. Since the action is non-automated, a process engine is not able to track the start or completion of such a task. As such, an engine is allowed to ignore the task in a process model.

BusinessRule Tasks are used to mark the execution of a business rule by a business rule engine. As before, an implementation technology needs to be specified in the definition of the task.

Script Tasks contain programs that can directly be executed by a process engine. The program needs to be specified as a *Script* in a *ScriptFormat* which the engine supports. BPMN does not specify a default format for scripts.

It can be seen from the task types that coordinating service interaction plays an important role in BPMN process models. The default implementation technology specified in the respective positions of the standard are Web Services. However, BPMN process models can easily be adjusted to refer to different service-oriented technologies. Since it is not required by the standard, such an adjustment is engine-dependent and nonportable.

Next to tasks, BPMN activities can be *SubProcesses* [26, Sect. 10.3.5]. These are a means for providing a hierarchical decomposition and structuring of a process model. As such, *SubProcesses* introduce block-structure into a BPMN

36

process model. Similar to the different task types, several types of *SubProcesses* do exist:

SubProcesses, in their ordinary form, resemble the structure of a top-level *process*. Two options for defining ordinary *SubProcesses* do exist. Either a *SubProcess* can be embedded into the control-flow graph of the parent process, or it can be defined globally and be called by a *CallActivity* [26, Sect. 10.3.6].

Event SubProcesses are specialized *SubProcesses* that are triggered by the occurrence of an event. In contrast to other activities, they are not connected to the control-flow graph of the process model through *SequenceFlows*. Instead, they are embedded loosely into the parent process and executed whenever their designated start event occurs. This can happen multiple times during the execution of the parent process.

Transactions are special *SubProcesses* that are controlled by a transactional protocol, such as WS-AtomicTransaction [142] or WS-BusinessActivity [143]. The protocol employed needs to be specified in the definition of the *Transaction* by a *TransactionMethod*.

Ad-Hoc SubProcesses represent a form of unstructured processes and do not use *SequenceFlows* to connect contained activities. Instead, the activities can be executed in any order. Activity execution may take place sequentially or in parallel, with parallel execution being the default setting. Moreover, each activity may also be executed multiple times. To ensure termination, an *Ad-Hoc SubProcess* needs to define a *CompletionCondition*. Activity instances that are still active when the *CompletionCondition* is evaluated as true may be canceled or allowed to terminate.

The last types of activities are *CallActivities* [26, Sect. 10.3.6] and *Global-Tasks* [26, Sect. 10.3.7]. All task types described above are also available in a global version, which means that they can be defined out of the scope of a process and without being embedded into the control-flow graph. A *CallActivity* can be used to reference such a globally defined task in the execution context of a process. Moreover, it can also be used to reference another *Process*, which is then executed in the same fashion as an embedded *SubProcess*.

Finally, all activities share a number of common attributes that can be used to define repetitive execution or compensation [26, Sect. 10.3.8]. *StandardLoopCharacteristics* can be used to implement an iterative execution of multiple instances of an activity. A *Condition* is used to control the amount of instances that are executed. Alternatively, *MultiInstanceLoopCharacteristics* can be used to implement the execution of multiple activity instances in parallel or sequentially. Activity instances in the context of a standard loop may depend on each other and subsequently work on the same data elements. In contrast to this, multi-instance activities have an isolated execution context. Furthermore, all activities can be marked for compensational execution instead of standard execution [26, Sect. 10.7]. Activities marked as compensational are called compensation handlers and are supposed to undo the results of the execution of previous activities. Fig. 2.11 summarizes the previous paragraphs and depicts the visual representation of all BPMN activities and their configuration options.

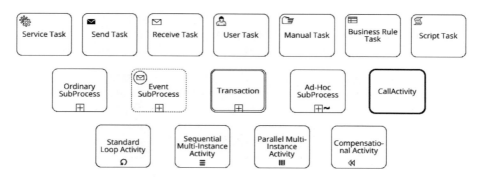

Figure 2.11.: Activities and Configuration Options in BPMN

Gateways in BPMN [26, Sect. 10.6] are used for routing the control-flow in a process model. Gateways are available in a *diverging* and a *converging* fashion. A diverging gateway is followed by multiple outgoing *SequenceFlows* and a converging gateway is preceded by multiple incoming *SequenceFlows*. A single gateway may be converging and diverging at the same time, but such structuring is generally not recommended [144]. The following types of gateways are available:

ExclusiveGateways are used to select a single branch among a set of *Sequence-Flows* for subsequent activation, or to merge a single activated *SequenceFlow* from a set of incoming *SequenceFlows*. The conditions that are evaluated are not attached to the gateway, but to the outgoing *SequenceFlows*. The semantics of this gateway correspond to *if-elseif-else* programming constructs.

EventBasedGateways are also used to select a single branch among a set of control-flow branches. In contrast to the *ExclusiveGateway*, the selection does not depend on a data-based condition, but on the occurrence of an event. Alternative control-flow branches are identified by an event and the event that occurs first leads to the activation of the associated control-flow branch. *EventBasedGateways* can be used to trigger the creation of a process instance and are also available in a parallel fashion, in which all specified events are expected to occur before execution can proceed, i.e., the gateway can act as a barrier.

ParallelGateways activate all subsequent control-flow branches in parallel or merge multiple parallel incoming control-flow branches.

InclusiveGateways form a combination of *Parallel-* and *ExclusiveGateways*. A number of subsequent branches can be activated in parallel, but the activation of each single branch depends on a condition.

ComplexGateways "*can be used to model complex synchronization behavior*" [26, p. 294]. They synchronize a number of parallel incoming branches and activate a number of subsequent branches in parallel. The diverging behavior of the *ComplexGateway* is identical to the *InclusiveGateway*. Its converging behavior corresponds to a cyclic barrier. A number of incoming control-flow branches, which may be a subset of the activated incoming branches, is expected to complete for the gateway to trigger the execution of subsequent branches.

Fig. 2.12 depicts the visual representation of gateways in BPMN and the configuration options for *SequenceFlows* when being combined with gateways.

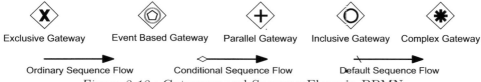

Exclusive Gateway   Event Based Gateway   Parallel Gateway   Inclusive Gateway   Complex Gateway

Ordinary Sequence Flow   Conditional Sequence Flow   Default Sequence Flow

Figure 2.12.: Gateways and SequenceFlows in BPMN

BPMN comes with a complex event model [26, Sect. 10.5] and numerous *Events* events exists. Events are identified through a combinatorial combination of a variety of event configuration options. A subset of these combinations are valid events [26, pp. 259/260]. Instead of listing all 63 admissible events, we describe the event configuration options here. First of all, events can either be *start*, *end*, or *intermediate* events. *StartEvents* have no incoming *SequenceFlows* and trigger the creation of a process instance. Vice versa, *EndEvents* mark the termination of a control-flow branch and have no outgoing *SequenceFlows*. *IntermediateEvents* occur during the execution of a process instance and are embedded into the control-flow graph by *SequenceFlows* in the same fashion as activities. They can be used to *throw* or *catch* an event. Moreover, events can be attached to the *boundary* of an activity, to *catch* an event thrown during the execution of an activity instance. Such intermediate boundary events can be *interrupting*, i.e., they stop the execution of the normal control-flow branch and continue with an exceptional branch. Alternatively, they can be *non-interrupting*, i.e., the execution of the normal control-flow branch continues as expected. Next to these configuration options, there are 13 different *event types*. These types are:

None events, which are a placeholder of no specific type.

Message events, which are used to send or consume a message in the same fashion as *Send-* or *ReceiveTasks*.

Timer events, which delay execution for a specified amount of time or until a specific point in time is reached.

Error events, which can be used to signal faults.

Escalation events, which can be used to trigger escalation management. For instance, this can be helpful if the execution of an activity takes too long.

Cancel events, which can be used to cancel a running transaction.

Compensation events are used to trigger the execution of compensational activities as described above.

Conditional events, which can be used to trigger conditional execution of a control-flow branch.

Link events are only relevant to visualization and are irrelevant to execution. They are used to connect the control-flow graph in large process models that do not fit into the space available on screen or paper.

Signal events, which can send or consume a signal. A signal is a notification that can be seen and consumed by multiple parties or control-flow branches.

Multiple events are a way to throw or catch one of a set of different event types.

ParallelMultiple events are a way to throw or catch all of a set of different event types.

Fig. 2.13 depicts the visual representation of event configuration options in BPMN. The complete set of all admissible events would be too long here, but can be found in [26, pp. 259/260].

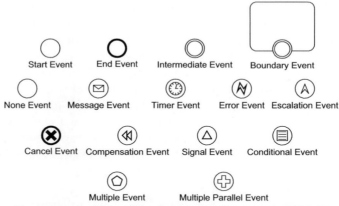

Figure 2.13.: Event Configuration Options in BPMN

An example of an executable process model in BPMN is shown in Fig. 2.8, as part of Sect. 2.2.2.1. An example of the serialization of the process model can be found in List. 2.1 in the same section. As a last point, it should be noted that, despite its popularity, the BPMN standard is quite imprecise, often lacks necessary technical details, and leaves much room for interpretation [145]. This severely complicates the implementation of standard-conformant process engines that behave in the same fashion. Consequently, the implementation of standard-conformant process models that result in the same execution behavior of process instances on different engines is challenging.

2.2.2.4. The Web Services Business Process Execution Language

The Web Services Business Process Execution Language [27] is an international standard that specifies a process language, which is primarily targeted at the orchestration of Web Services. It is maintained by the Organization for the Advancement of Structured Information Standards (OASIS) and has been finalized with version 2.0 in April 2007. The language "*defines a portable execution format for business processes that rely exclusively on Web Service resources*" [27, p. 7]. Since the publication of the standard, a plethora of BPEL engines has been developed and is available today. The tight link of BPEL to Web Services extends to further XML technologies, such as XSD and Extensible Stylesheet Language (XSL). Due to this technological dependence, the importance of BPEL is diminishing today. However, BPEL engines are in productive use and are still actively being developed. As a result, porting BPEL process models among engines is a realistic problem.

BPEL allows to specify two different types of process models[5]: *abstract* and *executable* process models [27, Sect. 13]. Abstract process models permit the usage of opaque and underspecified language elements, next to normal ones. As a result, abstract process models are not executable. Therefore, we do not consider abstract process models in this work. In contrast, executable process models are fully specified models and can be executed by an engine. Every BPEL process model is associated with at least one WSDL definition. This definition is implemented by the process model. This means that every BPEL process is also a Web service. BPEL supports block-structured and graph-oriented control-flow definition, although the largest part of the language is block-structured. In terms of terminology, BPEL refers to all nodes as activities, although specific activities serve as routing constructs, i. e., gateways, and others serve as events. The top-level language element is a *process*. Apart from activities, each process requires a number of mandatory elements: *Process types in BPEL*

Structure of a BPEL process model

Import elements are used to reference additional files needed by the process model, such as WSDL or XSD definitions and XSL transformations.

PartnerLinks correspond to role definitions [27, Sect. 6]. They link a process to the Web Service interface it implements or to external Web Services it invokes via a *partnerLinkType*. Each *partnerLink* is either specified as *myRole*, if the process implements this type and provides the operations specified by the *portType* of the service, or as *partnerRole* if it communicates with a service of that type.

Variables [27, Sect. 7] are used for storing and reading data during process instance execution. The types of variables can either be message types that are sent and received by a Web service, or custom defined XSD element types. Variables can be referenced by activities during execution and they can be defined with global visibility or within a *scope*.

---

[5]The BPEL specification uses the term *process definition* instead of process model. For reasons of consistency, we solely use the term process model here.

CorrelationSets [27, Sect. 7] are needed by a BPEL engine at run-time to direct incoming messages to a specific process instance. *CorrelationSets* are linked to specific parts of Web service messages via *propertyAliases*. When initialized with a certain value, all messages that have the same value in the referenced parts can be directed to the same process instance. Typically, *correlationSets* are initialized in a messaging activity and correlated upon in following messages.

MessageExchanges are optional elements that can be used to group pairs of activities for sending and receiving messages. They signal that two message-related activities, and the respective messages, belong together, with the second one being the reply to the first.

Scopes The remainder of the executable parts of BPEL separates in three areas: *scopes, basic activities,* and *structured activities. Scopes* are a means for the hierarchical decomposition of BPEL process models. They allow for the specification of the same elements as for a top-level *process* (cf. above), which technically is a global *scope.* Elements defined in a *scope* are only visible from within. Moreover, several types of *handlers* can be attached to a *scope* [27, Sect. 12]. Essentially, *handlers* are activities for event processing.

EventHandlers allow for the processing of incoming messages via *onMessage* activities or the handling of timeout expiration via *onAlarm* activities in parallel to the normal control-flow of a process instance.

FaultHandlers support fault handling similar to the exception handling strategies of common high-level programming languages. Faults can be caught by name, using a *catch* element, or all at once, using a *catchAll* element.

TerminationHandlers can be used to react to the forced termination of a *scope. TerminationHandlers* are executed before the activation of fault handling and start by disabling the *eventHandlers* attached to the *scope.* They trigger the termination of all activity instances that are still running and interrupt blocking instances.

CompensationHandlers are executed when the need for the compensation of a *scope* is signaled by the execution of specific activities. Their task is to undo, i. e., compensate for, the actions performed inside the *scope.* This is necessary for the execution of distributed transactions [146].

Basic activities Basic activities are atomic steps of work that cannot be decomposed further. BPEL defines the following set of basic activities [27, Sect. 10]:

Invoke activities are used to send a message to a Web service endpoint and, in case of a synchronous interaction, to wait for a reply. They reference the *partnerLink, portType,* and *operation* of the invoked Web service, and, if required, an *input-* and *outputVariable* to read and store message data. *Invoke* activities can also specify fault and compensation handling, in case a fault occurs during the Web service invocation.

Receive activities are used to wait for an incoming message. Similar to *invoke* activities, they reference a *partnerLink*, *portType*, and *operation*, as well as a *variable* in which the incoming message should be stored. *Receive* activities can be used to create a new process instance and, if part of a subsequent interaction, can be used to correlate on message data using *correlationSets*.

Reply activities are used in combination with *receive* activities to implement a synchronous interaction with the process instance. They link to the same *partnerLink* and *operation* as a previous *receive* activity and transmit the output message specified in this *operation*. Additionally, *receive* and *reply* can be linked by a *messageExchange*.

Assign activities are the primary means for data handling in BPEL. They can be used to copy data from variables to other variables or parts thereof, and can also be used to execute transformations in XSLT.

Throw activities can be used to trigger faults in the same fashion as is common for high-level programming languages. A *fault* is identified by its name and its structure needs to be defined in an imported schema. Moreover, a fault can carry data.

ReThrow activities work similar to *throw* activities, but can only be used within a *faultHandler*. They propagate a fault that was caught by the handler to the parent *scope* without changing associated fault data.

Wait activities are used to delay the execution of a process instance. Execution can either be delayed *for* a specific amount of time, or *until* a certain date.

Empty activities are mere placeholders and irrelevant to process execution.

ExtensionActivities are a means of adding language extensions into a process model. Such extensions will necessarily be tailored to particular engines and, in the sense of this work, be nonportable.

Exit activities can be used to immediately terminate a process instance without any fault, termination, or compensation handling.

The remaining group of activities in BPEL are structured activities. Structured activities enclose other activities and determine the order of their execution. This means that they correspond to gateways in the sense of Def. 6. The BPEL specification defines the following structured activities [27, Sect. 11]: *Structured activities*

Sequence activities execute enclosed activities in the order of their definition.

If activities allow for an exclusive choice among a set of different control-flow branches using a data-based boolean expression. As common in high-level programming languages, they can optionally be extended with a number of *elseif* cases and at most one *else* case.

While activities can be used to implement iterative looping behavior, given a
data-based boolean condition holds. The condition expression is evaluated
before the first execution of the loop.

RepeatUntil activities work similar to *while* activities, but execute contained activities repetitively until a specified boolean condition holds. The condition
expression is evaluated after the first execution of the loop.

Pick activities support the selection of one among a set of control-flow branches
based on the occurrence of an event. At least one message processing
activity must be contained within a *pick*, along with at least a second
event-processing activity. This can either be a message processing activity
or a timeout. The control-flow branch of whichever event occurs first, is
enabled for execution.

Flow activities enable parallel execution of contained activities. In their default
fashion, all activities contained within a *flow* are executed in parallel.
Additionally, *links* can be defined among activities to specify execution
order dependencies. The usage of links effectively enables a graph-oriented
control-flow definition inside a *flow* activity.

ForEach activities provide a means to execute contained activities for a given
amount of times, either sequentially or in parallel. The amount of times is
determined by an internal counter variable. A *completionCondition* can be
used to terminate the *forEach*, even if not all the enclosed activities have
terminated yet.

List. 2.2 shows an outline of a BPEL implementation for the travel grant
process from Fig. 2.8. It is intended as a simple outline for the serialization of a
BPEL process model.

Listing 2.2: Outline of a BPEL Process Model for the Travel Grant Process

```xml
<?xml version="1.0" encoding="UTF-8"?>
<process name="Travel Grant Application Process">
    <import ... />
    <partnerLinks .../>
    <variables .../>
    <correlationSets ... />

    <sequence>
        <receive name="Travel grant application received"
          />

        <invoke name="Check amount" />

        <if name="Amount too high?">
            <condition ... />
            <else>
```

```
          . . .
          </else>
      </if>

      <reply name="Application processed"/>
   </sequence>
</process>
```

As in the case of the BPMN model in List. 2.1, the listing omits parts of the
process model, because a complete version would be too long. The most notable
difference from the BPMN serialization in List. 2.1 is the lack of connectors
between activities (*SequenceFlows* in BPMN), which are omitted here due to the
block-structuredness of the process model and the usage of structured activities.

2.3. Software Quality Models and Portability

Parts of this section have been taken from [85].

This thesis centers on the portability of service-oriented and process-aware
software. Since portability is a quality characteristic of software, we describe the
foundations of software quality and quality models in the current section. As a
start, the term *software quality* can be defined as follows:

Definition 7: Software Quality

Software quality is *"the degree to which a software product satisfies stated
and implied needs when used under specified conditions"* [53, p. 17].

The vagueness in this definition is intentional. The stated and implied needs,
as well as the conditions of usage, on which software quality depends, differ
for different types of software and application scenarios. Therefore, also the
measurement and assessment of software quality is operationalized differently in
different areas.

In the following subsection, Sect. 2.3.1, we first motivate the importance of
the measurement and assessment of software quality and explain how software
measurement techniques can contribute to software quality. We describe the
combination of software measurement and agile software quality improvement
techniques, in particular continuous inspection. This leads to a discussion of
several software quality models that define the nature of software portability, in
particular the ISO/IEC 25010 standard for software quality [53] in Sect. 2.3.2.
Finally, we explain the relationship of portability and standard conformance in
Sect. 2.3.3.

2.3.1. Software Measurement Techniques for Quality Improvement

Motivation for software measurement Software quality is a decisive factor for software development project success or failure [147]. It is not only indispensable for meeting project requirements, but an improvement in software quality has also been found to lead to an improvement in development productivity [148]. A prerequisite for improving software quality is the ability to measure it. For instance, Reel states that *"only by measuring a system and analyzing those incremental measurements can you truly improve the system"* [147, p. 23]. The need for the measurement and assessment of software quality became evident already with the coining of the term *software crisis* and is voiced in foundational texts of this period [149]. Early works on software measurement and metrics, in particular [150, 151], are much-cited and still influential today. The quantification of the quality of software is an established branch of research and studies demonstrate that measurement and metrics can improve the quality of a software product [152, Chap. 9]. In a nutshell, this is the reason why we design a software quality measurement framework. Today, software measurement can be integrated into the software development process early and often, enabling *incremental* measurements. Among early applicable quality improvement techniques, especially code inspections and continuous quality audits have been found to make an impact [148]. Using such techniques, quality deficits can be identified early when the correction of defects is still cheap.

A particular agile quality assurance technique that makes use of software measurement and has the potential to improve quality [48,50–52,152] is *continuous inspection* [48, 49]. Continuous inspection is a term for the convergence of two quality assurance techniques, *software inspection* [153] and *continuous integration and delivery* [48,154]. Continuous inspection refers to the constant and automated inspection of a software product for every source code commit to enhance its quality [49].

Software inspection Software inspections, pioneered by Fagan [153], have a long tradition in software engineering [155, 156]. Ordinarily, these are manual tasks performed as a quality assurance technique next to other techniques such as unit testing. Essentially, an inspection is a review process where a team of reviewers individually scrutinize a software product according to a predefined set of criteria. The reviewers try to verify if the product meets its specifications and has a sufficient level of quality [157, pp. 16–25]. Afterwards, the reviewers gather in a meeting and produce a list of defects that can be handed to the authors of the software. Obviously, the inspection procedure requires a lot of communication and is therefore expensive to perform, especially in a repeated fashion. For these reasons, inspection tools have emerged during the last decade. These tools are static code analyzers that automatically highlight potential issues in code [158], [152, pp. 124–128]. The benefit of their usage is that an inspection can normally be performed within mere seconds and repeatedly. Of course, such a tool might not find all issues or detect false positives, but it offers unprecedented advantages in terms of efficiency [159]. Software inspections need not necessarily be limited to the detection of potential issues, but are also a good occasion to compute quality metrics to see if the software product meets predefined quality criteria.

Inspection tools can be used to much benefit, when combined with *Continuous Integration* (CI) [48]. The term emerged in the context of agile software development methods. It belongs to the concept of *continuous delivery* [154] which is specified in the first principle of the agile manifesto [160]. CI is a technique applied during software development that refers to the frequent integration of all parts of an application and the validation that they do indeed work together properly. In practice, a continuous integration server is set up and configured to build the software product and run the complete set of tests available every time a commit is made to the version control system [48]. This allows getting immediate feedback for the complete team in every stage of development and offers a variety of benefits [154, pp. 17–22], [48, pp. 29–32]. For instance, defects that are newly introduced into the code can be detected immediately and fixed at a point in time where the cost of correction is relatively low. CI has been embraced in practice and a variety of CI servers and tools is available today.

Continuous integration

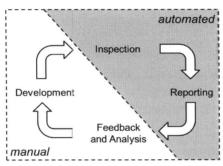

Figure 2.14.: Continuous Inspection Cycle adapted from [49]

With the proper tools, both of these techniques, software inspection and continuous integration, can be combined to continuous inspection [48, pp. 161–188], [49]. The idea depicted in the feedback cycle in Fig. 2.14 is to not just run tests for every commit to the version control system, but also to inspect the code automatically with available inspection software. That way, possible defects that are not captured in the tests can be discovered and fixed just as quickly. It might even be feasible to detect issues in the code that have not yet turned into concrete defects, but are likely to do so in the future. Moreover, this is an opportunity to compute quality metrics and compare them to previously configured thresholds [48, pp. 166–172],[154, pp. 137–140]. This way, it can be directly noticed if software quality deteriorates and counter measures can be taken before the deterioration turns into software errors. What is more, through this feedback, developers learn which patterns of code tend to reduce quality and which ones tend to improve quality and are encouraged to produce code of higher quality[6] [154, pp. 137–140].

Continuous inspection

---

[6]This effect of the influence of measurement on the persons being measured is known as the *Hawthorne effect*. Although it normally is disruptive for experiments, it can also be used to

The focus of this thesis is software portability. So, this section can be summarized in the following: Given inspection methods and tooling are available for detecting portability issues in code and measuring portability, these methods and tools can be used in today's ubiquitous CI environments through continuous inspection and, thus, have the potential to lead to code of higher quality, i. e., code that is more portable. *This is the motivation for developing methods and tools for measuring the portability of service-oriented and process-aware software.*

2.3.2. Portability and the ISO/IEC 25010 Quality Model

To use a technique such as continuous inspection, it is necessary to be able to capture software quality in the first place. The quality of software is generally perceived as a multi-dimensional property and this is where software quality models, e.g., [53–60, 62], come into play. Accordingly, the term software quality model can be defined as follows:

Definition 8: Software Quality Model

A software quality model is a *"defined set of characteristics, and of relationships between them, which provides a framework for specifying quality requirements and evaluating quality"* [53, p. 19].

Development of quality models   An abundance of such models has been developed during the last decades. A timeline of several renowned quality models is depicted in Fig. 2.15. Work on software quality began with the development of software metrics. Especially the cyclomatic complexity [151] and the metrics suite by Halstead [150] are to be mentioned here. Also the first quality models, especially by Boehm et al. [54], Gilb [55], or McCall et al. [56], are still influential today. These models served as the basis for the first software product quality standard, ISO/IEC 9126 [58]. This standard has had a tremendous impact on the evaluation of software quality and was the basis for subsequent models, such as Dromey's model [59], the FURPS model [62], or the SQALE model [60], a recent special-purpose quality model for estimating technical debt [161]. It has been revised in 2001 [57] and is superseded by the ISO/IEC standards framework for quality evaluation, ISO/IEC 25000 [162], called Systems and software Quality Requirements and Evaluation. The software product quality model of this series of standards is defined in [53] and marks the current pinnacle of software quality models. It is *"widely accepted both by industrial experts and academic researchers"* [163, p. 68]. Due to this importance, we align the quality measurement framework in this thesis to the ISO/IEC SQuaRE model.

As stated in Def. 8, quality models define a set of *quality characteristics* of software, sometimes also called *quality attributes* [55, Sect. 3.6]. Quality characteristics are defined as follows:

---

train developers in the fashion described in the text.

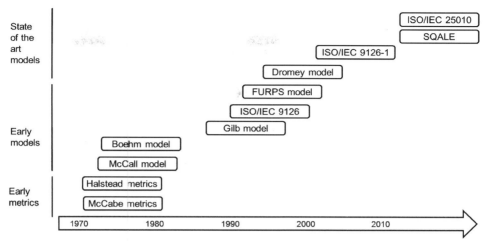

Figure 2.15.: Timeline of Software Quality Models adapted and extended from [163, Sect. 3.2]

Definition 9: Software Quality Characteristic

A software quality characteristic is a *"category of software quality that bears on software quality"* [53, p. 19].

Examples are characteristics such as *performance efficiency* or *usability* [53]. Also software *portability* is part of the models and all but the FURPS model [62] consider it as a major quality characteristic. The quality models provide a hierarchy of quality characteristics and divide major characteristics into a number of *subcharacteristics* that focus on more specific aspects[7]. For instance, the characteristic of performance efficiency can be divided into the subcharacteristics of *time behavior, resource utilization,* and *capacity* [53]. The main difference between different quality models [53–60, 62] lies in what quality characteristics and subcharacteristics they define and how many layers of characteristics they use.

As stated, we use the ISO/IEC quality model in its most recent revision, the ISO/IEC 25010 series [53]. This series is titled *"Systems and software engineering – Systems and software Quality Requirements and Evaluation (SQuaRE) – System and software quality models"*. The quality model from [53] is depicted in Fig. 2.16. It specifies eight top-level quality characteristics and one of these is portability, the focus of this work. The SQuaRE model defines portability as the *"degree of effectiveness and efficiency with which a system, product or component can be transferred from one hardware, software or other operational or usage environment to another.* [53, p. 15]. [53] further states that portability can be interpreted as an inherent capability of the software product, which is the interpretation we adopt. The scope of this work lies solely on software and not on hardware.

ISO/IEC SQuaRE

---

[7]This is called the *attribute hierarchy principle* [55, p. 135].

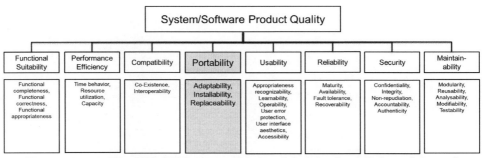

Figure 2.16.: The ISO/IEC 25010 Quality Model adapted from [53, p.4]

Hence, we reduce the scope of portability accordingly and define it as follows:

Definition 10: Portability

Portability is the *degree of effectiveness and efficiency with which a software product can be transferred from one software environment to another.*

As can be read from Fig. 2.16, portability has three subcharacteristics, *adaptability*, *replaceability*, and *installability*. The reasoning behind this structuring can be expressed through a sequence of decisions made when porting an application, as depicted in Fig. 2.17. If a software product needs to be ported, the starting

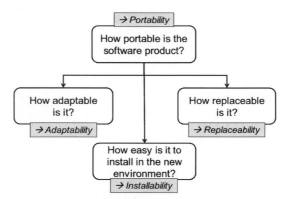

Figure 2.17.: Portability and its Subcharacteristics

point is the question whether it can be *directly ported* in its current form. If this is not the case, there are basically two options:

1. The nonportable parts of the software can be adapted for the new environment. The ease of this depends on its *adaptability*. In conformance to Def. 10, adaptability is defined as:

> **Definition 11: Adaptability**
>
> Adaptability is the *degree with which a software product can effectively and efficiently be adapted for different or evolving software environments.*

2. The software product can be *replaced* as a whole by an alternatively available software product that runs on the new platform. This depends on whether a suitable alternative is available. In contrast to portability or adaptability, this characteristic is not inherent to a software product, but depends on a comparison of software products. This is captured by the definition of replaceability:

> **Definition 12: Replaceability**
>
> Replaceability is the *degree to which a software product can replace another specified software product for the same purpose in the same environment* [53, p. 16].

Regardless of the decision taken, the new execution environment for the software product has to be *installed*. Moreover, the software product itself needs to be installed in the new environment. This is captured by the characteristic of installability, which is defined as:

> **Definition 13: Installability**
>
> Installability is the *degree of effectiveness and efficiency with which a software product can be successfully installed in a specified environment.*

[53, p. 7] clarifies that portability and its subcharacteristics are highly important for the maintainers and operators of a system. This is especially true for the installability of the system, since the operators of an organization will be the ones who have to perform the installation. As a consequence, an improvement of portability leads to an improvement of the working life of the operators. Enabling the quantification of these characteristics during development provides developers with feedback that allows them to develop software that is better to operate. This integration of development and operations is the central goal of the *DevOps* movement [124]. DevOps is a term for another agile practice that aims at improving IT performance and is strongly related to continuous integration and delivery. It is currently receiving widespread attention and is increasingly adopted in practice [164].

Each of the quality characteristics should be quantified to allow for meaningful decisions. The enabling of this quantification is one of the research objectives of this thesis. As stated at the beginning of this section, software quality and its measurement and assessment depends on stated and implied needs and conditions of software usage. This restriction has given rise to a number of approaches that

Portability and DevOps

51

try to make the ISO/IEC model more applicable in practice, such as [165–167]. Correspondingly, there is a need to tailor the ISO/IEC model for an evaluation of process-aware and service-oriented software and to develop metrics for this kind of software. At the time of writing, the ISO/IEC specification that is to contain concrete metrics [168] is still under development and not yet open to public scrutiny.

2.3.3. Standard Conformance and Portability

Service-oriented and process-aware software is standards-based software. As discussed before, a variety of standards for implementing process-aware and service-oriented software exist (cf. Sect. 2.2.1). Conformance to such a standard is a necessary prerequisite for software portability [29]. However, standard conformance is a two-fold aspect [45]: On the one hand, an application can be implemented in conformance to a standard, which is called *source code conformance*. On the other hand, a software execution environment, i. e., an engine, can implement a standard to enable the execution of application software that is source code-conformant. This corresponds to *implementation conformance* of the engine. Implementation conformance is more critical than source code conformance [45]. If there is no implementation conformance in engines, even applications that are source code-conformant cannot be executed. This means that the source code conformance of an application alone does not necessarily increase its portability. For this reason, we analyze implementation conformance as the basis for application portability in this work and define standard conformance accordingly:

Definition 14: Standard Conformance

Standard conformance is the degree to which a software product implements the features specified in a standard.

Building implementation-conformant execution environments and source code-conformant applications is a challenging task. Existing standards are complex and contain ambiguities, as discussed for particular specifications in [38, 39, 145, 169]. Moreover, they often have a large set of language elements. For instance, the BPMN specification lists 63 different types of events [26, Sect. 10.5]. As a result, the implementers of such a language often just implement a subset of the language or implement some language features in a way that differs from the original language specification. Only the elements of the language that are contained in the overlap of these subsets are truly portable from the source-code point of view. Other elements are portable to a limited degree, as depicted in Fig. 2.18. This implies that a practical porting of an application is often not feasible, despite the fact that multiple engines claim to support the standard it is implemented in.

The first research objective of this thesis is to provide evidence for and a general tendency of the portability of service-oriented and process-aware software.

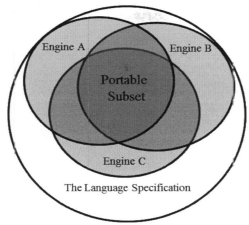

Figure 2.18.: Subsets of Supported Language Elements by Engines

Since portability depends on implementation conformance of engines, we build a *conformance benchmark* for process engines. This benchmark is described in Chap. 3. We benchmark engines for BPEL [27] and BPMN [26], since both are important for building executable service-oriented and process-aware software. The goal is to identify standard conformance-induced portability issues and to identify a tendency or degree of portability for every language element. This data is also the basis for subsequent metrics computation.

2.4. Software Metric Definition and Evaluation

Parts of this section have been taken from [170].

The second research objective of this thesis is the design and evaluation of a measurement framework for the assessment of the portability of service-oriented and process-aware software. To ensure scientific rigor in the definition and evaluation of this framework, a structured approach is needed. This approach is explained in the current section.

We discuss foundational theory of software metrics and metrics development, evaluation, and validation that stems from common metrics definition approaches [67, 68]. This forms the basis for the chapters of Part II of this thesis. The following subsection, Sect. 2.4.1, provides essential definitions and presents basic metric properties. In Sect. 2.4.2, we discuss the theoretical validation approaches used in this work, which includes a formal [69] as well as an informal approach [70]. Thereafter, in Sect. 2.4.3, we explain our method of operation for a practical evaluation of software metrics, along with the architecture of our prototypic implementation of a metrics suite, and a summary of the methods applied for hypothesis evaluation.

2.4.1. Basic Metric Properties

The purpose of software quality evaluation and assessment is to make the properties of a piece of software tangible through *measurement*. Measurement refers to the act of computing a *metric value* based on a piece of software [171, p. 3]. As such, it can be defined as follows:

> **Definition 15: Measurement**
>
> Measurement is *"the assignment of numerals to objects or events according to rules"* [172].

When it comes to software measurement, the objects or events of interest are software products. Measurement takes place either by analyzing their structure or by observing their behavior during execution. The terms *metric* and *measure* are often used interchangeably to denote a rule or function that performs the assignment of a numeral [53, 171, 173][174, p. 38]. In this thesis, we refer to the term *metric* as defined by [171]. There, the term *software quality metric* is defined as:

> **Definition 16: Software Quality Metric**
>
> A software quality metric is a *"function whose inputs are software data and whose output is a single numerical value that can be interpreted as the degree to which software possesses a given attribute that affects its quality"* [171, p. 3].

Measurement using software metrics is usually applied, either for the *assessment* of the quality of existing software or the *prediction* of future quality characteristics based on existing software and a predictive model [47]. The metrics derived in this work are directed at the assessment of the quality of existing software and not at the prediction of future quality characteristics.

Direct-ness and inter-nality Metrics can be *direct* or *indirect* [171, p. 3], *internal* or *external* [53, pp. 16f.], and possess a certain *scale* [172]. Direct metrics are metrics that do not depend on any other metric or measurement [171, p. 2] and a typical example for a direct metric are lines of code [174, p. 41]. In contrast, indirect metrics are computed from a combination of other, direct or indirect, metrics [171, p. 2]. Internal metrics are metrics that do only depend on the static attributes and structure of the software product, such as the source code [53, p. 17]. Consequently, such metrics can often be computed through static analysis. As opposed to this, external metrics depend on the behavior of an application and are computed at run-time [53, pp. 16f.]. The concepts of internality and externality are orthogonal to directness or indirectness. Direct or indirect metrics are also either internal or external.

Scale types The metric value that is assigned by a metric belongs to a certain value domain, which is determined by the scale type of the metric. The scale type delimits the mathematical operations that can be performed for a meaningful interpretation of the metric. Hence, it is the basis for the selection of proper statistical methods in an interpretation. Four scale types are frequently used, not only for software metrics [172][174, pp. 39f.]:

The nominal scale only differentiates between different values and is used for classification. It maps the measured attribute to a certain name or label and no relationships apart from equality and inequality can be observed among labels. Hence, the statistical methods that can be applied for a nominally scaled metric are limited. For instance, the total number of cases or the mode can be computed.

The ordinal scale extends the nominal scale by defining a natural order among the different labels. It can be observed that one label is considered "higher" than another, but there are no clear-cut distances between different labels. This allows for the computation of median values or percentiles.

The interval scale is similar to the ordinal scale in that it allows for an ordering of metric values, but in contrast to the ordinal scale the distance between the values are meaningful. For instance, it cannot only be observed that one value is higher than another, but also that the distance between the two is smaller or larger than the distance between another pair of values. Based on an interval scale, for instance, mean values, standard deviations, and correlations can be computed. Examples of an interval scale is temperature measured in Celsius.

The ratio scale is the most powerful scale and adds a meaningful null value to the interval scale. This implies that operations such as the coefficient of variation are possible.

When defining metrics in this thesis, we clarify their scale type, directness or indirectness, and internality or externality.

2.4.2. Theoretical Validation

Validation of new proposed metrics is a crucial but complex task [171]. Unfortunately, there is no strict consensus on metrics validation in the literature [175]. Instead, many different validity criteria for metrics [175], as well as threats to validity [174, Sect. 8.8], do exist. The importance of individual validity criteria and threats is context- and study-dependent. As [171, p. 10] states, *"validation does not mean a universal validation of the metrics for all applications. Rather it refers to validating the relationship between a set of metrics and a quality factor for a given application"*. In this thesis, we use the validity criteria defined in two established and often-cited validation frameworks [69, 70]. These frameworks have been applied in studies that are methodically similar to our work [65, 66, 176].

Validation approaches can be separated into formal approaches, e.g., [69, 177, 178], and informal approaches, e.g. [70, 179][171, pp. 10–13].

Informal approaches essentially bundle a number of validity criteria that are considered particularly important. Criteria that are mentioned often include aspects, such as repeatability, consistency, or discriminative power [171,179]. The evaluation of these criteria can be performed in a quantitative or qualitative fashion, depending on the validation framework.

Formal approaches take an axiomatic form. They specify a number of mathematical properties, for instance based on measurement theory, that a metric of a certain type should adhere to. Well-known formal validation approaches are, for instance, [69,177,178].

In this thesis, we apply a formal [69] and an informal [70] validation framework. The two frameworks are detailed more closely in the following subsections.

2.4.2.1. Formal Validation

The formal validation framework we use is the property-based software engineering measurement framework by Briand et. al. [69]. Its aim is to *"make the measure definition process more rigorous and less exploratory"* [69, p. 71]. It is a generic framework for validating mathematical properties of structural software metrics. The framework proposes several types of software metrics, being *size, length, complexity, cohesion,* and *coupling*. Each type of metric should fulfill certain mathematical properties.

Modular systems
    The formal model underlying [69] is that of a *modular system MS*. Such a system consists of the triple $< E, R, M >$, where E refers to the set of *elements* of the system, R to the set of *relations* among elements, i.e., $R \subseteq E \times E$, and M to a set of *modules*. Modules, in turn, consist of a subset of elements from E that are connected by relations from R. This means that modules form partitions of the elements and relations of the complete modular system. Fig. 2.19

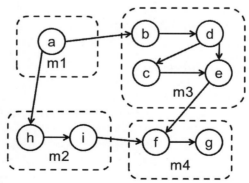

Figure 2.19.: Example of a Modular System adapted from [69, p. 71]

depicts an example of a modular system MS that consists of the four modules $M = \{m1, m2, m3, m4\}$, with the elements $E = \{a, b, c, d, e, f, g, h, i\}$ and the relations $R = \{< a, b >, < a, h >, < b, d >, < c, e >, < d, c >, < d, e >, < e, f >, < f, g >, < h, i >, < i, f >\}$. Each of the modules can be considered independently, for instance, $m3 =< E_{m3}, R_{m3} >=< \{\dot{v}, c, d, e\}, \{< b, d >, < c, e >, < d, c >, < d, e >\} >$. Although this is not the case in Fig. 2.19, modules may also overlap.

The metaphor of a modular system can directly be applied to service-oriented and process-aware software. The modular systems from [69] are directed graphs. Thus, they share the representation with process models as defined in Def. 6 and discussed in Sect. 2.2, which can also be represented as directed graphs. The elements of the modular system, the elements of set E, correspond to the nodes N of the process model, i.e., its activities, gateways, events, and basic elements. Analogously, the relations of the system, the elements of set R, correspond to the connectors C of a process model. For instance, a connector $c_1 \in C$ between two nodes $n_1, n_2 \in N$ implies a relation between the two, i.e., $< n_1, n_2 > \in R$. Moreover, a process model can be partitioned into multiple modules by labeling subsets of nodes and connectors. For instance, different control-flow branches could be considered as modules of the process model. The system from Fig. 2.19

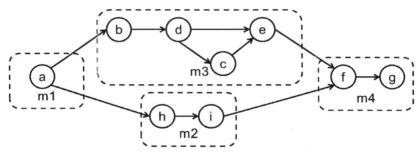

Figure 2.20.: A Process Model as a Modular System

can easily be rearranged in a directed form, which results in a visualization that is typical for process models. The visualization is depicted in Fig. 2.20. This demonstrates that the property-based software engineering measurement framework [69] is applicable for the formal validation of metrics for process-aware and service-oriented software.

The direct metrics defined in the course of this work are of two particular types: *size* and *complexity* [69]. Size metrics should fulfill the following properties[8]:

Non-negativity: Metric values for any system should be non-negative:

$$\forall.S =< E, R, M > \Rightarrow Metric(S) \geq 0 \tag{2.1}$$

Null value: Metric values for an empty system should be null:

$$\forall.S =< E, R, M >, E = \emptyset \Rightarrow Metric(S) = 0 \tag{2.2}$$

---

[8]In [180], Morasca proposes a refinement of the original framework [69] and demonstrates that not all the properties defined in [69] need to be discussed, for size and complexity metrics alike. Instead, only a subset of the original properties, from which the remaining properties follow, is strictly necessary. We still evaluate all properties defined in [69]. In contrast to [180], [69] has achieved wide-spread acceptance and is used in many studies. Relying on the same framework and axioms makes it easier to compare our work to these studies.

This means that an empty process model, i. e. a process model with no nodes, should have a size value of zero.

Additivity: The size of two disjoint modules of a system taken together should be identical to the sum of the two:

$$\forall.S =< E, R, M >, M = \{m_1, m_2\}, \ E_{m_1} \cap E_{m_2} = \emptyset \qquad (2.3)$$
$$\Rightarrow Metric(S) = Metric(m_1) + Metric(m_2)$$

These properties also apply to complexity metrics. Moreover, two additional properties should hold for complexity metrics:

Symmetry: Symmetry requires that the value of a complexity metric does not depend on the labeling used for the relations between elements. Two systems with identical elements but differently labeled relations should have the same complexity value:

$$\forall.S, S' : S = < E, R, M >, \ S' = < E, R', M > \qquad (2.4)$$
$$\Rightarrow Metric(S) = Metric(S')$$

Monotonicity: Monotonicity relates to additivity, which implies that the metric value for a combination of disjoint modules should be identical to the sum of the two. Monotonicity requires that the metric value for a combination of two non-disjoint modules should not decrease:

$$\forall.S =< E, R, M >, M = \{m_1, m_2\}, E_{m_1} \cap E_{m_2} \neq \emptyset \qquad (2.5)$$
$$\Rightarrow Metric(S) \geq Metric(m_1) + Metric(m_2)$$

It is important to note a difficulty in the interpretation of size and complexity, as defined by [69]. According to [69], the complexity of a system originates from the relations of the elements only and elements have no inherent complexity. [180] expands on this and clarifies that metrics which build on the relations of the system are complexity metrics, whereas metrics which build on system elements are size metrics. This view is debatable and [69, p. 73] concedes that "*it could be argued that [...] each element of E may have some complexity of its own*". In our case, system elements are the nodes of a process model. Each such element typically involves a variety of configuration options and settings that may even be interdependent. Thus, each element is also *complex* to a certain degree and, in some cases, the metrics defined in this work take this complexity into account. In this situation, the disambiguation into size or complexity metrics is not entirely clear and it is possible to put forward arguments for either type. If this is the case, we treat a metric as a complexity metric and, thus, validate more of the properties, rather than fewer.

2.4.2.2. Informal Validation

Software metrics should not only be mathematically sound, but also correctly reflect what they are intended to measure. This is often hard to prove formally. For instance, [67, p. 1107] states that *"the definition of a measure is itself a very human-intensive activity, which cannot be described and analyzed in a fully formal way"*. For this reason, informal validation approaches exist and complement a formal validation.

The informal theoretical validation framework we use is [70]. This framework builds on notable related informal validation approaches, in particular the IEEE standard 1061 [171] mentioned before, which defines a methodology for software quality metrics definition and validation. According to [171], direct metrics need not be validated, but are assumed to be valid due to the direct relationship to the characteristic which they measure. Kaner and Bond [70] criticize this assumption. They demonstrate, using the example of a direct metric from [171], that the directness of supposedly direct metrics is sometimes far from given. Their main point is that the existence of a causal relationship between a software metric and the quality characteristic it measures is seldom addressed. To better clarify the relation of the quality characteristic and metric, the authors propose a framework of ten questions. In these questions, they use the term *quality attribute* when referring to a *quality characteristic*. Another essential part is the *measurement instrument*, i. e., the tool or mechanism used to compute metric values. The ten questions to be answered for proposed metrics are [70]:

1. **What is the purpose of the metric?** The purpose of a metric influences the criticality of its validation. Examples of purposes are, for instance, project status evaluation, self-assessment and improvement, or providing information for stakeholders. The latter two are the primary purposes of the metrics presented in this thesis.

2. **What is the scope of the metric?** Depending on the size of the organization or project in which a metric is used, its scope can vary. Metrics can, for example, be directed at single persons, single projects of one or more workgroups, or at an entire company. The scope of the metrics in this work is generally a single, service-oriented and process-aware, project of one workgroup. They can be computed based on single process models or their execution engines.

3. **What attribute is the target of measurement?** The quality attribute to be measured should be clearly specified. If the attribute is unclear, then so is the value of the measurement. The top-level attribute this work focuses on is portability as defined in Sect. 2.3.2. Also the sub-attributes of portability, being installability, adaptability, and replaceability, are defined in this section.

4. **What is the natural scale of the attribute?** This question refers to scales of measurement as defined in Sect. 2.4.1. Although it is necessary to define

the scale type for a metric, this is not always possible for the measured attribute.

5. **What is the natural variability of the attribute?** There might exist an inherent variability for a quality attribute. This variability must be considered when interpreting it. For instance, programmer productivity varies naturally depending on the time of the day. If such a variation exists, this should be made clear.

6. **What is the metric and measurement instrument?** New metrics should be specified clearly, which can be achieved by a formal definition. Since the mechanism used to obtain metric values can also influence the result, it should also be clearly stated. Typical mechanisms are *counting* (e.g., lines of code, faults, control-flow branches), *matching* (e.g., program instructions, statements in a script), *comparing* (e.g., specifications, bug reports), or *timing* (e.g., duration of execution or installation). These mechanisms can be applied by a human or by a program. An automatic computation is clearly desirable, because it is more likely to result in objective metrics. Objective metrics are metrics that yield the exact same result for repeated computations [174, Sect. 3.1.2.]. In this work, we implement the metrics computation, as far as this is possible, in a metrics suite (cf. Sect. 2.4.3.2).

7. **What is the natural scale of the metric?** As stated before, the scale type of a metric needs to be defined. This scale may deviate from the scale of the attribute, and still allow for a valid quantification. In any case, the scale should be clearly specified.

8. **What is the natural variability of the instrument?** This question refers to possible measurement errors. Realistically, any practical measurement, regardless of whether it is performed by a human or by a program, has sources of errors. Since it is impossible to prove the absence of errors in the instrument, it is important to make clear what the primary sources of errors are.

9. **What is the relationship between attribute and metric?** This refers to the *construct validity* of the metric, i. e., if the metric really measures what it is intended to. The relationship between attribute and metric should be clarified by an underlying model. In particular, it should be clearly explained if and why there is a causal relationship between the two. The model that explains the relationship between the attributes we consider is the SQuaRE model explained in Sect. 2.3.2. The relationship between the metrics and each attribute is made clear in the respective chapters of the thesis.

10. **What are the side effects of using the instrument?** The results of a measurement may change depending on the effort put into the measurement process itself. Especially measurement performed by a human is prone to this error, as for example more time spent in measuring might result in

more desirable metric values without any change in the underlying attribute. Moreover, humans are good at modifying their behavior when being measured to produce more desirable metric values without any changes in the underlying attribute. If such side effects exist, they should be made clear.

2.4.3. Practical Evaluation

An evaluation of newly proposed metrics is crucial also from the practical point of view to complement a theoretical validation [171]. Metrics should be computed for realistic pieces of software to see how well they perform. This is necessary to demonstrate their applicability for assessing software quality and to exemplify their interpretation. Furthermore, it helps to verify what properties of the metrics hold in practice.

In this work, we perform a practical evaluation for the metrics we propose, by the means of an experiment. We gather large sets of service-oriented and process-aware applications, i. e., process models in BPEL 2.0 [27] or BPMN 2.0 [26], from public software repositories. Moreover, we implement the metrics computation for one of the two languages and compute metric values for gathered applications. Based on these values, we perform statistical analyses to verify a number of quality factors for the metrics[9].

2.4.3.1. Structure of the Experiments

The practical evaluation corresponds to an experiment. An experiment in the software engineering domain typically follows a series of steps and the structure and reporting of these steps is the topic of various publications [174, pp. 85ff.] [182, 183].

The first step is the scoping of the experiment and the statement of its goal, which we do during the discussion of the design of the experiment. This statement [183] clarifies the *objects of study*, the *purpose*, the *quality focus*, the *perspective*, and the *context* of the experiment. In our case, the objects of study are always pieces of service-oriented and process-aware software written in the languages mentioned above. The purpose of our experiment is to evaluate the quality of proposed metrics. The quality focus, i. e., the properties evaluated, depends on their nature. Hence, we evaluate different properties for different metrics. Properties we evaluate include for instance: *Goal statement*

Relation to Application Size: Software metrics, in particular complexity metrics, tend to produce very different values for applications of different size [184]. As a result, they cannot meaningfully be used for comparing applications of very different size. It can be considered a quality property of a metric, if it produces comparable values for applications of very different size.

Stability: On repeated executions of the experiment for different data, metric values should be similar. If they are vastly different, the mechanism of

---

[9]All statistical computations in this work are performed using the R software [181].

computation can be considered unstable. For instance after a given amount of time has passed and the applications that are the objects of study have been modified, the metrics should yield similar values. Only then, the mechanism of computation underlying the metrics can be considered as stable (or predictable in the terms of [171, p. 12]).

Discriminative Power: Metrics should assign different values to different pieces of software [171, p. 12]. If a metric assigns identical values to applications of very different quality, it can hardly be used for assessment and ranking.

The properties we evaluate are captured by experimental hypothesis. To conclude the goal statement, the perspective taken in the experiments is that of a software engineer, developer, or operator who builds and maintains process-aware and service-oriented software. Our evaluation is performed in the context of realistic software products obtained from third parties.

Source of applica-tions The next part of the experiment design, is the explanation of the origin and nature of the software applications used in the experiment and the design decisions made when obtaining them. The largest source for third party software used here is the Open Hub open source network[10]. At the time of writing, this network indexes and analyzes almost 700 thousand open source projects and offers the capability to search the code of these projects. To obtain software for analysis, we query the network, download the results of the query, and perform a variety of sanity checks to exclude broken or irrelevant results. The outcome are large sets of process models, in the languages we are looking for, that can be used for an evaluation of proposed metrics.

2.4.3.2. Implementation of a Metrics Suite

To allow for an objective computation of the metrics [174, Sect. 3.1.2.], we implement proposed metrics in a metrics suite, i. e., an application that automatically analyzes appropriate software artifacts and computes metric values. This is also necessary to perform the practical evaluation and to analyze thousands of process models. Without automated support, such a computation would not be feasible.

The metrics suite is essentially a static checker that parses and evaluates various software artifacts, similar to [158]. Its name is *prope*, which stands for *PRO*cess-aware information systems *P*ortability m*E*trics suite. The homepage of the tool is available at `https://uniba-dsg.github.io/prope/`. Prope uses a command line interface to trigger metrics computation and is implemented in Java. It is open source and freely available without charge under an MIT license.

Quality assurance Being our measurement instrument, prope is also a potential source of measurement errors. There is no way in which we can guarantee the absence of errors in the implementation. Since this thesis deals with software quality, we also tried to achieve a high level of quality in our tool. Therefore, we applied a variety of quality assurance techniques to reduce the amount of potential errors. To begin with, the code of prope is freely available and open to public scrutiny, which

---

[10]The network homepage is located at `https://www.openhub.net/`.

can lead to quality improvement [185, 186]. Moreover, we provide an excessive set of unit tests and, as suggested in Sect. 2.3.1, apply techniques of continuous integration and continuous inspection.

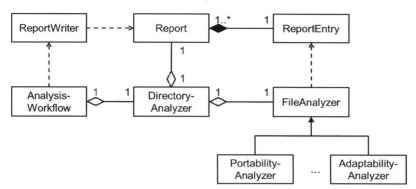

Figure 2.21.: Outline of the Metrics Suite

An outline of the structure of prope is depicted in Fig. 2.21. To perform an analysis and metrics computation for a set of software artifacts, prope requires two arguments: the type of the analysis to be performed and a file system path. The type of the analysis corresponds to one of the quality characteristics considered here, e.g., portability or installability, and the file system path identifies the location of the software artifacts to be analyzed. The execution of an analysis starts by instantiating an *AnalysisWorkflow*. This workflow controls the execution of an analysis run. It creates a *DirectoryAnalyzer* for the file system path that has been passed as an argument. This *DirectoryAnalyzer* recursively traverses the complete directory structure beginning with the initial path and schedules every file for an analysis by a *FileAnalyzer*. The *FileAnalyzer* corresponds to a plugin mechanism that can be extended to perform arbitrary analyses on software artifacts. The analyzers provided by prope depend on the quality characteristic for which metric values are to be computed and multiple implementations of this interface exist. A *FileAnalyzer* first determines if a given file is of interest to the current analysis type. If this is the case, the *FileAnalyzer* parses the file, computes relevant metrics for it, and produces a *ReportEntry*. Such an entry contains all metric values computed for the current file. When all files have been considered, the *DirectoryAnalyzer* aggregates all *ReportEntries* to a *Report* which is handed back to the *AnalysisWorkflow*. The workflow invokes a *ReportWriter* that serializes the results of the analysis. Currently, reports are written in CSV format.

Function-ing of the metrics suite

As indicated, the main extension point of prope are *FileAnalyzers*. These capture the actual mechanism of metrics computation. The functioning of specific *FileAnalyzers* is detailed as part of the practical evaluation in the different chapters of Part II. Using *FileAnalyzers*, it is easy to extend prope for the computation of additional metrics, even for different quality characteristics. Moreover, using its command line interface, prope can be integrated in enterprise

Plugin mecha-nism

level metrics suites, such as SonarQube[11]. That way, the metrics we propose are available for continuous integration and continuous inspection, as described in Sect. 2.3.1.

2.4.3.3. Hypothesis Evaluation

The last step in the practical evaluation is the computation of metric values for the applications obtained, using the implementation in the metrics suite, followed by the evaluation of the initially specified hypotheses. We discuss descriptive metric data and provide an interpretation of this data for the different applications. This serves as an example of the usage of the proposed metrics for quality assessment. Next, a number of statistical methods and tests are executed to evaluate the hypotheses stated in the design of the experiment. Using these tests, we check if the metrics satisfy expected quality properties. Frequently applied statistical techniques include:

- the Shapiro-Wilk test for normality [187] to see if metric values for a set of applications are distributed normally.

- the Mann-Whitney U test [188] for comparing the distributions of metrics values for different sets of applications. This test allows to see if the distributions of metric values differ significantly from each other.

- the Wilcoxon signed-rank test [189] for comparing the means of paired sets of metric values. The test is used to compare metric values for repeated executions of an experiment based on updated applications or an updated mechanism of computation. Using this test, we can see if the metric values of repeated executions differ significantly. Thus, we can evaluate stability (cf. Sect. 2.4.3.1).

- the square of the linear correlation coefficient, R^2, which allows to see if metric values for different metrics correlate with each other.

Lastly, the practical evaluation is concluded with a summary of the most important findings. This includes a final judgement on the appropriateness of the proposed metrics and, partly, the selection of a subset of the proposed metrics for quality assessment. All in all, the approach presented here allows to answer research question 2 and related subquestions, and addresses our second research objective.

---

[11]The project page of SonarQube can be found at http://www.sonarqube.org/. A prope plugin for this metric suite is currently under development.

3. A Conformance Benchmark for Process Engines

Parts of this chapter have been taken from [73, 74, 78, 82].

This chapter presents a benchmark of the standard conformance of a variety of process engines for the process languages BPEL 2.0 [27] and BPMN 2.0 [26]. The goal is to analyze the current state of the portability of process-aware and service-oriented software, i. e., to answer research question 1. As explained in Sect. 2.3.3, portability depends on the conformance of engines to the standards they claim to implement, i. e., their implementation conformance [45]. This is the reason for building a benchmark for process engines.

The results of the benchmark challenge the common assumption that contemporary standards are enough for enabling portability, i. e., it answers research question 1.1. Furthermore, it identifies existing portability issues and their implications and thereby answers research question 1.2. In summary, this chapter provides evidence that the portability of service-oriented and process-aware software is limited.

In the next section, we discuss common requirements for a benchmark and explain how we address these requirements here. In Sect. 3.2, we describe the design of the benchmark and its fully automatic implementation in the benchmarking tool betsy. We characterize the engines being tested and detail the test suites that cover the two languages BPEL [27], BPMN [26], as well as common workflow control-flow patterns [71]. Finally, the results of the execution of the benchmark are presented and interpreted in Sect. 3.3, which concludes the chapter and answers the research questions.

Structure of the chapter

3.1. Requirements for a Benchmark

Benchmarks are an important tool, for academic research and industry alike, to demonstrate the superiority of certain algorithms, tools, software products, or development processes [190]. Unfortunately, benchmarks are often complex and hard to build and interpret correctly [191]. Even seemingly small and technical issues can have a huge impact on the results and their validity. To make sure that a benchmark is valid and can correctly be interpreted, a number of requirements should be fulfilled [192]. These requirements relate to the software that automates the benchmark and the problem of the benchmarking itself. In the following, we detail the requirements from [192] and state how we address them in our benchmark.

Accessibility: The benchmark as well as its results should be easy to view and access. This is necessary, so that others can reproduce the results and double check their interpretation. It is not possible to assess the validity of a benchmark that cannot be accessed.

In our case, all of the software needed to perform the benchmark, with the exception of three commercial process engines, is open source and freely available without charge. We obtained three commercial BPEL engines under an academic license and are not permitted to distribute their executables or disclose their names. The remaining five BPEL engines and three BPMN engines, which we evaluate, are open source and available without cost.

Affordability: The costs of performing the benchmark must not be higher than the benefits gained from it. A benchmark should take up as little resources and time as is necessary to obtain valid results.

The primary cost factor for performing the conformance benchmark is execution time. Hardware costs are limited, and the benchmark can be performed on a single machine with no exceptional hardware requirements. The machine we executed the benchmark on was equipped with an Intel Core i7-2600 processor, 16 GB RAM, a 1 TB HDD, and was running Windows 7 Professional SP1. In this setting, a full conformance benchmark of all engines takes several dozen hours.

Clarity: The specification of the benchmark must be clearly stated and be as concise as possible so that others can look up and understand it with reasonable effort.

The specification of our benchmark is stated in the form of a testing methodology and a set of test suites consisting of conformance tests. These test suites detail the artifacts involved in a conformance test, the inputs to the test, the steps taken during test execution, and the expected results of the test. The test suites are described in a compact format and outlined in Sect. 3.2. Furthermore, all tests are listed in Appendix A.

Relevance: The benchmark should address a problem of realistic nature and size. The closeness to reality of the benchmark is dependent on its goal.

Our goal is to evaluate the standard conformance of a process engine. Every test in the benchmark is directly inferred from normative statements of a standard. The features we test are required to be supported by a conforming implementation of the standard and, hence, they are realistic. To allow for an isolated benchmarking of language features, the tests are as minimal as possible and, therefore, small in size. Nevertheless, they are relevant, since every test describes a feature an implementation has to support. Additionally, to cover larger-scale and realistic application scenarios, we include tests for the support for workflow control-flow patterns [71]. These patterns describe structures that are considered representative of realistic usage scenarios.

Solvability: A benchmark should produce meaningful results. There is no point in a benchmark that does not find differences between different systems or that is too trivial.

In Sect. 3.3, we describe a vast amount of unsuspected differences in standard conformance among the different engines which are uncovered by our benchmark. These differences in conformance have far reaching implications for application portability. Due to its size and specification coverage, the benchmark is also far from trivial.

Portability: The focus of this thesis, software portability, is not only relevant to process-aware and service-oriented software, but also to benchmarking. A benchmark that just works for one particular system is pointless. Instead, it should be abstract enough so that it is applicable to multiple systems. If there are too many customizations required to execute the benchmark on another system, its validity is put at risk. Differences in the results might originate from the customizations implemented and not the actual problem being tested.

The specification of our benchmark, as explained in Sect. 3.2, abstracts from a particular engine and also from a particular process standard. What is more, the benchmark is executed for a total of eleven different process engines and multiple revisions of these engines. Hence, the benchmark is sufficiently portable.

Scalability: The benchmark should work with systems of different maturity. It should be possible to work with research prototypes and industrial projects alike.

We benchmark open source and commercial engines, which are very different projects by nature. Although all of the engines are rated as mature by their respective distributors, it is clear from the benchmark results that some are much more complete than others. Hence, the benchmark scales to systems of varying origin and maturity.

3.2. Conformance Benchmark Design

The design of the benchmark consists of two main parts: The first part is a tool that is capable of installing, deleting, and communicating with a variety of process engines. The second part corresponds to three test suites of engine-independent conformance tests. The benchmarking tool instruments these tests to produce engine-specific deployment artifacts, deploys and executes these artifacts on the different engines, and evaluates the results of the execution. The outcome is a comprehensive overview of the support of a process engine for every feature of a standard.

In the following, we first describe the systems under test, i. e., the process engines we evaluate. Thereafter, we present the testing methodology and testing tool in Sect. 3.2.2. The remainder of the section details the three test suites.

3.2.1. **Systems under Test**

The benchmark addresses engines for BPMN [26] and BPEL [27]. The data we describe in this thesis stems from the evaluation of eight BPEL engines, five open source and three commercial ones, and three BPMN engines. It has to be remarked upfront that these are not all engines that exist for the two languages. Consequently, their selection might affect the external validity [174, p. 103], in particular generalizability, of the results. Arguably, benchmarking all existing engines is not feasible due to the associated effort and the licensing cost of several *Decisions* engines. However, the engines we selected are, to the best of our knowledge, *for* *engine* those that are most relevant to practice. Lacking market data on their usage, we *selection* cannot ultimately prove this assumption. Since we compare a relatively large amount of engines of open source and of commercial origin, we are confident that our results are generalizable to a larger population. Moreover, most of the engines received minor or patch version updates since the execution of the benchmark[12]. These updates resulted in minor changes in the benchmark data. None of these changes led to a different interpretation of the results or a different outcome of statistical tests applied. Hence, the results of the benchmark can be considered relatively stable.

In the following, we provide a brief overview over the engines under test. Table 3.1 shows the names, version numbers, licenses, and dates of release of the engines, with the exception of the three commercial BPEL engines. These engines are pseudonomized and further details cannot be unveiled due to the academic license under which the engines were obtained.

The BPEL engines we evaluate can be briefly characterized as follows:

Apache ODE: This engine can be considered as one of the most well-known and widely used open source BPEL engines. This is demonstrated by the fact that it is used in several open source Enterprise Service Buses (ESB's), such as WSO2. The project page of Apache ODE is available at http://ode.apache.org/.

bpel-g: bpel-g is a fork of the former reference implementation of the BPEL standard, the ActiveBPEL engine by Active Endpoints. The open source distribution of ActiveBPEL has been discontinued, but bpel-g is developed as a Google Code project and can be found at http://code.google.com/ p/bpel-g/.

OpenESB: The ESB product OpenESB includes a custom BPEL engine, which we evaluate. OpenESB was being developed by Sun prior to its acquisition by Oracle. Oracle open sourced OpenESB, which is now community-maintained. The project homepage of OpenESB is located at http://www. open-esb.net/.

Orchestra: Orchestra is a BPEL engine provided by the OW2 consortium, an open source community for infrastructure software. It uses a process

---

[12]The benchmark for BPEL engines was executed in July 2013 and for BPMN engines in October 2014.

Table 3.1.: Engines Under Test

Name	Version	License	Date of Release
BPEL			
Apache ODE	1.3.5	Apache License	02/2011
bpel-g	5.3	GPL	12/2012
OpenESB	2.3	CDDL	12/2009
Orchestra	4.9	LGPL	01/2012
Petals	4.1	LGPL	07/2012
E1	n.a.	commercial	n.a.
E2	n.a.	commercial	n.a.
E3	n.a.	commercial	n.a.
BPMN			
jBPM	6.0.0-Final	Apache License	11/2013
Activiti	5.16.3	Apache License	09/2014
camunda BPM	7.1.0-Final	Apache License	03/2014

virtual machine that is supposed to support the execution of different languages apart from BPEL, such as XPDL. Our focus in the evaluation relies solely on its BPEL conformance. Orchestra is available at `http://orchestra.ow2.org/`.

Petals: Similar to OpenESB, Petals ESB is an open source ESB that includes a custom BPEL engine, called EasyBPEL. Just like Orchestra, this product is developed by the OW2 consortium. After the benchmark had been executed, the Petals ESB project decided to discontinue the development of EasyBPEL. For completeness, we report on its support nonetheless. The documentation for EasyBPEL can be found at `http://research.petalslink.org/display/easyBPEL/EasyBPEL+Overview`.

Commercial BPEL Engines (E1–E3): The commercial engines under test come from major SOA middleware vendors. These vendors are also among the authors of the BPEL specification. Since we cannot disclose details, we pseudonimize the engines and refer to them as E1, E2, and E3 in the following.

Analogously, the BPMN engines we evaluate are:

jBPM: Similar to the Orchestra BPEL engine, jBPM was conceived as a general BPM platfrom and used a process virtual machine to support multiple process languages. From version 4.3 onwards, jBPM put its focus on the execution of BPMN processes specifically. The project website is located at `http://www.jbpm.org/`.

Activiti: The Activiti project was initiated by former developers of jBPM, with the intention to implement a new BPMN engine from scratch. Activiti's current main supporter is Alfresco and the project homepage can be found at `http://www.activiti.org/`.

Camunda BPM: Developed by the BPM software vendor camunda, this engine is a fork of Activiti. Prior to the forking in March 2013, developers from camunda were involved in the development of Activiti. The camunda BPM engine is available at `http://www.camunda.org/`.

3.2.2. **Benchmarking Methodology and Tool**

The intention of the benchmarking methodology presented in this section is to evaluate the standard conformance of a range of process engines in an isolated and reproducible fashion. We implemented a benchmarking tool that fully automates this methodology. The tool derives its name, *betsy*, from **BPEL/BPMN E**ngine **T**est **Sy**stem and is freely available at `https://github.com/uniba-dsg/betsy`. Betsy provides a domain model for defining conformance tests and automating the lifecycle of process engines. Furthermore, it executes these conformance tests in a conformance testing workflow. This section sketches the domain model and the testing workflow.

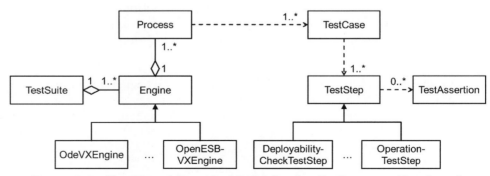

Figure 3.1.: Conceptual Domain Model for the Conformance Benchmark

Domain model   The domain model for specifying a benchmark is depicted in Fig. 3.1. This structure applies for benchmarks of BPEL and BPMN engines alike. Every execution of the tool is configured in a *TestSuite*. The key elements of this suite are *Processes* and *Engines*. A *Process* corresponds to a process model in either

BPEL or BPMN and bundles all engine independent artifacts that encapsulate a single language feature. In the case of BPEL, this is a BPEL process definition and related WSDL, XSD, and XSLT files. In the case of BPMN, it is a single file ending in .bpmn that includes a BPMN *Process*. A *Process* in the domain model is the basis for a single conformance test. An *Engine* represents one of the systems under test and defines methods for managing the lifecycle of a concrete engine instance in a specific version. Furthermore, it provides methods for deploying process models to that engine instance. Specific subclasses of this abstract class are implemented for every engine under test. This is also a major extension point of betsy and the conformance benchmark.

For each *Process*, a set of *TestCases*, consisting of several *TestSteps* that are verified through zero or more *TestAssertions* can be defined. A *TestCase* corresponds to a single valid control-flow path through a process model. Hence, multiple *TestCases* may be necessary to verify if the behavior of the language feature captured in the process model conforms to the standard. *TestSteps* correspond to steps in the traversal of the control-flow graph. For instance, this can be the creation of a process instance with specific input parameters or the sending of a message to a process instance. A *TestAssertion* captures expected behavior or output and can be validated after process execution. If all assertions pass, the test case is recorded as successful. If all *TestCases* linked to a *Process* are successful, the engine under test is considered to have passed the conformance test. Otherwise, the engine has failed the test.

TestAssertions are evaluated in different ways for BPEL and BPMN engines. For BPEL engines, betsy actively communicates with a running process instance by means of SOAP messages. In this case, *TestAssertions* are evaluated based on the payload of the messages received from the process instance as a reply. By sending messages at specific points during process instance execution, it is possible to verify if execution takes place as expected. In the case of BPMN, a fully standardized way of specifying message exchanges, working on all tested engines, is lacking, although a RESTful way of interaction is possible for some engines. [38] elaborates on this issue. Instead of actively communicating with a process instance, betsy evaluates execution traces written by the instance. For this reason, there is no communication between betsy and a BPMN process instance during execution.

The structure of process models used for capturing conformance tests reflects the difference between BPEL and BPMN. In both cases, we use a minimalistic process model, a *process stub* as the starting point for the implementation of every conformance test. The language elements used in the stub are of most basic nature and are confirmed to work on every engine under test. This ensures that they have no influence on the results of more sophisticated tests. For a conformance test, the process stub is extended with a specific language feature.

Process stub

Conformance tests for BPEL are necessarily based on WSDL. Every BPEL process model implements the same WSDL interface to enable a unified handling of all tests by betsy. To make sure that all engines support the interface, it is relatively simplistic. It contains a single *partnerLinkType* and several message definitions. All messages consist of one message part of a primitive type. The *portType* is made up of one asynchronous operation and two synchronous ones. The difference between the synchronous operations is that one of them defines a fault. The interface binding uses a document/literal style over HTTP, which is the most basic style available [105, Sec. 3]. Additionally, betsy provides a similarly structured web service interface, and Java implementation thereof, during execution. This is needed in the conformance tests for the *invoke* activity.

The process stub for BPEL conformance tests includes a synchronous operation. This is necessary to provide output and assert the correctness of the test execution. As a consequence, every BPEL conformance test requires the usage of *variables*, *assign* activities, and *reply* activities, next to an incoming message activity, either *receive* or *onMessage*, for instance creation. List. 3.1 outlines the structure of the process stub. The model starts with an incoming message activity (test prolog). This is followed by the implementation of the test, i. e., a language element in a particular configuration. Finally, the model is concluded by the transmission of the result (test epilog).

Listing 3.1: Outline of the BPEL Test Cases

```
<process>
    <partnerLinks />
    <variables />

    <sequence>
        <!-- Test Prolog-->
        <receive />

        <!-- Test implementation-->

        <!-- Test Epilog-->
        <assign />
        <reply />
    </sequence>
</process>
```

In the case of BPMN, a process model is not required make use of WSDL. Therefore, a single valid BPMN file is sufficient for implementing conformance tests. As before, a number of basic language elements are required. These are *none StartEvents*, *SequenceFlows*, *ScriptTasks*, and *none EndEvents*. *None Start-* and *none EndEvents* are of the most basic type, which the standard offers. They delineate the start and ending of the process model. As discussed above, active communication with the process instance is not possible in the same fashion as for BPEL conformance tests. Therefore, the tests use *ScriptTasks* to write execution traces to a log file. In the engine-independent specification of the conformance tests, the *ScriptTasks* only contain a token that describes the trace that should be written to the log file. The BPMN standard does not require support for a specific scripting language [26, Section 10.3.3]. Therefore, we inject a script in a language supported by an engine into the body of the *ScriptTask* on execution of a conformance test. Input data is provided to a process instance through process variables, which are initialized during the creation of the instance. Despite the difference in vocabulary, the resulting process model presented in List. 3.2 is very similar to its counterpart for BPEL conformance tests.

Listing 3.2: Outline of the BPMN Test Cases

```
<definitions>
    <process isExecutable="true">

        <!--Test Prolog-->
        <startEvent id="StartEvent">
            <outgoing>SequenceFlow_1</outgoing>
        </startEvent>
        <sequenceFlow id="SequenceFlow_1" sourceRef="
            StartEvent" targetRef="StartTask" />
        <scriptTask id="StartTask">
                <incoming>SequenceFlow_1</incoming>
                <outgoing>SequenceFlow_2</outgoing>
        </scriptTask>
        <sequenceFlow id="SequenceFlow_2" sourceRef="
            StartTask" targetRef="TestImplementation" />

        <!--Test implementation-->

        <!--Test Epilog-->
        <sequenceFlow id="SequenceFlow_3" sourceRef="
            TestImplementation" targetRef="EndTask" />
        <scriptTask id="EndTask">
                <incoming>SequenceFlow_3</incoming>
                <outgoing>SequenceFlow_4</outgoing>
        </scriptTask>
        <sequenceFlow id="SequenceFlow_4" sourceRef="
            EndTask" targetRef="EndEvent" />
        <endEvent id="EndEvent">
            <incoming>SequenceFlow_4</incoming>
        </endEvent>

    </process>
<definitions>
```

As discussed, in each conformance test, i.e., in each *Process*, we insert a *Benchmarking process* specific language feature in a particular configuration as test implementation. On execution, betsy links all *Processes* with all *Engines* in a *TestSuite* and executes all resulting tests sequentially. The execution logic of a benchmark is depicted

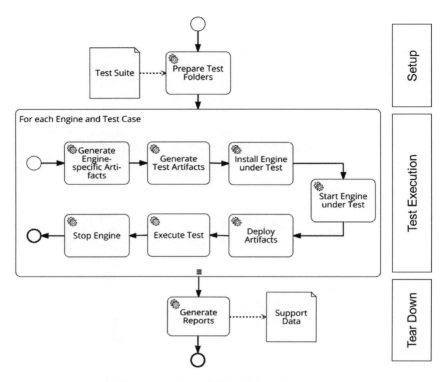

Figure 3.2.: Benchmarking Process

in Fig. 3.2 in BPMN notation. This process divides into phases of *setup, tear down* and *test execution*. The activity *Prepare Test Folders* corresponds to the setup phase and the activity *Generate Reports* to the tear down phase, which are executed exactly once, before and after the test execution phase, respectively. This latter phase corresponds to the execution of all *Processes* for all *Engines* in a *TestSuite*. Test execution takes place sequentially for each process and engine. Sequential execution of the tests implies a longer execution time, but is necessary to avoid side-effects that could occur when testing in parallel. Such side effects manifest for instance in blocked ports and could otherwise compromise the benchmark results.

During setup, the folder structure required for the test execution phase is built. The test execution in turn corresponds to multiple sequential steps. In the first step, a deployable artifact for a specific engine is created from the test files. If needed, this includes modifications to the standard-conformant process models, such as the addition of required engine-specific namespaces. Additionally, engine-specific deployment descriptors are generated. Second, test classes that trigger the execution of a process instance and validate its correctness are created from the *TestCases*. For BPEL, this involves a SoapUI[13] project configuration

---

[13]SoapUI is a unit testing tool for Web Services and RESTful services. It is available at

and JUnit[14] classes. For BPMN, the generation of a JUnit class that evaluates execution traces is sufficient. Third comes the installation of the engine under test. Each engine is installed anew for every test case execution. This is needed for test isolation, since the execution of a previous test case might have broken the engine installation. For instance, we found that a particular test resulted in an infinite loop for one engine, thereby crashing any future process instances executed on this engine. Fourth, the engine is started. Thereafter, the deployable artifact, which was created in the first step of the test execution phase, is deployed to the engine. In the sixth step, the test classes are executed, triggering the creation of a process instance, transmitting messages, and evaluating the result of the instance execution. Finally, the engine is stopped. Afterwards, the next test case is executed. During the tear down phase, all test results are aggregated to reports in CSV and HTML format. Table 3.2 summarizes the differences in the testing of BPMN and BPEL engines described in this section.

Table 3.2.: Differences in Testing BPMN and BPEL Engines

	BPMN	BPEL
Test Files	`.bpmn`	`.bpel, .wsdl, .xsd, .xslt`
Input Data	process variables	SOAP message content
Assertion Validation	execution traces	message exchanges
Test Execution	JUnit	SoapUI, JUnit

3.2.3. Conformance Test Suites

The next crucial ingredient of the conformance benchmark are the test suites of conformance test cases. In total, there are three test suites. These are a BPEL conformance test suite described in the following subsection, a test suite with workflow control-flow pattern implementations in BPEL described in Sect. 3.2.3.2, and a conformance test suite for BPMN described in Sect. 3.2.3.3.

All test cases have undergone quality assurance, to make sure that they correctly reflect the language standards. This includes an XSD validation of the process models, in-group peer review of all process models, as well as review of some process models by external experts. Moreover, an overwhelming majority of the test cases run on at least a single engine. The code used to perform the benchmark of BPEL engines is the v0.3.0 release of betsy and is available at `https://github.com/uniba-dsg/betsy/releases/tag/v0.3.0-icsoc2013`. The updated code for benchmarking BPMN engines can be found in betsy's v2.0.0 release, available at `https://github.com/uniba-dsg/betsy/releases/tag/2.0.0`.

`http://www.soapui.org/`. We use SoapUI for the testing of BPEL processes to transmit a series of SOAP messages and evaluate the replies.

[14]JUnit is the de-facto standard for unit testing in Java. It is available at `http://junit.org/`.

3.2.3.1. BPEL Conformance Test Suite

The source of all test cases are the normative requirements stated in the BPEL 2.0 standard [27]. A complete listing of all test cases can be found in Table A.1 in the appendix. Normative requirements are specified using common notational conventions [193] (i.e. MUST, MUST NOT, etc.). The test cases are classified into the activity groups defined in the specification and explained in Sect. 2.2.2.4: basic activities [27, pp. 84–97], structured activities [27, pp. 98–114] and scopes [27, pp. 115-147]. Each group also contains test cases for standard faults that are associated with the activities of the group. Table 3.3 provides an overview of the test suite and lists the number of conformance tests per activity.

Table 3.3.: BPEL Conformance Test Suite

Basic Activities		Structured Activities		Scopes	
Assign	19	Flow	9	Compensation	5
Empty	1	ForEach	11	CorrelationSets	2
Exit	1	If	5	EventHandlers	8
Invoke	12	Pick	5	FaultHandlers	6
Receive	5	RepeatUntil	2	MessageExchanges	3
Receive & Reply	11	Sequence	1	PartnerLinks	1
Rethrow	3	While	1	Scope-Attributes	3
Throw	5			TerminationHandlers	2
Validate	2			Variables	2
Variables	3				
Wait	3				
Σ	65		32		34

Design decisions   Although the BPEL standard is relatively precise, three aspects necessary for executable process models are left open: First, there is no required format for the specification of a partner reference that can be used in the assignment of *partnerLinks*. This is needed to enable dynamic assignment and runtime selection of services. In the benchmark, we use WS-Addressing *EndpointReferences* [194] (encapsulated in BPEL's *service-ref* container). Second, the URI scheme for identifying XSL stylesheets is not made clear. We use the filename of the stylesheet for its identification. Third, and probably most critical, is the underspecification of the behavior of the engine in case a fault is thrown during execution and not handled by the process instance, while at the same time, request-response operations are still open. Put differently, given a third party waits for a response from a process instance, it is not made clear what the third party will receive in case the instance crashes with a fault. Possible options are a timeout, a default response, or a propagation of the fault that led to the crash. In the test cases, we opt for the latter. This is also the fault propagation mechanism applied by most high-level programming languages and is a prerequisite for distributed fault handling [195].

3.2.3.2. Pattern Test Suite

The conformance test suites puts its focus on single language elements in isolation. Not all of these language elements are equally important in real-world applications. Moreover, it is possible that language elements that conform to the standard in isolation fail to conform when being combined with each other. To gain insights on the implications, which standard-conformance issues have in realistic application scenarios, additional tests are required. Such tests can be found in Workflow Control-Flow Patterns (WCPs) [71]. According to the authors of [71], these patterns capture scenarios that are frequently needed in real-world process-aware applications. Moreover, WCPs have frequently been used as a means for comparing different process languages or process management systems with respect to their expressiveness. Also BPEL and BPMN have been addressed by pattern-based analyses [196–198]. For this reason, we provide a test suite that benchmarks support for WCPs in BPEL engines.

Patterns often require the combination of multiple language constructs for their implementation. The focus of pattern-based analyses lies on how many patterns a language allows to implement and how directly a pattern can be implemented. The lower the amount of constructs needed for an implementation in a particular language, the more direct the support is considered, and hence the more expressive the language is [71]. The original pattern catalog [71] consists of 20 patterns. These are basic control-flow, advanced branching and synchronization, structural, multi-instance, state-based, and cancellation patterns. A discussion of the nature of every pattern is out of scope here, but can be found in [71] or on the homepage of the workflow patterns initiative located at http://www.workflowpatterns.com/. For a detailed description of pattern implementations in BPEL, we refer the interested reader to [196, 199].

In test suite at hand, we provide implementations of WCPs in BPEL that can be used by the benchmarking tool in the same fashion as conformance tests. The test cases are built by adapting the existing pattern implementations from [196]. The pattern tests use the same process stub and WSDL interface as the standard conformance tests. A pattern is considered to be *directly* supported (denoted as +), if at least one solution can be found, which uses no more than a single language construct to implement the pattern [71]. If a solution requires a combination of two constructs, it is counted as *partial support* (denoted as +/−) for the pattern, otherwise, there is *no direct support* (denoted as −). BPEL 2.0 provides no direct support for four out of the 20 patterns (*Multi-Merge, Discriminator, Arbitrary Cycles* and *Multiple Instances Without a Priori Runtime Knowledge*) [196, 199]. An engine can only improve this degree through the usage of nonstandard extensions. Since the goal of the benchmark is to evaluate standard conformance, we exclude these four patterns from the benchmark. Furthermore, three patterns (*Interleaved Parallel Routing, Milestone,* and *Cancel Activity*) are at most partially supported in standard-conformant BPEL. Implementations for these patterns are evaluated in the benchmark. Finally, for four patterns (*Multi-Choice, Synchronizing Merge, Multiple Instances Without Synchronization* and *Multiple Instances With a Priori Design Time Knowledge*) alternative solutions

Pattern test implementation

Table 3.4.: Workflow Control-Flow Patterns Test Suite

Patterns	BPEL	Tests
Basic Control-Flow Patterns		
WCP01: Sequence	+	1
WCP02: Parallel Split	+	1
WCP03: Synchronization	+	1
WCP04: Exclusive Choice	+	1
WCP05: Simple Merge	+	1
Advanced Branching and Synchronization Patterns		
WCP06: Multi-Choice	+	2
WCP07: Synchronizing Merge	+	2
WCP08: Multi-Merge	-	0
WCP09: Discriminator	-	0
Structural Patterns		
WCP10: Arbitrary Cycles	-	0
WCP11: Implicit Termination	+	1
Patterns with Multiple Instances (MI)		
WCP12: MI Without Synchronization	+	3
WCP13: MI With a Priori Design Time Knowledge	+	2
WCP14: MI With a Priori Runtime Knowledge	+	1
WCP15: MI Without a Priori Runtime Knowledge	-	0
State-based Patterns		
WCP16: Deferred Choice	+	1
WCP17: Interleaved Parallel Routing	+/-	1
WCP18: Milestone	+/-	1
Cancellation Patterns		
WCP19: Cancel Activity	+/-	1
WCP20: Cancel Case	+	1

are available in BPEL 2.0, which we cover in different tests. In summary, if an engine passes a pattern test, it provides either direct or partial support for a pattern, depending on the test. Table 3.4 shows the number of tests for the different WCPs in the test suite and the degree of pattern support (direct support, partial support, no direct support) that can be achieved with standard BPEL 2.0. The structure of the tests can be found in Table A.2 in the appendix.

3.2.3.3. BPMN Conformance Test Suite

The third test suite contains tests for assessing the standard conformance of BPMN 2.0 engines. Similar to the test suite for BPEL standard conformance, test cases are derived from the normative parts of the language standard [26]. As discussed in Sect. 2.2.2.3, the focus of this work is exclusively on the executable part of BPMN. Therefore, tests are derived from Chapter 10 of [26] which describes executable process models. The test suite is subdivided into the categories of *basics*, *activities*, *gateways*, *events*, and *errors*. The *activities* category comprises *Tasks*, *SubProcesses*, and *CallActivities*, as specified in [26, Chapter 10.3]. *Events* can be found in [26, Chapter 10.5] and *gateways* are defined in [26, Chapter 10.6]. Elements that are part of executable process models, but do not fall into the preceding categories, such as *SequenceFlows*,

Table 3.5.: BPMN Conformance Test Suite

Language Constructs		Tests
Basics		6
	Lane	1
	Participant	1
	SequenceFlow	4
Activities		12
	CallActivity	2
	Multiple Instantiation	5
	Looping	3
	SubProcess	1
	Transaction	1
Gateways		13
	ExclusiveGateway	3
	InclusiveGateway	2
	ParallelGateway	1
	ComplexGateway	1
	EventBasedGateway	2
	GatewayCombinations	4
Events		36
	Cancel	1
	Compensation	6
	Conditional	5
	Error	4
	Escalation	7
	Link	1
	Signal	6
	Terminate	1
	Timer	5
Errors		3
	InvalidGatewayCombinations	2
	ParallelGateway_Conditions	1

belong to the *basics* category. Finally, the *errors* category comprises process models that should be rejected by a BPMN engine. These are, for instance, invalid combinations of gateways. The resulting number of tests are listed in Table 3.5. An exhaustive description of all test cases can be found in Table A.3 in the appendix.

As indicated in Sect. 2.2.2.3, the BPMN standard is less precise than the BPEL standard. Implementers of BPMN have a relatively high degree of freedom of interpretation. As a result, it is challenging to write tests for standard conformance. For this reason, the test suite presented here covers only a subset of the executable part of BPMN. More precisely, it excludes specific types of tasks, e.g., *UserTask* or *BusinessRuleTask*. Furthermore, the definition of *MultipleEvents* and inter-process communication is not covered (intra-process communication in terms of communicating *SubProcesses* is included in the test suite). Since none of the engines we benchmarked provided the required support for WSDL interfaces, message-related events and tasks are omitted. Finally, *DataObjects* are also out of scope. The conformance evaluation of these elements remains for future work.

Test suite scope

3.3. Benchmarking Results and Implications

The engines under test, described in Sect. 3.2.1, were evaluated using the methodology and tool, discussed in Sect. 3.2.2, with the test suites from Sect. 3.2.3. The benchmark of BPEL engines for standard conformance and workflow control-flow pattern support was performed in July 2013. The standard conformance benchmark of BPMN engines took place in October 2014. Both benchmarks were executed on a single machine, using betsy with the Jenkins CI server, that runs a Windows 7 SP1 operating system and is equipped with an Intel Core i7-2600 processor, 16 GB RAM, and an a hard disk with 1TB of memory. These hardware specifications are more than sufficient for the benchmark. Repeated subsequent benchmark executions were performed for validation and resulted in the same data.

In the following, we first discuss the detailed results of the different test suites. Sect. 3.3.1 covers the standard conformance of BPEL engines, Sect. 3.3.2 deals with workflow control-flow patterns, and Sect. 3.3.3 focuses on BPMN engines. Thereafter, we discuss the implications these results have on application portability in Sect. 3.3.4 and answer the research questions addressed in this chapter.

3.3.1. Results for BPEL Engines

The amount of passed conformance tests aggregated by BPEL activity and engine can be found in Table 3.6 for basic activities, in Table 3.7 for structured activities, and in Table 3.8 for scopes. Additionally, the tables show the percentages of successful tests for each engine. In the last row, the average amount of successful tests for the three commercial engines, the top three open source engines, and all five open source engines can be found. Moreover, Fig. 3.3 depicts the aggregated amount of passed and failed tests by engine and activity group, i.e., basic activities (BA), scopes (S), and structured activities (SA). In the following, we first discuss the results for each particular engine, starting with commercial engines.

Engine E1: This engine passes the highest amount of tests, when compared to the other commercial engines. It fails eleven conformance tests, thus passing 92% of the test suite. Failed tests are confined to fault handling, XSL processing and specific service invocation settings. These failures occur for basic activities (nine tests) and structured activities (two tests). E1 passes all scope-related tests. Explained in more detail, the engine fails the tests that use XSLT and is unable to correctly invoke a Web service operation that does not expect an input message. Furthermore, it fails to throw an *invalidExpressionValue* fault given the *forEach* activity is configured with a negative *completionCondition* or a *startCounter* that is set too high.

Engine E2: Engine E2 passes only about half of all conformance tests. This is the worst rate among the commercial engines. The amount of failures is particularly high for basic activities, where 38 out of 65 tests fail. For scopes and structured activities, the situation looks better, with around two thirds

Table 3.6.: Number of Passed Conformance Tests for Basic Activities, Aggregated by Activity and Engine

Activity	Proprietary Engines			Open Source Engines					
	E1	E2	E3	bpel-g	ODE	OpenESB	Orchestra	Petals	Σ
Assign	15	7	15	15	10	13	11	8	19
Empty	1	1	1	1	1	1	1	1	1
Exit	1	1	1	1	1	1	1	1	1
Invoke	11	6	7	11	7	3	8	5	12
Receive	4	3	3	4	3	1	1	1	5
ReceiveReply	8	6	6	8	5	6	5	1	11
Rethrow	3	0	1	3	2	1	0	0	3
Throw	5	0	4	5	5	4	0	0	5
Validate	2	0	2	2	0	2	0	0	2
Variables	3	1	1	3	2	2	1	1	3
Wait	3	2	3	3	3	3	2	1	3
Σ	56	27	44	56	39	37	30	19	65
Percentage	86%	41%	68%	86%	60%	57%	46%	29%	
Ø	Commerical 65%			bpel-g, ODE, OpenESB 68%			Open Source 56%		

of successfully passed tests. The determining factor for this failure rate is the fault handling paradigm of E2. As discussed in Sect. 3.2.3.1, we expect a fault that reaches the root scope of the process to be propagated to third parties that still wait for a response from the process instance in an open request-response operation. In contrast to this, E2 does not propagate faults and a process instance fails silently instead. This behavior severely hampers the debugging of a process model and, as a result, the engine fails all tests for the *throw*, *rethrow*, and *validate* activities. Moreover, tests regarding the handling of faults from invoked services and other tests regarding standard faults are also unsuccessful. In total, this results in a failure of 32% of the complete test suite. The remaining amount of failed tests comes from features that are seemingly not implemented. *CompletionConditions* cannot be used in a *forEach* activity and *joinConditions* are not available in a *flow* activity. The scope-level definition of *correlationSets* or *partnerLinks* is not supported and so are *terminationHandlers*. Tests for *eventHandlers* are largely successful, although the *fromParts* syntax is not supported in an *onEvent* activity. Also delayed execution using the *until* element in an *onAlarm* activity is not possible. Nearly all tests for in-process fault handling are successful, with the exception of catching faults based on fault data in a *faultElement*. *CorrelationSets* have to be initialized in a synchronous operation, or E2 will be unable to correlate on a set in subsequent *eventHandlers*. When it comes to basic activities, *correlationSets* or *faultHandlers* cannot be defined for *invoke* activities and multiple features

Table 3.7.: Number of Passed Conformance Tests for Structured Activities, Aggregated by Activity and Engine

| Activity | Proprietary Engines | | | Open Source Engines | | | | | Σ |
	E1	E2	E3	bpel-g	ODE	OpenESB	Orchestra	Petals	
Flow	9	6	7	9	9	2	7	0	9
ForEach	9	4	6	9	3	9	0	2	11
If	5	4	4	5	4	4	4	4	5
Pick	5	5	5	5	5	4	4	1	5
RepeatUntil	2	2	2	2	1	2	2	0	2
Sequence	1	1	1	1	1	1	1	1	1
While	1	1	1	1	1	1	1	1	1
Σ	32	23	26	32	24	23	19	9	34
Percentage	94%	68%	76%	94%	71%	68%	56%	26%	
Ø	Commerical			bpel-g, ODE, OpenESB			Open Source		
	79%			77%			62%		

of the *assign* activity, i. e., all XPath extension functions, the assignment of *partnerLinks*, and the *keepSrcElementName* attribute, are unsupported.

Engine E3: The third commercial engine passes almost three quarters of the test suite. Among basic activities, E3 fails tests related to handlers attached to *invoke* activities, similar to E2, and the *toParts* syntax is unsupported. Moreover, it does not throw several standard faults, such as *correlationViolation* or *missingReply*. Also the throwing or rethrowing of faults based on *faultData* is not possible and *terminationHandlers* are unsupported. When it comes to structured activities, tests for the usage of *joinConditions* in *flow* activities fail. Finally, the *completionCondition* with the *successfulBranchesOnly* attribute set is not supported for the *forEach* activity. Also a truly parallel execution of the *forEach* activity fails, even when the *parallel* attribute is set.

bpel-g: Among the open source engines under test, bpel-g passes the highest amount of tests. In particular, all tests for scopes and all but two tests for structured activities are successful. Moreover, bpel-g also excels in throwing the standard faults in the expected situations. Failed tests are mainly confined to XSLT processing, which is not supported in the case of bpel-g, and the invocation of service operations that do not require input.

Apache ODE: This engine passes a fair part of the overall test suite, although several language features are not implemented. Similar to many other engines, numerous standard faults are not thrown as expected, *terminationHandlers* are unsupported, and so is the usage of *completionConditions* in the *forEach* activity. Moreover, the *toParts* and *fromParts* syntax is not supported for messaging activities and assignment alike. The same

Table 3.8.: Number of Passed Conformance Tests for Scopes, Aggregated by Activity and Engine

Activity	Proprietary Engines			Open Source Engines					
	E1	E2	E3	bpel-g	ODE	Op.ESB	Orch.	Petals	Σ
Compensation	5	5	5	5	4	5	2	0	5
CorrelationSets	2	0	2	2	2	1	0	0	2
EventHandlers	8	5	7	8	6	6	6	0	8
FaultHandlers	6	5	6	6	6	6	2	5	6
MessageExchanges	3	1	1	3	1	1	1	0	3
PartnerLinks	1	0	1	1	1	1	1	0	1
Scope-Attributes	3	2	3	3	2	3	1	1	3
Termin.Handlers	2	0	0	2	0	2	2	0	2
Variables	2	2	2	2	2	2	2	0	2
Σ	32	20	27	32	24	27	17	6	32
Percentage	100%	63%	84%	100%	75%	84%	53%	19%	
∅	Commerical			bpel-g, ODE, OpenESB			Open Source		
	82%			86%			66%		

applies to variable validation during assignment or the usage of the *validate* activity.

OpenESB: The OpenESB BPEL service engine is on par with Apache ODE and passes the same amount of tests, albeit different tests. One of its major drawbacks is its complete lack of support for links within *flow* activities. That way, a graph-oriented control-flow definition is not possible with OpenESB and process models are confined to the block-structured approach. Also truly parallel activity execution is not possible. Like in the case of Apache ODE, the *toParts* and *fromParts* syntax is not supported and many standard faults are not thrown as expected. The same applies to XSLT processing. Finally, the engine does not support the attachment of *faultHandlers* to *invoke* activities and the throwing and rethrowing of data in a fault.

Orchestra: The fourth open source engine passes around half of the overall test suite. The primary reason for failures lies in its fault handling paradigm, which is similar to that of the commercial engine E2. If a fault is propagated to the root scope of the process instance and third parties are still waiting on a reply in an open request response operation, Orchestra replies with an HTTP 200 OK status code instead of the fault. This results in a failure for all tests regarding the *throw* and *rethrow* activities, as well as numerous other tests for basic activities and scopes. Another severe issue is the failure of all tests that use message correlation in combination with asynchronous operations. As opposed to this, the amount of passed tests in the category of structured activities is almost as high as for Apache ODE and OpenESB. In

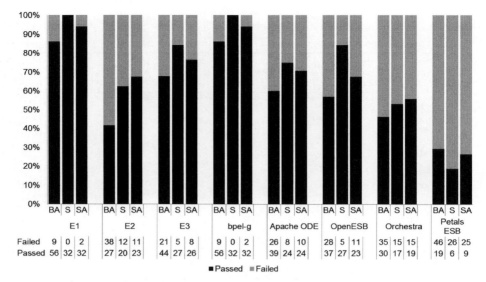

	BA	S	SA	BA	S	SA	BA	S	SA	BA	S	SA	BA	S	SA	BA	S	SA	BA	S	SA	BA	S	SA
		E1			E2			E3			bpel-g		Apache ODE			OpenESB			Orchestra			Petals ESB		
Failed	9	0	2	38	12	11	21	5	8	9	0	2	26	8	10	28	5	11	35	15	15	46	26	25
Passed	56	32	32	27	20	23	44	27	26	56	32	32	39	24	24	37	27	23	30	17	19	19	6	9

■ Passed ■ Failed

Figure 3.3.: Percentages of Passed and Failed Tests per Engine and Activity Group for BPEL

this category, however, Orchestra completely lacks support for the *forEach* activity.

Petals: Finally, the engine with the highest amount of failures is Petals. It fails almost three quarters of the complete test suite and, hence, BPEL support is minimal. In particular, the *flow, repeatUntil, validate, throw,* and *rethrow* activities are completely unsupported. The same applies to the scope-level definition of *correlationSets, eventHandlers, messageExchanges, partnerLinks, variables, compensationHandlers,* and *terminationHandlers.* Most critically, Petals does not pass a single test that involves message correlation. As a result, it cannot be used for implementing long-running interactions, which are among the primary motivations for using process-aware systems in the first place.

Based on these results, several observations can be made. To begin with, it becomes obvious that no single engine fully conforms to the BPEL standard. Moreover, the amount of passed tests and, hence, the degree of standard conformance achieved varies a lot among the different engines. This implies that research question 1.1 can be answered negatively for the case of the BPEL standard and BPEL engines. The existence of the relatively precise standard has not resulted in implementations that use the same execution model. Due to this varying degree of standard conformance, porting BPEL processes among different engines will be challenging.

Features with broad support As a next step, it can be observed which parts of the language are well-supported, and thus portable. First of all, basic language constructs for control-flow definition, e.g., the *sequence, if,* and *while* activities, are supported by practically every engine. Hence, conditional control-flow definition and repeated execution of activities is possible in a portable fashion. Moreover, basic facilities for enabling message exchanges do exist. In particular, the *invoke, receive,* and *reply* activities are supported in their simplest configuration. The same applies to data handling mechanisms using the *from* and *to* or *literal* syntax in the *assign* activity. Also basic support for fault handling using *faultHandlers* exists, as long as either a single fault is caught explicitly or all faults are caught regardless of their type. Finally, support for the *empty* and *exit* activities is in place. However, any slightly advanced features, e.g., graph-based control-flow definition, asynchronous messaging and message correlation, concurrency, compensation, or validation are often not supported or not implemented as specified by the BPEL standard. This implies that realistic process models that make use of these more advanced features will be hard to port among different engines.

Since the benchmark includes commercial and open source engines, it is worth to compare the two groups. To begin with, commercial engines pass between 53% and 92% of the conformance tests. For open source engines, the deviation is higher with 26% to 92% of successful conformance tests. On average, commercial engines pass 73% of the conformance test suite, whereas the open source engines only achieve 62%, so it looks as if commercial engines perform better. Using a binomial test, we can verify if this difference is significant. We tested if the probability of passing a conformance test is equal for open source engines and commercial engines at a significance level of 5% by comparing the amount of passed conformance tests in relation to the total amount of conformance tests for each group. With a resulting p-value of $2.5e^{-9}$, this hypothesis can be safely rejected in favor of the alternative: Open source engines pass significantly less tests than their counterparts. A cause for this observation may be that our test set of open source engines includes engines that could be considered premature, despite the fact that all of the vendors claim the maturity of the engines evaluated here. This argument is supported by the fact that the lowest ranking engine, Petals, only passes 26% of the tests. The comparison among commercial and open source engines changes, when excluding the engines with the most failures, Orchestra and Petals, and considering the top three open source engines, bpel-g, Apache ODE, and OpenESB. For these three engines, average standard conformance ranges at 75%, two percentage points above the corresponding value for commercial engines. Using binomial tests as before, we can confirm that there is no significant difference between the commercial and the top three open source engines. The number of successful conformance tests is clearly not lower (p-value of 0.81), but also not significantly higher (p-value of 0.23) for open source engines. To summarize this paragraph, commercial engines provide a higher degree of support, although the difference balances when only considering mature open source engines.

Commercial vs. OS engines

3.3.2. Workflow Control-Flow Pattern Support

The second part of the benchmark of BPEL engines is formed by the patterns test suite described in Sect. 3.2.3.2. Table 3.9 shows the results of this benchmark using the trivalent rating of direct support (+), partial support (+/-), and no direct support (-). The second column lists the highest degree of direct support for a pattern that can be achieved in standard BPEL. Patterns that cannot directly be implemented using standard BPEL, as discussed in Sect. 3.2.3.2, are omitted in the table. The last two rows show the percentages of the amount of times the engines achieve the same support rating as the BPEL standard.

Table 3.9.: Workflow Control-Flow Patterns Support By Engine

Pattern	BPEL	Comm. Eng.			Open Source Engines				
		E1	E2	E3	bpel-g	ODE	Op.ESB	Orch.	Pet.
Basic Control-Flow Patterns									
P01 Sequence	+	+	+	+	+	+	+	+	+
P02 Parallel Split	+	+	+	+	+	+	+	+	+
P03 Synchronization	+	+	+	+	+	+	+	+	+
P04 Exlusive Choice	+	+	+	+	+	+	+	+	+
P05 Simple Merge	+	+	+	+	+	+	+	+	+
Advanced Branching and Synchronization Patterns									
P06 Multi-Choice	+	+	+	+	+	+	+/-	+	+/-
P07 Synchronizing Merge	+	+	+	+	+	+	+/-	+	+/-
Structural Patterns									
P11 Implicit Termination	+	+	+	+	+	+	+	+	+
Patterns with Multiple Instances									
P12 MI Without Sync.	+	+	+	+/-	+	+	+/-	+/-	+/-
P13 MI W. Design T. Know.	+	+	+	-	+	+	+/-	+/-	+/-
P14 MI W. Runtime Know.	+	+	+	-	+	+	-	-	-
State-based Patterns									
P16 Deferred Choice	+	+	+	+	+	+	+	+	+
P17 Interl. Parallel Routing	+/-	+/-	+/-	+/-	+/-	+/-	-	-	-
P18 Milestone	+/-	+/-	+/-	+/-	+/-	+/-	+/-	-	-
Cancellation Patterns									
P19 Cancel Activity	+/-	+/-	+/-	+/-	+/-	+/-	+/-	+/-	+/-
P20 Cancel Case	+	+	+	+	+	+	+	+	+
Percentage		100%	100%	81%	100%	100%	63%	69%	56%
∅		Commerical			bpel-g, ODE, OpenESB			Open Source	
		94%			88%			72%	

The percentage values are relatively high, i.e., many engines support the pattern implementations we test for. In particular, four engines, two commercial and two open source ones, successfully support all control-flow patterns to the same degree as the BPEL standard. These are E1, E2, bpel-g, and Apache ODE. The remaining engines vary from 56% of pattern support to 81%. As before, several open source engines show a relatively small degree of support when compared to their commercial counterparts. Nevertheless, a lower degree of pattern support could have been expected for all engines, considering the results of the benchmark of standard conformance from the previous section.

All engines provide the same degree of support as BPEL for the basic control-flow patterns (WCP01–WCP05), the *Implicit Termination* structural pattern (WCP16), and the cancellation patterns (WCP19/20). In three cases, several engines partially support a pattern, which in standard BPEL is fully supported.

Finally, five patterns are not directly supported by at least one engine. The highest amount of differences lies in the category of multi-instance patterns. Here, in only half of the cases, the engines have the same degree of support as BPEL. For two of the patterns in this category, WCP12 and WCP13, three of the open source engines only support a workaround solution that grants partial support, but not a direct solution that is possible in standard BPEL. Moreover, the same engines fail to directly support the *Multiple Instances With a Priori Runtime Knowledge* pattern (WCP14). The commercial engine E3 also only supports WCP12 partially and fails to support the remaining multi-instance patterns. The three open source engines mentioned before fail the tests for the *Interleaved Parallel Routing* pattern (WCP17) and two of them do not pass the tests for the *Milestone* pattern (WCP18). When it comes to advanced branching and synchronization patterns, support is in place for all engines, although two open source engines only support the patterns using a workaround solution. All in all, the least supported pattern is the *Multiple Instances With a Priori Runtime Knowledge* pattern (WCP14), which is unsupported by half of the engines.

Interestingly, the sets of patterns for which open source and commercial engines achieve a lower degree of support than standard BPEL are almost disjoint. In comparison, commercial engines support more workflow control-flow patterns (94%) than open source engines (72%). Similar to the benchmark for standard conformance, this difference shrinks to an insignificant level (94% vs. 88%) when comparing only commercial and the three highest-ranking open source engines.

By looking at the detailed results of the tests, it becomes obvious that failures in pattern support are not caused by added issues that arise through the combination of language constructs. Instead, in all cases of failure, a pattern implementation *Reasons* does not work correctly, because a single language feature is not supported as *for lack* specified in the BPEL standard. Strictly speaking, all issues have already been *of support* discovered by the standard conformance benchmark discussed in the previous section. In six cases of failure, a pattern implementation does not work, because an engine does not fully support *links* in the *flow* activity. In three cases, support for the *forEach* activity is required and in nine cases also parallel execution of the activities contained therein. Finally, in two cases, engines do not provide proper support for required message correlation and in a single case, support for isolated scopes is missing. This demonstrates that standard-conformant implementations of the *flow* and *forEach* activities are crucial for pattern support. Put differently, a lack of truly parallel execution in an engine is the biggest obstacle to pattern support. Still, the impact of standard conformance on pattern support is little. For instance, Apache ODE, which passes only two thirds of the conformance tests, supports all workflow patterns that can be directly implemented in BPEL. Even the worst engine in terms of standard conformance, Petals, provides direct or partial support for 13 out of 16 patterns. The results of this section can be summarized as follows: workflow control-flow patterns can be implemented directly with only a moderate degree of standard conformance, but support for concurrent execution of activities is the decisive factor.

3.3.3. Results for BPMN Engines

The third test suite addresses BPMN engines. Table 3.10 presents the amount of successful tests for the three engines, grouped by language element. Furthermore, Fig. 3.4 depicts the percentages of successful tests aggregated by engine and construct group, i.e., basics (BA), activities (ACT), gateways (GW), events (EV), and errors (ERR). Next, we describe the results for each engine under test.

Table 3.10.: Number of Passed Conformance Tests for BPMN Engines

Category	Construct	Activiti	camunda BPM	jBPM	Total
basics	Lane	1	1	1	1
	Participant	1	1	1	1
	SequenceFlow	3	3	1	4
activities	CallActivity	0	0	0	2
	Multiple Instantiation	3	3	0	5
	Looping	1	1	1	3
	SubProcess	1	1	1	1
	Transaction	1	1	1	1
gateways	Exclusive	3	3	2	3
	Inclusive	2	2	1	2
	Parallel	1	1	1	1
	Complex	0	0	0	1
	EventBased	2	2	2	2
	GatewayCombinations	4	4	4	4
events	Cancel	1	1	0	1
	Compensation	2	2	5	6
	Conditional	0	0	0	5
	Error	4	4	4	4
	Escalation	0	0	6	7
	Link	0	1	1	1
	Signal	2	4	5	6
	Terminate	1	1	1	1
	Timer	3	5	3	5
errors	InvalidGatewayCombinations	2	2	2	2
	ParallelGateway_Conditions	1	1	1	1
Σ		39	44	44	70

Activiti: To begin with, Activiti and all other engines pass all error tests, i.e., they correctly reject process models that should be rejected according to the standard. From the overall test suite, Activiti passes 56% (39 out of 70) of the conformance tests. This is the lowest amount for all three engines. Nevertheless, Activiti passes nearly all of the tests for the *basics* category, with the exception of a special case of the usage of conditions with *SequenceFlows* [26, p. 427]. In the *activities* category, the engine passes the

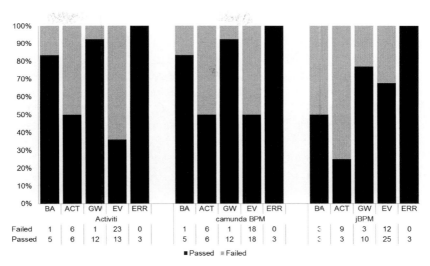

	BA	ACT	GW	EV	ERR		BA	ACT	GW	EV	ERR		BA	ACT	GW	EV	ERR
			Activiti						camunda BPM						jBPM		
Failed	1	6	1	23	0		1	6	1	18	0		3	9	3	12	0
Passed	5	6	12	13	3		5	6	12	18	3		3	3	10	25	3

■ Passed ■ Failed

Figure 3.4.: Percentages of Passed and Failed Tests per Engine and Construct Group for BPMN

tests for *SubProcesses* and *Transactions*. In contrast, tests for *GlobalTasks* or the usage of *CallActivities* fail. Furthermore, repeatable execution and multi-instance execution of tasks using the *MultiInstance* attributes is not fully supported. Several basic tests regarding *MultiInstance* behavior pass, but the standard looping mechanism using *StandardLoopCharacteristics* is not supported. A process model containing *StandardLoopCharacteristics* is not rejected by the engine, but is ignored during execution. Only in the case when the loop should be executed exactly once, i. e., no actual iteration occurs, the test is successful. In the gateways category, all tests, except for the *ComplexGateway*, pass. The events category is where most of Activiti's test failures belong to. Only roughly one third of all event-related tests are successful. Of the nine event types, only *Cancel*, *Error*, and *Terminate* events are fully supported. *Compensation* events are only correctly supported if used as an intermediate event, but compensation can also be triggered by a *Cancel* event. *Signal* events cannot be used as start or end events in (event) *SubProcesses* and such *SubProcesses* are not interrupted correctly by boundary events. Also *Timer* events are not supported as start events of event *SubProcesses*. Finally, all tests for *Conditional*, *Escalation*, and *Link* events fail.

camunda BPM: Since camunda BPM is a fork of Activiti, the results of the two engines are similar to a large degree. In particular, the test results for all categories except the events category are identical. In this category, camunda BPM performs considerably better. As a result, the engine has a higher amount of successful tests in total (44 out of 70). In contrast to Activiti, all tests for *Cancel*, *Error*, *Link*, *Terminate*, and *Timer* events pass and *Signal* events can also be used as end events for an event *SubProcess*. Apart from these differences, the same restrictions with respect to compensation and cancellation as for Activiti apply. Lastly, *Conditional* and *Escalation* events remain unsupported.

jBPM: jBPM successfully passes the same amount of conformance tests as camunda BPM (44 out of 70), but not the exact same test cases. Especially with respect to the *activities* category, support is limited and only one quarter of the tests pass. Only the default usage of *SubProcesses* and *Transactions* is supported, but tests for *CallActivities* or multiple instantiation fail. With respect to the standard looping mechanism, the same restrictions as for Activiti and camunda BPM apply. This is also the case for the *ComplexGateway*. Furthermore, jBPM fails several special cases in the gateways category. It does not support default *SequenceFlows* when used with an *InclusiveGateway* and gateways cannot be used with a mixed direction, i. e., they cannot merge and diverge control-flow at the same time. When it comes to the events category, jBPM passes all tests related to *Error*, *Link*, and *Terminate* events, as well as nearly all tests for *Signal*, *Compensation*, and *Escalation* events. Notably, it is the only engine to provide support for *Escalation* events. Three out of five tests for *Timer* events pass, but jBPM fails to support the usage of such events as start events in event *SubProcesses*. Finally, all tests for *Conditional* and *Cancel* events fail.

A clear-cut ranking of the three engines based on these results is not possible, since camunda BPM and jBPM pass the same amount of tests, with 64% of the overall test suite. Also Activiti, with 56% of passed tests, is not far of. Interestingly camunda BPM supports a superset of the language features supported by Activiti. Despite the fact that camunda BPM and jBPM pass the same amount of tests, camunda BPM passes all tests related to a single language construct more often. Successful tests for jBPM are more dispersed and more *Features with broad support* constructs are supported, although only in basic configuration. However, the amount of constructs supported by all three engines is small when compared to the large vocabulary of BPMN. Only unconditional *SequenceFlows*, none *StartEvents*, none *EndEvents*, *ScriptTasks*, *SubProcesses*, *Transactions*, *Lanes*, *Participants*, *ErrorEvents*, *TerminateEvents*, *EventBasedGateways* and *ParallelGateways* are fully supported. Successful conformance tests for the latter gateway by all engines can be considered surprising, since this gateway is used for defining parallelism. It turned out on closer investigation that none of the engines supports truly parallel execution of control-flow branches, but only pseudo-parallel interleaved execution. As discussed in the previous section, truly parallel execution is a decisive factor for the support for workflow control-flow patterns. As a result, it can be expected that the findings on workflow pattern support for BPEL engines generalize to BPMN engines as well. Finally, all engines are capable to execute combinations of different gateway types and to detect all tested erroneous process models.

Since all engines pass less than two thirds of the overall test suite, it is clear that they only implement a subset of the BPMN standard. Similar to BPEL, the standardization target has failed. As a result, even BPMN 2.0-conformant process models can not be directly executed on the engines and possibly require non-trivial adaptions. This reinforces the negative answer to research question 1.1: Conformance to the BPMN standard is not sufficient for enabling the portability of process models.

3.3.4. Implications on Application Portability

As can be seen from the previous sections, there is a high variance among the degree of standard conformance that engines provide. This means that the standardization target of BPEL and BPMN has not been reached. *In both cases, research question 1.1 can be answered negatively*: Current standards are not *question* enough for enabling the portability of service-oriented and process-aware software *1.1* among engines. For a conclusive answer, it might be worthwhile to evaluate the standard conformance provided by engines for other standards, such as XPDL, as well. Nevertheless, BPEL and BPMN are among the most widely used process standards today. Hence, a lack of conformance of the implementations of these standards is a significant insight. Furthermore, there is no indication that the situation is different in the case of other standards.

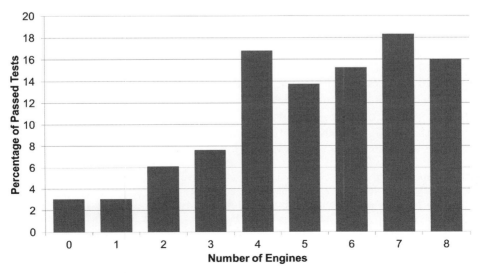

Figure 3.5.: Number of Engines By Percentage of Passed Tests for BPEL

Even if standards fail the standardization target and engines only implement a subset of the standard, the porting of applications might still be feasible. This is the case if engines implement *the same* subset of the standard. In this case, unsupported features cannot practically be used in any application. Features that are not used do also not present an obstacle for porting[15]. However, as discussed in Sect. 2.3.3, if each engine implements a varying subset of the standard, a loss of portability will be the likely result.

Guidelines for portable applications
To examine the size of the overlap in standard conformance for the tested engines, Fig. 3.5 displays different subsets of the BPEL conformance test suite tabled by the amount of engines that support a subset. Fig. 3.6 displays the same data for the BPMN conformance test suite. For the case of BPEL engines,

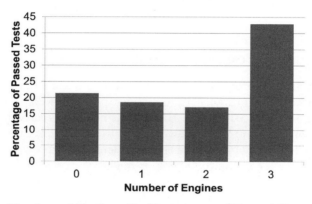

Figure 3.6.: Number of Engines By Percentage of Passed Tests for BPMN

only 21 of the 131 tests (16%) are passed by all eight engines under test. For BPMN engines, this number is somewhat higher with 30 of 70 tests (43%). It should be noted that these numbers are not suitable for a quality comparison of the BPEL and BPMN standards, or their engines. The number of BPMN engines we benchmark and the amount of tests of the BPMN test suite is much smaller than for BPEL. For this reason, it is not surprising that we find a higher overlap in features for BPMN engines. Increasing the number of tests or tested engines will likely result in a decrease of commonly supported features for BPMN engines, nearing the values found for BPEL engines.

Only the elements in the subsets that are supported by all engines are actually portable, as intended by the two standards. As· discussed in Sect. 3.3.1 and

---

[15]It is important to keep in mind that this is a practical assumption. It does not apply to many theoretic approaches, common in academia, that map higher-level specifications and models to standard-conformant process models. For instance, it is common to map process choreographies to sets of interacting processes, implemented in one of the above standards. Examples for such model-driven approaches are [130, 200, 201]. These approaches rely on the portability guarantees made by standards and make use of language features that are not supported on every engine. As the results presented here indicate, this leads to practical issues and any of the above approaches is limited to the engine with which its authors tested it. This restriction has been investigated in [76].

Sect. 3.3.3, these elements are very basic. In both cases, strictly sequential execution of basic tasks can be considered as portable. For BPEL, conditional branching and basic structured looping are portable as well. This is not the case for BPMN. There, pseudo-parallelism can be considered as portable, which does not apply to BPEL. The usage of any other advanced features, such as message correlation or compensation handling will be much less portable. When looking at real-world process models, studies have found that the most frequent language elements used in the models are also basic ones [202]. In the case of BPMN, nearly all of the eight most frequent elements are also supported by all of the engines under test. The implication of these results for portability can be expressed as follows: *To build truly portable applications, it is necessary to use only basic language features.* In particular, it is necessary to restrict control-flow to sequential execution. When considering realistic application scenarios, in the form of workflow control-flow patterns in Sect. 3.3.2, it becomes evident that only a moderate degree of standard conformance is needed to achieve widespread pattern support. However, one of the crucial features required is support for concurrent activity execution. Only half of the BPEL engines and none of the BPMN engines provides this feature in a standard-conformant fashion. Hence, another implication from the benchmark results is that *realistic application scenarios cannot necessarily be executed by a majority of the tested process engines.*

The common lack of standard conformance in engines can be summarized to frame an answer to research question 1.2: *There do exist portability issues in all but the most basic language elements, regardless of the language standard.* To built portable applications, it is necessary to limit process models to the usage of a moderate language vocabulary. Contemporary process engines are unable to execute many of the features needed in realistic application scenarios in a portable fashion. *Research question 1.2*

In summary, this section and the answers to research questions 1.1 and 1.2 conclude research question 1. *The current state of portability of service-oriented and process-aware software is dire*, since the degree of standard conformance in process engines and the amount of commonly implemented features is small. It is likely that many applications developed in practice cannot easily be ported among engines and their users are locked into the systems of an engine vendor. For this reason, the improvement of the portability of service-oriented and process-aware software is a relevant research goal. This is the motivation for the following part of this thesis, that presents a software metrics framework for the measurement and improvement of portability.

Part II.

Measurement Framework for Portability

4. Measuring Portability

Parts of this chapter have been taken from [77, 170].

As the evidence presented in Chap. 3 demonstrates, the standard conformance of process engines is limited. Consequently, standards-based portability of software artifacts is not guaranteed and the actual portability inherent to a piece of software is unclear. This leads to the topic of the current and the following chapters: Is it feasible to assess the portability of these software artifacts and how can such an assessment be achieved?

We evaluate the feasibility of portability assessment through the construction and validation of a measurement framework. The starting point of this framework in the current chapter is the core characteristic itself, portability. The aim of the chapter is to answer research question 2.1: *What are suitable metrics for measuring portability?* Together with the following three chapters, this chapter demonstrates the feasibility of measuring portability, answers research question 2, and forms one of the two main contributions of this thesis.

The chapter is organized as follows. First, we present our methodology for measuring portability in Sect. 4.1. Thereafter, we provide formal definitions of portability metrics in Sect. 4.2. Next, the metrics are validated theoretically in Sect. 4.3. Moreover, Sect. 4.4 evaluates the metrics with respect to their practical applicability. Finally, we summarize our findings in Sect. 4.5. *Structure of the chapter*

4.1. On the Measurement of Portability

In this section, we first discuss crucial considerations for measuring software portability, followed by the definition of a *degree of severity* with respect to portability. We outline design decisions made in this definition and present a running example used throughout the chapter.

As defined in Sect. 2.3.2, portability is the *"degree of effectiveness and efficiency with which a software product can be transferred from one software environment to another"*. This broad definition includes all subcharacteristics of portability as defined by the SQuaRE model. In this chapter, we focus on the feasibility of the porting, regardless of adaptation or replacement. Hence, we reduce the scope of the quality characteristic to *direct portability*:

> **Definition 17: Direct Portability**
>
> Direct portability is the degree of effectiveness and efficiency with which a software system can be transferred from one software environment to another, *without the need for adaptation or replacement.*

4. Measuring Portability

The goal of assessing direct portability is to determine how easy it is to take an existing piece of software to another execution environment with the purpose of executing it there. The viewpoint taken is that of a developer or operator, who has to perform the porting and possibly modify source code and configuration settings. Portability is perceived as an inherent property of an application that can be assessed independently of a concrete target environment.

Even though portability is a central part of most software quality models, e.g. [53–59], it is hard to quantify with justifiable effort [203]. In general, it is measured by contrasting the effort required for porting a piece of software to the effort of rewriting it from scratch. Assessing this effort empirically is difficult. To enable an automatable and objective assessment, as indicated in [54, 55], direct portability is computed based on lines of code. The number of portable lines of code is compared to the size of the overall code base. Although this principle is quite simple, it is nontrivial to distinguish automatically between portable and nonportable lines of code. Moreover, such a computation is coarse and its meaningfulness is limited. Any two lines of code have the same weighting, although their criticality might be vastly different.

Our goal is to provide a more accurate measurement and assessment of portability by taking into account domain knowledge of service-oriented and process-aware software. We map the basic mechanism for computing application portability to service-oriented and process-aware software and extend it by a definition of further metrics that consider the typical characteristics of this kind of software. Additionally, we enrich the computation with empirical data on language support in engines, obtained through the engine benchmarks described in Chap. 3. As mentioned before, we view portability as an inherent property of an application that can be computed, although a target engine on which the application should be executed is not yet known.

Porta-bility metrics based on standard confor-mance As argued in Sect. 2.3.3, software portability is strongly tailored to the standard conformance of execution environments. Only program elements that are supported by a majority, if not all, of the environments can be considered to be portable. As a consequence, the measurement of the portability of service-oriented and process-aware software should take process engines into account. If all engines support all of the specified language elements in the same manner with respect to semantics, then any compilable program will be portable to any engine. Thus, there are no portability issues. As demonstrated through the benchmark in Chap. 3, this is not the case. Each process engine, regardless of the language, supports a specific subset of the language elements. On the one hand, there is a basic subset of the total language that is supported by every engine. On the other hand, several language elements are limited to a subset of engines, causing portability issues. The more engines support a language element, the more portable it can be considered. The fewer engines support a language element, the more *severe* it is with respect to portability. This severity should be taken into account when computing portability metrics.

4.1.1. Degree of Severity

To enhance the assessment of portability, we introduce a *degree of severity* with respect to portability for each language element. This degree can be identified by the number of engines that do not support a particular element in a particular configuration. As discussed, the smaller the amount of engines supporting a language element is, the harder it will be to port code that uses this element. The conformance benchmarks, discussed in Chap. 3, allow to identify the amount of engines that support a particular language element in a particular configuration. The data set resulting from the benchmark lists for every language element whether it is supported by a given engine. Thus, this data lets us compute the number of engines that support, or fail to support, each language element. For illustration, Fig. 4.1 depicts the conceptual outline of the support of BPEL elements, grouped into elements supported by many, some, or few engines[16]. This enables the static checking of a process model for elements that are not supported by all engines and, thus, the assessment of the portability of the process model.

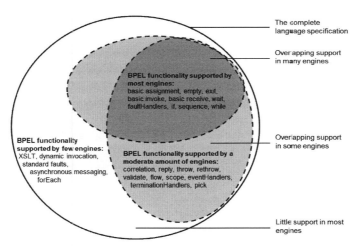

Figure 4.1.: Schematic Outline of BPEL Language Support – Dashed ellipses represent different subsets of language elements, e.g., the sets of elements supported by particular engines. Overlaps between the sets constitute subsets of elements that are supported by a higher amount of engines.

A single language element may have multiple different configurations or features *Test assertions for severity* that are of varying severity with respect to portability. This can happen if there are multiple different problematic configurations of the element. An example of such an element in BPEL is the *reply* activity [27, Sect. 10.4]. The activity may be used to report a fault to a client of the process, by setting its *faultName* attribute and it may be linked to a *receive* activity by setting its *messageExchange* attribute. Both of these attributes are independent of each other, but not fully

---

[16]The figure essentially maps Fig. 2.18 from Sect. 2.3.3 to BPEL.

portable, and differ in the amount of engines supporting them. Therefore, each of these configurations of an element should be captured separately. To enable their separate evaluation, we introduce the concept of a *test assertion* for static checking. A test assertion is a function used in code inspection that identifies a particular language element in a particular problematic configuration[17]. Each test assertion can be classified according to its severity. The portability metrics we propose in the following describe different aggregations of the degree of severity of every language element used in a process model, and identified by a test assertion, to a degree of portability for the overall model. The degree of severity is defined as follows:

Definition 18: Degree of Severity

$$D_{ta}(ta_{el}) = \sum_{i=1}^{N_{engines}} (1 - Supports(engine_i, el)), where \qquad (4.1)$$

- $el \in N \cup C, p =< N, C >$ is an element of the language specification in a particular configuration used in process model p; It corresponds to a node or connector in a process model p, as defined in Def. 6;
- ta_{el} is a test assertion which tests for the occurrence of el in p;
- $D_{ta} : (Assertion \to \mathbb{N}_0)$ is a function that assigns a natural number to a test assertion. A higher number corresponds to a higher degree of severity in terms of portability;
- $N_{engines}$ is the number of engines under consideration, the cardinality of the set of engines: $Engine = \{engine_1, \dots, engine_{N_{engines}}\}$;
- An engine, $engine_i$, can be represented by the set of language elements of the language vocabulary V, which it supports: $engine_i = (el_x, \dots, el_y) \subseteq V$;
- $Supports : (Engine \times Element \to [0, 1])$ is a function that returns 1 if an engine does support a language element and 0 otherwise, that is:

$$Supports(engine_i, el) = \begin{cases} 1 & \text{iff } el \in engine_i \\ 0 & otherwise \end{cases}$$

The degree of severity D_{ta} of test assertion ta_{el}, which checks for the usage of language element el in a process model p, reflects the position of el in Fig. 4.1. In other words, the degree represents the number of engines that do *not* support the feature (i.e., language element or specific configuration thereof) an assertion is checking. Any extension element that is found in a process model (i.e., an element that is not defined in the language specification and is not part of the

---

[17]This corresponds to the terminology used in related inspection tooling, in particular the Web Services Interoperability Organization (WS-I) test tools, available at `http://www.ws-i.org/deliverables/workinggroup.aspx?wg=testingtools`. There, a test assertion corresponds to a particular issue in a software artifact and is classified according to its severity.

vocabulary V) is considered to be supported by a single engine only. A high degree value means that the usage of the language element is an obstacle to portability.

4.1.2. Design Decisions

The degree of severity presented in the preceding section considers all engines to be of equal practical importance. Any engine that does not support the feature tested by a test assertion increases the degree of severity by one. For example, *Weighting of engines* the usage of *links* in the *flow* activity in BPEL is not supported by two engines in our benchmark, so the degree of severity of such an activity is equal to two. This identical weighting of engines is a questionable assumption, because, that way, the impact of experimental engines is larger than justified from their practical usage identified by their market share. For a more realistic computation, a lack of support in the engine with the biggest market share could be considered to be more severe than an issue in an experimental engine with just a small percentage of the overall market share. For instance, the degree value could be increased not by one for every engine, but instead with a value that is relative to the market share of the engine. However, as we lack independent data on engine usage, we cannot introduce a meaningful weighting into the degree computation. At least, all engines in our benchmark are considered as mature by their respective vendors. All in all, we consider the equal weighting of all engines in the degree computation a reasonable compromise.

Furthermore, we focus on the support for single language elements instead *Single language elements* of their combinations. As demonstrated with the evaluation of the support for workflow control-flow patterns in Sect. 3.3.2, combining language elements does not result in added portability issues. All failures in support for a pattern could be attributed to failures in singular language elements. For this reason, we consider it safe to use singular language elements in isolation for computing portability metrics.

Finally, this scheme of calculating metrics uses empirical data as a crucial *Metrics based on empirical data* ingredient for the weighting of the metrics. If this data, describing the language support in engines, changes, also the metrics values change. We claim that this is valuable, because it takes into account the evolution of engines, which are the decisive factor for portability. Moreover, it produces more practically relevant results than could be obtained with purely theoretically founded metrics.

4.1.3. Running Example

Fig. 4.2 depicts a simple BPEL process model[18], which we use as running example to demonstrate the metrics computation in this chapter. List. 4.1 contains a condensed version of the XML code of the same process model in which problematic areas are highlighted. In total, the process model consists of

---

[18]The visualization of the process model uses BPMN.

63 code elements, but, for conciseness, we limit List. 4.1 to the most important parts.

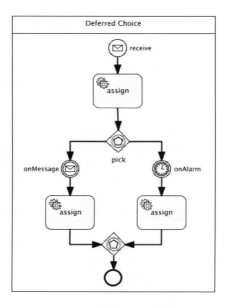

Figure 4.2.: Process Graph for the Running Example

Listing 4.1: Simplified XML Code of the Running Example

```
1   <process xmlns:sxt="http://extension/namespace" ...>
2     <import ... />
3     <partnerLinks>...</partnerLinks>
4     <variables>
5       <variable name="logMessage" ... />
6       <variable name="processInput" ... />
7     </variables>
8     <correlationSets>
9       <correlationSet name="CorSet" properties="
          ns:correlationId"/>
10    </correlationSets>
11    <sequence>
12      <receive operation="startProcessAsync" createInstance="yes"
          variable="processInput">
13        <correlations>
14          <correlation set="CorSet" initiate="yes"/>
15        </correlations>
16      </receive>
17      <assign>
```

```
18      <copy>
19        <from variable="processInput" part="inputPart"/>
20        <to>$logMessage/log:processId</to>
21      </copy>
22      <!-- Implementation of logging -->
23      <sxt:trace>
24        <sxt:log level="info" location="onComplete">
25          <from variable="logMessage"/>
26        </sxt:log>
27      </sxt:trace>
28    </assign>
29    <pick name="Pick" createInstance="no">
30      <onMessage operation="receiveAsyncMessage" variable="
            processInput" ...>
31        <correlations>
32          <correlation set="CorSet" initiate="no"/>
33        </correlations>
34        <assign>
35          <!-- Implementation of logging -->
36        </assign>
37      </onMessage>
38      <onAlarm> <for>'P0Y0M0DT0H0M5.0S'</for>
39        <assign>
40          <!-- Implementation of logging -->
41        </assign>
42      </onAlarm>
43    </pick>
44  </sequence>
45 </process>
```

The process is built for execution on the OpenESB BPEL service engine and is taken from [196]. It is also included in one of the libraries used in the practical evaluation in this chapter (cf. Sect. 4.4). It essentially implements a *deferred choice* between the occurrence of a timeout and the arrival of a message, and is a BPEL-based implementation of the *milestone* workflow control-flow pattern [71]. The process model starts with the reception of a message in a *receive* activity and, thereafter, waits for either a second message to arrive or a timeout to occur using a *pick* activity with an *onMessage* and an *onAlarm* event handler. Following each of these actions, there are *assign* activities. Portability issues in this process model exist for the *receive* and the *onMessage* activities in lines 12–15 and 30–33, as these use message correlation. Depending on the initialization of the correlation value, which in this case is done asynchronously, message correlation is only partly supported across engines. Moreover, the *onAlarm* event handler, used in lines 38–42, is not supported by every engine. Finally, all *assign* activities use

Issues in the running example

103

custom engine-specific extensions, two for each activity (an example is depicted in lines 22–27), for logging and monitoring purposes.

4.2. Portability Metrics

In this section, we propose several metrics that measure and assess portability from different viewpoints. Next to a basic metric used for comparison, we introduce a weighted mechanism of computation. Moreover, we define two metrics that focus on process-aware and service-oriented aspects respectively. In combination, these metrics form a comprehensive framework for quantifying portability.

4.2.1. Basic Portability Metric

From a conceptual point of view, portability metrics quantify the relation between the *cost* or *effort* of porting software and rewriting it from scratch [203]. As such, a portability metric for process-aware and service-oriented software can be based on the following definition:

Definition 19: Portability Metric

$$M_{port}(p) = 1 - \frac{C_{port}(p)}{C_{new}(p)}, where \qquad (4.2)$$

- $p =< N, C >$ is an executable process model as defined in Def. 6.
- $C_{port}(p) : (Process \rightarrow \mathbb{N}_0)$ is the cost of porting, a function that assigns a number from $\mathbb{N}_0$ to p; A higher number corresponds to a higher cost.
- $C_{new}(p) : (Process \rightarrow \mathbb{N}_0)$ is the cost of rewriting, a function that assigns a number from $\mathbb{N}_0$ to p; A higher number corresponds to a higher cost.
- $C_{new}(p) = 0 \rightarrow M_{port}(p) = 0$;
- $\forall p, \ C_{new}(p) \geq C_{port}(p)$.

$M_{port}(p)$ is a metric that quantifies the portability of a process model p. $C_{port}(p)$ is the cost of modifying the model so that it can be executed on another engine. $C_{new}(p)$ is the cost of rewriting it completely for a new engine. Def. 19 is based on the assumption that the cost of a rewrite is always at least as high as the cost of modification. This implies that the metric value ranges in the interval of zero and one, where zero indicates no portability and one full direct portability. Hence, the metric is defined on an *interval scale*. The difficulty in the equation is how to meaningfully determine the cost. The different metrics presented here propose different ways of calculating these values. Based on Def. 19, a portability metric is *indirect* [171, p. 2], since it depends on $C_{new}(p)$ and $C_{port}(p)$. Furthermore, it is *internal* [53, pp. 17], since it depends on the static structure of the process model. Finally, the metric is defined as zero for an empty program, where $C_{new}(p) = 0$.

A universally applicable way of calculating $C_{port}(p)$ and $C_{new}(p)$, which we *Classic computa-tion of portabil-ity* denote as the *basic* portability metric M_{basic}, is to take into account the lines of code that have to be rewritten for porting the software (as indicated in [54,55]). If it is to be redeveloped from scratch, all lines will have to be rewritten, so $C_{new}(p)$ amounts to the total lines of code of the program. $C_{port}(p)$ in turn amounts to the lines of code that have to be rewritten when porting it; that is, all lines of code for which portability issues can be detected. As the number of lines that have to be rewritten for porting cannot be larger than the number of lines that do actually exist, $C_{port}(p) \leq C_{new}(p)$ is satisfied. In the most extreme case, where all lines are nonportable, $C_{port}(p)$ will be equal to $C_{new}(p)$ and consequently $M_{basic}(p) = 0$, indicating no portability at all. In the other extreme, no line will have to be rewritten and $M_{basic}(p) = 1$. All in all, the metric quantifies the percentage of portable lines of code of the program.

To be able to automate the calculation of $C_{port}(p)$ and $C_{new}(p)$ in this setting, one aspect has to be clarified. Process languages are XML dialects with an XML serialization format and as such abstract from the notion of lines of code. Instead, XML elements, essentially the elements of the vocabulary of the process language, are the crucial unit, identifying a single statement or instruction. For that reason, we refer to language elements instead of lines of code. For M_{basic}, $C_{new}(p)$ refers to the total amount of elements in a process model, denoted as N_{el} being the cardinality of the sets of all model elements of p, i.e., $|p| = |N \cup C|$, and $C_{port}(p)$ to the number of elements for which portability issues can be diagnosed. This discussion is summarized in Def. 20:

Definition 20: Basic Portability Metric

$$M_{basic}(p) = 1 - \frac{\sum_{i=1}^{N_{el}} Issue(el_i)}{N_{el}}, where \qquad (4.3)$$

- $(el_1, \ldots, el_n) \in p = < N, C >$;
- $N_{el} = |p|$ is the number of elements in process model p;
- $Issue : (Element \rightarrow [0, 1])$ is a function that returns 1 if an element el is not fully portable and 0 otherwise; that is,

$$Issue(el) = \begin{cases} 1 & \text{iff } \exists\ engine_i, \text{such that } el \notin engine_i \\ 0 & otherwise \end{cases}$$

where $engine_i$ is defined as the set of elements supported, $engine_i = (el_x, \ldots, el_y)$ (cf. Def. 18).

To demonstrate the computation of the metric, we can compute it for the running example (cf. Sect. 4.1.3). This process model consists of 63 elements in total, and for nine elements, portability issues are detected. These are six usages of extension elements, the *onAlarm* event handler, the usage of correlations in the *receive* activity, and the usage of correlations in the *onMessage* eventHandler.

This results in the following metric value[19]: $M_{basic}(sample) = 1 - (9/63) = 0.86$.

4.2.2. Weighted Elements Portability Metric

M_{basic} transfers the classical abstract portability metric [203] to the area of process models. However, it does not make full use of the empirical data at hand. To be precise, it only confronts the amount of fully portable elements of a process model to all of them. Using the degree D_{ta} (cf. Def. 18), it is possible to relativize this observation, resulting in a more accurate assessment of the inherent portability of an application. This is the principle underlying the current and the following metrics.

The *weighted elements* portability metric M_{elem} takes the degree D_{ta} of elements into account. Here, the cost of rewriting a process model C_{new} is defined as follows:

$$C_{new}(p) = N_{el} * N_{engines} \tag{4.4}$$

This cost is identical to the amount of model elements N_{el} (as in the basic portability metric) multiplied with the number of engines under consideration $N_{engines}$. Effectively, every element is treated as if it is unsupported by any engine and has to be rewritten when being ported. The cost of porting, C_{port}, for M_{elem} is:

$$C_{port}(p) = \sum_{i=1}^{N_{el}} C_{el}(el_i) \tag{4.5}$$

The cost of porting, C_{port}, of a process model p is the sum of the element cost, C_{el}, for each element el_i. The element cost function for an element el_i of model p is defined as follows:

Definition 21: Element Cost Function

$$C_{el}(el_i) = \max_{j=1...N_{ta}} (Violates(ta_j, el_i) * D_{ta}(ta_j)), where \tag{4.6}$$

- N_{ta} is the number of assertions that test for portability issues;
- $Violates : (Assertion \times Element \rightarrow [0, 1])$ is the testing function that returns 1 if an assertion ta_j detects a portability issue for an element el_i and 0 otherwise.

As discussed, $D_{ta}(ta_j)$ denotes the degree of the test assertion ta_j (i.e., the number of engines that do not support the feature tested by a test assertion ta_j). This means that if an assertion ta_j does not find a violation for an element el_i (i.e., $Violates(ta_j, el_i) = 0$), the element cost for the combination of the two amounts to zero. If el_i violates the assertion, the element cost depends on the amount

---

[19]All metric values in this thesis are rounded to two decimal places.

of engines that do not support the feature tested by the assertion. The more engines that support the feature, the less the cost of porting it will be. The lower the amount of engines, the higher the cost. The *max* function takes into account that a single element can violate multiple assertions. As stated in Sect. 4.1.1, this can happen if there are multiple different problematic configurations of the element. We select the maximum of the degrees based on the assumption that the least portable part of the element will have the highest impact. This is a design decision and alternative schemes are possible. For instance, the arithmetic mean of the degrees of all violations could be computed. We tested several schemes for aggregating degrees during the practical evaluation of the metrics (cf. Sect. 4.4), but could not find significant differences in the metric values and therefore selected the simplest approach (i.e., the *max* function) here. Summarizing the above discussion, the weighted elements metric M_{elem} is defined as follows:

Design decisions for weighted computation

Definition 22: Weighted Elements Portability Metric

$$M_{elem}(p) = 1 - \frac{\sum_{i=1}^{N_{el}} \max_{j=1...N_{ta}} (Violates(ta_j, el_i) * D_{ta}(ta_j))}{N_{el} * N_{engines}} \qquad (4.7)$$

To exemplify the computation, we again refer to the running example: As discussed, there are 63 elements of code, for nine of which portability issues are detected. These are six usages of extension elements, which are naturally of limited portability and in our case have a degree of eight. The *onAlarm* event handler is unsupported by one engine and thus has a degree of one. The usage of correlations in the *receive* activity has a degree of three and in the *onMessage* eventHandler of two. So, the result for M_{elem} is the following: $M_{elem}(sample) = 1 - (6 * 8 + 1 + 3 + 2)/(63 * 9) = 0.9$.

4.2.3. Activity Portability Metric

As discussed in Sect. 2.2.2, the most central building block of process languages in general are activities, events, gateways, and the directed edges that connect them. These elements are also present in nonexecutable process models and the focus of visualizations for these models. For process complexity measures [204, 205], activities and the transitions among them are the dominant factor. From a conceptual point of view, activities, events, gateways, and connectors are of higher importance than the remaining elements of an executable process model, such as variable definitions or import statements. Therefore, it can be expected that the impact of using problematic activities on portability is more critical. If portability issues exist in activities and these have to be replaced when porting the process model, this might affect the control-flow behavior of process instances. In contrast to this, changes in the way in which documents are imported into the process model do not necessarily influence the definition of its control-flow

Non-functional changes and change propagation

structure. Changing the control-flow structure because of the porting of a process model means that a nonfunctional change requirement would trigger a functional change, which is a particularly undesirable kind of change propagation [206].

To provide a view on portability that focuses on control-flow, we define an additional portability metric, which we denote as *activity* portability metric M_{act}. This is a variation of the weighted elements metric. Here, instead of elements, we only consider problematic configurations of activities, events, gateways, and connectors (referring to Def. 6, the elements of sets C, A, E, and G, excluding B) when computing portability[20]. Portability issues that are linked to basic elements, i.e., the elements of set B, as for example process-level *import* statements or engine-specific language extensions, are omitted in the consideration of this metric. For M_{act}, C_{new} changes to:

$$C_{new}(p) = N_a * N_{engines} \qquad (4.8)$$

where N_a denotes the cardinality of sets $C \cup N \setminus B$ of a process model p. Analogously, C_{port} changes to:

$$C_{port}(p) = \sum_{i=1}^{N_a} C_{el}(a_i) \qquad (4.9)$$

This means that only the element cost C_{el} of the activities, events, gateways, and connectors is considered. The computation of C_{el} works as stated in Def. 21. Summarizing the above, M_{act} is defined as:

Definition 23: Activity Portability Metric

$$M_{act}(p) = 1 - \frac{\sum_{i=1}^{N_a} C_{el}(a_i)}{N_a * N_{engines}}, where \qquad (4.10)$$

- $(a_1, \ldots, a_n) \in C \cup N \setminus B$;
- $N_a = |C \cup N \setminus B|$ is the number of activities, events, gateways and connectors of process model p.

Looking at the running example, there is a total of seven activities, gateways, and events. Since the example is a block-structured BPEL process definition, there are no explicit connectors to be considered. The *receive* activity and the *onMessage* and *onAlarm* event handlers are of relevance here. Since it is not generally possible to tie language extensions to activities, except for *extensionActivities*, the logging-related extensions used in the running example do not count. Hence, the metric value is $M_{act}(sample) = 1 - (1+3+2)/(7*9) = 0.90$.

---

[20]This corresponds to the computation of portability also for nonexecutable process models as defined in Def. 5.

4.2.4. Service Communication Portability Metric

As discussed in Sect. 2.1.1 and Sect. 2.2.2.2, communication and composition relations among services are a decisive factor for service-oriented software. Conse-*Observ-* quently, metrics for such software center on communication-related properties [66]. *able* *behavior* Communication relationships describe the *observable behavior* of services; that is, *and* the messages they send and receive. Message sending and reception is performed *change* *propa-* using specific activities or events for sending, receiving, and replying messages. In *gation* terms of portability, these nodes are most critical. Single elements and perhaps even the control-flow structure of a process model may be changed for porting in a way that does not affect the observable behavior. However, this is unlikely if the elements that have to be changed, concern communication with other systems. In this case, these elements directly affect the observable behavior of process instances. Changing them (to enable portability), and consequently changing the observable behavior, influences third-party systems that interact with a process instance. This is undesirable.

The *service communication* portability metric M_{serv} allows to view the impact of communication related activities and events on portability. For this metric, the calculation of C_{new} and C_{port} is changed to include only the activities relating to service interaction (i.e., the elements of set S as defined in Def. 19):

Definition 24: Service Communication Portability Metric

$$M_{serv}(p) = 1 - \frac{\sum_{i=1}^{N_s} C_{el}(s_i)}{N_s * N_{engines}}, where \tag{4.11}$$

- $(s_1, \ldots, s_n) \in S \subset (A \cup E)$ as defined in Def. 6;
- $N_S = |S|$ is the number of communication activities or events of process model p, the cardinality of set S.

Effectively, this is a specialization of M_{act} that focuses solely on activities and events for service interaction. C_{port} is limited to only consider the element cost of these activities.

Coming to the example, there are two service-related nodes, the *receive* activity and the *onMessage* event handler. This results in the following metric value: $M_{serv}(sample) = 1 - (3 + 2)/(2 * 9) = 0.72$.

4.3. Theoretical Validation

In this section, we validate the proposed metrics theoretically using the two theoretical validation frameworks [69, 70] presented in Sect. 2.4.2. We begin with the evaluation of construct validity, followed by the discussion of measurement theory.

4.3.1. Evaluation of Construct Validity

In the following, we apply the validation framework from [70] and answer each question posed by the framework.

Purpose of the metrics: The purpose of the metrics is the assessment of software and provisioning of information for stakeholders: Developers and system ad-ministrators can be informed about the portability characteristics of their software. When the change of a process engine becomes necessary, the metrics help to make a decision on whether to invest in porting or rewriting software.

Scope of the metrics: Our metrics are of technical nature and are applicable during and after development. Since the metrics are computed at the level of a single executable process model, their scope is typically a single (service-oriented and process-aware) project of one workgroup.

Measured attribute: The metrics address a quality attribute of service-oriented and process-aware software. Specifically, they address its portability.

Natural scale of the attribute: Portability of software naturally ranges between two poles, full direct portability without a single modification and no portability of any part of the application. This resembles an interval scale.

Natural variability of the attribute: Being a technical attribute, portability is not subject to variations that are common for attributes involving human factors, such as the performance of a person depending on the time of the day. We can only determine the variability of the attribute by observing it in practice and considering the ranges in which in varies. Therefore, we defer this discussion to the practical evaluation in Sect. 4.4.

Definition of the metrics: The metrics and the functions for computing them have been formally defined in Sect. 4.2. They are direct and internal metrics that are computed at the level of a single executable process model. The measurement instrument used is *counting* (i.e., counting of portability issues in code). The measurement is automated.

Natural scale of the metrics: The metrics are defined on an interval scale of $[0; 1]$.

Natural variability of the instrument: To begin with, our metrics rely on empirical data of language support in engines; that is, the engine benchmarks described in Chap. 3 that list the amount of engines that support each language element. As a consequence, the main source of measurement error in the instrument stems from incomplete or faulty data. As already discussed in the respective chapter, we did not benchmark all engines that exist for the process languages, which is hardly feasible due to the effort associated with benchmarking and the licensing cost and strategy of several engine vendors. Hence, the data is not fully complete and an increase of the number of engines in the benchmark may also lead to a differing output of the measurement instrument. In Sect. 4.4, we show that such an increase does not significantly change the metric values, by contrasting the results based on two benchmarks from different points in time, which includes an increase in engines. Hence, this error can be considered negligible.

Another source of measurement errors are possible faults in the benchmark that indicate portability issues where there are none (false-positives) or do not discover certain issues (false-negatives). It is not possible to prove that no such errors exist, but since the total amount of tests performed in the benchmark is large (in the case of the BPEL conformance test suite with more than 130 tests for each of the engines) singular errors should not have a strong impact. Moreover, the benchmark code is available to public scrutiny and has been reviewed and corrected by experts from other groups.

The third possible source of measurement errors is the metric suite that performs a static analysis of process models based on benchmark data and computes metric values. As before, we cannot prove the absence of faults in this software tool. We try to reduce faults and maintain a high degree of quality of the suite by means of unit testing, continuous integration, continuous inspection, and open development of the tool.

Relationship between metrics and attribute: Our metrics are directly related to the measured attribute, portability. If for instance a nonstandard extension element is introduced in the process model, this will limit its overall portability. The usage of this element will be detected by our measurement instrument and influence the metric values accordingly.

Natural side effects of using the instrument: Since we have automated the measurement process fully, there is no room for human bias in the measurement instrument.

4.3.2. Measurement-Theoretic Validation

The second theoretical validation framework [69] is grounded in measurement theory and, as discussed in Sect. 2.4.2.1, defines certain types of metrics as well as the mathematical properties that should be satisfied by each type of metric. Although there is no direct fit of the portability metrics proposed here to this framework, it is important to discuss what kind of properties our metrics fulfill. The metrics presented here are formed by the relation of two metrics C_{port} and C_{new}, with different ways of calculating them. These metrics can be considered as complexity metrics [69]. Consequently, they fulfill the properties of *non-negativity*, *null value*, *symmetry*, *additivity*, and *monotonicity*. The purpose of relating C_{port} and C_{new} is to obtain a normalization which enables the comparison of programs of different sizes concerning their portability. Hence, our metrics are *normalized complexity metrics* which do no longer fulfill all properties of classical complexity metrics. Using different terminology, they could also be viewed as a *density* metric of portability. In the following, we discuss each of the different properties.

Non-negativity: Both, C_{port} and C_{new}, are obtained by adding up positive numbers, so they are always positive. From this follows that the property of non-negativity also applies to the normalized metrics: $M_{port}(p) \geq 0$

Null value: The null value property requires that the complexity of an empty system must be null. In our case, this corresponds to a process model $p = < N, C >$, with $N = \emptyset, C = \emptyset$. As a result, the cost values, $C_{new}(p)$ and $C_{port}(p)$, will be zero. For this special case, the metric value is defined as zero in Def. 19. Therefore, the metrics fulfill the property of null value.

Symmetry: Symmetry for complexity metrics requires that the complexity value does not depend on the labeling used for the relationships between elements. In our case, the relationship between elements translates to their ordering in the process graph. This means that two process models p and p' with an identical set of elements EL that have different orders *order* and *order'* with the same control-flow semantics should have the same metric values $M_{port}(p)$ and $M_{port}(p')$. Reordering is possible for a variety of elements, for example when used for parallel processing or event handling. The cost metrics calculate the cost on a per-element basis, so the ordering is irrelevant and the metrics are symmetrical. As a consequence, also the normalized metrics are symmetrical. In the notation of [69]:

$$(p=<EL, order> \wedge p'=<EL, order'>) \Rightarrow M_{port}(p) = M_{port}(p') \quad (4.12)$$

Additivity: Additivity requires that the complexity of a program that is composed of two disjoint modules is equal to the sum of their complexity. This applies to C_{port} and C_{new}, as specified in Def. 19. However, summing up the normalized portability metrics is meaningless, due to normalization. Hence, the portability metrics defined here are *not* additive.

Monotonicity: Monotonicity requires that the complexity of a program is no less than the sum of the complexity of two unrelated parts of it. In our case this can be illustrated by two parallel branches, p^1 and p^2 of the process model p. The complexity of the overall model should be at least as high as the sum of the complexity of the two branches. For C_{port} and C_{new}, this property clearly holds. However, this does not apply for the normalized metrics. Due to the normalization, the metric value $M_{port}(p)$ always is in the interval of $M_{port}(p^1)$ and $M_{port}(p^2)$ and not equal or higher than the sum of the two. Nevertheless, it is still monotonic. For instance, let $C_{port}(p^1) < C_{port}(p^2)$, $C_{new}(p^1) < C_{new}(p^2)$, and $M_{port}(p^1) < M_{port}(p^2)$. From the additivity of complexity metrics we get:

$$M_{port}(p) = \frac{(C_{port}(p^1) + C_{port}(p^2))}{(C_{new}(p^1) + C_{new}(p^2))} > \frac{C_{port}(p^1)}{C_{new}(p^1)} = M_{port}(p^1) \quad (4.13)$$

It follows that $M_{port}(p) > M_{port}(p^1)$: The portability of the process model will always be larger than the lower bound of the portability of two disjoint parts of it.

Summarizing the discussion, we can see that the metrics are normalized complexity metrics, or densities of portability, which fulfill the properties of non-negativity, null value, symmetry, and monotonicity. They fail to satisfy the property of additivity due to normalization.

4.4. Practical Evaluation

The practical evaluation in this section demonstrates the applicability of the metrics and exemplifies their interpretation. Furthermore, we verify what properties of the metrics hold in practice. We first explain the planning and design of the evaluation in Sect. 4.4.1 and outline the prototypic implementation of the metrics computation in Sect. 4.4.2. Thereafter, in Sect. 4.4.3, we discuss the results.

4.4.1. Design and Instrumentation

The goal of this evaluation is to analyze executable process models, for the purpose of assessing the metrics proposed in this chapter with respect to their practical properties. We perform the evaluation using process models implemented in *Goal statement* BPEL. The *context* [174, p. 90] of our evaluation can be characterized as follows: We perform an off-line experiment, meaning that we do not assess software that is currently in development in a project, but software that is already finished and available. We try to gather software that solves realistic problems, but without restricting it to a certain problem domain. The data gathering took place over an extended period of time, from 2013 to 2014, resulting in a variety of software artifacts.

Through the experiment, we validate a number of quality factors of the metrics. In particular, we evaluate the following hypotheses:

1. *Metric values are resilient to moderate changes in the data underlying their computation:* Engines constantly evolve and therefore also application portability is subject to slight changes over a longer period of time. If metric values do not change significantly, even if there are moderate changes in the data underlying their computation, then the current mechanism for computation can be considered robust and the interpretation of the portability values is meaningful.

2. *The metrics can be used for comparing process models of very different size:* Especially complexity metrics are prone to a distorting effect when it comes to code size [184]. Metrics tend to vary for programs of strongly differing size and, therefore, should be used with care when comparing such programs. It is a quality property of a metric to be resilient to changes in code size.

3. *The different metrics carry diverse information:* If the different metrics carry similar information from an information-theoretic viewpoint, then there is no point in computing all of them. Instead, the simplest one is sufficient and the remaining ones can be discarded.

4. *The weighted portability computation improves discriminative power:* A fundamental purpose of quality metrics is the ability to discriminate between different pieces of software. This ability is called the *discriminative power* of a metric. A metric that often assigns the same values to different pieces of software is not desirable, as it lacks this central property. The additional complexity introduced in the weighted metrics computation proposed here should be justified by an increase in discriminative power.

Objects of study When it comes to the *instrumentation* phase [174, pp. 101–102], our experiment objects are code documents, i.e., BPEL process models, for which the metrics can be computed. They come from a practical context and are of varying size. In total, we gathered five different process libraries for the evaluation. Three of them, $L1 - L3$ come from different BPEL engine vendors, being ActiveEndpoints, Apache ODE, and Oracle. These libraries are freely available and serve as documentation and tests for the respective engines. We obtained the fourth one, $L4$, manually from a set of different and more heterogeneous sources where BPEL processes are made publicly available, such as the BPEL-Unit [207] mailing list, Stack Overflow[21], and a collection of workflow patterns implemented in BPEL [196]. These libraries were collected in February 2013. In total, the amount of process models of these libraries adds up to a set of 215. The process models vary strongly in size, ranging from eight to 168 elements, and cover all features of BPEL. The size of each library varies from 22 to 86 process models. To evaluate the first hypothesis, we compare metric values for these libraries computed at two different points in time with updated benchmark data for the metrics computation, which includes: i) the benchmarks of two additional engines, ii) the benchmarks of the new revisions of four engines, iii) and an enhanced set of test assertions, due to more fine-grained test cases.

The remaining fifth library, $L5$, is a large-scale library collected from the Open Hub open source network. We queried the network in January 2014 for files ending in `.bpel`, resulting in 3312 hits which we downloaded for the analysis. From this set, we removed all process models from our own projects, which are also listed on Open Hub, as these are the input to the mechanism of the metrics computation and hence would introduce a bias into the library. Furthermore, we removed the process models from the Apache ODE project, as these are already included in one of the previous four libraries. From the remaining set, we analyzed only the process models that started with a valid BPEL *process* element with the proper BPEL 2.0 namespace and which contained messaging activities. That way, we exclude abstract processes, process models of different dialects, and minimalistic test cases for BPEL parsers. This ensures that the library consists of executable process models. The final set encompasses 1427 process models and is more than six times as large as the other four libraries taken together. It contains very diverse and large process models with up to 3845 elements of code. Due to its size and the fact that it comes from very different sources, we are confident that the process models give us a realistic view of the

---

[21]Stack Overflow is a question and answer site for programmers. Its homepage is located at `http://stackoverflow.com`.

usage of BPEL in practice, at least of its usage in the open source community, and thus allow for a meaningful interpretation of the portability metrics.

4.4.2. Portability Metrics Implementation

To be able to repeatedly calculate metric values from the extensive process libraries, we implemented a plugin for our metrics suite. The general structure of this suite is outlined in Sect. 2.4.3.2. In this section, we explain how we incorporate the computation of portability metrics into the metrics suite.

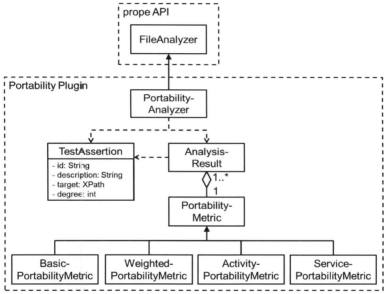

Figure 4.3.: Portability Plugin for the Metrics Suite

The portability metrics computation has initially been implemented in a static checking tool, the *BPEL Portability Profile* (bpp)[22]. During the progression of the dissertation project, it became obvious that it would be beneficial to bundle the computation of all metrics in a single tool, i.e., a metrics suite. Since the bpp tool had already been referenced in several publications, we decided to keep maintaining it and to integrate it in our metrics suite, prope, as a library. This is possible using the plugin mechanism for prope.

An outline of the structure of the portability plugin is depicted in Fig. 4.3. Whereas the main part of prope takes care of folder traversion and report generation, the portability metrics computation is implemented in a separate *FileAnalyzer*. This *PortabilityAnalyzer* is the facade for bpp and enables the interoperation of the APIs of prope and bpp. It parses files that end in .bpel and contain the BPEL 2.0 namespace. When it finds a valid BPEL process, it first tries to detect portability issues in it and groups them by the process

---

[22]See the project page, located at https://github.com/uniba-dsg/bpp, for details.

Test assertion implementation elements for which they are found. For the detection of issues, the tool has access to a large set of *TestAssertions*. Each assertion defines a normative requirement that should be respected to achieve portability and is associated with a degree of severity, the quantitative representation of its severity in terms of portability as described in Sect. 4.1.1. There is a test assertion for every language feature of BPEL that is not unanimously supported by all engines, as described in the benchmark (cf. Sect. 3.3.1). An assertion is identified by an id and is associated with an explanatory description. Furthermore, it contains a target, which is an XPath expression that selects all elements in the process model that are problematic with respect to the assertion, i.e., that violate the assertion. All test assertions are listed in tabular form in the appendix (cf. Appendix B)[23].

The *PortabilityAnalyzer* uses the assertions to detect all issues in the process model, by executing the XPath expressions that are associated with each assertion on the process model. These issues are grouped by the process elements, which results in a list of process elements for which one or more issues could be found, i.e., an *AnalysisResult*. Based on this result, different algorithms for computing portability, as defined by the metrics in Sect. 4.2, are implemented in separate classes for each distinct metric. All except the *BasicPortabilityMetric* make use of the degree of severity. The remaining implementations differ in the subsets of the process elements they select. Finally, all metric values computed for the process model are handed back to the main core of prope, which triggers the analysis of further files and, finally, writes all results to a report.

4.4.3. Results

In the following, we first describe the metric values we computed for the different process libraries. This serves as an exemplary assessment of the process libraries using the portability metrics. We contrast the initial four libraries with the extended fifth one and also look at the natural variability of BPEL process models. Thereafter, we evaluate the hypotheses stated above and provide a summary of the results.

4.4.3.1. Descriptive Statistics of the Process Libraries

Table 4.1 shows descriptive statistics for the process libraries with the different metrics. Additionally, Fig. 4.4 depicts boxplots for the different process libraries.

---

[23]It is important to note that the benchmark results presented in Sect. 3.3.1 are comprehensive point in time observations. To ensure the practical applicability of our tool, we update it every time we find differences in standard conformance, such as when a new patch version of an engine becomes available. As such updates do not justify the repetition of a full-fledged benchmark of all engines, the tool has diverged from the data presented in Sect. 3.3.1 to a certain degree. During the metrics evaluation in Sect. 4.4.3, we demonstrate that these updates do not harm the applicability of the metrics. This is essentially the focus of hypothesis 1. To sum up, the benchmark data from Sect. 3.3.1 shows the results at the time the benchmarks were made and the test assertions in the appendix show the state of the tool at the time of writing this thesis.

Table 4.1.: Descriptive Statistics for Process Libraries

Library	N	Statistics	M_{basic}	M_{elem}	M_{act}	M_{serv}	Ø
L1	22	Mean	0.84	0.87	0.99	0.99	0.92
		std(X)	0.13	0.12	0.01	0.05	0.11
L2	25	Mean	0.90	0.97	0.92	0.94	0.93
		std(X)	0.03	0.01	0.04	0.07	0.05
L3	82	Mean	0.94	0.98	0.96	0.94	0.95
		std(X)	0.06	0.02	0.04	0.10	0.07
L4	86	Mean	0.90	0.93	0.97	0.97	0.94
		std(X)	0.04	0.03	0.05	0.08	0.06
L5	1427	Mean	0.90	0.95	0.95	0.94	0.93
		std(X)	0.12	0.10	0.07	0.11	0.10
All	1642	Mean	0.90	0.95	0.95	0.94	0.94
		std(X)	0.11	0.10	0.06	0.11	0.10
Small Processes, Q_1	395	Mean	0.92	0.96	0.96	0.96	0.95
		std(X).	0.10	0.07	0.07	0.10	0.09
Large Processes, Q_4	409	Mean	0.89	0.96	0.94	0.94	0.93
		std(X)	0.11	0.09	0.06	0.09	0.09

Looking at $L1$, relatively low values for M_{basic} and M_{elem} with values of 0.84 and 0.87 respectively, along with relatively high standard deviations, contrast high values for M_{act} and M_{serv}. This reveals that the main portability issues do not lie in the control-flow and communication activities of the process models, these are indeed almost fully portable. The issues here reside mostly in the usage of nonstandard extensions. Such issues, as they relate to extensions for logging, etc., tend to be fixable.

For $L2$, values of M_{act} and M_{serv} are lower in total, and also lower than M_{elem}. This indicates the opposite structure than for $L1$. Portability issues mainly originate from the activities and the control-flow definition. Whereas the process models do not make heavy use of language extensions, they rely on configurations of activities that are of limited portability. Porting this process library is comparatively harder.

$L3$ achieves high and similar values for all metrics. M_{basic} and M_{serv} are lowest with values of 0.94 and M_{serv} has a comparably high standard deviation with 0.10. Again, the value of M_{serv} implies that most problems are found in service-related activities and thus porting this library could pose problems.

$L4$ shows similar values as $L1$, although with lower numbers in total. Portability issues mainly come from nonstandard elements that do not directly relate to activities or communication aspects.

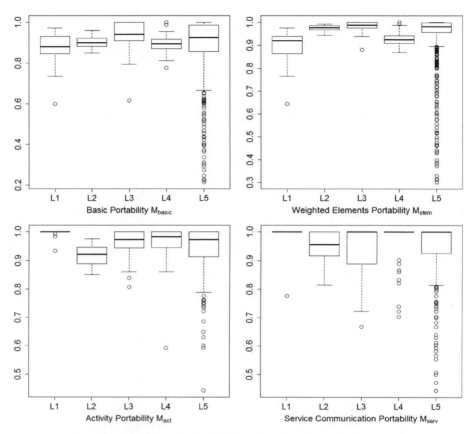

Figure 4.4.: Portability Values for the Process Libraries

The largest and hence the most diverse library, $L5$, is similar to $L3$, but at a lower degree of portability and standard deviations are higher. All in all, M_{basic} is lowest and has the highest standard deviation, which suggests that the main problems in this library are due to extension elements.

In total, $L3$ scores best when it comes to portability in general and a final decision is indicated by the aggregated metric values in the last column of Table 4.1. This is also illustrated by Fig. 4.4, where $L3$ clearly ranges at the top when looking at the plots for M_{basic} and M_{elem}. For M_{act} and M_{serv}, the situation is no longer that clear, due to the relatively large standard deviation in $L3$. The other libraries lie at the border of an acceptable level, with $L1$ scoring lowest and showing the highest degree of variation when it comes to M_{basic} and M_{elem}. Focusing on the process and communication view (M_{act} and M_{serv}), however, $L3$ is overtaken by $L1$ and $L4$.

Compari-
son of L5
and re- Due to its large size and origin, $L5$ can be seen as representative for the usage
mainder of BPEL in the open source community. This makes a closer comparison of $L5$ to

Table 4.2.: Mann-Whitney U Test for the Difference of $L5$ to $L1 - L4$

Library		M_{basic}	M_{elem}	M_{act}	M_{serv}
$L1 \longleftrightarrow L5$	p	0.01	$1.80e^{-8}$	$5.49e^{-6}$	0.01
	U	10902.5	4793.5	24387	19678
$L2 \longleftrightarrow L5$	p	0.07	0.15	$9.81e^{-5}$	0.03
	U	14131.5	14874	9874	14098
$L3 \longleftrightarrow L5$	p	0.01	0.00	0.70	0.41
	U	69070.5	69417.5	59967.5	55926.5
$L4 \longleftrightarrow L5$	p	0.00	$1.03e^{-15}$	0.01	0.00
	U	49946.5	29957	70898	71216

the other libraries worthwhile. In particular, it could be interesting to observe if the process models in $L5$ have a significantly higher or lower degree of portability for the different metrics, than the other libraries. We used the Shapiro Wilk test [187] to determine if metric values are normally distributed for the different process libraries[24]. As this was clearly not the case for all libraries except $L2$, we used a non-parametric test, the Mann-Whitney U test [188], for comparing the libraries. The null hypothesis in this case is that there are no significant differences in the distributions of the different process libraries, when compared to $L5$. Because we are doing four comparisons, one for each metric, we perform alpha-adjustment and reduce the significance level to $p < 0.05/4 = 0.0125$. The results of the test are depicted in Table 4.2. The null hypothesis can be rejected in all cases when comparing $L5$ to $L1$ and $L4$ respectively, so the differences between these libraries are significant. These two libraries are more portable when it comes to control-flow, but less portable according to M_{basic} and M_{elem}, indicating that there is a higher amount of nonstandard extensions used in these libraries. This is interesting, since $L1$ consists of process models which run on a commercial engine. In contrast to this, $L2$ and $L3$ do not show a significant difference to $L5$ for M_{basic} and M_{elem} or M_{act} and M_{serv} respectively. This implies that the process models in these libraries are representative for process models used in the open source community.

4.4.3.2. Natural Variability of Portability

For all metrics and process libraries, mean portability values are relatively high, ranging at values around 0.9. All standard deviations are relatively low, with the highest value of 0.13 for L_1 and M_{basic}. This indicates that the process models of each library do not deviate strongly and, despite their differences in functionality, do share a common level of portability. At a first glance, this level may seem

---

[24]Since we drop the assumption of normality in the following, we omit a presentation of the results of this test.

high. However, it is important to keep in mind, that the language and systems we consider here specifically aim to produce portable code. The question is what can be considered as high in this domain, or, in the terms of [70], what the natural variability of the attribute is (cf. Sect. 4.3.1). With the data at hand, we can provide a hint for the natural variability of the portability of BPEL process models in general. Considering the aggregated means and standard deviations of the different metrics for all process models, listed in the last column of Table 4.1, the data indicate that the portability naturally ranges at 0.94. Based on the evaluation, this value can be used as reference for the quality assessment of BPEL process models. Anything below this level can be considered to be of lower quality with respect to its portability.

As shown in Sect. 3.3.4, only 16 % of the total test set of the benchmark are passed by all engines under test. This implies that engines implement relatively disjoint sets of the language (cf. Fig. 4.1) and as a result lower portability values than the ones observed here could be expected. As discussed, disjointedness in standard conformance only results in portability issues if process models use features that are not well supported. If they mainly use features of the basic language subset that is widely supported, higher portability will be the result. The latter seems to be the case for all of the libraries. Even the process models from $L5$, which are most representative of practical BPEL usage, seem to use only a modest part of the language.

4.4.3.3. Variance of the Metrics Over Time

Hypothesis 1 addresses the resilience of the metrics to changes in the underlying data. This can be examined by testing whether the metric values have changed through the updates and additions of the engines over time, which we can find out by comparing newer data for $L1$ to $L4$ with older revisions. More precisely, we compare metric data computed based on benchmark results from February 2013 to metric data computed based on results from January 2014.

There are different ways of performing this comparison, such as by contrasting the mean or median values of repeated computations [171, p. 12]. Here, we use a statistical test to see if there are significant differences in the distributions of the metric values for repeated experiments. If there are no significant differences, we can infer that the mechanism for metrics computation is robust in the face of changes and the interpretation of the portability values is meaningful. To find out if there are significant differences, we use the Wilcoxon signed-rank test [189], a non-parametric test for comparing the means of paired sets of data, which is what we have here. Table 4.3 outlines the results. In no case, p-values become significant. This means that, based on the data, we cannot diagnose any significant changes in the metric values despite the updates in the underlying benchmark. It seems that the mechanism for metrics computation is at a mature state and robust in the face of changes.

Table 4.3.: Wilcoxon Test for the Difference of $L1 - L4$ at Different Points in
Time

Library		M_{basic}	M_{elem}	M_{act}	M_{serv}
L1	p	0.72	0.87	0.68	1
	W	126.5	123	32	2
L2	p	0.61	1	0.89	0.75
	W	131.5	162	168	106
L3	p	0.22	0.88	0.84	0.59
	W	1157.5	1432.5	1463.5	590.5
L4	p	0.84	0.99	0.59	0.53
	W	1657	1787.5	1409.5	159

4.4.3.4. Effect of Code Size

The second hypothesis addresses the usage of the metrics for the comparison
of process models of very different size. In general, a distorting effect can be
observed when comparing the complexity of programs with a different code
size [184]. Metrics values tend to vary in this case and therefore should be used
with care when comparing such programs. Resilience to changes in code size is
considered a quality property of a metric.

Table 4.4.: Mann-Whitney U Test for the Difference of Small and Large Process
Models

Statistics	M_{basic}	M_{elem}	M_{act}	M_{serv}
p	$5.65e^{-12}$	$2.42e^{-12}$	$2.2e^{-16}$	$8.32e^{-11}$
U	103270.5	103661.5	119881	97674.5

To investigate the effect of code size on our metrics, we extract two groups
of process models, large and small ones, from all of the libraries. Large process
models come from the fourth quartile in terms of the number of elements (i.e.,
the 25% largest models) and small process models from the first quartile (i.e.,
the 25% smallest models). Table 4.1 lists descriptive statistics for these sets in
the last two rows. The mean values and standard deviations for large and small
process models are very similar for all metrics. Still, when comparing the two
sets using the Mann-Whitney U test at a significance level of 0.0125, we can see
that there are significant differences between the two sets. The results of the
test can be found in Table 4.4. This means that our metrics, as common for
complexity metrics, should be treated with care if used to compare programs of
widely differing size.

121

4.4.3.5. Information Carried by the Metrics

Another important property, the focus of hypothesis 3, is the ability of the metrics to provide diverse information. This can be determined by looking at their correlation. If all metrics correlate strongly to each other, then, strictly speaking, they all carry similar information, in spite of their difference in point of view. If they all carry similar information, then there is no point in computing all of them. Instead, the simplest one is sufficient and the remaining ones can be discarded.

Table 4.5.: R^2 for Portability Metrics

	M_{basic}	M_{elem}	M_{act}	M_{serv}
M_{basic}	–	0.89	0.56	0.38
M_{elem}	0.89	–	0.49	0.37
M_{act}	0.56	0.49	–	0.64

The square of the linear correlation coefficient R^2 is suggested in [171] to evaluate correlation among software metrics. Table 4.5 outlines R^2 for the different metrics, aggregated for all process libraries. M_{basic} and M_{elem}, as well as M_{act} and M_{serv}, show a stronger correlation. All other combinations show a moderate correlation. Since the metrics are computed in a similar fashion, although with a different view, a moderate correlation should be expected. Nevertheless, this level is still acceptable. M_{basic} and M_{elem}, as well as M_{act} and M_{serv}, show a strong correlation which can be attributed to the strong similarity in their computation. So, from an information-theoretic viewpoint, M_{elem} is not superior to M_{basic} nor is M_{serv} to M_{act}. It is still beneficial to look at M_{elem} and M_{serv}, for reasons discussed in the following section.

4.4.3.6. Discriminative Power

Finally, hypothesis 4 addresses the discriminative power of the metrics. A metric should assign different values to different pieces of software, because otherwise there is not much use in a comparison of the metric values. In particular, the weighted metric, M_{elem}, should have a higher discriminative power than the basic metric, M_{basic}, to justify the added complexity for its computation.

Discriminative power can be measured by calculating the amount of unique metric values in the total set of values. The higher the amount of unique values, the better the metric is able to distinguish between different pieces of software and the higher its discriminative power is. For M_{basic} the discriminate power amounts to $379/1642 = 0.23$, for M_{elem} it is $531/1642 = 0.32$, for M_{act}: $224/1642 = 0.14$, and for M_{serv}: $81/1642 = 0.05$. Clearly, M_{elem} has the highest degree of discriminative power. In combination with the fact that it correlates strongly to M_{basic}, we claim that for that reason, M_{elem} is preferable to M_{basic} and the specialized metric indeed does have an added value. Both, M_{act} and M_{serv}, have a more limited degree of discriminative power which is expected as they abstract from certain aspects compared to M_{basic}. However, as demonstrated in the previous subsection, they do carry information different from M_{basic} and M_{elem} and highlight more critical portability issues.

4.5. Summary

In this chapter, we presented a measurement framework for quantifying and assessing the portability of service-oriented and process-aware software. The idea of using the amount of standard-conformant engines supporting certain language elements, discussed in Sect. 4.1, is an extension to classical portability metrics. Our measurement framework considers the portability of process models from different viewpoints, captured by dedicated metrics, that vary in their severity. We provide an extensive evaluation of the metrics, both from a theoretical and a practical angle. The metrics proposed in Sect. 4.2 are:

1. A basic portability metric that resembles the classical way of computation and serves as a means of comparison.
2. A weighted portability metric that, similar to the basic metric, considers all process elements and introduces engine support data into the computation.
3. An activity-oriented metric that limits the scope to the activities, events, and gateways of the process model.
4. A communication-oriented metric that limits the scope to the activities and events used for message sending and reception.

The theoretical properties these metrics fulfill are determined in the theoretical validation in Sect. 4.3. From a theoretical point of view, the metrics are normalized complexity metrics or densities of complexity. They satisfy the properties of non-negativity, null value, symmetry, and monotonicity, but not additivity. They are internal and indirect, target service-oriented and process-aware pieces of software, are obtained by counting issues in code, and have an interval scale.

The practical evaluation in Sect. 4.4 shows that the metrics are resilient to moderate changes in the data underlying the computation and carry diverse information. Furthermore, the evaluation demonstrates that the inclusion of engine support data in the computation improves the discriminative power of the metrics in comparison to the basic way of computation. However, as usual for complexity metrics, they cannot be used to compare process models of arbitrarily different size. By computing the metrics for various process libraries, we can also investigate the portability of BPEL process models in practice. Overall, the portability of real-world BPEL process models is quite high, which can be attributed to the fact that only a modest part of the language seems to be used in practice.

In combination, the proposed metrics and their theoretical and practical evaluation allows to answer research question 2.1: *What are suitable metrics for measuring portability?* The metrics framework provides a validated and practically tested way of achieving this.

5. Measuring Installability

Parts of this chapter have been taken from [79].

One of the three subcharacteristics of portability defined in the SQuaRE model in Sect. 2.3.2, and, hence, the next step in the measurement framework, is *installability*. In the same fashion as in the previous chapter, we define, validate, and evaluate a set of metrics for measuring the installability of process-aware and service-oriented software. The goal of this chapter is to answer research question 2.2: *What are suitable metrics for measuring installability?*

The organization of the chapter follows the framework of Part II of this thesis. *Structure* *of the* *chapter* We begin by discussing the nature of installability and how it can be measured in Sect. 5.1. Thereafter, we examine existing metrics that attempt this task and derive and formally define our metrics framework. Next comes the theoretical validation of the metrics in Sect. 5.2, followed by the practical evaluation in Sect. 5.3. Finally, the chapter is concluded with a summary in Sect. 5.4.

5.1. On the Measurement of Installability

In Sect. 2.3.2, installability was defined as the degree of effectiveness and effi- *Nature of* *installa-* ciency with which a software product can be successfully installed in a specified *bility* environment. When it comes to the installation of middleware-based software, which is the focus here, this definition has two focal points. The first one is the application to be installed. The second one is the middleware into which the application is installed. In our case, the application is an executable process model and the middleware a process engine. Especially at the enterprise-level, process engines are of considerable complexity. As a consequence of this complexity, also their installation can constitute a noticeable effort and should not be disregarded. This implies that a measurement framework for the installability of service-oriented and process-aware software should target two areas: i) The assessment of the installability of a process engine, and ii) the assessment of the installability of an executable process model into the process engine. The latter task, i. e., installing an application into a server environment, is commonly referred to as *deployment* [208]. Therefore, we subdivide the quality characteristic of installability into the subcharacteristics of *engine installability* and *deployability*.

It should be noted that the original definition of installability from [53] also *Uninstal-* *lation* considers uninstallation. In contrast, we do not consider uninstallation here. The reason for this is that in our setting, an uninstallation of a software system is rarely needed. In the times of cloud-provisioned execution environments, process-aware and service-oriented software systems are seldom installed directly into an operating system. Instead, the execution environment is virtualized, e.g., using virtual machines or containers, as discussed in Sect. 2.1.2.3. In such environments, an uninstallation can be performed simply by resetting the virtual machine state or discarding a container. A dedicated uninstallation procedure is not needed, since the system as a whole is being reset. The time and effort required for this task is constant, little, and independent of the software installed. Thus, we do not consider uninstallation here.

Existing metrics for instal- lability   When it comes to quantifying installability, only few metrics are available and some have been defined in the predecessors of SQuaRE, e.g., [209, 210]. However, in [209], all of them are marked as experimental. Furthermore, several of the defined metrics effectively measure the same thing. For instance, the metrics *effortless installation, installation ease*, and *ease of users manual installation operation* [209, p. 64] all measure the extent to which user actions are needed during the installation procedure. We condense this notion into a single metric, *installation effort*, in our measurement framework. The metric *operational installation effort reduction* [209, p. 64] is used to measure effort reduction in the case of changes in the installation procedure. As we do not focus on procedural changes, but want to assess installability as-is, the metric is of no relevance here. *Installation flexibility* [210, p. 37] relates the number of customizations implemented for the installation procedure, such as installation paths or port numbers, to the number of customizations required. The larger the extent to which customizations can be implemented is, the better. In the practical evaluation (cf. Sect. 5.3), we could implement all customizations needed in all cases. As a consequence, this metric did not bear any benefit here, and we decided to exclude it from our framework. The remaining metrics relevant here are *installation effort* and *ease of setup retry* [210, p. 37]. These metrics are adapted to and included in our framework, along with several new ones presented in the following.

Frame- work   Fig. 5.1 outlines the framework we use for measuring installability. As discussed earlier, the quality characteristic *installability* is subdivided into the subcharac- teristics *engine installability* and *deployability*. Each of the subcharacteristics can be measured by a set of direct and aggregated metrics. The metrics *ease of setup retry* (ESR) and *installation effort* (IE) stem from [209, 210]. Ease of setup retry is meant to characterize the reliability of the installation procedure. The intention of installation effort is to quantify the complexity of the installation procedure. In [209, 210], this is done by counting the number of steps required to perform the installation. We extended installation effort to also consider *average installation time* (AIT) and not only the *number of distinct steps* (NDS) of the installation procedure. When it comes to deployability, no corresponding metrics are available in [209, 210], so we develop a new set. This set consists of *deployment effort* (DE) which, like installation effort, is intended to quantify the effort required to achieve deployment. The metric considers *deployment descriptor sizes* (DDS) and the *effort of package construction* (EPC). Moreover, we introduce *deployment flexibility* (DF), to assess the degree of freedom an operator has when trying to achieve deployment.

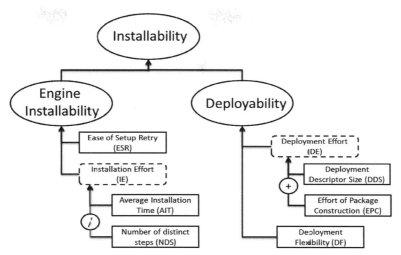

Figure 5.1.: The Framework for Measuring Installability – Ellipses denote quality attributes to be measured, rectangles denote metrics obtained through code analysis and benchmarking, and rounded dashed rectangles depict aggregated metrics that are computed by the combination of other metrics using the functions displayed in circles.

The deployability metrics DDS, EPC, and DE, as well as the installability metric NDS, are *internal* (i.e., they relate to static properties of the software). The remaining metrics are *external* (i.e., they relate to dynamic properties and can be computed during execution) [53, p. 27]. Apart from ESR, all metrics are defined on a ratio scale. In the following subsections, the metrics for the two quality characteristics are defined formally.

5.1.1. Measuring Engine Installability

Ease of setup retry (ESR) is intended to assess how easy it is to successfully repeat an installation [210, p. 37]. It relates the number of successful installations of the same engine e (N_{succ}) to the number of attempted installations in total (N_{total}). The computation of the metric requires the installation procedure to be repeated a suitable amount of times. Put formally:

Ease of setup retry

Definition 25: Ease of Setup Retry (ESR)

$$ESR(e) = \begin{cases} 0 & \text{if } N_{total}(e) = 0 \\ \frac{N_{succ}(e)}{N_{total}(e)} & otherwise \end{cases}, where \qquad (5.1)$$

- $N_{succ}(e) \in \mathbb{N}_0$ is the number of successful installation attempts of engine e;
- $N_{total}(e) \in \mathbb{N}_0$ is the total number of installation attempts of engine e;
- For $N_{total}(e) = 0$, ESR is defined as zero.

---

[210] refers to a manual installation procedure, but the metric is just as applicable to an automated procedure. If this procedure is completely deterministic, then $N_{succ}(e)$ and $N_{total}(e)$ will be identical and $ESR(e)$ equal to one. If it is not free of errors or side effects, installations may fail, resulting in a lower ESR value. This resembles an interval scale of $[0, 1]$.

Installa-
tion
effort
Installation effort (IE) is intended to provide a notion of the difficulty of the installation procedure. [210, p. 37] suggests to measure it as the relation of the amount of automatable installation steps and the total amount of prescribed steps. In our application scenario, the engine installation procedure can usually be automated fully, as demonstrated by our benchmarking tool in Chap. 3. As a consequence, relating automatable and manual installation steps would not result in a helpful metric value. Still, the engines do differ in the amount of steps they require for the installation. What is more, they do require a vastly different amount of time for the installation, which can vary in orders of magnitude when comparing certain engines. For that reason, we deviate in the measurement of installation effort from [210] and instead measure it through a combination of two other metrics: The total number of distinct steps (NDS) of the installation procedure and the average installation time (AIT). Hence, installation effort *Number* is an indirect metric. NDS is identical to the number of steps that need to be
of distinct
steps automated, and thereby partly corresponds to the metric defined in [210]. NDS includes every operation that needs to be performed for the installation, such as the copying of files and creation of directories or changes in the configuration of certain files. This number can be determined by a *heuristic evaluation* [211]. This is a technique commonly applied for assessing the usability of a user interface. In a heuristic evaluation, a domain expert examines the steps of a procedure in a user interface and judges their appropriateness and usability. Ported to our context, a heuristic evaluation can be performed to judge the complexity of an installation procedure, by counting the steps encoded in the installation script. It is important to note that this implies that the computation of NDS cannot be automated, but requires human inspection. An example of the steps in an installation script, required to install a BPEL engine, looks as follows:

1. Create or clean the installation directory

2. Uncompress the engine distribution to the installation directory

3. Uncompress the server core in the engine distribution

4. Copy the BPEL runtime to the server core

5. Copy the SOAP runtime to the server core

Average
installa-
tion
time
The average installation time can be computed by performing the distinct steps required a suitable amount of times and timing the duration. AIT and NDS can be aggregated to a notion of installation effort (IE) per installation step. This is captured in Def. 26:

Definition 26: Installation Effort (IE)

$$IE(e) = \begin{cases} 0 & \text{if } NDS(e) = 0 \\ \frac{AIT(e)}{NDS(e)} & otherwise \end{cases} \qquad (5.2)$$

- $NDS(e) \in \mathbb{N}_0$ refers to the number of steps required for installing engine e;
- For $NDS(e) = 0$, $IE(e)$ is defined as zero;
- $AIT(e) = time(e_{inst_1}), \ldots, time(e_{inst_n})$ refers to the arithmetic mean of the duration of multiple engine installations $e_{inst_1}, \ldots, e_{inst_n}$.

Note that an installation routine that consists of several simple steps is desirable over a single installation step that takes very long, even if the multiple step installation takes longer. The reasoning behind this is that simple and quick installation steps are easier to automate, to repeat in case of a failure, or to adapt to a new environment.

5.1.2. Measuring Deployability

Deployment is the task "*of readying [...] a component for installation in a specific environment*" [208]. Deployability characterizes the effort required to perform this task. There is no direct representation or corresponding metrics for this characteristic in the SQuaRE method. We derive new metrics from existing general-purpose quality measure elements from SQuaRE [212] as far as applicable.

Deployment normally consists of the execution of a single engine operation provided with the packaged application. Nevertheless, deployment can take different forms, multiple of which can be supported by an engine. The more options an engine supports, the more flexible it is and the easier deployment can be achieved. We capture this in the metric *deployment flexibility* (*DF*), which corresponds to the number of options available. The intention of the metric is to adapt *installation flexibility* from [210, p. 37] to this context. Typically, three different options are available:

1. a copy operation of a deployment archive into a specific directory, which is known as hot deployment,
2. the invocation of a deployment script or service,
3. a manual user operation using a GUI or web interface.

Deployment flexibility

> **Definition 27: Deployment Flexibility (DF)**
>
> $$DF(e) = |\{op_1, \ldots, op_n\}|, where \tag{5.3}$$
>
> - $\{op_1, \ldots, op_n\}$ refers to the set of the deployments options available for an engine e.

Deployment flexibility can be determined by a heuristic evaluation, similar to the number of distinct steps described in the previous section.

To be able to use one of the deployment operations for an application, this application must be prepared and, usually, be packaged for deployment. Next to packaging, this requires the construction of one or more deployment descriptors [208]. The construction of these descriptors may be partly automated or aided by graphical wizards, but in the end it is configuration effort that can take a significant amount of time to get right. The more complex the packaging is and the more extensive the descriptors are, the harder it is to deploy an application in a specific environment. We capture packaging with the metric *effort of package construction (EPC)* and deployment descriptors with the metric *deployment descriptor size (DDS)*. The effort of package construction can be measured in a similar fashion as the number of distinct steps for an installation procedure. That is, by counting each part of a prescribed folder structure that needs to be built and compression operations that need to be performed to construct the prescribed packaged application:

Effort of package construction

> **Definition 28: Effort of Package Construction (EPC)**
>
> $$EPC(app) = N_{fc}(app) + N_{dc}(app) + N_{co}(app), where \tag{5.4}$$
>
> - $N_{fc}(app) \in \mathbb{N}_0$ refers to the amount of folder creations needed for building the deployment package for application *app*;
> - $N_{dc}(app) \in \mathbb{N}_0$ refers to the amount of descriptor files needed in the deployment package for application *app*;
> - $N_{co}(app) \in \mathbb{N}_0$ refers to the amount of compression operations needed for building the deployment package for application *app*.

N_{fc} refers to the amount of folder creations, N_{dc} to the amount of descriptors, and N_{co} to the amount of compression operations required. Note that, due to the prescribed structure of a deployment package, the calculation of EPC can be automated. Taking the example of BPEL engines and process models, a very simple structure consists of a process file, a WSDL file, and a deployment descriptor file in one directory that is compressed to an archive. Decisive for EPC are the deployment folder, the descriptor file and the compression operation, so $EPC = 1 + 1 + 1 = 3$. However, the structure can be vastly more complex and depend on various nested archives with multiple descriptors.

The next part of deployment effort is the size of the descriptor files. The *Deployment descriptor size* deployment descriptor size for an application corresponds to the added size of all descriptor files needed:

Definition 29: Deployment Descriptor Size (DDS)

$$DDS(app) = \sum_{i=1}^{N_{desc}} size(dd_i), where \tag{5.5}$$

- $\{dd_1, ..., dd_{N_{desc}}\}$ refers to the set of descriptor files needed for the deployment package for application *app*; $N_{desc} \in \mathbb{N}_0$ refers to the cardinality of this set;
- $size(dd_i)$: *Descriptor* $\rightarrow \mathbb{N}_0$ is a function that returns the size of a descriptor file.

DDS is the sum of the size of all relevant descriptors $\{dd_1, ..., dd_{N_{desc}}\}$. For process-aware and service-oriented applications, typically two different types of descriptor files exist: i) Plain text files and i) XML configuration files. As plain text files and XML files differ in the ways in which they represent information, different ways of computing their size are needed. Here, we use two simple mechanisms to compute file sizes. For plain text files, a lines of code metric is appropriate. For the descriptors at hand, every non-empty and non-comment line in such files is a key-value pair with a configuration setting needed for deployment, such as a host or port configuration. We consider each such line, using a *LOC* function. For XML files, the notion of lines is not applicable, but instead information is structured in nested elements and attributes. To compute the size of XML files, we consider the number of elements, including simple content, and attributes, excluding namespace definitions, called N_{ea}. This represents an items of information in the same fashion as key-value pairs in plain text files. All in all, the size function for a descriptor *desc* is defined as follows:

Definition 30: Size Function

$$size(desc) = \begin{cases} LOC(desc), & \text{if } plain(desc) \\ N_{ea}(desc), & \text{if } xml(desc) \end{cases}, where \tag{5.6}$$

- $LOC(desc)$: *Descriptor* $\rightarrow \mathbb{N}_0$ is a function that returns the number of non-empty and non-comment lines of a descriptor file;
- $N_{ea}(desc)$: *Descriptor* $\rightarrow \mathbb{N}_0$ is a function that returns the number of elements and non-namespace attributes in an XML descriptor file;
- $plain(desc)$: *Descriptor* $\rightarrow$ *Boolean* is a function that determines if a descriptor file is a plain text file;
- $xml(desc)$: *Descriptor* $\rightarrow$ *Boolean* is a function that determines if a descriptor file is an XML file.

---

5. *Measuring Installability*

Listing 5.1 outlines a simple descriptor file for a single BPEL application. The descriptor consists of four elements and four non-namespace attributes that are set, so the total size of the descriptor is eight.

Listing 5.1: Example of a Simple Deployment Descriptor

```
<deploy xmlns=" ... " xmlns:bpel=" ... ">
    <process xmlns:tns=" ... " name="tns:SimpleService">
        <provide partnerLink="SimplePartnerLink">
            <service name="tns:SimpleServiceInterface" port="
                SimplePort"/>
        </provide>
    </process>
</deploy>
```

Deploy-ment effort To obtain the deployment effort of the complete application, the effort of package construction and deployment descriptor size can be added up to the indirect metric *deployment effort*:

Definition 31: Deployment Effort (DE)

$$DE(app) = EPC(app) + DDS(app), where \qquad (5.7)$$

- $EPC(app)$ is defined in Def. 28;
- $DDS(app)$ is defined in Def. 29.

The idea here is to capture every factor, independent of its nature, that increases the effort of deploying an application.

This concludes our measurement framework for installability. Next comes the theoretical validation of the metrics.

5.2. Theoretical Validation

In this section, we perform the theoretical validation of the proposed installability metrics. As before, we validate the metrics with respect to measurement theory [69] and construct validity [70]. We begin with the measurement-theoretic validation in the following section.

5.2.1. Measurement-Theoretic Validation

The measurement-theoretic validation framework [69] is tailored to internal software metrics. Here, only the metrics relating to descriptors and package sizes DDS, EPC, and DE, as well as installation scripts, NDS, are internal metrics. Hence, only they directly fit in this framework. The internal metrics

132

are size metrics in the sense of [69], which should fulfill the properties of *non-negativity*, *null value*, and *additivity*. Since a clarification of measurement-theoretic properties is valuable for all metrics, we nevertheless discuss these properties for all installability metrics.

Non-negativity: Nearly all of the metric values are obtained by counting occurrences of specific elements, being either operation steps (NDS), time units elapsed (AIT), successful installations and installation attempts (ESR), available deployment options (DF), or code constructs and lines of code (DDS and EPC). This implies that these metrics cannot yield negative values. The indirect metrics installation effort (IE) and deployment effort (DE) are aggregated through the summation or division of two non-negative metrics. As a result, they are also non-negative.

Null value: Deployment descriptor size (DDS) and the effort of package construction (EPC) are equal to zero for an empty program, as no descriptors or packages need to be built. Being the sum of the two, this also applies to deployment effort (DE). If there is nothing to install, the number of distinct steps for the installation (NDS) is equal to zero as well. The average installation time (AIT) of zero installations is also zero, similar to the ease of setup retry (ESR). In this case, IE is defined to be zero. The same applies to deployment flexibility (DF), as the set of available options is empty.

Additivity: Size metrics should be additive, meaning that the size of two disjoint systems taken together should be identical to the sum of the two. This property holds for deployment descriptor size (DDS) and the effort of package construction (EPC). If two applications app_1 and app_2 are packaged separately and can be deployed on their own, the sizes of their descriptors and packages are completely independent of each other. Hence, if they are deployed on the same engine, forming a system app together, the values for DDS and EPC of that system will be equal to the sum of the values of the two applications. Since deployment effort (DE) refers to the sum of DDS and EPC, additivity also holds for this metric.

Furthermore, additivity holds for the number of distinct steps of the installation (NDS). Given two engines are installed, the installation operations need to be completed for each of them.

However, additivity does not hold for the remaining metrics. The average installation time (AIT), ease of setup retry (ESR), and installation effort (IE) are average values or aggregated thereof, so adding them up is meaningless. Also the number of deployment options (DF) does not necessarily increase with the number of engines.

Summarizing the discussion, it can be seen that all metrics are non-negative and provide null values. The internal metrics are additive, whereas the external metrics fail to satisfy this property.

5.2.2. **Evaluation of Construct Validity**

When it comes to the second theoretical validation framework [70], the attribute in the sense of [70] that is being measured by the metrics is installability. As before, the measurement instrument is our metrics suite. In the following, we answer the ten aspects specified by [70].

Purpose of the metrics: Similar to the metrics for the other quality characteristics, the primary purpose of the metrics at hand is the information of stakeholders. They inform developers and operators about the installability characteristics of their applications. This can be used for private self-assessment of a workgroup or for the information of third parties, such as customers and maintainers. The metrics can also be used for decision making, for instance when selecting one of a set of systems for deployment into production.

Scope of the metrics: The scope of the metrics is typically a single project from one workgroup that consists of multiple process-aware and service-oriented applications and engines.

Measured attribute: The attribute to be measured is the installability of the software, the ease with which it can be installed in an environment. As discussed in Sect. 5.1, uninstallability is negligible. The installation effort metrics (NDS, AIT, and IE) measure the complexity of the installation routine of an engine and the ease of setup retry (ESR) measures the reliability of the installation. The deployment effort metrics (DDS, EPC, and DE) measure the size of deployment artifacts and DF the flexibility of the deployment operation.

Natural scale of the attribute: We have no knowledge on the natural scale of installability or deployability per se, but it is reasonable to assume that applications differ in their installability or deployability in a way that allows to build an ordering. This implies that installability can be observed at least on an ordinal, and possibly on a ratio scale.

Natural variability of the attribute: We have no knowledge on the natural variability of installability or deployability. However, it can reasonably be expected that installability or deployability varies depending on the environment into which a piece of software is installed or the size of the system to be installed or deployed. This claim is also supported by the practical evaluation in Sect. 5.3.

Definition of the metrics and the instrument: All metrics are formally defined in Sect. 5.1. They are computed by *counting* code constructs or elements, by *matching* installation steps or product functions, and by *timing* task executions [70, p. 4].

Natural scale of the metrics: Ease of setup retry (ESR) is measured on an interval scale of $[0; 1]$. All other metrics are measured on a ratio scale [212, p. 36]

Natural variability of the measurement instrument: Human judgement usually involves a margin of error, so metrics determined by heuristic evaluation $(NDS$ and $DF)$ can yield inaccuracies. The rate of failed installations (ESR) and the time elapsed during installation $(AIT$ and $IE)$ likely depends on physical constraints such as the number of processors or memory available, and will be different on different hardware. However, this is rather an inherent natural variability and not a computational error. We compute the descriptor size metrics $(EPC, DDS,$ and $DE)$ based on whitelisting of relevant descriptor files. In case we omitted a file type, there is an error in the measurement instrument.

Relationship of the attribute to metrics values: Except for installation effort (IE) and deployment effort (DE), which are aggregated from the other metrics, all of the metrics are direct in the sense of [171]. Changes to the underlying attributes are directly reflected in the metrics. For instance, if more installations fail, the ease of setup retry (ESR) decreases. If the installation procedure gets more complex, it will likely involve more steps (NDS) or take longer (AIT). If deployment gets more complex, it will likely involve more steps to construct deployment packages (EPC) or require larger descriptors (DDS). If a new option for deployment is available, deployment flexibility (DF) increases.

Natural side-effects of using the metrics: The measurement of human behavior is prone to side-effects, as humans could adapt their behavior to produce desirable metric values without changing the underlying attribute. Here, we measure code artifacts, so there is no room for this type of error.

5.3. Practical Evaluation

By performing a practical and experimental evaluation, we can demonstrate the interpretation of the metrics and the properties that hold for them in practice.

In Sect. 5.3.1, we explain the goal and design of the evaluation, as well as experimental hypotheses. This is followed by the description of our prototypic implementation of the installability metrics in the prope tool in 5.3.2. Thereafter, we discuss the results of the evaluation in Sect. 5.3.3.

5.3.1. Design and Instrumentation

The goal of the evaluation is the assessment of the proposed metrics with respect to their practical properties, by evaluating the installability and deployability characteristics of a set of process models and engines. More precisely, we use a *Goal statement* set of BPEL engines and process models that can be executed by these engines.

5. Measuring Installability

The evaluation corresponds to an off-line experiment. We have a closer look at the following metric quality factors:

1. *Installability metrics allow for a distinction of different engines:* The purpose of the metrics is the information of stakeholders and decision support. To achieve this purpose, the metrics should uncover differences in the installation characteristics of different engines.

2. *The average installation time can be interpreted in a meaningful way:* The average installation time is computed through the arithmetic mean. Hence, it is vulnerable to outliers in the data, which limits its applicability. Installation times, however, do typically not differ strongly. Therefore, it could be expected that this effect is minimal.

3. *Deployability metrics allow for a distinction of different engines:* Similar to installability metrics, deployability metrics should also uncover differences and allow for the construction of rankings of different software systems. Although deployability values are computed based on concrete applications, it can be expected that there are similarities in the deployability of applications depending on the engines used.

4. *Process model size affects deployability:* It can be expected that the size of a process model influences its deployability. In particular, larger applications can be expected to require more effort for deployment.

Objects of study   With respect to instrumentation, the objects we evaluate are software artifacts and their runtime environments. In particular, we evaluate BPEL process models and engines, along with the artifacts required for executing the first on the latter. It should be noted that, although we focus on BPEL engines to make sure that the metrics are applicable for assessing service-oriented and process-aware software, the metrics framework as a whole can be applied to a larger variety of environments. For instance in [84], the framework has been adapted to assess the installability characteristics of Platform-as-a-Service (PaaS) environments.

The engines used in the evaluation are the five open source engines included in the benchmark (cf. Sect. 3.2.1) and the former ActiveBPEL engine in version 5.0.2. The latter is the predecessor of the bpel-g engine. Although the open source version is deprecated by now, we decided to include it in the evaluation, because it differs strongly in its installability characteristics from its successor. Data on the size of installation routines and deployment artifacts for these engines can be gathered with the help of our conformance benchmarking tool betsy, presented in Chap. 3. In the context of the benchmark, the installation of an engine and deployment of an application is performed for every test case. To be able to gather the data needed for the computation of metrics like the average installation time (AIT), we modified the installation procedure to print timing data in a suitable format into the log files, so that we could parse these files with our metrics computation tool, prope. Furthermore, we performed a heuristic evaluation of the installation scripts to compute metrics such as the number of distinct steps (NDS). The advantage of using the conformance benchmark for this task is that the installation procedure of engines is automated and, thereby, reproducible. Moreover, it works in the same fashion for all engines. This similarity enables a reasonable direct comparison of different engines, the lack of which is a common drawback in software comparisons [185].

To gather the data needed for the calculation of the metrics, we repeated the installation routine of each engine 150 times, after a warm-up phase of three installations, on a machine running Windows 7, 64bit with an i7 quadcore processor, 16 GB of RAM, and a 1 TB SATA drive with 7200 RPM. This is the same machine used to perform the conformance benchmark described in Chap. 3. The hardware requirements are far above the requirements specified for any of the engines. After performing the benchmark, we mined the log files of these runs and analyzed the installation scripts.

The BPEL process models used for the evaluation of deployability are custom-built and of identical functionality. This is necessary to allow for the direct comparison of the deployability values for the same piece of software, when executed on different engines. In this case, the only part that differs are the deployment-related artifacts. To be more precise, the process models for the evaluation correspond to the set of test cases that are passed by all of the engines used in this evaluation. This amounts to 36 process models from the test suites for BPEL (cf. Sect. 3.2.3.1 and 3.2.3.2). This way, a direct comparison of the deployability of the engines is possible.

Finally, to demonstrate that deployability metrics can also be used for comparing separate applications with different functionality, we examine the applications that form the ActiveBPEL process library. This library has also been used for evaluating the portability metrics in Chap. 4. With the help of this library, we can observe the impact of process size on deployability.

5.3.2. Installability Metrics Implementation

As before, the metrics computation has been implemented in the prope tool in the form of a plugin for installability. The structure of this plugin is depicted in Fig. 5.2.

It has to be emphasized that the computation cannot be automated for all of the metrics presented in Sect. 5.1. This applies to metrics that are obtained through a heuristic evaluation, i.e., the number of distinct steps NDS and deployment flexibility DF. Since the values of NDS are needed for the computation of installation effort, they are encoded into prope for the engines used in this evaluation.

The installability plugin provides two separate implementations of a *FileAnalyzer*. The first, the *DeploymentPackageAnalyzer*, computes deployability metrics, whereas the second, the *AverageInstallationTimeCalculator*, computes metrics for engine installability. The *DeploymentPackageAnalyzer* parses application *Deploya-* packages that are ready for deployment. First, it uncompresses deployment *bility* packages, as well as further packages contained therein. Thereafter, it analyzes

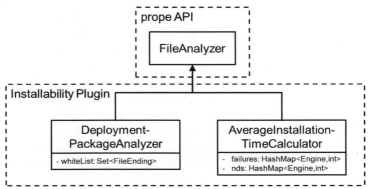

Figure 5.2.: Installability Plugin for the Metrics Suite

all deployment descriptor files. The relevant files are identified by a whitelist based on their file ending. This list is exhaustive for the engines considered in the evaluation, but needs to be extended if further engines are to be considered. If a deployment descriptor is found, the *DeploymentPackageAnalyzer* computes its size depending on its type, as described in Sect. 5.1.2. The number of elements and non-namespace attributes of an XML descriptor are computed based on the document object model of the descriptor.

Engine installability The *AverageInstallationTimeCalculator* is essentially a log file parser. It consumes log files written by betsy and selects the time stamps of specific events. In particular, it scans for messages that confirm a successful installation of an engine and extracts the duration of this installation. Moreover, it scans for messages that signal an installation failure and uses this to compute the amount of failed installation attempts. Based on the encoded values for NDS, this data enables the *AverageInstallationTimeCalculator* to compute all metrics related to engine installability.

5.3.3. Results

We first discuss results for the metrics related to engine installability in Sect. 5.3.3.1 and evaluate hypotheses 1 and 2. Thereafter, we discuss results for deployability in Sect. 5.3.3.2 and construct a ranking of the engines by considering the combination of the two characteristics. Thereby, we evaluate hypothesis 3. Finally, we investigate the relation between process model size and deployability, thus evaluating hypothesis 4, in Sect. 5.3.3.3.

5.3.3.1. Engine Installability

Table 5.1 lists the metrics that characterize engine installability. The installation procedure for all engines consists of the setup of a core server environment into which the engine needs to be copied or installed with a vendor-provided installation script, along with the setting of environment-specific configurations.

Table 5.1.: Engine Installability Metrics ($N = 150$ runs)

Metric	OpenESB	Petals	ODE	bpel-g	Orchestra	ActiveBPEL
NDS	7	5	6	6	7	6
AIT [sec]	133.88	3.13	3.31	3.01	42.53	22.91
CV_{time}	0.02	0.11	0.51	0.37	0.22	0.06
IE	19.13	0.63	0.55	0.50	6.08	3.82
ESR	1	0.90	1	1	1	1

The data presented in Table 5.1 allows for several observations. Most engines require a similar amount of steps for installation (i.e., have a similar value for NDS). All but the engine with the lowest amount of steps, Petals, have a fully deterministic installation procedure (i.e., after one installation attempt, it is always possible to deploy and execute an application on the engine). For Petals, every tenth installation attempt is a failure, as seen in the value for ease of setup retry (ESR). In this case, the engine signals a successful installation, but certain components are missing which results in failures during later operation. We were unable to ultimately determine the reasons for these installation failures, but this underlines the necessity of computing a metric such as ESR. For the average installation time (AIT), the engines differ strongly with up to two orders of magnitude. OpenESB forms an outlier with a very high installation time. This is due to one step, where a vendor-provided installation script is called which consists of a number of uncompression operations that take a comparably high amount of time. The same applies for Orchestra and ActiveBPEL, albeit to a lesser degree.

Being a mean value, AIT is vulnerable to outliers in the data. Given there is a *Interpretation of AIT* high deviation in the data, AIT would not allow for a meaningful interpretation. This is the focus of hypothesis 2. To determine whether this is the case here, we computed the *coefficient of variation* (CV_{time}), which describes the relation between the mean value and the standard deviation of a variable. If the value of CV_{time} is larger than one, the underlying distribution is considered as having a high variation. Otherwise, it is considered as having a low variation. Low values apply for all our observations of AIT, which means that this metric indeed allows for a meaningful interpretation on its own.

A ranking of engines based on engine installability can be constructed by *Ranking engines based on installability* looking at the installation effort, IE. Three engines, Petals, Apache ODE, and bpel-g, have quite low values, resulting from their relatively low average installation time. However, considering the frequent installation failures of Petals, this engine should be used with care. For the remaining engines, there is a clear difference in terms of installation effort, with OpenESB ranking last. This demonstrates that the metrics can be used for a meaningful interpretation and confirms hypothesis 1.

5.3.3.2. Application Deployability

Table 5.2 lists deployability metrics for the set of applications, aggregated by the engines. To get an overall view of the metric values for the applications, we present the mean values and standard deviations.

Table 5.2.: Deployability Metrics of Functionally Identical Process Models ($N = 36$)

Metric		OpenESB	Petals	ODE	bpel-g	Orch.	ActiveBPEL
DF		2	2	3	2	2	2
DDS							
	$Mean$	73.92	78.5	10.69	9.11	0	21.36
	$std(X)$	7.37	6.31	1.75	2.81	0	5.96
EPC	$Mean$	14	9	2	2	1	5
DE							
	$Mean$	87.92	87.5	12.69	11.11	1	26.36
	$std(X)$	7.37	6.31	1.75	2.81	0	5.96

For the effort of package construction (EPC), the mean alone allows for a meaningful interpretation. As all deployment packages are built in a very similar fashion, standard deviations for EPC are equal to zero in all cases. The values of all metrics vary strongly for the different engines. For instance, OpenESB and Petals require descriptor sizes of more than 70 elements in the mean. For the other engines, this value is much lower. One special case is formed by Orchestra. There, no deployment descriptors are required. All information needed is read from the source files, such as WSDL definitions, directly. Due to the self-descriptiveness of Web Services artifacts, such a strategy is possible and Orchestra demonstrates that it is feasible. Nevertheless, only few engines make use of this feature and, instead, require the duplication of information in deployment descriptors. When looking at EPC values, it can be seen that the engines that require the largest deployment descriptors are also the ones that require the most complex archives (i.e., several nested archives containing zip and war files). For all other engines, archives are simply necessary for grouping all relevant files together, so that they can be deployed by linking a single file. Moreover, when looking at the number of deployment options available (DF), it can be seen that nearly all *Ranking engines* engines offer a similar level of flexibility. DE aggregates the deployment effort *based on* for a direct comparison that allows for a ranking of the engines. This is the focus *deploya-* of hypothesis 3. Orchestra clearly excels with respect to deployability, followed *bility* by ODE and bpel-g. The deployment effort for ActiveBPEL is more than twice as high as for these engines. OpenESB and Petals require an effort that is a multitude of the effort required for the other engines.

Engine installability and deployability metrics can be also be combined to rank engines. Firstly, it can be seen that both, ODE and bpel-g, provide a balanced level of good values for the installability and deployability metrics, with bpel-g being slightly ahead. Although it excels in terms of deployability, Orchestra takes somewhat longer to install (AIT and IE) and therefore ranks third. Even though ActiveBPEL is quicker than Orchestra in its installation, the deployment is much more complicated (DE), leading to rank four. Finally, OpenESB and Petals both have relatively complex files with large descriptors (DDS and DE). OpenESB takes long to install (AIT and IE) and the installation of Petals is not stable (ESR).

Combination of engine installability and deployability

5.3.3.3. Application Size and Deployability

The final hypothesis concerns the impact of application size on deployability. To evaluate this hypothesis, Table 5.3 depicts results for deployability of the applications from the ActiveBPEL library.

Table 5.3.: Deployability of Applications of Different Size

$N_{services}$	Applications	$\overline{DDS}$	$\overline{EPC}$	$\overline{DE}$
1	11	31.36	9	40.36
2	3	43.67	9.33	53.0
5	5	105.0	9	114.0

Table 5.3 also includes metrics that characterize the complexity or size of the applications in the library. A basic metric for expressing the size of a service-oriented system, and, hence, the size of a service-oriented and process-aware applications is the *number of services*, $N_{services}$, provided or used in the application [66]. The applications in the library involve either one, two, or five services, and Table 5.3 depicts deployability metrics for these groups, along with the number of applications in each group.

EPC values are almost constant, although slightly higher than the ones presented in Sect. 5.3.3.2, due to the package structure typical in the library. Moreover, they are unaffected by the growth in application size. In contrast to this, as proposed in hypothesis 4, descriptor sizes increase with the number of services. Here, a linear regression analysis confirms that there is a linear relation between application size and deployment descriptor size. The corresponding scatterplot is depicted in Fig. 5.3. Since deployment descriptor size is the decisive input to deployment effort, the linear relation also holds for deployment effort and application size. This result demonstrates that an application with many services of possibly fine granularity will be comparably harder to deploy than one with a few services of lower granularity. This is an important observation when considering the current trend of microservices development, which favors the construction of software based on many fine-granular services instead of fewer services of lower granularity.

Relation of number of services and descriptor size

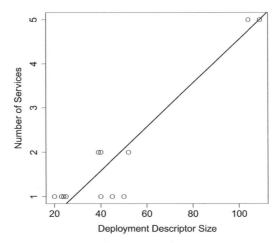

Figure 5.3.: Scatterplot for the Number of Services and Deployment Descriptor Size

5.4. Summary

In this chapter, we presented a measurement framework for quantifying and assessing the installability of service-oriented and process-aware software. The installability of such software can be subdivided into the installability of the engine and the deployability of an application onto the engine. We proposed metrics for these two characteristics in Sect. 5.1, which form a significant extension of prior metrics proposed in respectice ISO/IEC standards [209, 210]. In particular the metrics related to application deployability are new. The metrics fall into the categories of direct and indirect, as well as internal and external metrics. All internal metrics are size metrics.

The theoretical evaluation in Sect. 5.2 shows that all internal size metrics satisfy the properties of non-negativity, null value, and additivity. External metrics do not satisfy additivity. The purpose of the metrics is the information of stakeholders and decision support. They are computed by counting, matching, or timing and are defined on an interval or a ratio scale.

The practical evaluation in Sect. 5.3 demonstrates that installability and deployability metrics can be used for ranking and comparing engines, as well as single applications. The coefficient of variance shows that the average installation time allows for a meaningful interpretation. Moreover, there is a linear relationship between the number of services involved in an application and its deployability.

In summary, the framework presented in this chapter provides a suitable way for assessing the installability of service-oriented and process-aware software, i.e., it forms an answer to research question 2.2: *What are suitable metrics for measuring installability?*. The metrics presented in this chapter form a theoretically valid and practically applicable framework for achieving this.

6. Measuring Adaptability

Parts of this chapter have been taken from [80, 83, 85].

According to the SQuaRE model [53], if software cannot be ported directly to another platform, it might be possible to adapt it for the new platform. The quality model tackles this aspect in the context of the quality characteristic of *adaptability*. Akin to the methodology applied in the previous chapters, we answer the following research question here: *What are suitable metrics for measuring adaptability?*

Similar to the other chapters of Part II, we first discuss the nature of adapt- *Structure* ability and how it can be measured, followed by the formal definition of a set of *of the chapter* metrics that are made for assessing service-oriented and process-aware software, in Sect. 6.1. In particular, we propose two different modes of computation for adaptability. Thereafter, in Sect. 6.2, the metrics are validated with respect to their theoretical properties. This is followed by a practical evaluation of the metrics in Sect. 6.3. In contrast to the previous two chapters, we perform the practical evaluation in this chapter based on BPMN process models. Finally, the chapter is concluded in Sect. 6.4 with a summary.

6.1. On the Measurement of Adaptability

Like the other quality characteristics, the term adaptability has different meanings in different contexts and subject areas. In Sect. 2.3.2, we defined adaptability as *Design-* the *"degree with which a software product can effectively and efficiently be adapted* *time* *for different or evolving software environments.".* The change of a software *adapt-* environment typically involves the recompilation or repackaging of an application. *ability* The changes made to the application in the interim are *design-time* changes. In other words, adaptability, as defined here, does not refer to run-time changes to a piece of software. This is a different interpretation as, for instance, in the subject area of autonomous systems, where adaptability refers to whether a system can change its structure to cope with changing requirements, such as a different system load, at run-time [213].

Design-time adaptability, as defined here, is often measured at the software *Ap-* architecture level. A common conceptual approach used in similar work [214,215], *proaches* is to start with the assessment of adaptability at the level of an atomic system *for mea-* element. For instance, every element can be tagged with an *adaptability score.* *suring* Then, these atomic scores are aggregated at one or more levels to indices or *design-* *time* *degrees of adaptability*, until the complete system is considered as a whole. This *adapt-* approach is outlined in Fig. 6.1. The focus here is on service-oriented and process- *ability* aware software, i. e., executable process models. Hence, the most atomic system

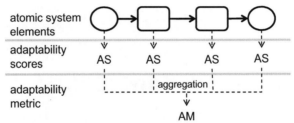

Figure 6.1.: Mechanism for Computing Adaptability

elements that can be considered for the start of an adaptability computation are the nodes, i. e., activities, events, gateways, and basic elements, and connectors of a process model, as defined in Def. 6. So, when evaluating the adaptability of process models written in a particular language, it is first necessary to assign an adaptability score to each type of element in that language.

Alter-
native
represen-
tations
The idea we put forward here is to consider the *amount of alternative representations* a process language offers for a specific language element. The more of such alternative representations exist, the easier and more likely it is that one can find a semantically equivalent alternative when modifying the process model for porting. In other words, the more alternatives exist, the more adaptable the element is. A practical example for BPMN are *ReceiveTasks*, atomic tasks that consume a message. One straight-forward alternative for such a task, among others, is an *IntermediateMessageCatchEvent* which provides semantically identical behavior. Another example for multiple alternative implementations of the same functionality in BPMN is repetitive execution of a task through *StandardLoopCharacteristics*. As demonstrated by the benchmark in Chap. 3, this particular looping mechanism is not supported by any engine and, hence, needs to be adapted in a process model that is to be used for execution. Any of the following language constructs can be used to define iterative execution of a task and hence can be used as an alternative to *StandardLoopCharacteristics*:

1. A combination of an *ExclusiveGateway* and *SequenceFlows*
2. A combination of an *InclusiveGateway* and *SequenceFlows*
3. A combination of a *ComplexGateway* and *SequenceFlows*
4. Enclosing the task in a loop *SubProcess*
5. Enclosing the task in an *Ad-hoc SubProcess*
6. Enclosing the task in an event *SubProcess*

Usually, a given BPMN engine only supports a subset of these options. For instance, the Activiti engine does support the combination of certain *Gateways* and *SequenceFlows*, as well as event *SubProcesses*, but no loop or *Ad-hoc SubProcesses*. Given a process with a task that uses *StandardLoopCharacteristics* needs to be ported to the Activiti engine, the code needs be adapted to a solution that Activiti supports. To summarize the above discussion, the adaptability score of a task with *StandardLoopCharacteristics* is equal to six. The adaptability score $AS(e)$ can be formally defined as:

Definition 32: Adaptability Score

$AS(e)$ is the cardinality of the set of alternatives $ALT_e = \{alt_1^e, \ldots, alt_n^e\}$ available for an element e.

$$AS(e) = \mid ALT_e \mid, where \tag{6.1}$$

- $e \in V$ is an element of the vocabulary V of the process language (cf. Def. 6);
- $alt_i^e \in V$ is a semantically equivalent alternative to language element e.

The set of alternatives, and, thus, the adaptability score, needs to be determined for every language element of a process language.

The next step towards computing an adaptability metric, as depicted in Fig. 6.1, is the normalization and aggregation of the scores for all elements of a complete process model.

6.1.1. Adaptability Metrics Definition

For the definition of an adaptability metric based on adaptability scores, two crucial aspects have to be addressed:

1. *How to turn the scores into a meaningful relative value?* Absolute values are common for software metrics, but often hard to interpret. This is easier with relative values, which range in a certain interval, as for instance percentage values. That way, values close to the upper bound of the interval can be identified as referring to high quality and vice versa.
2. *How to normalize this value with respect to process model size?* Different process models can be expected to have different sizes. Metric values should be normalized with respect to process model size, because otherwise they cannot meaningfully be used to compare process models of different sizes.

The first aspect can be addressed by introducing an *adaptability degree* $AD(e)$ *Relativi-* that turns an adaptability score as defined in the previous section into a relative *zation* value:

Definition 33: Adaptability Degree

The adaptability degree $AD(e)$ of an element e is a function that maps an element e to a value in the interval of zero and one, i.e., a percentage scale.

$$AD(e) \rightarrow [0, 1]. \tag{6.2}$$

Similar to the measurement of portability, discussed in Chap. 4, it is a design choice of our approach to map degree values to the interval of $[0, 1]$. Strictly speaking, we could choose any interval, but the reason we choose $[0, 1]$ is one of understandability. This interval resembles a percentage scale and this scale is easily understood by most people. This eases the interpretation of the metric to some degree and thus lowers the barrier for its adoption. The question of what values in this scale refer to *high* or *low* depends on how the mapping is achieved. This is the central difference between the different metrics we introduce below. Hence, we redefine the adaptability degree for each adaptability metric in the following sections.

Normal-ization   The second problem can be solved by following the approach taken by similar studies [214, 215] and computing the arithmetic mean of all adaptability degrees of the different elements of a process model. Hence, an adaptability metric $AM(p)$ of a process model p is defined as follows:

Definition 34: Adaptability Metric

$$AM(p) = \begin{cases} 0 & \text{if } p = \emptyset \\ \overline{AD(e_1), \ldots, AD(e_n)} & otherwise \end{cases} \quad (6.3)$$

- $p = < N, C >$ is an executable process model (cf. Def. 6) that consists of the elements $e_1, \ldots, e_n$;
- For an empty process model, $p = \emptyset$, $AM(p)$ is defined as zero, i.e., $AM(p) = 0$;
- For a nonempty process model, $p = \{e_1, \ldots, e_n\}$, $AM(p)$ is defined as the arithmetic mean of adaptability degrees of the elements of the model: $\overline{AD(e_1), \ldots, AD(e_n)}$.

In the following, we propose different ways of computing an adaptability degree for a given process element, and, hence, different adaptability metrics.

6.1.1.1. Binary Adaptability Degree

A first option for computing adaptability degrees is a *binary mapping*. Here, $AD(e) \rightarrow \{0, 1\}$ applies, i.e., every element is mapped to a degree of zero or one. Such a mapping is, for instance, used in [214].

Threshold mapping   This mapping is achieved by applying a threshold on the adaptability score for an element. The score, as specified in Def. 32, is an absolute representation of the adaptability of an element, the higher the better. When comparing the elements of one language, it is possible to distinguish high adaptability scores with respect to all scores of the language from low ones. In the binary mapping, we assign a degree value of *one* to elements with high scores and a value of *zero* to elements with low scores. To achieve this, a suitable threshold value needs to be found. For instance, the threshold can be defined at 50%. This means that elements that have lower adaptability scores than 50% of all language elements are mapped to zero and elements that have higher or equal scores to 50% of all language elements are mapped to one. Put formally:

Definition 35: Binary Adaptability Degree

$$AD_{binary}(e) = \begin{cases} 1, & \text{if } AS(e) \geq (t * R) \\ 0, & otherwise \end{cases}, where \qquad (6.4)$$

- $R \in \mathbb{N}_0$; R is a reference value, the maximum adaptability score achieved by any element in the language under consideration, i.e., $\forall e \in V, AS(e) \leq R$;
- $t \in]0, 1[$; t marks a threshold that is used to discriminate between high and low adaptability values.

As a consequence, a *binary adaptability metric* $AM_{binary}(p)$ is based on the binary adaptability degree: $AM_{binary}(p) = \overline{AD_{binary}(e_1), \ldots, AD_{binary}(e_n)}$. An appropriate threshold value t that results in meaningful metric values can only be fixed based on practical experiments. In the practical evaluation in Sect. 6.3, we evaluate several threshold values and select the most appropriate one.

6.1.1.2. Weighted Adaptability Degree

The binary degree maps the score values to the boundaries of the interval of $[0, 1]$. It could be expected that the utilization of the full scale of this interval leads to a more fine-grained and precise quantification of adaptability. A similar reasoning underlies the definition of weighted portability metrics, defined in Sect. 4.2. Here, we define a *weighted mapping* as the basis for a weighted adaptability degree:

Definition 36: Weighted Adaptability Degree

$$AD_{weighted}(e) = AS(e)/R, where \qquad (6.5)$$

- R refers to the maximum adaptability score as defined in Def. 35;
- $\forall e, AS(e) \leq R$; implies that $AD_{weighted}(e) \rightarrow [0, 1]$.

As a result, the adaptability degree of every language element is relative to the most adaptable element of the language. This leads to the desired normalization to the interval of $[0, 1]$. A *weighted adaptability metric* $AM_{weighted}(p) = \overline{AD_{weighted}(e_1), \ldots, AD_{weighted}(e_n)}$ is based on the weighted adaptability degree.

6.1.2. Example for Adaptability Computation

In this section, we demonstrate an exemplary computation of the proposed adaptability metrics. We use two synthetic process models, $PM1$ and $PM2$, which are implemented in BPMN and depicted in Fig. 6.2.

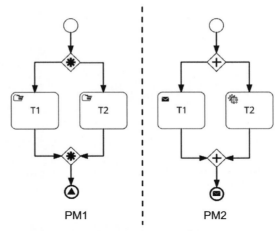

Figure 6.2.: Example for Adaptability Computation

Language
elements
used
Both process models have a similar graph structure, but use different elements of the vocabulary of BPMN, which vary in their adaptability score. The first process model, $PM1$ relies on language elements that can hardly be adapted. In particular, these are *ComplexGateways*, *ManualTasks*, and a *SignalEndEvent*. As indicated in its name, the *ComplexGateway* is the most advanced gateway construct in BPMN. It is used to model complex synchronization behavior that may involve conditional activation based on a number of incoming branches and conditional activation of outgoing branches. Due to its complex configuration, it cannot generally be adapted by another language element of BPMN. The same applies to *ManualTasks*, which serve as unique placeholders for actions performed without automatic support. For the final *SignalEndEvent*, semantically equivalent alternatives that represent ordered termination and produce a notification do exist. For instance, a *MessageEndEvent* could be used to implement similar behavior. In contrast, $PM2$ uses elements that can be considered as more adaptable. These are *ParallelGateways*, a *SendTask*, a *ServiceTask*, and a *MessageEndEvent*. For the *ParallelGateway*, straight-forward alternatives, such as an *InclusiveGateway* that is configured to activate all subsequent control-flow branches, do exist. Message-related elements in BPMN are duplicated in the form of message-related tasks and message-related events and, as a result, several alternatives are available for the *SendTask* and the *MessageEndEvent*. Also for a *ServiceTask*, alternatives that do trigger the execution of an application or service, such as a *ScriptTask*, do exist.

*Metric
values*
The adaptability metrics should consider $PM2$ as more adaptable than $PM1$. This is clearly the case, which can be seen in the metric values listed in Table 6.1[25]. The table lists the values for the binary adaptability metric with a threshold set at 60% and the weighted metric. In both cases, the metric values for $PM1$ are much lower than for $PM2$, with 0.17 compared to 0.50 for the binary metric and

---

[25]The details of the metrics implementation are clarified in Sect. 6.3.2.

0.21 compared to 0.55 for the weighted metric. This demonstrates that both metrics measure what they are intended to.

Table 6.1.: Adaptability Metric Values for the Example

Process Model	$AM_{bin.}$	$AM_{weighted}$
$PM1$	0.17	0.21
$PM2$	0.50	0.55

6.2. Theoretical Validation

In this section, we validate the binary and the weighted adaptability metrics theoretically. The starting is the clarification of the measurement-theoretic properties of the metrics in Sect. 6.2.1. Thereafter, we discuss construct validity in Sect. 6.2.2.

6.2.1. Measurement-Theoretic Validation

Similar to the portability metrics presented in Chap. 4, we classify the metrics defined here as complexity metrics. Since the metrics are computed by the arithmetic mean, we deal with normalized complexity metrics, or densities of complexity, with the same restrictions and properties as before. Complexity metrics should fulfill the properties of *non-negativity, null value, symmetry, monotonicity*, and *additivity* [69].

Non-negativity: Complexity metrics should yield non-negative values. Since the adaptability score is defined as the cardinality of a set, it is always non-negative. Moreover, adaptability degrees are mapped to the interval of $[0, 1]$. The arithmetic mean of a set of values in this interval, i.e., an adaptability metric as defined in Def. 34, is always non-negative.

Null value: The complexity of an empty system should be zero. In our case, an empty system corresponds to a process model p with no elements, i.e., $p = \emptyset$. For this case, $AM(p)$ is defined as zero in Def. 34.

Symmetry: The labeling for representing the relationships among system elements should not affect the metric value. Here, the labeling refers to the ordering of elements in the process graph. The reordering of elements in the process graph, without altering control-flow semantics, is possible for a variety of elements, for instance in the case of parallelism. In the notation of [69], symmetry means that two process models $p =< E, R >$ and $p' =< E, R' >$ with identical elements E and control-flow semantics but different element ordering R and R' should have the same metric value. We compute adaptability on a per-element basis through the adaptability degree. This degree is fixed independently of an elements position in the process graph, so symmetry holds: $AM(p) = AM(\{e_1, \ldots, e_n\}) = AM(p')$

Monotonicity and Additivity: When two unrelated parts of a system are taken together, the resulting metric value should at least be equal to the sum of the combined parts. This means that complexity metrics should be additive and monotonous. Additivity holds for adaptability degrees, but not for the metrics, due to normalization. We apply the arithmetic mean to achieve a normalization with respect to the size of a process model and adding up the mean values of two process fragments is not meaningful. Hence, additivity in the sense of [69] does not hold for reasons of normalization. Nevertheless, adaptability metrics are still monotonous. For instance, let $p^1 = \{e_1, \ldots, e_i\}$ and $p^2 = \{e_j, \ldots, e_n\}$ be two unrelated parts of process model p:

$$AM(p) = AM(p^1 \cup p^2) = AM(\{e_1, \ldots, e_n\}) = \qquad (6.6)$$
$$\frac{AD(e_1,) + \ldots + AD(e_i) + AD(e_j) + \ldots + AD(e_n)}{N_{|p^1 \cup p^2|}}$$
$$\geq min(AM(p^1), AM(p^2))$$

The metric value of two process fragments taken together cannot be lower than the metric value of the less adaptable of the two fragments and therefore the metrics are monotonous. This is the same result as for the portability metrics, discussed in Sect. 4.3.2.

To summarize the above discussion, adaptability metrics are normalized complexity metrics, or densities of complexity, which fulfill the properties of non-negativity, null value, symmetry, and monotonicity.

6.2.2. Evaluation of Construct Validity

The *attribute*, [70] to be measured in the current chapter is adaptability and the *measurement instrument* remains the metrics suite, prope.

Purpose of the metrics: The purpose is the facilitation of private self-assessment and improvement, and the information of developers and system administrators about the adaptability characteristics of a process model. When having to port a process model, the metrics can help to make the decision whether it is worth to invest in its adaptation.

Scope of the metrics: The scope of the metrics is a single project of one workgroup. The metrics are applicable during and after development.

Measured attribute: The metrics try to measure the *adaptability* of a process model, the ease with which the elements of a given process model can be modified at design-time without changing the execution semantics of the model.

Natural scale of the attribute: The scale of the attribute is intrinsic to the attribute itself and independent of the way in which we try to quantify it. At the current time, we cannot tell what the scale of adaptability is, but it can reasonably be assumed that process models differ in their adaptability in a way that allows us to construct a natural ordering. Hence, the attribute of adaptability, at the very least, has an ordinal scale.

Natural variability of the attribute: We do not know in which ranges adaptability typically varies. Being a technical attribute inherent to a process model, we know that it is not subject to variation common for human attributes, such as developer productivity depending on the time of the day.

Definition of the metrics and the instrument: All the metrics, the functions that assign values to the attribute, are formally defined in Sect. 6.1.1. Adaptability scores of elements are fixed values and obtained through *counting*. Adaptability degrees and metrics are computed based on this. The *measurement instrument* is a plugin for our metrics suite in which we implemented the metrics computation. The structure of this plugin is explained as part of the practical evaluation in Sect. 6.3.

Natural scale of the metrics: The metrics are defined in Def. 34 on an interval scale of $[0, 1]$.

Natural variability of the measurement instrument: This question refers to the *measurement error* of the instrument, in our case a static analyzer. Since we compute the metrics through static analysis, there is no variability of the instrument for subsequent analyses of the same process model.

There is no way in which we can guarantee the absence of errors in our software. For instance, programming errors that impact the metric values the tool produces might exist. We try to limit the amount of errors by open sourcing the tool and making all code available to public scrutiny, by providing an excessive set of unit tests for the tool itself, and by applying techniques of continuous integration and inspection during development.

Another source of measurement error are the adaptability scores encoded in the tool. These are based on human judgment and, naturally, we can err in our understanding of the semantics of BPMN elements. We tried to minimize these errors through in-group peer review and by making all scores publicly available as part of the tool implementation. Moreover, it is possible that we did not consider all potential alternatives that exist for a particular language element when judging its score. If this is the case, the element is considered as less adaptable by our tool than it is in reality. As a consequence, the metric values computed by our measurement instrument can be treated as a lower bound of the adaptability of a process model.

Relationship of the attribute to metrics values: As discussed in Sect. 6.1, the adaptability of an element is related to the number of alternatives available to that element. The more alternatives exist for a given language element, the more adaptable this element can be considered. Based on this assumption, our metrics are *directly* [171] related to process elements. Given elements with a higher degree of adaptability are introduced into the process model, this will be detected by our measurement instrument and the resulting metric value will increase accordingly.

Side-effects of using the metrics: Similar to the portability metrics, we automated the metrics computation fully. Hence, there is no room for human bias in the measurement instrument.

6.3. Practical Evaluation

As before, the practical evaluation of the adaptability metrics demonstrates the feasibility of their computation and exemplifies their interpretation.

In the next section, we first describe the design and instrumentation of the evaluation. This is followed in Sect. 6.3.2 by an outline of the functioning of their prototypic implementation in a plugin to our metrics suite. Finally, Sect. 6.3.3 describes the results of the evaluation.

6.3.1. Design and Instrumentation

Goal statement
The goal of this evaluation is to analyze real-world process models for the purpose of assessing the metrics and selecting the most appropriate ones. To meet this goal, we evaluate software that is finished and available, i.e., we perform an off-line experiment. Using the evaluation, we can validate several quality factors for the different metrics, addressed by the following hypotheses:

1. *The weighted adaptability computation improves discriminative power in comparison to a binary computation:* The ability to distinguish between different pieces of software, the *discriminative power*, is an important quality factor of a software metric. We expect that the weighted computation, due to more fine-grained scoring, outperforms the binary computation with respect to this quality factor.

2. *The metrics can be used for comparing process models of different size:* Another important quality factor of a software metric is the ability to allow for a comparison of programs of very different size. This is often problematic, especially with complexity metrics [184].

3. *The metric values are resilient to minor changes in the underlying data:* Minor modifications to process code should not result in significant changes to the metric value, since this would imply that the mechanism of computation is unstable.

Objects of study
A practical evaluation needs to be based on real-world process models and, therefore, on a particular process language. In this evaluation, we use process models implemented in BPMN [26]. Therefore, we need concrete data in the

form of BPMN process models. As before, we gathered this data from numerous open source projects with the help of the Open Hub Open Source network. To obtain our primary data set, we queried the network in May 2014 for files that:

1. have the file extension `bpmn`, `bpmn2`, or `xml`,

2. contain the keyword *definitions*, the top-level element of a BPMN-compliant file, and

3. contain the BPMN 2.0 namespace.

We downloaded and analyzed the resulting files using the plugin for our metrics suite described in the following section. We tried to parse every file downloaded from Open Hub and if we could find a valid *definitions* element and at least one *process* element beneath it, we computed the adaptability metrics for it. This resulted in almost three thousand BPMN process models. We re-performed the query in October 2014, to obtain a second version of the same data set at a later point in time. This is necessary for evaluating hypothesis 3.

6.3.2. Adaptability Metrics Implementation

To implement the approach, it is necessary to set adaptability scores, as defined in Def. 32, for every relevant element of BPMN. As discussed in Sect. 2.2.2.3, *Score setting* we limit the evaluation to BPMN *processes* [26, pp. 143–314], since these form the executable part of the language and, hence, the target of our metrics. Other types of process models, such as collaborations or process choreographies are not considered. We reviewed the specification and set scores for all elements that are permitted in BPMN processes. These are *activities*, including *tasks* and *subProcesses*, *gateways*, and *events*. Thus, we cover all control-flow aspects of BPMN, but abstract from data-flow here. Moreover, we omit language elements that are relevant to the visualization of the process model only, such as *lanes*. The result is a total of 94 language elements for which we set a score.

After setting the scores, we extended our metrics suite, prope, with a plugin *Plugin structure* for computing the adaptability of BPMN process models. The structure of this plugin is depicted in Fig. 6.3. As before, the plugin is hooked into the architecture of prope through a custom implementation of a *FileAnalyzer*. This *AdaptabilityAnalyzer* starts with a number of sanity checks on a given file, using a *BpmnInspector*. These sanity checks include the checking of the usage of correct namespaces and the validation of referential integrity of the elements in the process model using the *BPMNspector* tool[26]. If a process model does not pass these checks, it is excluded from further analysis. After the initial validation, the *AdaptabilityAnalyzer* continues with the computation of adaptability metrics using different implementations that follow the definitions from Sect. 6.1.1. In particular, the implementation of the binary adaptability metric can be configured with different threshold values that are used as cutoff criterion. The metric

---

[26]The project page of this BPMN file validation tool can be found at http://www.bpmnspector. org/.

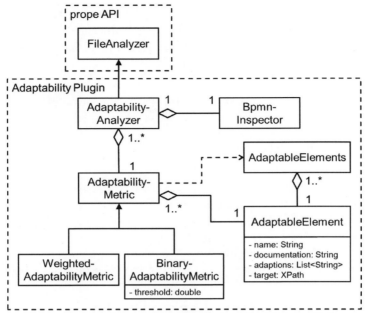

Figure 6.3.: Adaptability Plugin for the Metrics Suite

implementations themselves utilize *AdaptableElements* that are representations of concrete BPMN elements and their adaptability score. Each *AdaptableElement* is identified by its name and a list of possible adaptations. This list corresponds to the set of alternative representations, as defined in Def. 32. Hence, the size of the list is the adaptability score of the element. Moreover, an *AdaptableElement* contains a documentation that explains design decisions for the configuration of the list of adaptions and an XPath expression that is used to locate the element in a BPMN process model. The set of all these elements is constructed via a factory class, *AdaptableElements*. Since the *AdaptableElements*, and particularly the list of adaptions, is imperative for the computation of the adaptability metric values, they are listed in tabular form in Appendix C.

6.3.3. Results

In the following sections, we first describe the nature and construct usage of the gathered process models in Sect. 6.3.3.1. Thereafter, we present and discuss descriptive metric data in Sect. 6.3.3.2 and evaluate the hypotheses to determine the most useful metrics in Sect. 6.3.3.3 to 6.3.3.5.

6.3.3.1. BPMN Process Models and Usage of Elements

The process models we obtained can be seen as representative of the open source *Correct-* usage of BPMN, since they are all gathered from freely accessible projects. As *ness* *checks* indicated in the previous section, we performed several correctness checks, such as the correct usage of namespaces and the validation of element references, on the process models and excluded them from the analysis if they did not pass these checks. For instance, despite the fact that a file contains the correct BPMN 2.0 namespace, a process model defined in it might use a different one. The amount of such process models in our data set is negligible and more than 99% of the analyzed process models are using the correct BPMN namespace. When it comes to referential integrity, we could detect issues, such as an *EventDefinition* referenced in an event but not found in the process model, in 8% of the cases. This step reduced the initial set of process models from 2995 to 2745. Finally, 12% of the process models, a total of 327, are explicitly marked as executable, i.e., the *isExecutable* flag of the *process* element is set to *true*.

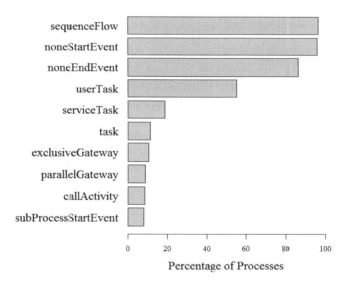

Figure 6.4.: Occurence Frequency of BPMN Elements

In an influential paper [202], which also had impact on the current version of BPMN [216], zur Muehlen and Recker analyzed the usage of BPMN elements in process models and found that only a very small subset of the existing elements were actually used in practice. As this information can be used to refine the computation of our metrics, we reproduced this analysis for the process models at hand. The plot in Fig. 6.4 depicts the occurrence frequency of selected BPMN elements, i.e., the percentage of process models in which the elements occur. We limit the figure to the ten most frequent elements found in the process models. Although the evaluation from [202] uses an older revision of BPMN, our results largely reinstate theirs. By far the most common elements in BPMN process models that occur in almost all cases are *SequenceFlows* and ordinary *Start-* and *EndEvents*. The next most frequent elements are two specific types of *tasks*.

Occurrence frequency

This is similar to [202] where *tasks* are not separated by a specific type. The occurrence frequency of elements is important to the metrics computation for the following reason: The most frequent elements will need to be present in every process model and adapting them is simply not an option. If included in the adaptability computation, these elements would introduce noise into the metric value. For instance, *SequenceFlows* are very common in any process model and including them in the computation would introduce a strong weighting towards the adaptability of *SequenceFlows* in general. Since they cannot be adapted, this weighting would be noise. Based on the data depicted in Fig. 6.4, we can exclude the most common elements from the metrics computation, being the elements that occur in more than two thirds of all process models. These are *SequenceFlows* and ordinary *Start-* and *EndEvents*.

6.3.3.2. Comparison of the Metrics

Table 6.2 lists descriptive statistics for the process models, sorted into executable and nonexecutable models, i. e., process models that have the *isExecutable* flag set to *true* or *false* respectively. We computed the weighted metric as defined in Sect. 6.1.1.2, and the binary metric, as defined in Sect. 6.1.1.1, with the thresholds set at 20%, 40%, 60%, and 80% of the most adaptable element of the language to see which threshold performs best. The metric values are very similar

Table 6.2.: Descriptive Statistics for the Process Libraries

Process Group	N	Statistics	$AM_{bin.}$, $t = 0.2$	$AM_{bin.}$, $t = 0.4$	$AM_{bin.}$, $t = 0.6$	$AM_{bin.}$, $t = 0.8$	$AM_{weighted}$
executable	327	*Mean*	0.91	0.88	0.60	0.09	0.56
		std(X)	0.14	0.16	0.15	0.16	0.14
		Disc.Pow.	0.08	0.09	0.12	0.09	0.21
nonexecutable	2418	*Mean*	0.96	0.93	0.59	0.09	0.59
		std(X)	0.12	0.14	0.19	0.16	0.12
		Disc.Pow.	0.02	0.02	0.02	0.01	0.05

for the two process groups, but there are strong differences among the different

Differences in metric distributions

metrics. A first step is to examine if there are significant differences between the adaptability of executable and nonexecutable process models. To determine this, we first performed the Shapiro-Wilk test to see if the metric values are normally distributed. Since this is clearly not the case, we chose a nonparametric test, the Mann-Whitney U test [188] to find out if there are differences in the distributions of the metric values for the two process groups. The null hypothesis here is that there are no significant differences in the distributions of the metric values for the two process groups. Here, p-values do not reach a significant level for any of the metrics, so the null hypothesis cannot be rejected and there seem to be no significant differences between executable and nonexecutable process models in the data at hand. The reason for this might be that most process models we obtained are in fact used for execution, but not marked with the respective flag. In the following, we evaluate the previously stated hypotheses regarding the quality of the metrics.

6.3.3.3. Hypothesis 1 – Discriminative Power

We can show that our metrics perform better when analyzing process models marked for execution and we can filter for the metrics that are particularly good. This can be achieved by looking at the *discriminative power* of the metrics, their ability to differentiate between different process models. The better a metric differentiates between different process models, the better it can be used for quality comparison and ranking of process models. To determine the discriminative power, we removed all duplicate metric values from the different data sets, resulting in a list of unique metric values for each metric and process group. By comparing the amount of unique values to the total amount of values, we obtained the percentage of unique values for the process models in the different sets. These percentage values are listed in the third row of each process group in Table 6.2. It can be seen that the discriminative power is much higher for executable process models and in particular the weighted adaptability degree performs best. Looking at the binary degrees, a threshold set at 60% yields best results. This narrows the scope of the useful metrics to the weighted metric and the binary metric with a threshold set at 60%.

6.3.3.4. Hypothesis 2 – Process Model Size

A further quality characteristic of software metrics is the ability to compare systems of different size. Typically, metrics tend to produce very different values when the system size differs a lot [184], thus rendering them insufficient for comparing systems of a very different size. To investigate how well our metrics perform in the face of process models of different size, we extracted two sets of process models. These are small and large models separated into executable and nonexecutable groups. The set of small process models refers to the first quartile with respect to the number of elements in the process model, i.e., the 25% smallest models. In the same fashion, the set of large process models corresponds to the fourth quartile with respect to the elements in the process models. We use the Mann-Whitney U test [188] as above to see if the metrics for small and large process models differ in their distribution. The null hypothesis here is that there are no significant differences in the distributions of the metric values for the two process groups. We limit this comparison to $AM_{weighted}$ and AM_{binary} with a threshold set at 60%.

Table 6.3 depicts the results of this test separated by process groups. Because we are doing four tests, we have to adjust the significance level to $0.05/4 = 0.0125$. In all but one case, p-values become significant, meaning that the distributions of the process groups for the metrics really are different. Consequently, these metrics should be treated with care when comparing process models of very different size. The only exception to this is $AM_{weighted}$ for executable process

Table 6.3.: Descriptive Statistics and Mann-Whitney U Test for Differences in Process Model Size

Process Group	N_{small}	N_{large}	Statistics	$AM_{bin.,}$ $t : 60\%$	$AM_{weighted}$
executable	62	80	$\tilde{x}_{small}$	0.67	0.62
			$\tilde{x}_{large}$	0.58	0.53
			p	0.004	0.09
			U	2559	2803
nonexecutable	573	564	$\tilde{x}_{small}$	0.67	0.62
			$\tilde{x}_{large}$	0.43	0.54
			p	$2.2e^{-16}$	$2.2e^{-16}$
			U	220285	213544

models. Here, no significant differences of the metric values for small and large process models could be detected. This means that the metric really can be used for comparing process models of different size.

6.3.3.5. Hypothesis 3 – Stability

A third quality factor for the metrics addresses their resilience to variances over time. Repeated measurements should produce similar results to demonstrate the stability of the mechanism of computation, i.e., the *predictability* of the metric value. One way to test this aspect, recommended by [171, p. 12], is by checking if metric values of repeated measurements differ only up to a certain *accuracy* threshold. This can be evaluated with the following formula, adapted from [171, p. 12]:

$$\left| \frac{AM(p_2) - AM(p_1)}{AM(p_2)} \right| < Acc.Threshold \tag{6.7}$$

By comparing the metric values of different snapshots of our data set over time, we can evaluate this aspect. For this reason, we repeated the data gathering described in Sect. 6.3.1 five months later and obtained a second snapshot of the data. This data set is slightly smaller, with 2719 instead of 2997 process models, but contains a larger amount of executable process models with 565 instead of 327 cases. Since we do not compare single process models, but different sets of process models, we replace the metric values in equation 6.7 with the median values of the different sets. As [171] leaves no hint for a suitable accuracy threshold, we set it to 0.05, meaning that the difference in metric values of repeated measurement should be no higher. The median values and results are depicted in Table 6.4. In nearly all cases, median values are identical. In case of the weighted metric for executable process models, the result is 0.04 which is still below the threshold.

Table 6.4.: Descriptive Statistics and Accuracy for Repeated Measurements

Process Group	N_1	N_2	Statistics	$AM_{bin.}$ $t : 60\%$	$AM_{weighted}$
executable	327	565	$\tilde{x}_1$	0.63	0.59
			$\tilde{x}_2$	0.63	0.57
			Acc.	0	0.04
nonexecutable	2418	1921	$\tilde{x}_1$	0.67	0.62
			$\tilde{x}_2$	0.67	0.62
			Acc.	0	0

6.4. Summary

In this chapter, we proposed a set of metrics for measuring and assessing the adaptability of service-oriented and process-aware software. Adaptability in this context refers to the design-time adaption of executable process models to enable their execution on a different engine. In Sect. 6.1, we proposed and formally defined a set of metrics that capture this quality characteristic, based on the notion of alternative representations of process elements. The idea is that elements for which a higher amount of standard-conformant alternative representations exist can be considered as more adaptable.

The proposed metrics are internal complexity metrics. The theoretical validation in Sect. 6.2 shows that the metrics fulfill related measurement-theoretic properties, i.e., non-negativity, null value, symmetry, and monotonicity. Due to the normalization of the metrics with respect to process model size, they fail to satisfy additivity. Moreover, the metrics are defined on an interval scale and are computed by counting. Their purpose is status assessment and the information of stakeholders.

We implemented the metrics computation for BPMN process models and gathered a large set of real-world process models for the practical evaluation in Sect. 6.3. The occurrence frequency of process elements in the gathered process models shows that only a small part of the vocabulary of BPMN is used in practice. We used this information to refine the metrics computation. The analysis of the discriminative power of the metrics shows that the weighted adaptability metric and the binary adaptability metric with a threshold set at 60% perform best. However, the former is the only metric that allows for the meaningful comparison of process models of different size. Finally, all metrics produce stable results.

In summary, the weighted adaptability metric outperforms the other proposed metrics. Hence, it is our answer to research question 2.3 and we can recommend it as a theoretically valid and practically tested mechanism for computing the adaptability of service-oriented and process-aware software.

7. Measuring Replaceability

Parts of this chapter have been taken from [85].

If software is not directly portable, nor easy to adapt, the remaining alternative, specified by the SQuaRE model [53], is to *replace* it. Replacement might also be required when upgrading an execution environment and a high degree of replaceability reduces the risk of vendor lock-in [53, p. 16]. This quality characteristic forms the concluding part of the measurement framework. It is addressed by research question 2.4, the target of this chapter: *What are suitable metrics for measuring replaceability?* As discussed in Sect. 2.3, the SQuaRE model defines replaceability as the *"degree to which a product can replace another specified software product for the same purpose in the same environment"* [53, p. 16]. In terms of this work, a *product* refers to a piece of service-oriented and process-aware software, whereas the environment is the engine. The definition indicates that replaceability is not computed based on a single piece of software, but based on a paired comparison of an original piece of software and a replacement candidate. This constitutes a notable difference to the quality characteristics that have been the focus of the previous chapters. As opposed to these characteristics, replaceability is no inherent property of a piece of software.

In this chapter, we deviate from the methodology applied for the previous three quality characteristics. The reason for this deviation is that a large amount of metrics that seem applicable for assessing replaceability has already been proposed, validated, and evaluated, e.g., [217–227]. What is more, comparative studies that evaluate these metrics do already exist [228]. Adding yet another set of replaceability metrics on top of the existing body of metrics is neither desirable, nor likely to form a novel contribution. Instead of proposing new metrics, we review existing metrics and discuss their suitability for our area of application, the replaceability evaluation of executable software. We propose an extension to existing metrics that is necessary to support our use case and evaluate the resulting metrics computation. The proposed extension is orthogonal to the definition of existing metrics and does not change their way of computation. A theoretical validation of existing metrics is not required, since this is part of the sources in which they are defined.

We start by explaining the nature of replaceability in Sect. 7.1. This is followed by a review of existing metrics in Sect. 7.2. The review includes a discussion of desirable properties for replaceability metrics and presents a categorization of existing metrics. Moreover, we select a subset of applicable metrics based on their targeted area of application, provide a closer discussion of these metrics, and ultimately choose two metrics for an evaluation. Next, Sect. 7.3 states deficiencies of these metrics for replaceability assessment, proposes an extension to cope with these deficiencies, and evaluates the selected metrics using a set of synthetic process models. This allows to decide on which metric fits best. Finally, Sect. 7.4 concludes with a summary.

7.1. On the Measurement of Replaceability

As indicated in the previous section, the quality characteristic of replaceability, as defined by the SQuaRE model [53], differs from the other characteristics related to portability. These characteristics of portability, installability, and adaptability are inherent properties of a single piece of software or software system. They can be computed based on the static attributes or dynamic behavior of the piece of software alone. In contrast, replaceability, as defined above, is the degree to which a software product can replace another software product. This implies that replaceability cannot be evaluated for a single isolated piece of software, but requires a paired combination of two pieces: the currently installed software product and a candidate for its replacement. In our case, this translates to a currently enacted executable process model and one or more replacement candidates. If the change of an engine becomes necessary, for instance due to an upgrade, and a process model is neither directly portable to this engine, nor easy to adapt, it could be replaced by an alternative that can be executed on this engine. Clearly, this is only possible if alternatives to the original model do exist. Consequently, the evaluation of replaceability is not always possible or desired.

An eventual source of replacement candidates are process model repositories [229, 230]. Management of such repositories is a common task for enterprises that adopt process-aware and service-oriented technologies. If replacement candidates are available in such a repository, replaceability can be computed for all paired combinations of the enacted model and its alternatives to determine the best fitting replacement candidate.

Replace-ability and similarity Though denoted as replaceability by the SQuaRE model [53], in its core, replaceability translates to *similarity* [231]. Process models are more likely to be replaceable with each other, if they are highly similar. As a consequence, metrics for evaluating process model similarity seem suited for evaluating replaceability. This opens up a large space of related work. Process model similarity is important for a wide array of application scenarios apart from replaceability assessment [231]. A few of these application scenarios, without claiming completeness, are process or service discovery [218, 221, 225, 232], compliance assurance [233], pattern support assessment [196], the facilitation of process change [222], or process clustering for efficient process model repository management [234]. As a result of this wide applicability, many similarity metrics have been proposed in the literature, e.g., [217–227]. In the following section, we discuss common properties and classifications of similarity and replaceability metrics and review existing metrics that seem suitable for our area of application.

7.2. Review of Existing Metrics

Similarity metrics, and, therefore, also replaceability metrics, measure the distance between objects [235, 236]. The smaller the distance between the objects is, the more similar and, thus, the more replaceable they are. In our case, the objects are executable pieces of software. Based on the definition of a similarity metric given in [228, Sect. 2.4], a replaceability metric for service-oriented and process-aware software can formally be defined as follows:

Definition 37: Replaceability Metric

$$REPL(p^1, p^2) = \frac{1}{1 + dist(p^1, p^2)}, where \qquad (7.1)$$

- $dist : Process \times Process \rightarrow \mathbb{R}_0^+$ is a function that computes the distance between two process models.
- $p^1, p^2 \in P$, where P is the set of all process models and $(P, dist)$ forms the *metric space* [235].

The crucial difference between replaceability metrics lies in their definition of the distance function.

Since replaceability is no structural property of a software system, the property-based software engineering measurement framework [69] is not applicable here. Nevertheless, a set of properties that apply to the distance function are defined in the literature [235]. These properties are *symmetry, non-negativity, identity,* and the *triangle inequality*:

Symmetry: Distance values for pairs of objects must be identical, regardless of the order of in which the objects are compared.

$$\forall p^1, p^2 \in P, dist(p^1, p^2) = dist(p^2, p^1) \qquad (7.2)$$

Non-negativity: Distance values cannot be negative.

$$\forall p^1, p^2 \in P, dist(p^1, p^2) \geq 0 \qquad (7.3)$$

Identity: The distance between identical objects must be zero.

$$\forall p^1, p^2 \in P, p^1 = p^2 \rightarrow dist(p^1, p^2) = 0 \qquad (7.4)$$

Triangle inequality: The distance between two objects must not be larger than the added distance between the two objects and a third.

$$\forall p^1, p^2, p^3 \in P, dist(p^1, p^2) \leq dist(p^1, p^3) + dist(p^3, p^2) \qquad (7.5)$$

Similarity metrics for process models can further be classified depending on the entities which form the basis of the computation. This results in a classification in terms of *labels, structure,* or *behavior* [237].

Label Similarity: Metrics based on label similarity compute the similarity of process models based on the names, i.e., the labels, assigned to their elements. If the labels of two elements found in the models p and p' are identical, these elements are considered to be identical as well. If all elements of p are also found in p', and no more, regardless of the structuring of the process graph, then p and p' are considered to be identical and $REPL(p, p') = 1$. Examples of metrics for label similarity can be found in [217–220, 226].

The problem with label similarity is that the labels assigned to process elements are normally written in natural language and, hence, they are seldom identical. For instance, the label of an activity in p might be "Check Order", whereas p' contains an activity labeled "Order Checking". Though the labels are not identical, their distance could be considered as small. Certain natural language comparison techniques, such as the string edit distance [238], or semantic techniques that utilize a thesaurus, as for instance found in [218, 239], can be used to improve the similarity computation among labels.

Structural Similarity: Metrics based on structural similarity compare the structure of the process graphs of two models. The smaller the distance between the structure of the graphs, the more similar they are. The distance between graphs can be measured through the graph edit distance of process models [232]. This distance corresponds to the number of insertions, deletions, and substitutions of process elements that are needed to transform the graph of one process model into another. The higher this number is, the greater is the distance. Structural similarity metrics have for instance been defined in [218, 222, 232].

Behavioral Similarity: Metrics based on behavioral similarity focus on the execution behavior of process models [221]. They are often computed based on the execution traces of process models or the execution dependencies among the activities of two models. First, possible traces or execution dependencies are computed based on the model. Then, these traces or dependencies are compared to the traces or dependencies belonging to another model. The higher the overlap between these sets of traces or dependencies is, the higher is the similarity of the process models. Behavioral similarity metrics can for example be found in [218, 225, 227].

A crucial problem of approaches in this area is the requirement to map the nodes in one process model to one or more nodes in the other model. This is necessary to identify if traces really are similar. To achieve this, approaches for behavioral similarity often make use of approaches for label similarity.

As indicated above, an abundance of similarity metrics has been defined in all of these categories, e.g., in [217–227]. This has led researchers to refrain from the definition of new metrics and perform comparative studies on metrics performance instead. One such study, which is used as the foundation of this chapter, is [228]. In this work, Becker and Laue perform a review of existing metrics, classify them according to the area of application they are directed at, and compute metric values for a set of synthetic process models. Based on this computation, they provide suggestions on the quality and appropriateness of the different metrics for different use cases. Here, we use the classification and results from [228] to narrow the set of relevant metrics and to decide which metrics are a potential fit for our use case.

[228] distinguishes seven application areas for similarity metrics: i) The sim- *Metric* plification of change in process variants, ii) process merging, iii) facilitation of *use cases* reuse, iv) management of process model repositories, v) automation of process execution, vi) compliance assurance with normative models, and vii) service discovery. The areas of process execution automation and service discovery are closest to our focus of application. [228] emphasizes the importance of these areas for SOA, which coincides with the focus of this thesis. The authors remark that *"automation is usually concerned in SOA applications"* and service discovery is *"closely connected to the goal of automation"* [228, Sect. 4.2]. For these areas of application, the authors recommend behavioral metrics that compute similarity based on the dependencies among the nodes of the process graph in favor of metrics based on label or structural similarity. In particular, these metrics are *dependency graphs* [223] and their improvement in *TAR-similarity* [224], the *string edit distance of sets of traces* [225], *causal behavioral profiles* [227], and *causal footprints* [218]. From this set of metrics, we consider TAR-similarity and causal behavioral profiles to be applicable for a replaceability computation. The reasons for excluding the remaining metrics are explained in the following subsections.

7.2.1. Direct Precedence Relationships Among Activities

The metrics captured by dependency graphs [223], TAR-similarity [224], and the string edit distance of sets of traces [225], are all based on a similar idea: They compute the similarity of process models by considering direct precedence relationships among the activities in a process model.

In [223], the direct precedence relationships among activities correspond to *Depen-* the so-called *dependency graph* of a process model. To determine process model *dency* similarity, first, all direct precedence relationships of two models, i. e., their *graphs* dependencies graphs, are computed. In a second step, these sets of direct precedence relationships are compared and the higher their overlap is, the more similar the two process models are[27]. More precisely, the distance between the dependency graphs is equal to the number of dependencies that are not present in both of the graphs. In the case of [223], direct precedence relationships among activities are considered, regardless of gateways that might be placed between two activities. This means that conditional branching or parallelism in a process model is not taken into account. This is a clear drawback of the approach.

---

[27]Essentially, the distance between two dependency graphs corresponds to the Jaccard distance [240] between the sets of dependencies.

TAR-similarity

An extension of dependency graphs that tries to tackle this issue is formed by TAR-similarity [224]. The term TAR stems from the *transition adjacency relation*, which is a special form of a direct precedence relationship. The TAR does not only consider direct control dependencies among activities, but also takes into account the interleaving of activities that are executed in parallel. This means that if a process model uses inclusive (OR) or parallel (AND) gateways, there is a larger amount of dependencies in the dependency graph, which is called the TAR set here. Apart from this, TAR-similarity is computed in the same fashion as dependency graphs, i. e., by comparing the amount of shared adjacency relations of the TAR sets, TAR_1 and TAR_2, of two process models, p^1 and p^2, to all relations. Based on the definition of the similarity metric in [224], the distance function, *dist*, from Def. 37, can be defined as follows:

$$dist_{TAR}(p^1, p^2) = \frac{|(TAR_1 \cup TAR_2)|}{|(TAR_1 \cap TAR_2)|} - 1 \qquad (7.6)$$

Projected-TAR

Although TAR-similarity takes gateways into account, it is still limited to direct adjacency relations. An improvement of TAR-similarity that tries to eliminate the requirement of directness can be found in the projected TAR [241]. This extension tries to relax the restriction of direct dependencies, by first computing a projection of the original process model that eliminates so-called silent steps in the model. The TAR-similarity is then computed based on the projected model. The problem with the approach presented in [241] is that it cannot automatically be determined which parts of the process model are considered as silent. Here, human judgment is required. As a result, the projected TAR is a subjective metric in the sense of [174, Sect. 3.1.2]. For this reason, we omit the projected TAR from further consideration.

Edit distance of sets of traces

Another metric that is quite similar to dependency graphs and TAR-similarity is the string edit distance of sets of traces [225]. This metric is based on the analysis of execution traces, instead of a dependency graph. However, as the traces are computed based on the process graph, the difference between sets of traces and a dependency graph is mainly one of terminology. A more notable difference of this metric lies in the fact that it does not necessarily focus on binary, i. e., direct, relations only. Instead, it also takes larger sets of activity sequences into account, which are called *words of length n*, or *n-grams*. An n-gram is a trace of the process model that includes exactly n subsequent activities. To calculate the string edit distance of sets of traces, all possible n-grams for a process model have to be computed. Thereafter, the distance of two process models corresponds to the aggregated string edit distance of all n-grams. Although [225] does not address the computational complexity of this approach, it is clear that the calculation is challenging. To begin with, the amount of traces of a process model explodes when parallelism is involved. On top of that, all n-grams of these traces have to be computed, which quickly reaches computational boundaries. Additionally, for the metrics computation, a pairwise comparison of all elements of the potentially high amount of n-grams is required. As a result, the usage of a high value of n is not feasible in practice and n-grams of length two, called bi-grams, are most frequent. In this case, the string edit distance of sets of traces corresponds to TAR-similarity. For this reason, we only consider TAR-similarity further.

7.2.2. Causal Footprints

Causal footprints are a behavioral similarity metric proposed in [218]. A causal footprint of a process model corresponds to the set of its activities and the execution dependencies among them. These execution dependencies are not limited to direct precedence relationships. To obtain a causal footprint, a set of look-back links and a set of look-ahead links is computed for every activity in a process model. The set of look-back links of an activity A corresponds to the set of all activities that may precede the execution of A. Similarly, the set of look-ahead links of A corresponds to the set of all activities that may be executed after A has finished. Note, that it is not necessary that all activities in the set of look-back or look-ahead links are executed. Instead, the execution of at least one of the activities from each set is sufficient. The causal footprint of a process model corresponds to all sets of look-back and look-ahead links of the activities in the model. The sets of look-ahead and look-back links are treated as vectors, and the similarity of two process models is computed through the cosine of their vectors.

Based on their observations in [228], Becker and Laue discourage the usage of causal footprints, due to their computational inefficiency. Despite the usage of the reference implementation of causal footprints and a very moderate test set of only eight small process models, they experienced computation times that were more than five times as large as for any other similarity metric. This puts the feasibility of the practical application of causal footprints into question. Hence, we do not consider causal footprints any further.

7.2.3. Causal Behavioral Profiles

As the name indicates, causal behavioral profiles [227] refer to a behavioral similarity metric. Like the other metrics, its mechanism of computation bases on relations between activities. These relations are not limited to direct precedence relations, as for the metrics discussed in Sect. 7.2.1. Instead, the metric considers four categories of behavioral relations between activities. Given two activities, A_1 and A_2, these relations are: i) Strict order relation (A_1 is always executed before A_2), ii) co-occurrence relation (if A_1 is executed in a process instance, A_2 must be executed as well, and vice versa), iii) exclusiveness relation (A_1 and A_2 are never executed in the same process instance), and iv) concurrency relation (A_1 may be executed before A_2, but also the other way round). The set of all behavioral relations among the activities of a process model is its *behavioral profile*.

The similarity of two process models is computed by comparing their behavioral profiles. More precisely, the amount of shared execution relations among activities is compared to the amount of all execution relations. In this sense, causal behavioral profiles are very similar to TAR-similarity. The main difference between the two lies in what kind of relations among activities are considered. Behavioral profiles are necessarily larger than TAR sets, since they include a relation for every pair of activities in a process model. However, there is an additional notable distinction. To be able to compare the execution relations among activities of the two process models, it is necessary to establish which activities in the two models correspond to each other. Only then, it is possible to determine if two behavioral relations are the same. If it is the case that, for a specific activity, there are no corresponding activities in the partner process model, all behavioral relations that involve this activity are ignored. As [227] puts it: *"Solely activities that are aligned by the correspondence relation are considered"*. This is a significant difference from TAR-similarity, for which such relations are still part of the TAR sets. Furthermore, it implies that causal behavioral profiles heavily depend on a proper correspondence function. Weidlich et al. use a trace equivalence correspondence function based on execution traces and activity labels, but require that the function must be injective. This means it is not applicable if there are activities in the first process model for which no corresponding activity in the second process model can be found.

7.2.4. Summary of the Review

The results of the review are summarized in Table 7.1. The table depicts

Table 7.1.: Reviewed Similarity Metrics for Replaceability Evaluation

Metric	Ref.	Object in Focus	Issues
Dependency Graphs	[223]	direct precedence relations	gateways are ignored superseded by TAR-similarity
TAR-similarity	[224]	direct precedence relations	
Edit Distance of Set of Traces	[225]	n-grams	inefficient for larger n
Causal Footprints	[218]	look-back and look-ahead links	inefficient computation
Causal Behavioral Profiles	[227]	behavioral relations among activities	

the metrics that seem suitable for our area of application, according to the categorization specified in [228]. Dependency graphs are excluded from further consideration, since they are superseded by TAR-similarity. When using bi-grams, the edit distance of sets of traces corresponds to TAR-similarity as well. For this reason, it is sufficient to use TAR-similarity as representative for the mechanism of computation underlying these three metrics. Causal footprints are omitted from further consideration, because of their computational inefficiency. Finally, causal behavioral profiles are considered in the evaluation. To form a conclusion, based on the review, we evaluate TAR-similarity and causal behavioral profiles as candidates for a replaceability metric.

7.3. Metrics Improvement and Selection

Evaluating the replaceability of executable software is not what the designers of similarity metrics originally had in mind. Due to this, existing similarity metrics share a number of deficiencies for a replaceability evaluation, which we discuss in the following subsection, Sect. 7.3.1. Thereafter, in Sect. 7.3.2, we propose an extension that is supposed to improve their applicability for evaluating replaceability of service-oriented and process-aware software. Finally, we evaluate the extension using a set of synthetic process models, similar to [228], in Sect. 7.3.3, to determine which of the remaining similarity metric is best for our use case.

7.3.1. Deficiencies of Existing Metrics for Replaceability Evaluation

To be applicable in many settings and use cases, all metrics discussed in Sect. 7.2 are computed on the basis of a formalism, such as Petri nets, or other abstractions of concrete process models. To enable the metrics computation, a process model has to be translated into the formalism. During this translation, language-specific execution semantics of particular language elements, except for control-flow routing constructs, are mostly lost. This is acceptable in general-purpose application scenarios, in particular those that deal with nonexecutable and abstract process models anyway. In fact, such scenarios are what most metrics have been designed for. For instance, only three out of the 22 metrics evaluated in [228] are targeted at similarity assessment of executable process models by their authors. This results in several problems when trying to use the metrics for an evaluation of the replaceability of executable software. These problems may render certain metrics unsuitable for this use case.

To understand these issues, it is important to recall the purpose of a replace- *Issues of existing techniques* ability evaluation here: To investigate how well a given software product can replace a second software product in a given execution environment, because the second one contains language elements that are not supported. As a consequence, the concrete language elements have to be taken into account during the replaceability evaluation. Abstracting from the concrete vocabulary of the language, which is what practically all metrics do, defeats the purpose of the evaluation to begin with. The deficiencies for a replaceability evaluation resulting from this abstraction level can be summarized a follows:

1. *Generality*: In most cases, similarity is computed based on the activities and connectors among them. The vocabulary of a process language may not be limited to these sets of elements. For instance, in the case of BPMN,

activities and gateways clearly fit to this model. However, it needs to be stated, in what way events fit into the above categories. Moreover, it is seldom made clear how a metric should deal with hierarchical decomposition in a process model.

2. *Node Mapping*: Practically all approaches assume that it is possible to map the nodes, in particular the activities, or their execution traces between two process models, i. e., that it is possible to determine if an activity of process model p_1 *corresponds* to one or more activities of process model p_2. This is referred to as the *matching problem* in [242]. In the definition of most structural or behavioral metrics, this aspect is left open or, if discussed at all, deferred to approaches that determine the correspondence between activities based on their labels. This underspecification is problematic, due to the impact of the node mapping on the similarity metric. As [228, Sect. 7] puts it, *"the quality of the mapping between nodes [...] has a significant contribution to the quality of a similarity measure"*. This is even more evident when it comes to executable software. Activity labels on their own are of no importance for the execution semantics of activities. As a consequence, relying on activity labels only for finding corresponding activities is a questionable assumption. Instead, the execution semantics of a concrete activity, as for instance captured in its type (e.g., message sending, script execution, business rule execution, etc.) are a decisive factor. When considering a process language, such as BPMN, a variety of node types with different execution semantics exist. None of the approaches explicitly takes these types into account.

Solutions to the issues   All in all, the issue of generality can be resolved with relative simplicity. In the case of BPMN, as done in [228], events can be included in the replaceability evaluation by considering them as nodes of a process model in the same fashion as activities. Hierarchical decomposition is more difficult to incorporate. It can be achieved by either treating a *SubProcess* as a single node in the same fashion as tasks and events, or by ignoring the decomposition and embedding the contents of a *SubProcess* into the parent process. The latter is the strategy favored by the metrics we consider for evaluation here [224, 227].

The issue of constructing a node mapping is more critical. By ignoring node types, and, hence, parts of the execution semantics of the process model, a similarity metric risks to rate process models as similar, although they are dissimilar in reality, or vice versa. This can be demonstrated by considering the similarity of the BPMN process models depicted in Fig. 7.1[28]. These are a reference model, RM, a first variant of the reference model, V1, and a second variant of the reference model, V2. The structure of the process graph is identical in all cases and so are the labels of the nodes. We use identical labels and structure to eliminate any influence of label or structural similarity and enable

---

[28]The structure of the models is identical to the structure of the reference model from [228]. We adjusted the types of the activities from ordinary tasks to specific BPMN tasks and introduced events in V1.

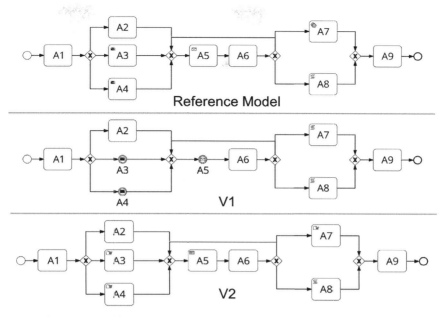

Figure 7.1.: Process Models for Replaceability Computation

an isolated consideration of the node types. When ignoring node types, the dependency graphs and execution traces for the process models, as well as their causal footprints and behavioral profiles are identical. As a result, all process models are considered identical to each other with the discussed metrics. This is problematic, since two of the models are less similar, when taking the concrete node types into account. At first glance, it may seem that V2 is more similar to the reference model than V1, since V1 uses events, whereas V2 only uses activities. However, the opposite is true: The execution semantics of V1 are identical to RM, although it uses events instead of activities. In V1, *Send-* (A3, A4) and *ReceiveTasks* (A5) are replaced by *Send-* and *ReceiveEvents*. These process elements have the same execution semantics in BPMN. Furthermore, the *ServiceTask* (A7) in RM is replaced by a *ScriptTask*. A script implemented in a programming language can be used to emulate almost any other task, including a *ServiceTask*. Therefore, V1 and the reference model are in fact fully replaceable. In contrast, in V2, activity A5 is not a *ReceiveTask* that blocks until a message is received from an external party, but a *BusinessRuleTask*, which has very different execution semantics. Thus, it cannot be considered as corresponding to activity A5 of the reference model. The same reasoning applies to activities A3, A4, and A7, which are *ManualTasks* in V2, but *Send-* and *ServiceTasks* in the reference model. Similar to [228], the process models depicted in Fig. 7.1 can be used for evaluating replaceability metrics. A suitable replaceability metric should consider V2 less fit to replace RM than V1 and RM.

Although mentioned before, it is important to emphasize that so-called *semantic* mapping approaches, as for instance found in [218, 239], focus on the semantic similarity of node labels, but not on execution semantics of nodes. As most approaches address the similarity of abstract process models, executable models have been neglected so far. Such models require a more restrictive notion of node correspondence, which, as indicated in [228, Sect. 7], may render metrics unsuitable.

To address this issue, we propose a node mapping approach that takes execution semantics of nodes into account. The aim of this mapping approach is to operationalize the metrics for the replaceability evaluation of service-oriented and process-aware software. Our mapping approach is described in the next section.

7.3.2. Node Mapping and Correspondence

Nearly all approaches require the usage of a function that maps the nodes in one process model to one or more nodes in another one. Formally, we define the mapping function as follows:

Definition 38: Mapping Function

$$map(p^1, p^2) \rightarrow MAP, where \qquad (7.7)$$

- $map : Process \times Process \rightarrow MAP$ is a function that computes the mapping set MAP.
- $\forall a_i \in p^1 \wedge a_j \in p^2, (a_i, a_j) \in MAP \leftrightarrow corresponds(a_j, a_i)$, i. e., the mapping set MAP of two process models p^1 and p^2 consists of all *corresponding* pairs of activities.
- $corresponds : Activity \times Activity \rightarrow Boolean$ is a function that determines if an activity corresponds to another one.

The crucial aspect in this definition is the correspondence function *corresponds* that is used to construct the mapping set MAP. It is possible that, for an activity a_i from p^1 no corresponding activity a_j from p^2 is found. Moreover, there may be multiple activities from p^2 that correspond to a_i. Hence, the mapping is not necessarily total or injective. This can be problematic, since some approaches require an injective mapping. However, such a requirement is questionable from a practical point of view.

As discussed in the previous section, most approaches decide on node correspondence based on the similarity of node labels only. This ignores execution semantics of nodes and, therefore, is problematic for the evaluation of the replaceability of executable software. Here, we draw on a previous definition of the similarity of the execution semantics of process elements to define an improved correspondence function. In Chap. 6, we have already considered the similarity of the execution semantics of process elements for measuring the adaptability of process models. There, we defined the *set of alternatives*, *ALT*, for an element as part of Def. 32. This set contains all semantically equivalent alternative process elements that can be used to replace a certain element. As such, it can be reused to take execution semantics into account when evaluating node correspondence:

Definition 39: Node Correspondence Function

$$corresponds(n_i, n_j) = \begin{cases} true & \leftrightarrow\ n_j \in ALT_{n_i} \\ false & otherwise \end{cases} \quad (7.8)$$

Where ALT_{n_i} is the set of alternatives, as defined in Def. 32.

Based on this correspondence function, nodes with similar execution semantics are considered as corresponding nodes in the replaceability computation. This function can easily be combined with approaches for label similarity. For instance, two nodes can be considered as corresponding if their labels are identical *and* their types correspond to each other.

As a final design decision, it has to be noted that the correspondence function could be defined to return a real number instead of a boolean value. Such a return value could be used to denote a relative correspondence of process elements. The relative correspondence could also be used to influence the overall similarity value, as for instance done in [218]. Since the metrics we selected for the evaluation here do not use such a weighting, a boolean return value of the correspondence function is sufficient.

7.3.3. Discussion of Metrics Performance

To evaluate how well the metrics perform with the node mapping and correspondence functions from Sect. 7.3.2, and to determine their suitability for replaceability assessment, we compute the metric values for the BPMN process models depicted in Fig. 7.1[29]. As such, our evaluation is similar to the one performed in [228].

As stated in Sect. 7.3.1, a suitable metric should find V1 to be very similar, if not identical, to the reference model. At the same time, the metric should find V2 to be dissimilar from the reference model. The two metrics that remain from the review presented in Sect. 7.2 are TAR-similarity [224] and causal behavioral profiles [227]. In the following, we discuss the values of these metrics, when computed using the mapping function defined in Sect. 7.3.2 and judge the results, which can be found in Table 7.2. To determine corresponding nodes, we combine the correspondence function and label identity.

TAR-similarity: In the case of TAR-similarity, the TAR set of the reference model, TAR_{RM}, resolves to $\{(A1, A2), (A1, A3), (A1, A4), (A2, A5), (A3,$

---

[29]We did not re-implement the metrics computation in the prope tool, since the implementation primarily serves as a proof of feasibility. For the metrics at hand no such proof is needed, as they have already been implemented as part of [228]. This implementation can be found at http://sourceforge.net/projects/prom-similarity/.

Table 7.2.: Results of the Metrics Evaluation

Metric	$RM \leftrightarrow V1$	$RM \leftrightarrow V2$
Desired Result	1	< 1
TAR-similarity	1	0.16
Causal Behavioral Profiles	1	1

$A5)$, $(A4, A5)$, $(A5, A6)$, $(A6, A7)$, $(A6, A8)$, $(A7, A9)$, $(A8, A9)\}$. For V1, the nodes A3, A4, A5, and A7 are events and tasks that differ in their type from their counterparts in the reference model. However, based on the correspondence function, they correspond to the respective tasks in the reference model. Thus, the TAR set of V1, TAR_{V1}, resolves to the same set as for the reference model, TAR_{RM}. Hence, $dist(RM, V1) = 0$ and $REPL(RM, V1) = 1$. Put differently, the TAR-similarity metric rates the reference model and V1 as fully replaceable. This is a desirable result.

When considering V2, the tasks A3, A4, A5, and A7 do not correspond to their counterparts in the reference model based on the correspondence function. Therefore, the TAR set of V2, TAR_{V2} resolves to $\{(A1, A2)$, $(A1, A3_{V2})$, $(A1, A4_{V2})$, $(A2, A5_{V2})$, $(A3_{V2}, A5_{V2})$, $(A4_{V2}, A5_{V2})$, $(A5_{V2}, A6)$, $(A6, A7_{V2})$, $(A6, A8)$, $(A7_{V2}, A9)$, $(A8, A9)\}$. Consequently, $TAR_{RM} \cap TAR_{V2}$ is limited to $\{(A1, A2), (A6, A8), (A8, A9)\}$. Since $\mid TAR_{RM} \cup TAR_{V2} \mid$ resolves to nineteen, the replaceability metric bears the following value: $REPL(RM, V2) = 1 / (19 / 3) \approx 0.16$. The reference model and V2 are not considered as identical.

Summarizing the results, TAR-similarity, when computed based on our mapping function, passes the evaluation, as it rates RM and V1 as replaceable and RM and V2 as dissimilar.

Causal Behavioral Profiles: Although the source defining causal behavioral profiles [227] uses BPMN process models as example, it states that it is necessary to map the models into a formal representation. This mapping is not clarified in the paper, but deferred to another paper [243]. The applicability of this mapping for BPMN 2.0 process models is questionable, since it refers to an outdated version of BPMN and, therefore, ignores aspects that are imperative to the execution semantics of a BPMN 2.0 process, such as different task types. Nevertheless, using our mapping and correspondence function, metrics computation for the process models is rather straight-forward. The structure of the three process models is identical, hence, their behavioral profiles are also identical, given they are computed based on node labels or execution traces. As before, the distinguishing difference lies in the nodes that differ between the models: A3, A4, A5, and A7. In the case of the reference model and V1, these nodes are considered to correspond to their counterparts by our correspondence function. Therefore, the two process models are considered to be identical and fully replaceable. Similar to TAR-similarity, this is the desired result.

However, the assessment of the replaceability of the reference model and the V2 uncovers a crucial problem. For A3, A4, A5, and A7, no corresponding nodes can be found for the reference model in V2 and vice versa. In this case, as described in Sect. 7.2.3, all behavioral relations involving these nodes are omitted from the behavioral profiles. This means, replaceability is solely computed by considering the behavioral relations among A1, A2, A6, A8, and A9. These relations are completely identical in both models. Therefore, the result is the same as for the comparison of the reference model and V1: For causal behavioral profiles, $REPL(RM, V2) = 1 = REPL(RM, V1)$ applies, and the two models are considered fully identical. This is not a desirable result, since we expect $REPL(RM, V2) < REPL(RM, V1)$.

This finding indicates that causal behavioral profiles are not applicable for our use case of computing replaceability. It seems that our notion of node correspondence is too restrictive for a meaningful application of the metric.

The result of the discussion in this section can be expressed as follows: TAR-similarity has been found to be applicable for the evaluation of the replaceability of service-oriented and process-aware software. In contrast, causal behavioral profiles have not passed the test, and we cannot recommend this metric for our application scenario.

7.4. Summary

In this chapter, we discussed how the replaceability of service-oriented and process-aware software can be evaluated and found TAR-similarity [224] to be the most promising candidate metric. Hence, we can answer research question 2.4, concerning what metrics are most suitable for evaluating replaceability, with a recommendation for TAR-similarity.

Essentially, as explained in Sect. 7.1, replaceability can be reduced to a problem of similarity. For the computation of this property, a large body of metrics, discussed in Sect. 7.2, does already exist. These existing metrics can be classified as either labeling, structural, or behavioral metrics. They are based on the computation of the distance between objects. A proper distance function fulfills the desirable properties of symmetry, non-negativity, identity, and triangle inequality. Using the metrics categorization presented in [228], dependency graphs, TAR-similarity, the string edit distance of sets of traces, causal footprints, and causal behavioral profiles seem appropriate to our use case. From this set of metrics, TAR-similarity [224] and causal behavioral profiles [227] are most promising and the remaining metrics can be excluded due to their computational inefficiency or because they have been superseded by one of the two previous metrics.

To perform a conclusive evaluation of the selected metrics in Sect. 7.3, we discussed problems of the metrics for replaceability assessment. The main issue is that the metrics in their current form fail to take node types into account. This can be resolved by the usage of proper node mapping and correspondence functions, which we defined. The subsequent evaluation with a set of synthetic process models demonstrates that TAR-similarity is better suited for a replaceability evaluation than causal behavioral profiles. As a result, it is the metric we recommend for a practical application.

Part III.

Discussion and Conclusion

8. Related Work

Parts of this chapter have been taken from [74, 77, 79, 80, 83, 85, 170].

In this chapter, we discuss work that is related to this thesis and that presents alternative views of, or approaches to, the aspects addressed in this work. Related work that has directly influenced and laid the foundations for the studies performed here, has already been discussed throughout the previous chapters of the thesis and will not be repeated here. Thus, the chapter complements the existing discussion of related work and provides a wider view of the topic.

We start by discussing alternative languages and standards that can be used to *Structure* implement service-oriented and process-aware software in Sect. 8.1. Thereafter, we *of the* examine approaches that can be used to tackle portability issues, but which do not *chapter* necessarily rely on standard-conformance in Sect. 8.2. This is followed by related work on benchmarking and testing of process engines and models in Sect. 8.3. Next, we outline approaches for measuring further quality characteristics of service-oriented or process-aware software, apart from the ones relevant here, in Sect. 8.4. Finally, Sect. 8.5 to 8.8 discuss alternative notions and interpretations of the quality characteristics considered in this work and alternative approaches for measuring them.

8.1. Alternative Languages and Standards

Considerable effort has been put into the development of process standards and languages. The languages used in this thesis, BPEL [27] and BPMN [26], were described in Sect. 2.2.2. Apart from these two, several more languages with varying focus exist. For instance, [25] discusses fifteen languages for specifying business process models, but only a small minority of these languages actually allow to specify executable process models. Notable competitors of BPEL and BPMN are the *XML Process Definition Language* (XPDL) 2.2 [31], the *Windows Workflow Foundation* (WF) 4.5 [28], and *Yet Another Workflow Language* (YAWL) [244]. The usage of XML-technologies is ubiquitous in this area. Enabling the portability of process models among editors and engines is a central aim of these languages and the reason to provide an XML serialization format. Each of the languages has specific areas of focus and application.

XPDL is a process language and standard promoted by the workflow manage- *XML* ment coalition. Its initial version was published in 1993 and the standard has *Process* undergone multiple revisions and extensions since that time. Process models are *Defini-* specified in a graph-oriented style. The primary focus of XPDL is the storage and *tion* interchange of process models. This means, it is specifically tailored to porting *Language* process models between tools of different vendors. However, its main purposes are

179

documentation, monitoring, and simulation [31, p. 10] and not primarily execution. To this end, process models in XPDL also include information that relates to the visualization of process models. Prior to the publication of BPMN 2.0 in 2011, XPDL was frequently used as a serialization format for BPMN process models [245]. Hence, some BPMN engines consumed this format for deploying process models and BPMN was only used for visualization purposes. Since the publication of BPMN 2.0, this separation is no longer needed and process models can be implemented and visualized directly in the BPMN format. Nevertheless, there are still engines that only consume XPDL process models, but claim to be BPMN 2.0-compliant. In revision 2.2, XPDL also addresses BPMN 2.0 and its conformance classes. As such, XPDL can still be used to provide an alternative serialization format for BPMN process models. Nonetheless, it is expected that newer process engines head for direct support of the BPMN format [245]. Due to this, BPMN can be considered to be of more importance, when it comes to process execution.

Windows Workflow Foundation
Most of the contemporary process engines are implemented in Java or in a language that is part of the Java ecosystem. When it comes to Java's most notable competitor, the .NET framework promoted by Microsoft, there is only one major process language available natively. This language is WF [28], which is the designated process language of the .NET framework and which is currently available in version 4.5. WF is somewhat closer to ordinary high-level programming languages than other process languages, since process models can be specified in either C# or in an XML dialect called extensible application markup language. There is a graphical visualization format for process models and the language provides different styles of control-flow definition that include block-structuredness and graph-orientation. Moreover, WF is tightly integrated with the Windows Communication Foundation to support service-orientation. Due to its clear focus on the development of executable software, WF is a good candidate for implementing service-oriented and process-aware applications. Since the .NET framework is also a specification that may be implemented by different runtime environments, the portability of code among its implementations is an issue. Currently, however, only the official .NET implementation by Microsoft supports WF. Open source implementations, such as Mono[30], might provide support for the language in the future, but at the moment no such implementation is available. Therefore, the porting of WF-based applications is only a theoretical problem so far.

Yet Another Workflow Language
YAWL [244] is an academic workflow language based on Petri nets that was originally developed as a reference implementation for workflow patterns [71]. YAWL has had impact in academia, especially on work that concerns the formal verification of safety and lifeness properties of process models. Nowadays, the language has shifted from a purely academic application and is also used in commercial systems. YAWL captures functionality that is typically needed in workflow management systems, i.e., workflow patterns, with dedicated language constructs to allow for a convenient and straight-forward process model definition.

---

[30]The homepage of the Mono project is available at http://www.mono-project.com.

Similar to the other languages, YAWL does provide an XML serialization format for process models. Since it is based on Petri nets, process models are defined in a graph-oriented style. However, like for WF, only a single engine is currently available. This is the reference implementation of the language. To the best of our knowledge, there is no project or initiative that intends to provide an alternative implementation. As a consequence, the issue of porting process models among different YAWL implementations is likely to remain a theoretical one.

8.2. Approaches for Mitigating Portability Issues

In this thesis, we approach the problem of application portability based on the conformance of implementations to standards. There are other directions from which this problem can be addressed, especially if the modification and refinement of standards is considered as an option. The approaches discussed in this section can be categorized into i) approaches that specify formal execution semantics for existing languages, ii) approaches that provide alternate specification languages, which are compiled to process models, iii) approaches that compile process models to different notations, and iv) approaches that refine and restrict existing standards based on their practical usage.

The languages and standards considered here, e. g., BPMN [26] or BPEL [27], *Formal execution semantics* are informal specifications. As a consequence, they are not free of ambiguities or underspecifications, as discussed for the case of BPMN in [38, 145]. Ambiguities and underspecifications can lead to implementations that behave differently. This behavior is the cause of portability issues. One approach to resolve these issues, taken in related work, is to refine existing standards with a formal, and, therefore, unambiguous, definition of execution semantics. If implemented correctly by every implementation, such a formal definition would ensure that all implementations behave identically. Frequently, a formalization of a standard is achieved by translating the constructs defined in the standard into a formal notation. For process languages, frequently applied formal notations include Petri nets [246] or process algebras, such as the π-calculus [247]. [248] provides an overview of challenges and translation approaches for different languages to Petri nets. Concrete approaches that translate BPEL process models to Petri nets can, for instance, be found in [249–251], and for BPMN in [243, 252]. Often, the primary focus of such translation approaches is to enable the verification of behavioral properties of the interaction of multiple process instances. The clarification of the execution semantics defined in a standard can be considered as a by-product. We have to emphasize that our work does not focus on cross-process instance behavior. Although a formal specification may help to reduce portability issues in theory, implementers of a standard are not required to take these formalizations into account in order to claim support for a standard. Unfortunately, such work is rarely considered in practice by engine vendors, leading to differences in the interpretation of language elements and to portability issues. Even if engine vendors did take formalizations into account, there is no guarantee that the formalization itself would be implemented correctly. In this work, we take a practical point of view and concede the unavoidable imperfectness of standard implementations. For that reason, we base the metrics computation in this thesis on the informal semantics defined in the respective standards and the factual behavior of process engines only, and not on a formalization thereof.

Alternate specification languages
A way to preempt the occurrence of portability issues can be seen in the application of model-driven development approaches. Such approaches often try to make formalizations more applicable in practice by defining alternate specification languages. These languages can be used by developers to implement or specify an application and this specification is compiled to a process model for execution on an engine. For instance, [253] tries to tackle the problem of portability of BPEL process models through a formal specification that refines ambiguous aspects, similar to approaches discussed above. The formalization is accomplished by a formal language called B*lite* [39]. This language is intended to be used by developers and can be compiled to executable BPEL code for a specific engine. [254] takes the same approach, by defining a domain specific language that should make BPEL programming easier. This additional step of compilation can preempt portability problems, if the compilation of the original model to the vocabulary supported by a particular engine is correct. The downside of such approaches is that its users need to learn another language besides the target implementation language. This requirement is often problematic from a practical point of view. Here, we do not try to preempt portability issues, but instead to call attention to them via benchmarking, quantification, and quality assessment.

Process code reduction and compilation
[255] is similar to [253, 254], although the authors take the opposite direction. Their approach is to reduce an existing process model to the usage of a subset of the language, through idempotent transformations of the model elements. The approach is implemented for BPEL and the subset of the language that results from the idempotent transformations is called Core BPEL. The advantage of this approach is that the original process models can be implemented according to the existing language and there is no requirement for developers to learn another language on top. The result of the transformation is a process model that uses a smaller set of the language constructs. This approach has the potential to solve portability issues by eliminating constructs that are rarely supported. However, it could also reduce portability, if the core subset is not well supported. A similar, but more general approach, proposed in [256], is to provide a virtual machine for various process languages. The idea is to compile process models to a separate format, called process intermediate representation, which can be executed on a process virtual machine. This is beneficial to bridge the usage of different process languages and execute them on the same engine. In this case, the problem of portability is transferred from the original language to the compiled format, the process intermediate representation. Similar to Core BPEL, this format has the potential to eliminate portability issues during compilation, but also to introduce new issues, if it is not implemented in the same fashion by multiple implementations.

An alternative and practically-oriented approach, taken by [61], is to modify the standard specification itself, by considering the implementation of the standard in practice. This is different from the previously discussed approaches, which try *Standards refinement and restriction* to refine the standard based on theoretical considerations. The solution proposed in [61] is quite straight-forward: Problems of ambiguity in the specification can be resolved by adopting the interpretation a majority of implementations use in practice and modifying the standard specification accordingly. This principle is close to our work, since we also consider the way engines implement the standard in practice. However, lacking influence on the respective standardization committees, it is not our intent to refine and change the specifications, as in [61]. A comparable approach that has achieved some improvement in the refinement of Web Services standards has been taken by the WS-I. Since Web Services standard implementations turned out to be not as interoperable as expected, the WS-I defined restrictions on existing standards, in the form of so-called profiles, e. g., [257–259], that need to be adhered to if interoperability is a target. These profiles have been accepted in practice. This approach is quite close to our work, when it comes to quantifying portability. The WS-I profiles define test assertions that check the artifacts produced by Web Services standard implementations for aspects that are considered as non-interoperable. Similarly, in Chap. 4, we define test assertions that check process models for elements that can be considered as nonportable. In both cases, test assertions are used to highlight issues. Ultimately, this does not fix interoperability or portability issues, but serves as a means to draw attention to them to enable their resolution. We think this is valuable, since the WS-I approaches are among the few initiatives that have had significant impact in practice and, thus, have demonstrated their feasibility.

8.3. Benchmarking and Testing of Process Engines

So far, the conformance benchmarking of process engines is a niche area that did not receive widespread attention. Nevertheless, it builds on lower-level testing approaches for process engines and models, in particular on unit testing approaches. Performance benchmarking approaches for process engines are more frequent. Finally, there exists a variety of approaches for conformance checking in the area of service-orientation and process-awareness.

Conformance tests evaluate the correctness of the implementation of singular *Lower-level testing techniques* language features in isolation. For this reason, they are quite similar to unit tests for process models. The unit testing of BPEL process models received considerable attention, but even here more work is called for [260]. In this area, the BPELUnit project [207] is widely recognized. BPELUnit allows for the construction of unit and integration tests for BPEL process models that run on specific engines. The benchmarking tool presented in this work is similar to BPELUnit, as it allows for the automatic deployment of BPEL process models and execution of test cases for these models for specific engines. In fact, the benchmarking tool internally uses unit testing frameworks, soapUI and JUnit, to automate test execution and reporting. Using BPELUnit in this thesis was not an option, since it supports fewer and less up-to-date engines. To the best of our knowledge, there are no unit testing frameworks specifically tailored to

BPMN process models and engines so far. Instead, unit testing methodologies are engine-specific and unit tests are usually implemented using lower-level testing frameworks, such as JUnit. Ultimately, unit testing tools are enabling technologies for conformance testing, but differ in the system under test. For unit tests, the system under test is the process model and for conformance tests, the system under test is the process engine.

Perfor-
mance
bench-
marking
Performance benchmarking approaches share the system under test with our conformance benchmark, the process engine, but evaluate a different software quality characteristic, i. e., performance. The most important performance benchmarking approaches related to our work are SOABench [63] for BPEL engines, the BenchFlow project [261] for BPMN engines, and *GENESIS2* [262] as a general purpose testbed generation framework. Essentially, all of these approaches develop testbed environments that can be used to generate testbeds for particular types of systems. Each approach defines a domain model to automatically generate and execute test cases for a given system. Performance benchmarking approaches necessarily have a more complex domain model and benchmarking procedure, since a more fine-grained control of the testing environment is required. Otherwise, the gathering of accurate performance data would not be possible. Among the performance testing approaches in BPEL [64], SOABench [63] forms one of the few approaches that is not limited to a single engine. A central limitation of SOABench is the size of its set of test cases used to perform the benchmark, which comprises only four process models. When it comes to benchmarking the performance of BPMN engines, the BenchFlow project is currently underway. In comparison to SOABench, BenchFlow [261] aims at the construction of a more realistic set of performance tests. To this end, the project tries to gather real-world process models as the basis for performance test cases. Since real-world process models are not necessarily portable to every engine under test, the benchmark presented in this thesis can serve to inform the BenchFlow project on which process models are actually applicable. GENESIS2 [262] is a testbed generation framework that targets service-oriented applications in general and is not strictly limited to process-aware applications as well. Moreover, it also can be used for correctness and integration testing. Since it includes performance characteristics and quality of service aspects, we consider it as a performance testing approach here. The framework takes a Web Services-based system and generates interceptors on the basis of the Web service definitions used in the system. These interceptors allow to intercept messages exchanged at run-time, and thus to test a single component in the system, such as a process model, in isolation. This can also be used to verify performance aspects and quality of service parameters.

Confor-
mance
checking
Finally, conformance checking is a frequently applied term in research on SOA and process-aware information systems, albeit not in the meaning used in this work. Instead of checking the conformance of an implementation to a software standard in the sense of [263, pp. 203–208] or [264], as done here, conformance checking often refers to the verification of behavioral properties of a concrete process model. For instance, it is verified that a process model behaves as specified

by (conforms to) an abstract process model. In this case, conformance checking is necessary to verify the functional correctness of a larger system. Oftentimes, model-driven development approaches require these verification techniques to ensure that generated execution artifacts comply with the higher-level models from which they have been generated. Examples of approaches using this type of conformance checking are [265–269].

8.4. Metrics for Process-Aware and Service-Oriented Software

Portability is a special aspect of software quality and, as specified in the SQuaRE model in Sect. 2.3.2, there are many more quality characteristics that can be considered with the help of software metrics. In this section, we provide an overview of related work on measurement for different quality characteristics in service-oriented and process-aware information systems, with a focus on approaches that are particularly relevant to executable software. It has to be emphasized that the topic of metrics and measurement in this area is vast and this section should be considered as a short and selective summary of important points and not as a conclusive discussion of the subject, which would likely form a thesis of its own.

The two quality characteristics that are most often considered in SOC are performance and maintainability. The latter is generally assessed by operationalizing metrics that stem from object-oriented design to the service-oriented context. In particular, these are cohesion and coupling metrics. Metric frameworks that measure cohesion and coupling for service-oriented systems have for example been presented in [65, 66, 270]. These works also include metrics for further structural properties of service-oriented systems, such as size and complexity. Other structural aspects addressed include, for instance service granularity [271], or reusability and composability [272]. The common ground the metrics presented in this thesis share with the above metric frameworks is that computation takes place based on structural properties of a given application. When it comes to external metrics in SOA, the by far most frequent target of study are performance-related characteristics. The specification of performance guarantees in service-level agreements is important in SOA. To verify if service providers fulfill the level of quality of service that they have guaranteed, it is necessary to monitor service performance and compute related metrics [273]. Performance characteristics that are frequently considered are latency, throughput, or the resource consumption in terms of memory and processing power required by a service. Examples of studies that use such performance-related metrics are, for instance, [274–276], as well as the performance benchmarking approaches discussed in Sect. 8.3.

The dichotomy of structural metrics primarily focused on maintainability and complexity on the one hand, and external metrics primarily focused on performance on the other hand, can also be found for process-aware information

Metrics in PAIS systems. An overview of the usage of metrics in business process modeling and execution is given in [277]. Structural quality metrics for process models also build upon classical object-oriented metrics [204], focus on syntax- or semantics-related errors in a process model [278], relate to the static complexity of the model during design-time [279], or the dynamic complexity of process instances during run-time [205, 280]. Performance metrics for service-oriented software can easily be transferred to process-aware services, as further studies, apart from the ones already mentioned in the context of performance benchmarking, for instance, [281, 282], show. Since process modeling, especially for non-executable models, is a human-intense task, the measurement of related quality characteristics, such as understandability and comprehensibility [133, 283] has been addressed as well.

8.5. Related Work on Portability Measurement

As discussed in Chap. 4, portability is commonly measured as the relation between the cost of porting a software product and the cost of rewriting it from scratch. Notable quality models [54, 55] indicate that this cost can be computed in terms of program size, i. e., by relating portable to nonportable lines of code. Also the respective ISO/IEC standards [209, 210] measure portability with a single metric based on standard conformance. This metric contrasts the amount of items that conform to a standard to the amount of items that require standard conformance. In Chap. 4, we built upon these approaches.

Related measurement techniques Apart from the notion described above and used in this thesis, there is little work on quantifying portability. For instance, [284] uses a similar definition of a degree of portability as done here. However, the author recommends computing the cost of porting and the cost of rewriting based on a number of further cost functions, instead of lines of code. For example, the cost of porting in [284] is defined as the sum of the cost for manual modification, the cost of testing and debugging, and the cost of documentation. However, [284] does not prescribe how the latter cost functions should be computed based on a software product, but uses cost estimates from domain experts. A more recent work on portability measurement is [285]. This work proposes a portability coefficient based on the size of a software product in terms of the number of its components. This number is combined with the number of external interactions of the program during execution. As before, the result is contrasted for the reference system and the new system to obtain the coefficient. Whereas these approaches are defined on a generic software product level, to the best of our knowledge, there is no study that operationalizes portability measurement for service-oriented or process-aware software in detail. Furthermore, there is no work that supports an automated calculation of portability based on source code, instead of manually established estimates by domain experts.

Application migration Recently, software portability is shifting more into the focus of research in distributed systems, in particular for cloud environments [46]. The reason for this is that applications are increasingly deployed to infrastructure- or platform-as-a-service environments to leverage performance or cost benefits. This trend introduces new platform dependencies and potentials for vendor lock-in. A high degree of application portability can protect from this lock-in effect. Research on portability in cloud environments is still in its early stages [32, 33, 286]. So far, portability of cloud applications has not been measured in terms of a degree or coefficient of portability inherent to an application, as done in this thesis. Rather, the value of porting is quantified by comparing operational costs or application performance before and after an application migration. Examples of such studies are [287–289].

8.6. Related Work on Installability Measurement

In this work, we adopt the SQuaRE definition of installability. This means, we consider installability as the effectiveness and efficiency with which a software product can be installed in a given environment. Corresponding metrics from existing ISO/IEC standards [209, 210] have already been discussed in Chap. 5. However, alternative notions for installability, and the related characteristic deployability, exist.

Installability need not necessarily be viewed as an inherent property of a software product. As an alternative, it can be considered as the ability to install *Co-existence* several software products next to each other in the same environment, as done in [290, 291]. Component-, or package-based software systems, such as most Linux distributions, are built from package repositories. A software product that is installed into the system might require other packages in particular versions to be installed as well. These package versions can conflict with the versions required by other software products, resulting in a failure of the installation. This property is also covered in the SQuaRE model, but there it is denoted as *co-existence* [53, p. 11], a subcharacteristic of the quality characteristic of compatibility.

We consider deployability as the ease with which an application can be deployed *Deploya-bility* onto a middleware product. In contrast, the characteristic can also be seen as the cost of the deployment of an application onto the nodes of a network. In this setting, the cost of deployment is dependent on the amount or positioning of the nodes in the network on which an application has to be deployed to function properly [292, Sect. 2.6]. This interpretation of deployability is important in large scale IoT systems [293]. Here, we do not consider the network-wide deployment of an application, but instead the ease of deploying it on a single host. This view is orthogonal to a network-wide deployment and our framework could be combined with such an approach. When it comes to the quality characteristic of deployability in the sense of the work at hand, recent work [294] suggests practices for enabling deployability, but without defining concrete metrics. Finally, a software development process-oriented view and quantification of deployability is to consider it as the duration of the release cycles of a software product [295].

An alternative to automated measurement that has also been used for measuring *Installa-bility* installability, deployability, and, in particular, usability in different domains is a *measure-ment* heuristic evaluation or cognitive walkthrough [211]. As discussed in Sect. 5.1.1, using these methods, a user steps through a procedure, such as an installation, and judges its appropriateness for the task at hand. These techniques are especially useful for the evaluation of user interfaces [211]. In [296], they are also used to analyze the installability and deployability of an application for anonymous web browsing. In this work, we use heuristic evaluation to quantify the complexity of an installation procedure, but we evaluate installation scripts instead of user interfaces.

8.7. Related Work on Adaptability Measurement

Adaptability, as it is addressed in Chap. 6, is defined as the degree to which a software product can effectively and efficiently be adapted for different or evolving execution environments. Our focus lies on structural adaptions to a software product that are made at design-time, such as the change of a process model to enable its execution on a different engine. This opposes other common definitions of adaptability, which are discussed in the following.

Adapter synthesis   A number of studies in the field of SOA deals with the topic of adapter synthesis, e. g., [297–299], which resolves to an application integration problem [75]. In a distributed setting, two service-oriented and process-aware applications might need to interact with each other to achieve a desired goal. This can be challenging, if the message signatures or message transmission sequences expected by the two applications do not fit together. Adapter synthesis targets the automatic generation of an adapter that mediates message sequences between the two applications to enable their interoperation. In this context, adaptability refers to the ability to generate such an adapter.

Autonomous systems   Another area, where adaptability is of high importance, is autonomous systems [213]. There, adaptability refers to the ability of an application to change its structure at run-time to cope with changing requirements, such as a different load. In the area of cloud computing, this property is also referred to as elasticity [300]. In the context of service-oriented or process-aware systems, this kind of adaption typically takes place at the level of a service instance or activity and is called service rebinding. For instance, an application may dynamically change a service provider it invokes at run-time, i. e., it may rebind the service to another provider, and try to select a provider that offers the best quality of service [301]. The difficulty here lies in the appropriate specification of quality requirements as the basis for service selection and the determination of an optimal service provider based on these requirements. Approaches that focus on this kind of adaptability can, for instance, be found in [301–303]. The problem is also addressed by cloud process engines, for which it is necessary to decide where service instances should be placed [304]. We have to emphasize that the focus of this work lies on structural design-time adaptability and not on run-time adaptability or elasticity.

Structural adaption and measurement   When it comes to the enablement of structural design-time adaptions, a common approach is to parameterize an application at design-time. At run-time, parameterized parts can be exchanged and modified with predefined variations, thus making an application more flexible and adaptable. To this end, aspect-oriented programming concepts are applied and examples of such approaches are [305, 306]. Furthermore, features that increase the adaptability of process-aware systems have been captured in change patterns [307]. However, the measurement and quantification of the structural design-time adaptability inherent to a software product is less frequently addressed. Adaptability metrics defined in the ISO/IEC standards [209, 210] focus predominantly on the observation of user behavior in response to changes in an application, for instance, to see if users can adapt easily to a new software environment. This contrasts our use case, which concerns how easily a process model implemented in a specification language can be changed, in a way that still complies to the specification, to enable it to run on a different implementation of the specification. As discussed in Chap. 6, related studies that measure design-time adaptability [214, 215] do so at the architectural level. They provide an adaptability score at the level of atomic system elements and aggregate this score to a global degree of adaptability. In similar work [308], the authors define numerous metrics for measuring run-time adaptivity, but their metrics suite also includes structural and architectural adaptability metrics. Like in the studies mentioned before, these metrics depend on the identification of adaptable or adaptive program elements, which are aggregated to several adaptability indices for the complete application. This is also the path we take in this thesis.

8.8. Related Work on Replaceability Measurement

As discussed in Chap. 7, replaceability refers to the degree to which a software product can replace another software product in the same environment. As such, it corresponds to the notion of similarity. Existing replaceability or similarity metrics have already been reviewed in Chap. 7. This section elaborates on additional notions that are related to replaceability. Moreover, it discusses approaches for the evaluation of node mapping functions.

Several notions used in the literature can be considered to bear a similar *Related* meaning as replaceability or similarity. These are substitutability [309], bi- *notions* simulation [310], or equivalence [311]. Substitutability refers to the ability of one service to fully replace, i. e., to substitute, another service. Hence, substitutability has a boolean value. Conceptually, if the replaceability of two services is equal to one, they are substitutable. Bi-simulation is a consistency relation among two process-aware and service-oriented applications and concerns their communication relations. Two applications bi-simulate each other if they provide the same communication behavior from an external point of view. The inner structure and the control-flow graph of the applications may be vastly different, as long as the observed behavior is identical. Finally, equivalence in process-aware services is introduced in [311] as a multifaceted aspect. It is used to refer to the invocation of similar, i. e., equivalent, services in an application. Equivalence consists of three different equivalence properties. These are i) label equivalence, which refers to the similarity of the labels used in the two services, ii) attribute equivalence, which corresponds to similarity in context, such as input or output parameters of two services, and iii) position equivalence, which refers to the position of their invocation in the control-flow graph of an application.

Work on node mapping As discussed in Chap. 7, a crucial basis for a replaceability computation is the node mapping function that determines corresponding nodes in two process models. It could be seen in the chapter that a suitable mapping function depends on the application domain and may render given similarity metrics more or less suitable for a domain. Recent work [226, 242, 312] shifts the interest from the definition of new similarity metrics to the evaluation of node mapping functions and the prediction of their quality. Mapping functions are evaluated in terms of precision and recall, by observing to what degree the outcome of the mapping function corresponds to human judgment. A considerable hinder to these evaluation approaches, and the evaluation performed in this thesis, is the unavailability of a sufficiently large corpus of process models that can be used as a benchmark for similarity metrics and mapping functions. Recent initiatives try to establish such process corpora [312, 313]. However, a universally accepted corpus for similarity metric and node mapping function evaluation is not yet available.

9. Summary and Conclusion

This final chapter completes the thesis and reflects on the main contributions and findings. We begin by summarizing the contributions presented throughout the dissertation in Sect. 9.1. This is followed by an overview of the limitations of the work and a discussion of selected aspects that offer promising areas of future work in Sect. 9.2. Finally, Sect. 9.3 ends the thesis with concluding remarks.

9.1. Summary of Contributions

This thesis revolved around two research objectives, proposed in Sect. 1.1. The first research objective centered on the investigation of standard-conformance induced portability issues that exist in service-oriented and process-aware software. The second research objective concerned the design and evaluation of a software measurement framework for quantifying portability. These two objectives have been captured by two central research questions, which were split up into a number of subquestions. The subquestions have been answered throughout the main part of the thesis. In the following, we summarize the answers to these questions and the central contributions made.

9.1.1. Evidence for Portability Issues

The first research question addressed the current state of the portability of service-oriented and process-aware software. This question was split into research question 1.1, regarding the sufficiency of contemporary standards and their implementations for enabling application portability, and research question 1.2, regarding the nature of existing portability issues and their implications.

As discussed in Sect. 2.3.3, a core driver and prerequisite for enabling appli- *Confor-* cation portability is the standard conformance of process engines, which is also *mance* called implementation conformance. Process engines that conform to a standard *bench-* enable the execution of applications that are implemented in that standard. *mark* Consequently, a comprehensive standard conformance benchmark of multiple process engines, presented in Chap. 3, formed the basis for answering the research questions. In Sect. 3.1, we outlined the requirements for such a benchmark, being accessibility, affordability, clarity, relevance, solvability, portability, and scalability, and explained how the benchmark addresses them. This was followed by a description of the benchmark design in Sect. 3.2. The benchmarking methodology was detailed through a domain model that allows to specify test suites of standard conformance tests. Moreover, the execution of the benchmark was implemented in a fully automated benchmarking tool, called betsy. This tool enables the isolated testing and evaluation of process engines. A central advantage of the benchmark is that it works similarly, regardless of the actual standard for which standard conformance is evaluated and regardless of a concrete engine that is being evaluated. As a consequence, it is possible to extend the benchmarking methodology and tool with support for additional standards and engines. The fact that the benchmark in this work includes multiple engines and different standards demonstrates this extensibility. We implemented the benchmark for the two process standards, BPMN 2.0.2 [26] and BPEL 2.0 [27]. The final benchmark data encompasses the evaluation of a total of eleven process engines that claim to support either of these standards. The core of the benchmark are three test suites, which are used to evaluate process engines. Two of these test suites support the benchmarking of BPEL engines and one is tailored to BPMN engines. The test suite for BPMN engines and one of the test suites for BPEL engines cover standard conformance. They comprise tests for asserting the correct implementation of the features that are required for building executable process models, as defined in the respective standards. The implementation of each conformance test is aimed at minimality and feature isolation. For BPEL, there is a second test suite that consists of implementations of workflow control-flow patterns [71]. The purpose of this test suite is to evaluate support in process engines for realistic usage scenarios. Moreover, the pattern test suite enables the investigation of dependencies among portability issues that may arise when combining language features.

Insuffi-ciency of standards When it comes to research question 1.1, regarding the sufficiency of standards and their implementations for enabling application portability, the data that resulted from the benchmark showed that contemporary standards and their implementations do not reach this aim. These results were presented in Sect. 3.3. Only a minority of the language features that are required to be supported by a conforming implementation of the respective standard were supported by all, or nearly all, engines under test. This observation holds for BPEL engines and BPMN engines alike. None of the two standards was able to secure broad support of its feature set in practice. Thus, both standards failed their standardization target. In both cases, only a subset of the language features are actually implemented in most engines and can be considered as portable. This subset is limited to the most basic language elements, such as support for sequential activity instance execution and conditional control-flow branching. More advanced features, most notably truly parallel activity instance execution, are rarely supported. As a consequence, application portability cannot be guaranteed, even for applications that are intended to be portable by being implemented in conformance to a standard.

Implica-tions of porta-bility issues From these results, a number of implications follow, which regard research question 1.2. To build portable service-oriented and process-aware applications, it is necessary to limit an application to the most basic feature set of a language standard. This is a problem, since several of the more advanced features, such as truly parallel activity instance execution or compensation, are indispensable for implementing certain types of use cases. Nevertheless, the evaluation of the second test suite for BPEL, the workflow control-flow patterns test suite, showed that several realistic application scenarios can still be expected to be implementable in a portable fashion. Even engines with only a moderate degree of standard conformance were able to support a majority of the usage scenarios that are captured by the workflow control-flow patterns. However, the lack of truly parallel activity instance execution is clearly an inhibiting factor. Besides, the evaluation of workflow pattern support did not uncover portability issues that were triggered by the combination of language features. A lack of support for a particular pattern could always be traced back to a singular standard conformance issue in an engine.

As a summary, these contributions could be used to frame an answer to research question 1. *The portability of service-oriented and process-aware software based on language standards is clearly problematic, because the degree of standard conformance in contemporary engines is limited.* Neither of the two standards fulfills its goal of defining *"a portable execution format for business processes"* (BPEL) [27, p. 7], or enabling the *"portability of Process definitions"* (BPMN) [26, p. 20]. As a consequence, the assessment of the portability of existing applications, as a means of improving their portability, could be confirmed as a relevant research goal. This motivated the second research objective of this thesis. *Summary*

9.1.2. Measurement Framework for Portability

The second research objective targeted the design and evaluation of a measurement framework for portability. In Sect. 2.3.2, the ISO/IEC SQuaRE model for software quality was selected as theoretical basis for this measurement framework, because it can be considered as one of the most important quality models today. The model defines portability as one of eight major software quality characteristics. Furthermore, it defines three subcharacteristics of portability, being installability, adaptability, and replaceability. As a consequence, the measurement and assessment of portability and its subcharacteristics were addressed by a separate research question each. Moreover, each characteristic was the topic of a separate chapter of Part II.

The analysis of each quality characteristic started with a discussion of its nature and an explanation of how the characteristic is commonly measured. This was followed by the formal definition of a set of metrics that capture the characteristic for service-oriented and process-aware software. Subsequently, each set of metrics was validated theoretically with two validation frameworks. On the one hand, a formal validation framework was used to address the measurement-theoretic properties of the metrics. On the other hand, an informal validation framework was applied to enhance the definition of the metrics and to clarify their relationship to the characteristic they are intended to measure. This was followed by a practical evaluation of the metrics. First, the goal of the evaluation and experimental hypotheses were stated. Second, a large set of real-world applications were gathered from public open source software repositories. Third, the metrics computation was implemented in a prototypic metrics suite, called *Metric derivation and evaluation* prope. Fourth, using the metrics suite, metric values were computed for the gathered applications. Based on this data, we could perform a variety of statistical tests to verify a number of quality properties of the metrics and could evaluate the experimental hypotheses. The quality properties included, for instance, the discriminative power of the metrics, their stability, or their relation to application size. In parts, this analysis allowed us to recommend a subset of the proposed metrics for practical usage.

Porta-
bility   Portability was discussed in Chap. 4. In the context of this thesis, portability was defined as the degree of effectiveness and efficiency with which an executable process model can be transferred from one process engine to another, without the need for modification. Four different metrics were proposed to measure this characteristic: i) a basic portability metric, used as a means of comparison, ii) a weighted elements portability metric that takes all elements of a process model into account, iii) an activity portability metric that reduces the focus of measurement to the nodes of a process model, and iv) a service communication portability metric that reduces the focus of measurement to the nodes relevant to service interaction. The computation of the metrics relies on a degree of severity with respect to portability for every language element. This degree is computed based on the relative support of a language element in process engines. The data necessary for this computation was provided by the engine benchmarks described in Chap. 3. Introducing this data into the metrics computation improves the practical relevance of the resulting metric values. From a measurement-theoretic point of view, the metrics can be considered as normalized complexity metrics or densities of complexity. They satisfy the properties of non-negativity, null value, symmetry, and monotonicity. Due to their normalization with respect to application size, they fail to satisfy additivity. The metrics are direct and internal, are obtained by counting issues in code, and have an interval scale. The practical evaluation was performed on the basis of more than 1600 BPEL process models and provided several insights: First, it showed that the metrics and their mechanism of computation is stable, since repeated executions of the evaluation based on modified data yielded similar results. Second, the metrics have been found to carry diverse information, as there was only a moderate correlation among their values for the data at hand. Third, the evaluation showed that the inclusion of engine support data in the computation improves the discriminative power of the metrics in comparison to the basic way of computation. Fourth, it could be seen that the metrics cannot be used to compare process models of arbitrarily different size, which is usual for complexity metrics. Finally, we found that the portability of the gathered process models was relatively high, despite the limited degree of standard conformance in engines. This finding could be attributed to the fact that only a moderate part of the language is actually used in practice.

Installa-
bility   The topic of Chap. 5 was the quality characteristic of installability. Installability was defined as the effectiveness and efficiency with which a software system can be installed. In the context of this thesis, the quality characteristic was subdivided into two further subcharacteristics. These were the installability

of the process engine and the deployability of an application onto the engine. Several metrics for assessing each of the subcharacteristics were proposed and defined formally. Engine installability was addressed by considering the duration of the installation, the amount of steps required for the installation, and the reliability of the installation routine. Deployability was assessed through the size of the different deployment artifacts and the flexibility of the deployment. The theoretical evaluation showed that nearly all metrics are size metrics and satisfy the necessary properties of non-negativity, null value, and additivity. Proposed size metrics are internal, whereas metrics related to installation duration are external. The metrics are computed either by counting, matching, or timing and are defined on an interval or on a ratio scale. In the practical evaluation, the engine installability of six BPEL engines was evaluated based on data from 150 installation runs. Moreover, the evaluation included the assessment of the deployability of almost 40 applications to said engines, and the assessment of an external process library coming from an engine vendor. This showed that installability and deployability metrics alike can be used for ranking and comparing engines, as well as single applications. It could be demonstrated that the average installation time allows for a meaningful interpretation, despite being an average value. Moreover, a linear relationship between the number of services involved in an application and its deployability could be determined.

In Chap. 6, the quality characteristic of adaptability was discussed. Adaptability refers to the degree with which an application can effectively and efficiently be adapted for different process engines at design-time. The proposed metrics assess adaptability by considering the amount of alternative representations for every language element that exist in a process language. The more alternatives that are available for a language element, the more adaptable it can be considered. Consequently, the adaptability of an application can be assessed by computing the average adaptability of all language elements the application is made up of. A binary metric, which is configurable with a threshold, and a weighted metric were proposed and formally defined to capture this notion. Similar to the metrics for assessing portability, the adaptability metrics can be considered as internal complexity metrics. As such, they fulfill the same measurement-theoretic properties, are also defined on an interval scale, and are computed through counting. To evaluate the metrics practically, almost three thousand BPMN process models were gathered from public open source software repositories. The occurrence frequency of process elements in the gathered process models showed that only a small part of the vocabulary of BPMN is used in practice. As such, this result was similar to the observation made for the usage of the vocabulary of BPEL in the context of the evaluation of portability metrics. The observed occurrence frequency of process elements was used to refine the metrics computation. The subsequent analysis of the discriminative power of the metrics showed that the weighted adaptability metric and the binary adaptability metric, with a threshold set at 60%, perform best. Furthermore, the weighted adaptability metric was also found to allow for the meaningful comparison of process models of different size. A repeated execution of the complete evaluation based on data gathered

Adapt-ability

several months later confirmed that the mechanism of computation is stable.

Replace-
ability
The final quality characteristic, addressed in Chap. 7, was replaceability. Replaceability captures the degree to which an application can replace another application in the same environment. As such, its assessment requires a paired comparison of two applications. Moreover, this assessment boils down to an assessment of similarity, because similar applications can more easily be used to replace each other. When it comes to process model similarity, a large body of metrics does already exist. For this reason, the evaluation of replaceability metrics differed from the evaluation of the other quality characteristics. Instead of proposing new metrics, several existing metrics were selected based on a relevance and suitability assessment. Thereafter, an extension for these metrics was proposed and evaluated. Existing metrics can be classified as either labeling, structural, or behavioral metrics and are computed on the basis of the distance between objects. The distance function fulfills the properties of symmetry, non-negativity, identity, and triangle inequality. Ultimately, the metrics TAR-similarity and causal behavioral profiles were selected based on their target application area and practical properties. For the application of these metrics, a proper node matching function was required. Such a function was defined based on the notion of alternative representations for process elements stemming from the adaptability metrics proposed in Chap. 6. A practical evaluation based on several synthetic process models showed that TAR-similarity is best suited for evaluating replaceability in the context of this work.

Summary
Each study, discussed above, answers its associated research question, regarding the identification of suitable metrics for measuring a particular software quality characteristic. In combination, the studies allow to frame a concluding answer to research question 2: *It is feasible to measure the portability of service-oriented and process-aware software. The framework presented in this thesis can be considered as one way to achieve this task.* All metrics proposed have been theoretically validated. An implementation and automated computation of nearly all metrics that enables the evaluation of thousands of applications was possible. Finally, the comprehensive practical experiments emphasize the practical suitability of the metrics and the feasibility of their application. Using this framework, the portability of service-oriented and process-aware software can be made visible. Ultimately, this visibility is necessary to improve application portability.

9.2. Limitations and Open Problems

Scientific work is hardly ever fully complete without limitations and areas that deserve further investigation. Of course, this restriction also applies to this thesis. Many of the limitations of the work at hand have been discussed throughout the different chapters. For instance, there are more process languages that could be considered and also more process engines that could be evaluated in a standard conformance benchmark. Moreover, the metrics proposed for measuring associated quality characteristics should not be viewed as a final say. Different mechanisms of computation are possible and have been indicated in the design decisions discussed. Future work may show that there are more suitable or more efficient ways of assessing application portability. Whereas we have broached these issues throughout the thesis, this section addresses several limitations that have not yet been sufficiently discussed. At least as importantly, we consider these limitations as promising sources of future work.

The first aspect discussed in the following subsection is the combination and ranking of the metrics. The second one, discussed in Sect. 9.2.2, concerns effort prediction for application porting and migration. Finally, Sect. 9.2.3 concerns the investigation of the practical usage of process languages.

9.2.1. Metrics Combination and Ranking

In this thesis, we defined a measurement framework that consists of metrics for assessing four different quality characteristics. Each set of metrics addresses one characteristic and helps in decision making during application migration, as outlined in Sect. 2.3.2. Hence, the framework is beneficial and can be applied in its current form. Still, the amount of metrics is high and the metrics are defined at a quite fine-granular level, for instance at the level of process elements. For this reason, it would be helpful to offer a way to compose or aggregate all metrics to a global portability indicator that can be interpreted based on a single value [314].

A variety of options exists for performing a metrics aggregation [315]. These range from simple statistical measures, such as mean or median values, to more sophisticated statistical techniques, such as distribution fitting [316] or inequality indices like the Gini [317] or Atkinson [318] index. A central issue with metric aggregation techniques is that the importance of individual metrics can vary strongly depending on the requirements of a concrete project. Hence, it is difficult to provide a universally acceptable aggregation for a metrics framework. Since individual metrics essentially translate to quality requirements for a software project, it is possible to apply requirements prioritization techniques for building an aggregation, as was done in similar work [278]. Among existing prioritization techniques, the *analytic hierarchy process* [319] has been identified as particularly useful [320]. Thus, the application of the analytic hierarchy process to our metrics framework seems to be a promising area of future work.

The analytic hierarchy process [319] builds on a pair-wise comparison of all requirements, in our case of all metrics. Decision makers compare each pair of requirements and decide which one is more important for the project at hand, using a scale of different levels of importance. The results of the choices of multiple decision makers for a pair of requirements can be merged by computing the arithmetic mean of the importance relations. This pair-wise comparison is performed for every level of the hierarchy of requirements, i.e., for the quality characteristics and the metrics. The relative priorities of each hierarchy level are propagated down to the lower levels. This means that if a top-level requirement is found to be more important, an example could be that installability is considered more important than adaptability, also the lower-level requirements, i.e., the metrics for installability, have a higher impact on the aggregation. To provide a general indication for a suitable aggregation of the metrics presented here, it would be possible to perform a survey among domain experts. A questionnaire could be used to table the metrics pair-wise and domain experts could use this questionnaire to perform the ranking. Consequently, the meaningfulness of the results of such a study depends on the availability of a sufficiently large set of domain experts that are able to compare the proposed metrics.

9.2.2. Effort Prediction

As stated in Sect. 2.4, the goal of the metrics in this thesis is quality measurement and assessment. Based on quality assessment, a second common target of software metrics is quality or effort prediction [47]. More recently, also the prediction of technical debt [161] is gaining traction. In that sense, the thesis lays the foundation for further work on predicting the effort associated with porting or migrating software.

There are several ways to approach effort estimation. For instance, in [321], Sun and Li present an effort estimation approach for cloud application migration that can directly be applied in our setting. To estimate the effort required for a migration project, the authors propose to estimate the effort for the different phases of performing an application migration separately and to sum up the results. For determining the effort associated with an individual phase, two central ingredients are required. Firstly, these are structural properties of the application, such as the size of the artifacts to be migrated. This corresponds to the metrics proposed in this work, which mostly relate to structural properties of an application. Secondly, the size and skills of the team that performs the migration is taken into account. Each person is ranked by her skills and each skill rank is associated with a weighting factor which influences the estimated effort. For instance, an expert is considered to have a high success probability for a given task, whereas a novice is considered to have a low success probability. The consideration of skill is orthogonal to the metrics presented in this thesis. More precisely, the metrics can be used to characterize the size of the artifacts to be migrated and the likelihood of a successful porting or adaptation, whereas skill factors could be used to translate metric values into effort estimates.

A second way to estimate effort could be operationalized similar to the methods applied in well-known industry effort estimation models, such as COCOMO2 [322]. This model comes in various flavors and is applicable at different stages of development. Most close to our use case is the so-called post-architecture model, which concerns development and maintenance effort for a software product [323]. Similar to the approach from [321], effort or cost is estimated based on the structural properties of the software product and several weighting factors or cost drivers that influence the resulting effort estimates. The size of the system is measured in lines of code or function points and takes adaptions and reuse into account. As before, this is close to the metrics presented here, which largely base on application size or process elements. Hence, the metrics seem applicable as an input to the post-architecture model. The weighting factors for estimating effort stem from a database of previous projects and their de facto effort. This is one of the primary reasons for the industry acceptance of COCOMO2. As such, it is also a major challenge for effort prediction based on our metrics. The project database that underlies COCOMO2 builds on projects that have been executed during the 1990s. These projects did not apply the principles of service-orientation or process-awareness, but relied on development methodologies and technologies that were available at that time. It is not clear if the relation among size and effort is the same for these projects, as opposed to projects that build service-oriented and process-aware software. Hence, a new project database is needed for meaningfully estimating effort values. Such data would need to be gathered in a series of industry projects that perform a migration of a process-aware and service-oriented application. A lack of access to such projects could be compensated for, to a limited degree, using student projects at a university. For instance, a representative amount of skilled students could perform the migration of a set of applications and the effort required could be correlated with the metric values for the applications. The problem with this approach is that studies based on student projects can never fully be used as representative for real industry projects. Hence, observing the effort required in industry projects and the relation to our metrics forms a promising, but also quite challenging, area of future work.

9.2.3. Practical Usage of Process Languages

In this thesis, we evaluated application portability based on standard conformance. A major finding of the conformance benchmark presented in Chap. 3 was that a large part of the respective languages and many of the more advanced language features are rarely supported by their implementations. As a result, a low degree of portability could be expected in realistic applications. Nevertheless, during the practical evaluation of the portability metrics in Sect. 4.4, average portability values of real-world applications were still relatively high. This can be attributed to the fact that many of the advanced features of a process language are used very seldom in practice. Such a restricted language usage has already been indicated by earlier work [202]. The analysis of the usage of BPMN elements as part of the practical evaluation of adaptability metrics in Sect. 6.3 reinstates these findings.

These research results question the suitability of the vocabulary provided by contemporary process languages. It seems that many of the features that are required to be implemented by an engine might not actually be needed in practice. Unfortunately, it is not entirely clear if these features are not used, because they are not needed, or because they are not properly implemented. To gain more insights on this aspect, more work, especially of empirical kind, that analyses realistic and industry scale process models is required. Much of the established work on the necessary features of process languages, such as the workflow patterns [71], bases the relevance of features solely on theoretical argumentation or the claims of its authors. This is problematic. As discussed by

Börger [145], workflow patterns and also a large part of BPMN lack empirical evidence of their relevance. If many of the features in contemporary languages are irrelevant from a practical point of view, their importance to portability is also reduced. The metrics proposed here already take this into account, since only language elements that are actually used in an application do influence the resulting metric value. Nevertheless, if fewer language features would be required to be implemented in a process engine, it would be easier for engine vendors to implement a larger part of the standard. As a result, it is likely that there would be a larger set of language features that are supported by a majority of engines. This in turn, would increase application portability. To summarize this section, more empirical work is needed to determine the actual functionality required in realistic service-oriented and process-aware applications.

9.3. Closing Remarks

This chapter tied together the central findings of this thesis and summarized the results. Both research objectives have been addressed by a number of comprehensive studies that advance the state of knowledge. Moreover, this chapter pointed out selected limitations of this work and discussed how these limitations can be leveraged as promising areas of future work.

Ultimately, this thesis demonstrates that software portability in contemporary distributed applications is a challenging and relevant topic. It shows that standards alone cannot be used as a free ticket for achieving application portability. Moreover, the research points out that portability is a multi-faceted aspect that is hard to pin down accurately. Nevertheless, there are also many directions from which application portability can be approached and improved. Given the recent surge of work on application portability in cloud environments, we hope that this thesis can serve to motivate further work and inform future researchers.

Bibliography

[1] G. Coulouris, J. Dollimore, T. Kindberg, and G. Blair, *Distributed Systems: Concepts and Design*, 5th ed. Addison-Wesley, 2012, ISBN: 978-0273760597, international edition. (Cited on page 3.)

[2] A. S. Tanenbaum and M. van Steen, *Distributed Systems: Principles and Paradigms*, 2nd ed. Prentice Hall, 2007, ISBN: 978-0132392273. (Cited on page 3.)

[3] M. van Steen, G. Pierre, and S. Voulgaris, "Challenges in very large distributed systems," *Internet Services and Applications*, vol. 3, no. 1, pp. 59–66, May 2012. (Cited on page 3.)

[4] M. Dumas, W. M. P. van der Aalst, and A. H. M. ter Hofstede, *Process-Aware Information Systems: Bridging People and Software Through Process Technology*. Wiley, 2005, ISBN: 978-0-471-66306-5. (Cited on pages 3, 4, 25, and 26.)

[5] M. P. Papazoglou and D. Georgakopoulos, "Service-oriented Computing," *Communications of the ACM*, vol. 46, no. 10, pp. 24–28, October 2003. (Cited on pages 3, 4, 18, 19, 20, and 33.)

[6] M. Armbrust, A. Fox, R. Griffith, A. D. Joseph, R. H. Katz, A. Konwinski, G. Lee, D. A. Patterson, A. Rabkin, I. Stoica, and M. Zaharia, "A View of Cloud Computing," *Communications of the ACM*, vol. 53, no. 4, pp. 50–58, April 2010. (Cited on page 3.)

[7] L. Atzori, A. Iera, and G. Morabito, "The Internet of Things: A survey," *Computer Networks*, vol. 54, no. 15, 2010. (Cited on page 3.)

[8] P. A. Bernstein, "Middleware: A Model for Distributed System Services," *Communications of the ACM*, vol. 39, no. 2, 1996. (Cited on page 3.)

[9] D. Spinellis, "Portability: Goodies vs. the Hair Shirt," *IEEE Software*, vol. 30, no. 4, pp. 22–23, July/August 2013. (Cited on page 3.)

[10] S. Dustdar and M. Aiello, "Service Oriented Computing: Service Foundations," in *Service Oriented Computing*, ser. Dagstuhl Seminar Proceedings, no. 05462, Internationales Begegnungs- und Forschungszentrum für Informatik (IBFI), Schloss Dagstuhl, Germany, 2006. (Cited on pages 3 and 19.)

[11] SOA Manifesto Working Group, "SOA Manifesto," in *SOA Symposium*, Rotterdam, The Netherlands, October 2009. (Cited on pages 3 and 18.)

[12] M. A. Vouk, "Cloud Computing – Issues, Research and Implementations," *Journal of Computing and Information Technology*, vol. 16, no. 4, pp. 235–246, 2008. (Cited on page 3.)

[13] J. Hoppermann, P. D. Hamerman, and G. Lawrie, *The 10 Most Important Technology Trends in Business Application Architecture Today*, Forrester Research, 2013. (Cited on page 3.)

[14] Y. Wei and M. B. Blake, "Service-Oriented Computing and Cloud Computing: Challenges and Opportunities," *IEEE Internet Computing*, vol. 14, no. 6, 2010. (Cited on page 3.)

[15] M. Papazoglou, *Web Services: Principles and Technology*. Prentice Hall, 2007, ISBN: 978-0321155559. (Cited on pages 3, 11, 18, and 20.)

[16] R. T. Fielding, "Architectural Styles and the Design of Network-based Software Architectures," Ph.D. dissertation, University of California, Irvine, CA, USA, 2000. (Cited on pages 3, 11, 18, 20, and 22.)

[17] J. Lewis and M. Fowler, *Microservices*, March 2014, http://martinfowler.com/articles/microservices.html. (Cited on pages 3, 11, 18, 20, 23, 24, and 25.)

[18] M. P. Papazoglou, P. Traverso, S. Dustdar, and F. Leymann, "Service-Oriented Computing: State of the Art and Research Challenges," *IEEE Computer*, vol. 40, no. 11, pp. 38–45, November 2007. (Cited on page 4.)

[19] S. Dustdar and W. Schreiner, "A survey on web services composition," *International Journal of Web and Grid Services*, vol. 1, no. 1, pp. 1–30, August 2005. (Cited on pages 4, 17, 19, and 33.)

[20] M. Weske, *Business Process Management: Concepts, Languages, Architectures (Second Edition)*. Springer-Verlag, Berlin, Heidelberg, 2012, ISBN: 978-3642286155. (Cited on pages 4, 25, 26, 27, 28, 29, 33, and 34.)

[21] N. Russell, "Foundations of Process-Aware Information Systems," Ph.D. dissertation, Queensland University of Technology, June 2007. (Cited on pages 4 and 25.)

[22] M. Kohlbacher, "The effects of process orientation: a literature review," *Business Process Management Journal*, vol. 16, no. 1, pp. 135–152, 2010. (Cited on pages 4 and 26.)

[23] W. M. P. van der Aalst, "Business Process Management: A Comprehensive Survey," *ISRN Software Engineering*, pp. 1–37, 2013. (Cited on pages 4, 17, and 25.)

[24] W. M. P. van der Aalst and K. van Hee, *Workflow Management: Models, Methods, and Systems.* MIT Press, 2004, ISBN: 978-0262720465. (Cited on page 4.)

[25] H. Mili, G. Tremblay, G. B. Jaoude, E. Lefebvre, L. Elabed, and G. E. Boussaidi, "Business Process Modeling Languages: Sorting Through the Alphabet Soup," *ACM Computing Surveys*, vol. 43, no. 1, November 2010. (Cited on pages 4 and 179.)

[26] ISO/IEC, *ISO/IEC 19510:2013 – Information technology - Object Management Group Business Process Model and Notation*, November 2013, v2.0.2. (Cited on pages 4, 5, 11, 12, 20, 26, 28, 34, 35, 36, 37, 38, 39, 40, 52, 53, 61, 65, 68, 73, 78, 88, 152, 153, 179, 181, 192, and 193.)

[27] OASIS, *Web Services Business Process Execution Language*, April 2007, v2.0. (Cited on pages 4, 5, 11, 12, 20, 26, 28, 33, 34, 41, 42, 43, 53, 61, 65, 68, 76, 99, 179, 181, 192, and 193.)

[28] B. White, *Pro WF 4.5.* Apress, December 2012, ISBN-13: 978-1-4302-4383-0. (Cited on pages 4, 5, 179, and 180.)

[29] D. Rowley, "The Business of Application Portability," *ACM StandardView*, vol. 4, no. 2, pp. 80 –87, June 1996. (Cited on pages 4 and 52.)

[30] R. Khalaf, A. Keller, and F. Leymann, "Business processes for Web Services: Principles and applications," *IBM Systems Journal*, vol. 45, no. 2, pp. 425–446, 2006. (Cited on pages 4, 7, and 32.)

[31] WfMC, *Process Definition Interface – XML Process Definition Language*, August 2012, v2.2. (Cited on pages 4, 5, 27, 28, 179, and 180.)

[32] D. Petcu, G. Macariu, S. Panica, and C. Crǎciun, "Portable Cloud applications – From theory to practice," *Future Generation Computer Systems, Elsevier*, vol. 29, no. 6, pp. 1417–1430, August 2013. (Cited on pages 5 and 187.)

[33] S. Kolb and G. Wirtz, "Towards Application Portability in Platform as a Service," in *8th International IEEE Symposium on Service-Oriented System Engineering*, Oxford, UK, April 2014, pp. 218–229. (Cited on pages 5 and 187.)

[34] S. Qanbari, F. Li, and S. Dustdar, "Towards Portable Cloud Manufacturing Services," *IEEE Internet Computing*, vol. 18, no. 6, pp. 77–80, November/December 2014. (Cited on page 5.)

[35] P. Hoenisch, S. Schulte, S. Dustdar, and S. Venugopal, "Self-Adaptive Resource Allocation for Elastic Process Execution," in *IEEE Sixth International Conference on Cloud Computing*, Santa Clara, CA, USA, June 2013, pp. 220–227. (Cited on page 5.)

[36] OASIS, *Topology and Orchestration Specification for Cloud Applications Version 1.0*, November 2013. (Cited on page 5.)

[37] T. Binz, G. Breiter, F. Leymann, and T. Spatzier, "Portable Cloud Services Using TOSCA," *IEEE Internet Computing*, vol. 16, no. 3, pp. 80–85, 2012. (Cited on page 5.)

[38] C. Gutschier, R. Hoch, H. Kaindl, and R. Popp, "A Pitfall with BPMN Execution," in *Second International Conference on Building and Exploring Web Based Environments (WEB 2014)*, Charmonix, France, April 2014, pp. 7–13. (Cited on pages 5, 7, 52, 71, and 181.)

[39] A. Lapadula, R. Pugliese, and F. Tiezzi, "A Formal Account of WS-BPEL," in *10th International Conference on Coordination Models and Languages*, Oslo, Norway, June 4-6 2008, pp. 199–215. (Cited on pages 5, 7, 52, and 182.)

[40] DZone Research, *2014 Guide To Enterprise Integration*, 2014. (Cited on page 5.)

[41] W3C, *HTML5: A vocabulary and associated APIs for HTML and XHTML*, October 2014. (Cited on page 5.)

[42] ——, *Cascading Style Sheets Level 2 Revision 2 (CSS 2.2) Specification*, September 2014. (Cited on page 5.)

[43] S. R. Choudhary, H. Versee, and A. Orso, "WEBDIFF: Automated identification of cross-browser issues in web applications," in *26th IEEE International Conference on Software Maintenance*, Timisoara, Romania, September 2010. (Cited on page 5.)

[44] A. Mesbah and M. R. Prasad, "Automated Cross-Browser Compatibility Testing," in *33rd International Conference on Software Engineering*, Honolulu, Hawaii, USA, May 2011, pp. 561–570. (Cited on page 5.)

[45] S. R. Walli, "The myth of application source-code conformance," *ACM StandardView*, vol. 4, no. 2, pp. 94–99, 1996. (Cited on pages 5, 7, 52, and 65.)

[46] D. Petcu and A. V. Vasilakos, "Portability in clouds: approaches and research opportunities," *Scalable Computing: Practice and Experience*, vol. 15, no. 3, pp. 251–270, September 2014. (Cited on pages 5 and 186.)

[47] N. E. Fenton and S. L. Pfleeger, *Software Metrics: A Rigorous and Practical Approach*. PWS Publishing, 1997, ISBN: 0-534-95425-1. (Cited on pages 6, 54, and 198.)

[48] P. M. Duvall, S. Matyas, and A. Glover, *Continuous Integration: Improving Software Quality and Reducing Risk*. Addison-Wesley Professional, 2007, ISBN-13: 978-0321336385. (Cited on pages 6, 46, and 47.)

[49] P. Merson, A. Aguiar, E. Guerra, and J. Yoder, "Continuous Inspection: A Pattern for Keeping your Code Healthy and Aligned to the Architecture," in *3rd Asian Conference on Pattern Languages of Programs*, Tokyo, Japan, March 2014. (Cited on pages 6, 8, 46, and 47.)

[50] T. Dybå and T. Dingsøyr, "Empirical studies of agile software development: A systematic review," *Information and Software Technology*, vol. 50, no. 9–10, pp. 833–859, 2008. (Cited on pages 6 and 46.)

[51] D. Karlström and P. Runeson, "Combining Agile Methods with Stage-Gate Project Management," *IEEE Software*, vol. 22, no. 3, pp. 43–49, 2005. (Cited on pages 6 and 46.)

[52] M. Huo, J. M. Verner, L. Zhu, and M. A. Babar, "Software Quality and Agile Methods," in *28th International Computer Software and Applications Conference*, Hong Kong, China, December 2004, pp. 520–525. (Cited on pages 6 and 46.)

[53] ISO/IEC, *Systems and software engineering – System and software Quality Requirements and Evaluation (SQuaRE) – System and software quality models*, 2011, 25010:2011. (Cited on pages 6, 8, 11, 12, 45, 48, 49, 50, 51, 54, 98, 104, 125, 127, 143, 161, 162, and 187.)

[54] B. Boehm, J. Brown, and M. Lipow, "Quantitative Evaluation of Software Quality," in *2nd International Conference on Software Engineering*, San Francisco, USA, October 1976, pp. 592–605. (Cited on pages 6, 8, 48, 49, 98, 105, and 186.)

[55] T. Gilb, *Principles of Software Engineering Management*. Addison Wesley, 1988, ISBN-13: 978-0201192469. (Cited on pages 6, 8, 48, 49, 98, 105, and 186.)

[56] J. McCall, P. Richards, and G. Walters, "Factors in Software Quality – Concept and Definitions of Software Quality," General Electric Company, Sunnyvale, California, USA, Tech. Rep., 1977. (Cited on pages 6, 8, 48, 49, and 98.)

[57] ISO/IEC, *Software engineering – Product quality – Part 1: Quality model*, 2001, 9126-1:2001. (Cited on pages 6, 8, 48, 49, and 98.)

[58] ——, *Software engineering – Product quality* , 1991, 9126:1991. (Cited on pages 6, 8, 48, 49, and 98.)

[59] R. G. Dromey, "A Model for Software Product Quality," *IEEE Transactions on Software Engineering*, vol. 21, no. 2, pp. 146–162, February 1995. (Cited on pages 6, 8, 48, 49, and 98.)

[60] J.-L. Letouzey and M. Ilkiewicz, "Managing Technical Debt with the SQUALE Method," *IEEE Software*, vol. 29, no. 6, pp. 44–51, 2012. (Cited on pages 6, 48, and 49.)

[61] T. Hallwyl, F. Henglein, and T. Hildebrandt, "A standard-driven implementation of WS-BPEL 2.0," in *25th ACM Symposium on Applied Computing*, Sierre, Switzerland, March 2010, pp. 2472–2476. (Cited on pages 7, 182, and 183.)

[62] R. B. Grady, *Practical Software Metrics for Project Management and Process Improvement.* Prentice Hall, 1992, ISBN-13: 978-0137203840. (Cited on pages 8, 48, and 49.)

[63] D. Bianculli, W. Binder, and M. L. Drago, "Automated Performance Assessment for Service-Oriented Middleware: a Case Study on BPEL engines," in *19th International Conference on the World Wide Web*, Raleigh, North Carolina, USA, April 2010, pp. 141–150. (Cited on pages 8 and 184.)

[64] C. Röck, S. Harrer, and G. Wirtz, "Performance Benchmarking of BPEL Engines: A Comparison Framework, Status Quo Evaluation and Challenges," in *26th International Conference on Software Engineering and Knowledge Engineering*, Vancouver, Canada, July 2014. (Cited on pages 8 and 184.)

[65] M. Perepletchikov, C. Ryan, K. Frampton, and Z. Tari, "Coupling Metrics for Predicting Maintainability in Service-Oriented Designs," in *18th IEEE Australian Software Engineering Conference*, Melbourne, Australia, April 2007, pp. 329–340. (Cited on pages 8, 19, 55, and 185.)

[66] H. Hofmeister and G. Wirtz, "Supporting Service-Oriented Design with Metrics," in *Proceedings of the 12th International IEEE Enterprise Distributed Object Computing Conference*, Munich, Germany, September 2008, pp. 191–200. (Cited on pages 8, 19, 55, 109, 141, and 185.)

[67] L. Briand, S. Morasca, and V. Basili, "An Operational Process for Goal-Driven Definition of Measures," *IEEE Transactions on Software Engineering*, vol. 28, no. 12, pp. 1106–1125, 2002. (Cited on pages 11, 53, and 59.)

[68] V. R. Basili, G. Caldiera, and H. D. Rombach, "The Goal Question Metric Approach," *Encyclopedia of Software Engineering*, vol. 2, pp. 528–532, 1994. (Cited on pages 11 and 53.)

[69] L. Briand, S. Morasca, and V. Basili, "Property-based software engineering measurement," *IEEE Transactions on Software Engineering*, vol. 22, no. 1, pp. 68–86, 1996. (Cited on pages 12, 53, 55, 56, 57, 58, 109, 111, 112, 132, 133, 149, 150, and 163.)

[70] C. Kaner and W. Bond, "Software Engineering Metrics: What Do They Measure and How Do We Know?" in *10th International Software Metrics Symposium*, Chicago, USA, September 2004, pp. 1–12. (Cited on pages 12, 53, 55, 56, 59, 109, 110, 120, 132, 134, and 150.)

[71] W. M. P. van der Aalst, A. H. M. ter Hofstede, B. Kiepuszewski, and A. P. Barros, "Workflow Patterns," *Distributed and Parallel Databases, Springer*, vol. 14, no. 1, pp. 5–51, July 2003. (Cited on pages 12, 65, 66, 77, 103, 180, 192, and 199.)

[72] J. Lenhard and G. Wirtz, "Building Orchestrations in B2Bi – The Case of BPEL 2.0 and BPMN 2.0," in *4th Central-European Workshop on Services and their Composition (ZEUS)*, Bamberg, Germany, February 2012. (Cited on page 13.)

[73] S. Harrer and J. Lenhard, "Betsy – A BPEL Engine Test System," University of Bamberg, Bamberger Beiträge zur Wirtschaftsinformatik und Angewandten Informatik, no. 90, July 2012, technical report. (Cited on pages 13 and 65.)

[74] S. Harrer, J. Lenhard, and G. Wirtz, "BPEL Conformance in Open Source Engines," in *5th IEEE International Conference on Service-Oriented Computing and Applications*, Taipei, Taiwan, December 17-19 2012, pp. 237–244. (Cited on pages 13, 65, and 179.)

[75] S. Kolb, J. Lenhard, and G. Wirtz, "Bridging the Heterogeneity of Orchestrations - A Petri Net-based Integration of BPEL and Windows Workflow," in *5th IEEE International Conference on Service-Oriented Computing and Applications*, Taipei, Taiwan, December 17-19 2012. (Cited on pages 13 and 188.)

[76] J. Lenhard and G. Wirtz, "Detecting Portability Issues in Model-Driven BPEL Mappings," in *25th International Conference on Software Engineering and Knowledge Engineering*, Boston, Massachusetts, USA, June 2013, pp. 18–21. (Cited on pages 13 and 92.)

[77] ——, "Measuring the Portability of Executable Service-Oriented Processes," in *17th IEEE International Enterprise Distributed Object Computing Conference*, Vancouver, Canada, September 2013, pp. 117–126. (Cited on pages 13, 97, and 179.)

[78] S. Harrer, J. Lenhard, and G. Wirtz, "Open Source versus Proprietary Software in Service-Orientation: The Case of BPEL Engines," in *11th International Conference on Service Oriented Computing (ICSOC)*, Berlin, Germany, December 2-5 2013, pp. 99–113. (Cited on pages 13 and 65.)

[79] J. Lenhard, S. Harrer, and G. Wirtz, "Measuring the Installability of Service Orchestrations Using the SQuaRE Method," in *6th IEEE International Conference on Service-Oriented Computing and Applications*, Kauai, Hawaii, USA, December 16-18 2013, pp. 118–125. (Cited on pages 14, 125, and 179.)

[80] J. Lenhard, "Towards Quantifying the Adaptability of Executable BPMN Processes," in *6th Central-European Workshop on Services and their Composition*, Potsdam, Germany, February 2014, pp. 34–41. (Cited on pages 14, 31, 32, 143, and 179.)

[81] S. Harrer, J. Lenhard, G. Wirtz, and T. van Lessen, "Towards Uniform BPEL Engine Management in the Cloud," in *CloudCycle14 Workshop*. Stuttgart, Germany: Gesellschaft für Informatik e.V. (GI), September 2014, pp. 259–270. (Cited on page 14.)

[82] M. Geiger, S. Harrer, J. Lenhard, M. Casar, A. Vorndran, and G. Wirtz, "BPMN Conformance in Open Source Engines," in *9th International IEEE Symposium on Service-Oriented System Engineering (SOSE)*, San Francisco Bay, USA, March/April 2015. (Cited on pages 14 and 65.)

[83] J. Lenhard, M. Geiger, and G. Wirtz, "On the Measurement of Design-Time Adaptability for Process-Based Systems," in *9th International IEEE Symposium on Service-Oriented System Engineering (SOSE)*, San Francisco Bay, USA, March/April 2015. (Cited on pages 14, 143, and 179.)

[84] S. Kolb, J. Lenhard, and G. Wirtz, "Application Migration Effort in the Cloud – The Case of Cloud Platforms," in *8th IEEE International Conference on Cloud Computing (CLOUD)*, New York, USA, June/July 2015. (Cited on pages 14 and 136.)

[85] J. Lenhard, "Improving Process Portability through Metrics and Continuous Inspection," in *Advances in Intelligent Process-Aware Information Systems*, M. Reichert, R. Oberhauser, and G. Grambow, Eds. Springer-Verlag, Germany, 2016, to appear. (Cited on pages 14, 45, 143, 161, and 179.)

[86] C. Peltz, "Web Services Orchestration and Choreography," *IEEE Computer*, vol. 36, no. 10, pp. 46–52, October 2003. (Cited on pages 17, 19, 33, and 34.)

[87] M. P. Papazoglou, P. Traverso, S. Dustdar, and F. Leymann, "Service-Oriented Computing: A Research Roadmap," *International Journal of Cooperative Information Systems*, vol. 17, no. 2, pp. 223–255, 2008. (Cited on pages 18 and 33.)

[88] M. Perepletchikov, C. Ryan, K. Frampton, and H. Schmidt, "Formalising Service-Oriented Design," *Journal of Software*, vol. 3, no. 2, pp. 528–532, 2008. (Cited on page 18.)

[89] M. N. Huhns and M. P. Singh, "Service-Oriented Computing: Key Concepts and Principles," *IEEE Internet Computing*, vol. 9, no. 1, pp. 75–81, January/February 2005. (Cited on page 18.)

[90] W3C, *Web Services Architecture*, February 2004. (Cited on pages 18, 19, 20, and 21.)

[91] D. Karastoyanova and A. P. Buchmann, "Components, Middleware and Web Services," in *IADIS International Conference WWW/Internet*, Algarve, Portugal, November 2003, pp. 967–970. (Cited on page 18.)

[92] M. Stal, "Web Services: Beyond Component-Based Computing," *Communications of the ACM*, vol. 45, no. 10, pp. 71–76, October 2002. (Cited on page 18.)

[93] A. Becker, T. Widjaja, and P. Buxmann, "Value Potentials and Challenges of Service-Oriented Architectures," *Business & Information Systems Engineering*, vol. 3, no. 4, pp. 199–210, 2011. (Cited on page 18.)

[94] S. Kumar, V. Dakshinamoorth, and M. Krishnan, "Does SOA Improve the Supply Chain? An Empirical Analysis of the Impact of SOA Adoption on Electronic Supply Chain Performance," in *40th Hawaii International Conference on System Sciences*, Waikoloa, HI, USA, January 2007. (Cited on page 18.)

[95] H. Luthria and F. Rabhi, "Using Service Oriented Computing for Competitive Advantage," in *15th Americas Conference on Information Systems*, San Francisco, CA, USA, August 6-9 2009. (Cited on page 18.)

[96] T. Kaczmarek and K. Węcel, "Hype over Service Oriented Architecture Continues," *Wirtschaftsinformatik*, vol. 50, no. 11, pp. 52–59, 2008. (Cited on page 18.)

[97] C. Pautasso, O. Zimmermann, and F. Leymann, "RESTful Web Services vs. "Big" Web Services: Making the Right Architectural Decision," in *17th International World Wide Web Conference*, Beijing, Chaina, April 2008. (Cited on pages 18, 20, 21, 22, and 23.)

[98] N. Gold, A. Mohan, C. Knight, and M. Munro, "Understanding Service-Oriented Software," *IEEE Software*, vol. 21, no. 2, pp. 71–77, March/April 2004. (Cited on page 18.)

[99] OASIS, *Reference Models for Service Oriented Architecture 1.0*, August 2006. (Cited on page 18.)

[100] P. Offermann, M. Hoffmann, and U. Bub, "Benefits of SOA: Evaluation of an implemented scenario against alternative architectures," in *Workshops Proceedings of the 13th IEEE International Enterprise Distributed Object Computing Conference*, Auckland, New Zealand, September 1-4 2009, pp. 352–359. (Cited on page 18.)

[101] Z. Mahmood, "Service Oriented Architecture: Potential Benefits and Challenges," in *11th WSEAS International Conference on Computers*, Agios Nikolaos, Crete, Greece, July 2007. (Cited on page 18.)

[102] R. C. Martin, *Agile Software Development, Principles, Patterns, and Practices*. Prentice Hall, 2002, ISBN: 0-13-597444-5. (Cited on page 19.)

[103] S. Newman, *Building Microservices*, M. Loukides and B. MacDonald, Eds. O'Reilly Media, February 2015. (Cited on pages 20, 23, 24, 25, and 33.)

[104] A. Schönberger, C. Wilms, and G. Wirtz, "A Requirements Analysis of Business-to-Business Integration," Otto-Friedrich-Universität Bamberg, Bamberger Beiträge zur Wirtschaftsinformatik und Angewandten Informatik, Tech. Rep. 83, December 2009, iSSN 0937-3349. (Cited on page 21.)

[105] W3C, *Web Services Description Language (WSDL) 1.1*, March 2001. (Cited on pages 21 and 72.)

[106] ——, *Web Services Description Language (WSDL) Version 2.0 Part 1: Core Language*, June 2007. (Cited on pages 21 and 23.)

[107] ——, *Simple Object Access Protocol (SOAP) 1.1*, 2000. (Cited on page 21.)

[108] ——, *SOAP Version 1.2 Part 1: Messaging Framework (Second Edition)*, 2007. (Cited on page 21.)

[109] ——, *Extensible Markup Language (XML) 1.1 (Second Edition)*, August 2006. (Cited on page 21.)

[110] ——, *XML Schema Part 0: Primer Second Edition*, October 2004. (Cited on page 21.)

[111] ——, *Hypertext Transfer Protocol – HTTP/1.1*, June 1999. (Cited on page 22.)

[112] OASIS, *WS-Security Core Specification 1.1*, 2006. (Cited on page 22.)

[113] ——, *Web Services Reliable Messaging (WS-ReliableMessaging) Version 1.2*, February 2009. (Cited on page 22.)

[114] Open Grid Forum, *Web Services Agreement Specification (WS-Agreement*, March 2007. (Cited on page 22.)

[115] W3C, *Web Services Policy 1.5 - Framework*, September 2007. (Cited on page 22.)

[116] A. Schönberger, J. Schwalb, and G. Wirtz, "Interoperability and Functionality of WS-* Implementations," *International Journal of Web Services Research*, vol. 9, no. 3, pp. 1–22, 2012. (Cited on page 22.)

[117] E. Wilde and C. Pautasso, *REST: From Research to Practice*. Springer, August 2011, ISBN: 978-1441983022. (Cited on pages 22 and 23.)

[118] P. Adamczyk, P. H. Smith, R. E. Johnson, and M. Hafiz, *REST and Web Services: In Theory and in Practice*. Springer, 2011, REST: From Research to Practice, ISBN: 978-1441983022. (Cited on pages 22 and 23.)

[119] IETF, *Simple Mail Transfer Protocol*, October 2008. (Cited on page 23.)

[120] W3C, *Web Application Description Language (WADL)*, February 2009. (Cited on page 23.)

[121] IETF, *HTTP Over TLS*, May 2000. (Cited on page 23.)

[122] S. Soltesz, H. Pötzl, M. E. Fiuczynski, A. Bavier, and L. Peterson, "Container-based Operating System Virtualization: A Scalable, High-performance Alternative to Hypervisors," in *2nd EuroSys Conference*, Lisbon, Portugal, March 2007, pp. 275–287. (Cited on page 25.)

[123] M. Miglierina, "Application Deployment and Management in the Cloud," in *16th International Symposium on Symbolic and Numerical Algorithms for Scientific Computing*, Timisoara, Romania, September 22-25 2014, pp. 422–428. (Cited on page 25.)

[124] M. Loukides, *What is DevOps?* O'Reilly Media, 2012, ISBN: 1-4493-3910-7. (Cited on pages 25 and 51.)

[125] W. van der Aalst and K. van Hee, *Workflow Management: Models, Methods, and Systems.* The MIT Press, 2004, ISBN: 978-0262720465. (Cited on page 25.)

[126] J. vom Brocke and M. Rosemann, Eds., *Handbook on Business Process Management 1*, ser. International Handbooks on Information Systems. Springer-Verlag, Berlin, Heidelberg, 2015, ISBN: 978-3642450990. (Cited on page 25.)

[127] U. Zdun, C. Hentrich, and S. Dustdar, "Modeling Process-Driven and Service-Oriented Architectures Using Patterns and Pattern Primitives," *ACM Transactions on the Web*, vol. 1, no. 3, September 2007. (Cited on page 25.)

[128] W. M. P. van der Aalst, A. H. M. ter Hofstede, and M. Weske, "Business process management: A survey," in *International Conference on Business Process Management.* Eindhoven, The Netherlands: Springer Berlin Heidelberg, 2003. (Cited on page 25.)

[129] WfMC, *The Workflow Reference Model*, January 1995, v1.1. (Cited on pages 25, 26, 27, and 28.)

[130] C. Ouyang, M. Dumas, Wil M. P. van der Aalst, Arthur H. M. ter Hofstede, and J. Mendling, "From Business Process Models to Process-Oriented Software Systems," *ACM Transactions on Software Engineering and Methodology*, vol. 19, no. 2, 2009. (Cited on pages 25 and 92.)

[131] H. Schuster, D. Georgakopoulos, A. Cichocki, and D. Baker, "Modeling and Composing Service-Based and Reference Process-Based Multi-enterprise Processes," in *12th Conference on Advanced Information Systems Engineering*, Stockholm, Sweden, June 2000, pp. 247–263. (Cited on page 25.)

[132] H. Fernández Fernández, E. Palacios-González, V. García-Díaz, B. C. Pelayo G-Bustelo, O. Sanjuán Martínez, and J. M. Cueva Lovelle, "SBPMN – An

easier business process modeling notation for business users," *Computer Standards & Interfaces*, vol. 32, no. 1–2, pp. 18–28, 2010. (Cited on page 26.)

[133] H. A. Reijers and J. Mendling, "A Study into the Factors that Influence the Understandability of Business Process Models," *IEEE Transactions on Systems, Man and Cybernetics – Part A*, vol. 41, no. 3, pp. 449–462, 2011. (Cited on pages 26 and 186.)

[134] B. Myers, "Taxonomies of Visual Programming and Program Visualization," *Journal of Visual Languages and Computing*, vol. 1, no. 1, pp. 97–123, 1990. (Cited on page 27.)

[135] F. Leymann, "BPEL vs. BPMN 2.0: Should You Care?" in *2nd International Workshop on BPMN*, Potsdam, Germany, October 2010. (Cited on page 27.)

[136] S. Schulte, D. Schuller, P. Hoenisch, U. Lampe, R. Steinmetz, and S. Dustdar, "Cost-Driven Optimization of Cloud Resource Allocation for Elastic Processes," *International Journal of Cloud Computing*, vol. 1, no. 2, pp. 1–14, October–December 2013. (Cited on page 28.)

[137] D. Chappell, "The Workflow Way: Understanding Windows Workflow Foundation," Microsoft Corporation, Tech. Rep., April 2009. (Cited on page 28.)

[138] O. Kopp, D. Martin, D. Wutke, and F. Leymann, "The Difference Between Graph-Based and Block-Structured Business Process Modelling Languages," *Enterprise Modelling and Information Systems, Gesellschaft für Informatik e.V. (GI)*, vol. 4, no. 1, pp. 3–13, 2009. (Cited on page 30.)

[139] J. Mendling, K. Lassen, and U. Zdun, "On the Transformation of Control Flow between Block-Oriented and Graph-Oriented Process Modeling Languages," *International Journal of Business Process Integration and Management*, vol. 3, no. 2, pp. 96–108, 2008. (Cited on page 31.)

[140] A. Schönberger, "The CHORCH B2Bi Approach: Performing ebBP Choreographies as Distributed BPEL Orchestrations," in *Second International Workshop on Services Computing for B2B*, Miami, Florida, USA, July 2010. (Cited on page 34.)

[141] OASIS, *Web Services - Human Task (WS-HumanTask) Version 1.1*, August 2010. (Cited on page 36.)

[142] ——, *Web Services Atomic Transaction (WS-AtomicTransaction) Version 1.2*, February 2009. (Cited on page 37.)

[143] ——, *Web Services Business Activity (WS-BusinessActivity) Version 1.1*, April 2007. (Cited on page 37.)

[144] B. Kiepuszewski, A. H. M. ter Hofstede, and C. J. Bussler, "On Structured Workflow Modeling," in *12th International Conference on Advanced Information Systems Engineering*, Stockholm, Sweden, June 2000. (Cited on page 38.)

[145] E. Börger, "Approaches to modeling business processes: a critical analysis of BPMN, workflow patterns and YAWL," *Software & Systems Modeling*, vol. 11, no. 3, pp. 305–318, 2012. (Cited on pages 40, 52, 181, and 200.)

[146] B. Limthanmaphon and Y. Zhang, "Web Service Composition Transaction Management," in *15th Australasian Database Conference*, Dunedin, New Zealand, January 18-22 2004, pp. 171–179. (Cited on page 42.)

[147] J. S. Reel, "Critical Success Factors in Software Projects," *IEEE Software*, vol. 16, no. 3, pp. 18–23, May/June 1999. (Cited on page 46.)

[148] M. S. Krishnan, C. H. Kriebel, S. Kekre, and T. Mukhopadhyay, "An Empirical Analysis of Productivity and Quality in Software Products," *Management Science*, vol. 46, no. 6, pp. 745–759, June 2000. (Cited on page 46.)

[149] F. Brooks, *The Mythical Man-Month*. Addison-Wesley, 1975, ISBN: 0-201-00650-2. (Cited on page 46.)

[150] M. H. Halstead, *Elements of Software Science*. Prentice Hall, 1977, ISBN-13: 978-0444002051. (Cited on pages 46 and 48.)

[151] T. McCabe, "A Complexity Measure," *IEEE Transactions on Software Engineering*, vol. 2, no. 4, pp. 308–320, December 1976. (Cited on pages 46 and 48.)

[152] C. Jones, *Software Engineering Best Practices – Lessons from Successful Projects in the Top Companies*. McGraw-Hill, 2010, ISBN: 978-0-07-162162-5. (Cited on page 46.)

[153] M. Fagan, "Design and Code Inspections to Reduce Errors in Program Development," *IBM Systems Journal*, vol. 15, no. 3, pp. 182–211, 1976. (Cited on page 46.)

[154] J. Humble and D. Farley, *Continuous Delivery*. Addison-Wesley, 2010, ISBN: 0321601912. (Cited on pages 46 and 47.)

[155] A. Aurum, H. Petersson, and C. Wohlin, "State-of-the-Art: Software Inspections after 25 Years," *Software Testing, Verification and Reliability*, vol. 12, no. 3, pp. 133–154, February 2002. (Cited on page 46.)

[156] M. Ciolkowski, O. Laitenberger, H. D. Rombach, F. Shull, and D. E. Perry, "Software Inspections, Reviews & Walkthroughs," in *24th International Conference on Software Engineering*, Orlando, Florida, USA, May 2004, pp. 641–642. (Cited on page 46.)

Bibliography

[157] IEEE, *IEEE Std 1028-2008, IEEE Standard for a Software Reviews and Audits*, 2008, revision of IEEE Std 1028-1997. (Cited on page 46.)

[158] J. Foster, M. Hicks, and W. Pugh, "Improving Software Quality With Static Analysis," in *7th ACM SIGPLAN-SIGSOFT Workshop on Program Analysis for Software Tools and Engineering*, San Diego, California, June 2007, pp. 83–84. (Cited on pages 46 and 62.)

[159] J. Zheng, L. Williams, N. Nagappan, W. Snipes, J. P. Hudepohl, and M. A. Vouk, "On the Value of Static Analysis for Fault Detection in Software," *IEEE Transactions on Software Engineering*, vol. 32, no. 4, pp. 240–253, 2006. (Cited on page 46.)

[160] K. Beck, M. Beedle, A. van Bennekum, A. Cockburn, W. Cunningham, M. Fowler, J. Grenning, J. Highsmith, A. Hunt, R. Jeffries, J. Kern, B. Marick, R. C. Martin, S. Mallor, K. Shwaber, and J. Sutherland, "The Agile Manifesto," The Agile Alliance, Tech. Rep., 2001. (Cited on page 47.)

[161] P. Kruchten, R. L. Nord, and I. Ozkaya, "Technical Debt: From Metaphor to Theory and Practice," *IEEE Software*, vol. 29, no. 6, November / December 2012. (Cited on pages 48 and 198.)

[162] ISO/IEC, *Systems and software engineering – System and software Quality Requirements and Evaluation (SQuaRE) – Guide to SQuaRE*, 2014, 25000:2014. (Cited on page 48.)

[163] R. Ferenc, P. Hegedűs, and T. Gyimóthy, "Software Product Quality Models," in *Evolving Software Systems*, T. Mens, A. Serebrenik, and A. Cleve, Eds. Berlin Heidelberg: Springer, 2014, ISBN: 978-3-642-45397-7. (Cited on pages 48 and 49.)

[164] Puppet Labs, IT Revolution Press, ThoughtWorks, *2014 State of DevOps Report*, June 2014. (Cited on page 51.)

[165] K. Mordal-Manet, F. Balmas, S. Denier, S. Ducasse, H. Wertz, J. Laval, F. Bellingard, and P. Vaillergues, "The Squale Model – A Practice-based Intdustrial Quality Model," in *25th IEEE International Conference on Software Maintenance*, Edmonton, Alberta, Canada, September 2009, pp. 531–534. (Cited on page 52.)

[166] S. Wagner, K. Lochmann, L. Heinemann, M. Kläs, A. Trendowicz, R. Plösch, A. Seidi, A. Goeb, and J. Streit, "The Quamoco product quality modelling and assessment approach," in *34th International Conference on Software Engineering*, Zurich, Switzerland, June 2012, pp. 1133–1142. (Cited on page 52.)

[167] I. Heitlager, T. Kuipers, and J. Visser, "A Practical Model for Measuring Maintainability," in *6th International Conference on the Quality of Information and Communications Technology*, Lisbon, Portugal, September 2007, pp. 30–39. (Cited on page 52.)

[168] ISO/IEC, *Systems and software engineering – Systems and software Quality Requirements and Evaluation (SQuaRE) – Measurement of system and software product quality*, 2013, 25023. (Cited on page 52.)

[169] F. Kossak, C. Illibauer, V. Geist, J. Kubovy, C. Natschläger, T. Ziebermayr, T. Kopetzky, B. Freudenthaler, and K.-D. Schewe, *A Rigorous Semantics for BPMN 2.0 Process Diagrams*. Springer, 2014, ISBN: 978-3-319-09930-9. (Cited on page 52.)

[170] J. Lenhard and G. Wirtz, "Portability of Executable Service-Oriented Processes: Metrics and Validation," *Service Oriented Computing and Applications*, 2015, (submitted for review). (Cited on pages 53, 97, and 179.)

[171] IEEE, *IEEE Std 1061-1998 (R2009), IEEE Standard for a Software Quality Metrics Methodology*, 1998, revision of IEEE Std 1061-1992. (Cited on pages 54, 55, 56, 59, 61, 62, 104, 120, 122, 135, 152, and 158.)

[172] S. S. Stevens, "On the Theory of Scales of Measurement," *Science*, vol. 103, no. 2684, pp. 677–680, 1946. (Cited on pages 54 and 55.)

[173] N. Fenton, "Software Measurement: A Necessary Scientific Basis," *IEEE Transactions on Software Engineering*, vol. 20, no. 3, pp. 199–206, 1994. (Cited on page 54.)

[174] C. Wohlin, P. Runeson, M. Höst, M. C. Ohlsson, B. Regnell, and A. Wesslén, *Experimentation in Software Engineering*. Springer-Verlag, Berlin, Heidelberg, 2012, ISBN: 978-3642290435. (Cited on pages 54, 55, 60, 61, 62, 68, 113, 114, and 166.)

[175] A. Meneely, B. Smith, and L. Williams, "Validating Software Metrics: A Spectrum of Philosophies," *ACM Transactions on Software Engineering and Methodology*, vol. 21, no. 4, November 2012. (Cited on page 55.)

[176] D. Basci and S. Misra, "Measuring and Evaluating a Design Complexity Metric for XML Schema Documents," *Journal of Information Science and Engineering*, vol. 25, no. 5, pp. 1405–1425, 2009. (Cited on page 55.)

[177] E. Weyuker, "Evaluating Software Complexity Measures," *IEEE Transactions on Software Engineering*, vol. 14, no. 9, pp. 1357–1365, 1988. (Cited on pages 55 and 56.)

[178] N. Fenton and A. Melton, "Deriving structurally based software measures," *Journal of Systems and Software*, vol. 22, no. 3, pp. 177–187, 1990. (Cited on pages 55 and 56.)

[179] N. F. Schneidewind, "Methodology For Validating Software Metrics," *IEEE Transactions on Software Engineering*, vol. 18, no. 5, pp. 410–422, 1992. (Cited on pages 55 and 56.)

[180] S. Morasca, "Refining the Axiomatic Definition of Internal Software Attributes," in *Second International Symposium on Empirical Software Engineering and Measurement (ESEM)*, Kaiserslautern, Germany, October 2008, pp. 188–197. (Cited on pages 57 and 58.)

[181] R Core Team, *R: A Language and Environment for Statistical Computing*, R Foundation for Statistical Computing, Vienna, Austria, 2013. [Online]. Available: http://www.R-project.org (Cited on page 61.)

[182] A. Jedlitschka, M. Ciolkowski, and D. Pfahl, *Reporting Experiments in Software Engineering*. Springer, 2008, Guide to Advanced Empirical Software Engineering, ISBN: 978-1-84800-043-8. (Cited on page 61.)

[183] V. R. Basili and H. D. Rombach, "The TAME Project: Towards Improvement-Oriented Software Environments," *IEEE Transactions on Software Engineering*, vol. 14, no. 6, pp. 758–773, 1988. (Cited on page 61.)

[184] K. E. Emam, S. Benlarbi, N. Goel, and S. Rai, "The Confounding Effect of Class Size on the Validity of Object-Oriented Metrics," *IEEE Transactions on Software Engineering*, vol. 27, no. 7, pp. 630–650, 2001. (Cited on pages 61, 113, 121, 152, and 157.)

[185] D. Spinellis, *Quality Wars: Open Source Versus Proprietary Software*. O'Reilly Media, Inc., 2011, Making Software, ISBN: 978-0-596-80832-7. (Cited on pages 63 and 137.)

[186] A. Mockus, R. T. Fielding, and J. D. Herbsleb, "Two Case Studies of Open Source Software Development: Apache and Mozilla," *ACM Transactions on Software Engineering and Methodology*, vol. 11, no. 3, pp. 309–346, 2002. (Cited on page 63.)

[187] S. Shapiro and M. B. Wilk, "An analysis of variance test for normality (complete samples)," *Biometrika*, vol. 52, no. 3–4, pp. 591–611, 1965. (Cited on pages 64 and 119.)

[188] H. B. Mann and D. R. Whitney, "On a Test of Whether one of Two Random Variables is Stochastically Larger than the Other," *Annals of Mathematical Statistics*, vol. 18, no. 1, pp. 50–60, 1947. (Cited on pages 64, 119, 156, and 157.)

[189] F. Wilcoxon, "Individual Comparisons by Ranking Methods," *Biometrics Bulletin*, vol. 1, no. 6, pp. 80–83, 1945. (Cited on pages 64 and 120.)

[190] C. Jones, *Software Assessments, Benchmarks, and Best Practices*. Addison-Wesley, 2000, ISBN: 978-0201485424. (Cited on page 65.)

[191] W. F. Tichy, "Should Computer Scientists Experiment More?" *IEEE Computer*, vol. 31, no. 5, pp. 32–40, 1998. (Cited on page 65.)

[192] S. E. Sim, S. Easterbrook, and R. C. Holt, "Using Benchmarking to Advance Research: A Challenge to Software Engineering," in *25th International Conference on Software Engineering*, Portland, Oregon, USA, May 2003. (Cited on page 65.)

[193] IETF, *Key words for use in RFCs to Indicate Requirement Levels*, March 1997, rFC 2119. (Cited on page 76.)

[194] W3C, *Web Services Addressing 1.0 - Core*, May 2006. (Cited on page 76.)

[195] C. Guidi, I. Lanese, F. Montesi, and G. Zavattaro, "On the Interplay Between Fault Handling and Request-Response Service Interactions," in *8th International Conference on Application of Concurrency for System Design*, Xi'an, China, June 2008, pp. 190–198. (Cited on page 76.)

[196] J. Lenhard, A. Schönberger, and G. Wirtz, "Edit Distance-Based Pattern Support Assessment of Orchestration Languages," in *19th International Conference on Cooperative Information Systems*, Hersonissos, Crete, Greece, October 2011, pp. 137–154. (Cited on pages 77, 103, 114, and 162.)

[197] P. Wohed, W. M. P. van der Aalst, M. Dumas, and A. H. M. ter Hofstede, "Analysis of Web Services Composition Languages: The Case of BPEL4WS," in *22nd International Conference on Conceptual Modeling*, Chicago, Illinois, USA, October 2003, pp. 200–215. (Cited on page 77.)

[198] P. Wohed, W. M. P. van der Aalst, M. Dumas, A. H. M. ter Hofstede, and N. Russell, "On the Suitability of BPMN for Business Process Modelling," in *Business Process Management*, Vienna, Austria, September 2006, pp. 161–176. (Cited on page 77.)

[199] J. Lenhard, "A Pattern-based Analysis of WS-BPEL and Windows Workflow," Otto-Friedrich Universität Bamberg, Bamberger Beiträge zur Wirtschaftsinformatik und Angewandten Informatik, no. 88, March 2011. (Cited on page 77.)

[200] A. Schönberger, C. Pflügler, and G. Wirtz, "Translating Shared State Based ebXML BPSS models to WS-BPEL," *International Journal of Business Intelligence and Data Mining*, vol. 5, no. 4, 2010. (Cited on page 92.)

[201] J. Mateo, V. Valeor, and G. Díaz, "An Operational Semantics of BPEL Orchestrations Integrating Web Services Resource Framework," in *Web Services and Formal Methods*, Clermont-Ferrand, France, September 2011. (Cited on page 92.)

[202] M. zur Muehlen and J. Recker, "How Much Language is Enough? Theoretical and Practical Use of the Business Process Modeling Notation," in *Advanced Information Systems Engineering (CAiSE)*, Montpellier, France, June 2008. (Cited on pages 93, 155, 156, and 199.)

[203] M. Glinz, "A Risk-Based, Value-Oriented Approach to Quality Requirements," *IEEE Computer*, vol. 25, no. 8, pp. 34–41, March/April 2008. (Cited on pages 98, 104, and 106.)

[204] I. Vanderfeesten, J. Cardoso, J. Mendling, H. Reijers, and W. M. P. van der Aalst, *Quality Metrics for Business Process Models*. Future Strategies, May 2007. (Cited on pages 107 and 186.)

[205] J. Cardoso, "Business Process Quality Metrics: Log-Based Complexity of Workflow Patterns," in *On the Move to Meaningful Internet Systems 2007: CoopIS, DOA, ODBASE, GADA, and IS*. Springer, 2007, pp. 427–434. (Cited on pages 107 and 186.)

[206] A. E. Hassan and R. C. Holt, "Predicting Change Propagation in Software Systems," in *20th IEEE International Conference on Software Maintainance*, Chicago, Illinois, USA, September 2004, pp. 284–293. (Cited on page 108.)

[207] D. Lübke, "Unit Testing BPEL Compositions," in *Test and Analysis of Service-oriented Systems*. Springer, 2007, pp. 149–171, ISBN 978-3540729112. (Cited on pages 114 and 183.)

[208] C. Szyperski, "Component Technology - What, Where, and How," in *25th International Conference on Software Engineering*, Portland, Oregon, USA, May 2003. (Cited on pages 125, 129, and 130.)

[209] ISO/IEC, *Software engineering – Product quality – Part 2: External metrics*, 2003, 9126-2:2003. (Cited on pages 126, 142, 186, 187, and 189.)

[210] ——, *Software engineering – Product quality – Part 3: Internal metrics*, 2003, 9126-3:2003. (Cited on pages 126, 127, 128, 129, 142, 186, 187, and 189.)

[211] J. Nielsen, "Usability Inspection Methods," in *ACM Conference on Human Factors in Computing Systems*, April 1994, pp. 413–414. (Cited on pages 128, 187, and 188.)

[212] ISO/IEC, *Systems and software engineering – Systems and software Quality Requirements and Evaluation (SQuaRE) – Quality measure elements*, 2012, 25021. (Cited on pages 129 and 135.)

[213] M. Salehie and L. Tahvildari, "Self-Adaptive Software: Landscape and Research Challenges," *ACM Transactions on Autonomous and Adaptive Systems*, vol. 4, no. 2, 2009. (Cited on pages 143 and 188.)

[214] N. Subramanian and L. Chung, "Metrics for Software Adaptability," in *Proc. Software Quality Management*, Loughborough, UK, April 2001. (Cited on pages 143, 146, and 189.)

[215] D. Perez-Palacin, R. Mirandola, and J. Merseguer, "On the Relationships between QoS and Software Adaptability at the Architectural Level," *Journal of Systems and Software*, vol. 87, no. 1, pp. 1–17, 2014. (Cited on pages 143, 146, and 189.)

[216] M. zur Muehlen and J. Recker, "We Still Don't Know How Much BPMN is Enough, But We Are Getting Closer," in *Seminal Contributions to Informations Systems Engineering: 25 Years of CAiSE*, 2013, pp. 445–451. (Cited on page 155.)

[217] R. Akkiraju and A. Ivan, "Discovering Business Process Similarities: An Empirical Study with SAP Best Practice Business Processes," in *8th International Conference on Service Oriented Computing (ICSOC)*, San Francisco, CA, USA, December 7-10 2010, pp. 515–526. (Cited on pages 161, 162, and 164.)

[218] R. M. Dijkman, M. Dumas, B. F. van Dongen, R. Käärik, and J. Mendling, "Similarity of Business Process Models: Metrics and Evaluation," *Information Systems*, vol. 36, no. 2, pp. 498–516, 2011. (Cited on pages 161, 162, 164, 165, 167, 168, 171, and 173.)

[219] Z. Yan, R. Dijkman, and P. Grefen, "Fast Business Process Similarity Search with Feature-Based Similarity Estimation," in *18th International Conference on Cooperative Information Systems (CoopIS)*, Crete, Greece, 2010, pp. 60–77. (Cited on pages 161, 162, and 164.)

[220] M. Minor, A. Tartakovski, and R. Bergmann, "Representation and Structure-Based Similarity Assessment for Agile Workflows," in *7th International Conference on Case-Based Reasoning (ICCBR)*, Belfast, Northern Ireland, UK, August 13-16 2007, pp. 224–238. (Cited on pages 161, 162, and 164.)

[221] M. Kunze, M. Weidlich, and M. Weske, "Behavioral Similarity – A Proper Metric," in *9th International Conference on Business Process Management*, Clermont-Ferrand, France, August, September 2011, pp. 166–181. (Cited on pages 161, 162, and 164.)

[222] C. Li, M. Reichert, and A. Wombacher, "On Measuring Process Model Similarity Based on High-Level Change Operations," in *27th International Conference on Conceptual Modeling*, Barcelona, Spain, October 2008, pp. 248–264. (Cited on pages 161, 162, and 164.)

[223] J. Bae, J. Caverlee, L. Liu, and W. B. Rouse, "Process Mining, Discovery, and Integration using Distance Measures," in *International Conference on Web Services*, Chicago, USA, September 2006, pp. 479–488. (Cited on pages 161, 162, 164, 165, and 168.)

[224] H. Zha, J. Wang, L. Wen, C. Wang, and J. Sun, "A workflow net similarity measure based on transition adjacency relations," *Computers in Industry*,

vol. 61, no. 5, pp. 463–471, 2010. (Cited on pages 161, 162, 164, 165, 166, 168, 170, 173, and 175.)

[225] A. Wombacher and C. Li, "Alternative Approaches for Workflow Similarity," in *7th International Conference on Services Computing*, Miami, Florida, USA, July 2010, pp. 337–345. (Cited on pages 161, 162, 164, 165, 166, and 168.)

[226] C. Klinkmüller, I. Weber, J. Mendling, H. Leopold, and A. Ludwig, "Increasing Recall of Process Model Matching by Improved Activity Label Matching," in *11th International Conference on Business Process Management*, Beijing, China, August 26-30 2013, pp. 211–218. (Cited on pages 161, 162, 164, and 190.)

[227] M. Weidlich, J. Mendling, and M. Weske, "Efficient Consistency Measurement Based on Behavioral Profiles of Process Models," *IEEE Transactions on Software Engineering*, vol. 37, no. 3, pp. 410–429, 2011. (Cited on pages 161, 162, 164, 165, 167, 168, 170, 173, 174, and 175.)

[228] M. Becker and R. Laue, "A Comparative Survey of Business Process Similarity Measures," *Computers in Industry*, vol. 63, no. 2, pp. 148–167, 2012. (Cited on pages 161, 163, 165, 167, 168, 169, 170, 171, 172, 173, and 175.)

[229] M. L. Rose, H. A. Reijers, W. M. van der Aalst, R. M. Dijkman, J. Mendling, M. Dumas, and L. García-Bañuelos, "APROMORE: An Advanced Process Model Repository," *Expert Systems with Applications*, vol. 38, no. 6, pp. 7029–7040, 2011. (Cited on page 162.)

[230] Z. Yan, R. Dijkman, and P. Grefen, "Business Process Model Repositories – Framework and Survey," *Information and Software Technology*, vol. 54, no. 4, pp. 380–395, 2012. (Cited on page 162.)

[231] Z. Zhou, W. Gaaloul, F. Gao, L. Shu, and S. Tata, "Assessing the Replaceability of Service Protocols in Mediated Service Interactions," *Future Generation Computer Systems*, vol. 29, no. 1, pp. 287–299, 2013. (Cited on page 162.)

[232] R. M. Dijkman, M. Dumas, and L. García-Bañuelos, "Graph Matching Algorithms for Business Process Model Similarity Search," in *Business Process Management Conference*, Ulm, Germany, September 2009, pp. 48–63. (Cited on pages 162 and 164.)

[233] P. Fettke, P. Loos, and J. Zwicker, "Business Process Reference Models: Survey and Classification," in *Business Process Management Workshops*, Nancy, France, September 2005, pp. 469–483. (Cited on page 162.)

[234] R.-H. Eid-Sabbagh, "Towards Automatic Generation of Process Architectures for Process Collections," in *4th Central-European Workshop on*

Services and their Composition, Bamberg, Germany, February 2012, pp. 88–95. (Cited on page 162.)

[235] P. Zezula, G. Amato, V. Dohnal, and M. Batko, *Similarity Search: The Metric Space Approach*, ser. Advances in Database Systems.   Springer, 2006, vol. 32, iSBN 978-0-387-29146-8. (Cited on page 163.)

[236] S. Santini and R. Jain, "Similarity Measures," *IEEE Transactions on Pattern Analysis and Machine Intelligence*, vol. 21, no. 9, pp. 871–883, 1999. (Cited on page 163.)

[237] M. Dumas, L. García-Bañuelos, and R. Dijkman, "Similarity Search of Business Process Models," *IEEE Data Engineering Bulletin*, vol. 32, no. 3, pp. 23–28, 2009. (Cited on page 163.)

[238] V. I. Levenshtein, "Binary Codes Capable of Correcting Deletions, Insertions, and Reversals," *Soviet Physics Doklady*, vol. 10, no. 8, pp. 707–710, 1966. (Cited on page 164.)

[239] M. Ehrig, A. Koschmider, and A. Oberweis, "Measuring Similarity between Semantic Business Process Models," in *Asia-Pacific Conference on Conceptual Modelling (APCCM)*, Ballarat, Australia, January/February 2007, pp. 71–80. (Cited on pages 164 and 171.)

[240] M. Levandowsky and D. Winter, "Distance between Sets," *Nature*, vol. 234, no. 5, pp. 34–35, November 1971. (Cited on page 165.)

[241] J. Prescher, J. Mendling, and M. Weidlich, "The Projected TAR and its Application to Conformance Checking," in *Entwicklungsmethoden für Informationssysteme und deren Anwendung (EMISA)*, Vienna, Austria, September 13–14 2012, pp. 151–164. (Cited on page 166.)

[242] M. Weidlich, T. Sagi, H. Leopold, A. Gal, and J. Mendling, "Predicting the Quality of Process Model Matching," in *11th International Conference on Business Process Management*, Beijing, China, August 26-30 2013, pp. 203–210. (Cited on pages 170 and 190.)

[243] R. Dijkman, M. Dumas, and C. Ouyang, "Semantics and Analysis of Buisness Process Models in BPMN," *Information and Software Technology*, vol. 50, no. 12, pp. 1281–1294, 2009. (Cited on pages 174 and 181.)

[244] W. M. P. van der Aalst and A. H. M. ter Hofstede, "YAWL: Yet Another Workflow Language," *Information Systems*, vol. 30, no. 4, pp. 245–275, 2005. (Cited on pages 179 and 180.)

[245] M. Chinosi and A. Trombetta, "BPMN: An introduction ot the standard," *Computer Standards & Interfaces*, vol. 34, no. 1, pp. 124–134, January 2012. (Cited on page 180.)

[246] W. M. P. van der Aalst, "The Application of Petri Nets to Workflow Management," *Journal of Circuits, Systems and Computers*, vol. 8, no. 1, pp. 21–66, 1998. (Cited on page 181.)

[247] F. Puhlmann, "Why do we actually need the Pi-Calculus for Business Process Management?" in *9th International Conference on Business Information Systems*, Klagenfurt, Austria, August 2006. (Cited on page 181.)

[248] N. Lohmann, E. Verbeek, and R. M. Dijkman, "Petri Net Transformations for Business Processes - A Survey," *Transactions on Petri Nets and Other Models of Concurrency II*, vol. 2, pp. 46–63, 2009. (Cited on page 181.)

[249] S. Hinz, K. Schmidt, and C. Stahl, "Transforming BPEL to Petri Nets," in *3rd International Conference on Business Process Management*, Nancy, France, September 2005. (Cited on page 181.)

[250] W. Tan, Y. Fan, and M. Zhou, "A Petri Net-Based Method for Compatibility Analysis and Composition of Web Services in Business Process Execution Language," *IEEE Transactions on Automation Science and Engineering*, vol. 6, no. 1, pp. 94–106, 2009. (Cited on page 181.)

[251] H. Kang, X. Yang, and S. Yuan, "Modeling and Verification of Web Services Composition based on CPN," in *IFIP International Conference on Network and Parallel Computing Workshops*, Dalian, China, September 2007. (Cited on page 181.)

[252] I. Raedts, M. Petkovic, Y. S. Usenko, J. M. van der Werf, J. F. Groote, and L. J. Somers, "Transformation of BPMN Models for Behaviour Analysis," in *5th International Workshop on Modelling, Simulation, Verification and Validation of Enterprise Information Systems*, Funchal, Portugal, June 2007, pp. 126–137. (Cited on page 181.)

[253] L. Cesari, A. Lapadula, R. Pugliese, and F. Tiezzi, "A tool for rapid development of WS-BPEL applications," in *25th ACM Symposium on Applied Computing (SAC)*, Sierre, Switzerland, March 2010, pp. 2438–2442. (Cited on page 182.)

[254] B. Simon, B. Goldschmidt, and K. Kondorosi, "A Human Readable Platform Independent Domain Specific Language for BPEL," in *Second International Conference on Networked Digital Technologies*, Prague, Czech Republic, July 2010, pp. 537–544. (Cited on page 182.)

[255] E. Højsgaard and T. Hallwyl, "Core BPEL: Syntactic Simplification of WS-BPEL 2.0," in *27th ACM Symposium on Applied Computing*, Trento, Italy, 2012, pp. 1984–1991. (Cited on page 182.)

[256] T. M. Prinz, "Proposals for a Virtual Machine for Business Processes," in *7th Central-European Workshop on Services and their Composition*, Jena, Germany, February 2015, pp. 10–17. (Cited on page 182.)

[257] WS-I, *Basic Profile Version 1.2*, November 2010. (Cited on page 183.)

[258] ——, *Basic Profile Version 2.0*, November 2010. (Cited on page 183.)

[259] ——, *Reliable Secure Profile Version 1.0*, November 2010. (Cited on page 183.)

[260] Z. Zakaria, R. Atan, A. Ghani, and N. Sani, "Unit Testing Approaches for BPEL: A Systematic Review," in *16th Asia-Pacific Software Engineering Conference*, Penang, Malaysia, December 2009, pp. 316–322. (Cited on page 183.)

[261] M. Skouradaki, D. H. Roller, F. Leymann, V. Ferme, and C. Pautasso, "On the Road to Benchmarking BPMN 2.0 Workflow Engines," in *6th ACM/SPEC International Conference on Performance Engineering*, Austin, Texas, USA, January / February 2015. (Cited on page 184.)

[262] L. Juszczyk and S. Dustdar, "Script-based Generation of Dynamic Testbeds for SOA," in *8th IEEE International Conference on Web Services*, Miami, Florida, USA, July 2010. (Cited on page 184.)

[263] A. P. Mathur, *Foundations of Software Testing*. Dorling Kindersley, 2009, ISBN-13: 978-81-317-1660-1. (Cited on page 184.)

[264] ISO/IEC, *ISO/IEC 9646-1:1994 – Information technology – Open Systems Interconnection – Conformance testing methodology and framework – Part 1: General concepts*, 1994. (Cited on page 184.)

[265] W. M. P. van der Aalst, N. Lohmann, P. Massuthe, C. Stahl, and K. Wolf, "From Public Views to Private Views - Correctness-by-Design for Services," in *4th International Workshop on Web Services and Formal Methods*, Brisbane, Australia, September 2007, pp. 139–153. (Cited on page 185.)

[266] M. Geiger, A. Schönberger, and G. Wirtz, "Towards Automated Conformance Checking of ebBP-ST Choreographies and Corresponding WS-BPEL Based Orchestrations," in *23rd International Conference on Software Engineering and Knowledge Engineering*, Miami, Florida, USA, July 2011. (Cited on page 185.)

[267] W. M. van der Aalst, M. Dumas, C. Ouyang, A. Rozinat, and E. Verbeek, "Conformance Checking of Service Behavior," *ACM Transactions on Internet Technology*, vol. 8, no. 3, pp. 29–59, May 2008. (Cited on page 185.)

[268] A. Both and W. Zimmermann, "Automatic Protocol Conformance Checking of Recursive and Parallel BPEL Systems," in *6th European Conference on Web Services*, Dublin, Ireland, November 2008, pp. 81–91. (Cited on page 185.)

[269] J. García-Fanjul and J. T. Claudio de la Riva, "Generation of Conformance Test Suites for Compositions of Web Services Using Model Checking," in *Testing: Academic & Industrial Conference – Practice and Research Techniques*, Windsor, United Kingdom, August 2006, pp. 127–130. (Cited on page 185.)

[270] M. Perepletchikov, C. Ryan, and K. Frampton, "Cohesion Metrics for Predicting Maintainability in Service-Oriented Software," in *7th International Conference on Quality Software*, Portland, Oregon, USA, October 2007, pp. 328–335. (Cited on page 185.)

[271] W. Xiao-Jun, "Metrics for Evaluating Coupling and Service Granularity in Service Oriented Architecture," in *1st International Conference on Information Engineering and Computer Science*, Wuhan, China, December 2009. (Cited on page 185.)

[272] R. Sindhgatta, B. Sengupta, and K. Ponnalagu, "Measuring the Quality of Service Oriented Design," in *7th International Conference on Service Oriented Computing*, Stockholm, Sweden, November 2009, pp. 485–499. (Cited on page 185.)

[273] P. Bianco, G. A. Lewis, and P. Merson, "Service Level Agreements in Service-Oriented Architecture Environments," Software Engineering Institute, Carnegie Mellon University, Tech. Rep., 2008. (Cited on page 185.)

[274] P. Brebner, L. O'Brien, and J. Gray, "Performance Modeling for Service Oriented Architectures," in *30th International Conference on Software Engineering*, Leipzig, Germany, May 2008, pp. 953–954. (Cited on page 185.)

[275] P. Leitner, C. Inzinger, W. Hummer, B. Satzger, and S. Dustdar, "Application-Level Performance Monitoring of Cloud Services Based on the Complex Event Processing Paradigm," in *5th IEEE International Conference on Service-Oriented Computing and Applications*, Taipei, Taiwan, December 2012. (Cited on page 185.)

[276] V. C. Emeakaroha, I. Brandic, M. Maurer, and S. Dustdar, "Low Level Metrics to High Level SLAs - LoM2HiS framework: Bridging the gap between monitored metrics and SLA parameters in Cloud environments," in *2010 High Performance Computing and Simulation Conference*, Caen, France, June / July 2010. (Cited on page 185.)

[277] L. S. González, F. G. Rubio, F. R. González, and M. P. Velthuis, "Measurement in business processes: a systematic review," *Business Process Management Journal*, vol. 16, no. 91, pp. 114–134, January 2010. (Cited on page 186.)

[278] S. Overhage, D. Birkmeier, and S. Schlauderer, "Quality Marks, Metrics and Measurement Procedures for Business Process Models: The 3QM-Framework," *Business & Information Systems Engineering*, vol. 4, no. 5, pp. 229–246, 2012. (Cited on pages 186 and 197.)

[279] G. Muketha, A. Ghani, M. Selamat, and R. Atan, "Complexity Metrics for Executable Business Processes," *Information Technology Journal*, vol. 9, no. 7, pp. 1317–1326, 2010. (Cited on page 186.)

[280] A. Ghani, K. T. Muketha, and W. P. Wen, "Complexity Metrics for Measuring the Understandability and Maintainability of Business Process Models using Goal-Question-Metric (GQM)," *International Journal of Computer Science and Network Security*, vol. 8, no. 5, pp. 219–225, 2008. (Cited on page 186.)

[281] B. Wetzstein, S. Strauch, and F. Leymann, "Measuring Performance of WS-BPEL Service Compositions," in *5th International Conference on Networking and Services*, Valencia, Spain, April 2009, pp. 49–56. (Cited on page 186.)

[282] B. Wetzstein, P. Leitner, F. Rosenberg, I. Brandic, F. Leymann, and S. Dustdar, "Monitoring and Analyzing Influential Factors of Business Process Performance," in *13th IEEE International Enterprise Distributed Object Computing Conference*, Auckland, New Zealand, August / September 2009. (Cited on page 186.)

[283] K. Figl and R. Laue, "Cognitive Complexity in Business Process Modeling," in *23rd International Conference on Advanced Information Systems Engineering*, London, UK, June 2011, pp. 452–466. (Cited on page 186.)

[284] J. Mooney, "Issues in the Specification and Measurement of Software Portability," West Virginia University, USA, Tech. Rep., 1993. (Cited on page 186.)

[285] F. A. Talib, A. Abran, and D. Giannacopoulos, "Designing a Measurement Method for the Portability Non-Functional Requirement," in *8th International Conference on Software Process and Product Measurement*, Ankara, Turkey, November 2013, pp. 38–43. (Cited on page 186.)

[286] B. Di Martino, "Applications Portability and Services Interoperability among Multiple Clouds," *IEEE Cloud Computing*, vol. 1, no. 1, pp. 74–77, May 2014. (Cited on page 187.)

[287] A. Khajeh-Hosseini, D. Greenwood, and I. Sommerville, "Cloud Migration: A Case Study of Migrating an Enterprise IT System to IaaS," in *3rd IEEE International Conference on Cloud Computing*, Miami, Florida, USA, July 2010. (Cited on page 187.)

[288] M. Hajjat, X. Sun, Y.-W. E. Sung, D. Maltz, S. Rao, K. Sripanidkulchai, and M. Tawarmalani, "Cloudward Bound: Planning for Beneficial Migration of Enterprise Applications to the Cloud," *Computer Communication Review*, vol. 40, no. 4, October 2010. (Cited on page 187.)

[289] B. C. Tak, B. Urgaonkar, and A. Sivasubramaniam, "To Move or Not to Move: The Economics of Cloud Computing," in *3rd USENIX Conference on Hot Topics in Cloud Computing*, Portland, Oregon, USA, June 2011. (Cited on page 187.)

[290] J. Vouillon and R. D. Cosmo, "On Software Component Co-Installability," *ACM Transactions on Software Engineering and Methodology*, vol. 22, no. 4, October 2013. (Cited on page 187.)

[291] F. Mancinelli, J. Boender, R. D. Cosmo, J. Vouillon, B. Durak, X. Leroy, and R. Treinen, "Managing the Complexity of Large Free and Open Source Package-Based Software Distributions," in *21st IEEE/ACM International Conference on Automated Software Engineering*, Tokyo, Japan, September 2006, pp. 199–208. (Cited on page 187.)

[292] IETF, *Metrics for the Evaluation of Congestion Control Mechanisms*, March 2008, IETF Network Working Group. (Cited on page 187.)

[293] M. Vögler, J. M. Schleicher, C. Inzinger, S. Nastic, S. Sehic, and S. Dustdar, "LEONORE - Large-Scale Provisioning of Resource-Constrained IoT Deployments," in *9th IEEE International Symposium on Service-Oriented System Engineering*, San Francisco Bay, CA, USA, March / April 2015. (Cited on page 187.)

[294] S. Bellomo, N. Ernst, R. Nord, and R. Kazman, "Toward Design Decisions to Enable Deployability: Empirical Study of Three Projects Reaching for the Continuous Delivery Holy Grail," Software Engineering Institute, Carnegie Mellon University, Tech. Rep., 2015. (Cited on page 187.)

[295] M. Mäntylä, F. Khomh, B. Adams, E. Engström, and K. Petersen, "On Rapid Releases and Software Testing," in *29th IEEE International Conference on Software Maintenance*, Eindhoven, The Netherlands, September 2013, pp. 20–29. (Cited on page 187.)

[296] J. Clark, P. van Oorschot, and C. Adams, "Usability of Anonymous Web Browsing: An Examination of Tor Interfaces and Deployability," in *3rd Symposium on Usable Privacy and Security*, Pittsburgh, USA, July 2007. (Cited on page 188.)

[297] Z. Zhou, S. Bhiri, H. Zhuge, and M. Hauswirth, "Assessing Service Protocol Adaptability Based on Protocol Reduction and Graph Search," *Concurrency and Computation: Practice and Experience*, vol. 23, no. 9, pp. 880–904, June 2011. (Cited on page 188.)

[298] C. Gierds, A. J. Mooij, and K. Wolf, "Reducing Adapter Synthesis to Controller Synthesis," *IEEE Transactions on Services Computing*, vol. 5, no. 1, pp. 72–85, March 2012. (Cited on page 188.)

[299] M. Dumas, B. Benatallah, and H. R. M. Nezhad, "Web service protocols: Compatibility and adaptation," *IEEE Data Engineering Bulletin*, vol. 31, no. 3, pp. 40–44, September 2008. (Cited on page 188.)

[300] H.-L. Truong and S. Dustdar, "Programming Elasticity in the Cloud," *IEEE Computer*, vol. 48, no. 3, pp. 87–90, March 2015. (Cited on page 188.)

[301] A. Michlmayr, F. Rosenberg, P. Leitner, and S. Dustdar, "End-to-End Support for QoS-Aware Service Selection, Binding, and Mediation in VRESCo," *IEEE Transactions on Services Computing*, vol. 3, no. 3, pp. 193–205, July 2010. (Cited on page 188.)

[302] D. Ardagna, M. Comuzzi, E. Mussi, B. Pernici, and P. Plebani, "PAWS: A Framework for Executing Adaptive Web-Service Processes," *IEEE Software*, vol. 24, no. 6, pp. 39–46, November 2007. (Cited on page 188.)

[303] A. Mosincat and W. Binder, "Transparent Runtime Adaptability for BPEL Processes," in *6th International Conference on Service-Oriented Computing*, Chicago, USA, September 2008, pp. 241–255. (Cited on page 188.)

[304] P. Hoenisch, C. Hochreiner, D. Schuller, S. Schulte, J. Mendling, and S. Dustdar, "Cost-Efficient Scheduling of Elastic Processes in Hybrid Clouds," in *8th IEEE International Conference on Cloud Computing*, New York, USA, June / July 2015. (Cited on page 188.)

[305] D. Karastoyanova and F. Leymann, "BPEL'n'Aspects: Adapting Service Orchestration Logic," in *7th IEEE International Conference on Web Services*, Los Angeles, CA, USA, July 2009, pp. 222–229. (Cited on page 189.)

[306] A. Charfi, T. Dinkelaker, and M. Mezini, "A Plug-in Architecture for Self-Adaptive Web Service Compositions," in *7th IEEE International Conference on Web Services*, Los Angeles, CA, USA, July 2009, pp. 35–42. (Cited on page 189.)

[307] B. Weber, S. Rinderle, and M. Reichert, "Change Patterns and Change Support Features - Enhancing Flexibility in Process-Aware Information Systems," *Data and Knowledge Engineering, Elsevier*, vol. 66, no. 3, pp. 438–466, July 2008. (Cited on page 189.)

[308] C. Raibulet and L. Masciadri, "Metrics for the Evaluation of Adaptivity Aspects in Software Systems," *International Journal on Advances in Software*, vol. 3, no. 1 & 2, pp. 238–251, 2010. (Cited on page 189.)

[309] C. Stahl and K. Wolf, "Deciding Service Composition and Substitutability Using Extended Operation Guidelines," *Data & Knowledge Engineering*, vol. 68, no. 9, pp. 819–833, 2009. (Cited on page 189.)

[310] G. Decker and M. Weske, "Behavioral Consistency for B2B Process Integration," in *19th International Conference on Advanced Information*

Systems Engineering, Trondheim, Norway, June 2007, pp. 81–95. (Cited on page 189.)

[311] S. Rinderle-Ma, M. Reichert, and M. Jurisch, "On Utilizing Web Service Equivalence for Supporting the Composition Life Cycle," *International Journal of Web Services Research*, vol. 8, no. 1, pp. 44–67, 2011. (Cited on page 189.)

[312] U. Cayoglu, R. Dijkman, M. Dumas, P. Fettke, L. García-Bañuelos, P. Hake, C. Klinkmüller, H. Leopold, A. Ludwig, P. Loos, J. Mendling, A. Oberweis, A. Schoknecht, E. Sheetrit, T. Thaler, M. Ullrich, I. Weber, and M. Weidlich, "Report: The Process Model Matching Contest 2013," in *5th International Workshop on Process Model Collections: Management and Reuse*, Eindhoven, The Netherlands, September 2014. (Cited on page 190.)

[313] T. Thaler, J. Walter, P. Ardalani, P. Fettke, and P. Loos, "The Need for Process Model Corpora," in *Free Models Initiative 2014*, Vienna, Austria, March 2014. (Cited on page 190.)

[314] K. Mordal, N. Anquetil, J. Laval, A. Serebrenik, B. Vasilescu, and S. Ducasse, "Software quality metrics aggregation in industry," *Journal of Software: Evolution and Process*, vol. 25, no. 10, pp. 1117–1135, August 2012. (Cited on page 197.)

[315] B. Vasilescu, A. Serebrenik, and M. van den Brand, "You Can't Control the Unfamiliar: A Study on the Relations Between Aggregation Techniques for Software Metrics," in *27th IEEE Seventh International Conference on Software Maintenance*, Williamsburg, Virginia, USA, September 2011, pp. 313–322. (Cited on page 197.)

[316] G. Concas, M. Marchesi, S. Pinna, and N. Serra, "Power-Laws in a Large Object-Oriented Software System," *IEEE Transactions on Software Engineering*, vol. 33, no. 10, pp. 687–707, October 2007. (Cited on page 197.)

[317] C. Gini, "Measurement of inequality and incomes," *The Economic Journal*, vol. 31, pp. 124–126, 1921. (Cited on page 197.)

[318] A. B. Atkinson, "On the measurment of inequality," *Journal of Economic Theory*, vol. 2, no. 3, pp. 244–263, 1970. (Cited on page 197.)

[319] T. Saaty, *The Analytic Hierarchy Process.* McGraw-Hill, New York, 1980. (Cited on page 197.)

[320] J. Karlsson, C. Wohlin, and B. Regnell, "An Evaluation of Methods for Prioritizing Software Requirements," *Information and Software Technology*, vol. 39, no. 14–15, pp. 939–947, 1998. (Cited on page 197.)

[321] K. Sun and Y. Li, "Effort Estimation in Cloud Migration Process," in *7th IEEE International Symposium on Service-Oriented Engineering*, San Francisco Bay, USA, March 2013. (Cited on page 198.)

[322] B. W. Boehm, C. Abts, A. W. Brown, S. Chulani, B. K. Clark, E. Horowitz, R. Madachy, D. J. Reifer, and B. Steece, *Software Cost Estimation with COCOMO II.* Prentice Hall, 2000, ISBN-13: 978-0130266927. (Cited on page 198.)

[323] B. Clark, S. Devnani-Chulani, and B. Boehm, "Calibrating the COCOMO II Post-Architecture Model," in *20th International Conference on Software Engineering*, Kyoto, Japan, April 1998, pp. 477–480. (Cited on page 198.)

Part IV.

Appendix

A. Conformance Test Suites

This section lists all conformance tests and test cases used in the conformance benchmark discussed in Chap. 3. For each conformance test, we list a name that describes the feature being tested for, a description that characterizes the underlying process models, and a list of test cases that are used to evaluate the feature. For pattern tests cases, we omit a description row. since the description of a pattern can be looked up in the original source. The tables have been generated automatically from the source code of the betsy tool.

The next section, Appendix A.1, contains the conformance test suite for BPEL and the test suite for workflow control-flow patterns. Appendix A.2 lists the test suite for BPMN.

A.1. BPEL Test Cases

In the case of BPEL, there is at least one test step for every test case. Each test step is described by its *input, expected* output, and invoked *operation.* The *input* equals to the payload of the message sent to a process instance during the test step. Correspondingly, *expected* is the payload of the reply message that is required for a passing test. If there is no assertion on the output payload, *expected* is left empty. *Operation* corresponds to the type of Web service operation being invoked in the test step, which can either be synchronous or asynchronous.

Table A.1 lists the BPEL conformance test suite described in Sect. 3.2.3.1 and Table A.2 lists the workflow control-flow patterns test suite described in Sect. 3.2.3.2.

Table A.1.: BPEL Conformance Test Cases

Property	Conformance Test
Name	Assign-Validate
Description	A receive-reply pair with an intermediate assign that has validate set to yes. The assign copies to a variable that represents a month and the validation should fail for values not in the range of one to twelve.
Test case: Input Value 13 should return validation fault	input expected operation 13 invalidVariables synchronous
Name	Assign-Property

Continued on next page

Table A.1 – *Continued from previous page*

Description	A receive-reply pair with an intermediate assign that copies from a property instead of a variable.		
Test case: Good-Case	input	expected	operation
	5	5	synchronous

Name	Assign-PartnerLink		
Description	A receive-reply pair with an intermediate assign that assigns a WS-A EndpointReference to a partnerLink which is used in a subsequent invoke.		
Test case: Good-Case	input	expected	operation
	5	0	synchronous

Name	Assign-PartnerLink-UnsupportedReference		
Description	A receive-reply pair with an intermediate assign that assigns a bogus refernce to a partnerLink which is used in a subsequent invoke. The reference scheme should not be supported by any engine and fail with a corresponding fault.		
Test case: Good-Case	input	expected	operation
	1	unsupportedReference	synchronous

Name	Assign-MismatchedAssignmentFailure		
Description	An assignment between two incompatible types. A mismatchedAssignmentFailure should be thrown.		
Test case: Good-Case	input	expected	operation
	1	mismatchedAssignment	synchronous

Name	Assign-Literal		
Description	A receive-reply pair with an intermediate assign that copies a literal.		
Test case: Good-Case	input	expected	operation
	5	1	synchronous

Name	Assign-Expression-From		
Description	A receive-reply pair with an intermediate assign that uses an expression in a from element.		
Test case: Good-Case	input	expected	operation
	5	5	synchronous

Name	Assign-Expression-To		
Description	A receive-reply pair with an intermediate assign that uses an expression in a to element.		
Test case: Good-Case	input	expected	operation
	5	5	synchronous

Name	Assign-Int		

Continued on next page

Description	A receive-reply pair combined with an assign and an invoke inbetween. The assign copies an int value as an expression to the inputVariable of the invoke. The invocation fails if the value copied is not an int (but, for instance, a float).		
Test case: Good-Case	input	expected	operation
	1	10	synchronous

Name	Assign-SelectionFailure		
Description	A receive-reply pair with an intermediate assign that uses a from that retuns zero nodes. This should trigger a selectionFailure.		
Test case: Good-Case	input	expected	operation
	1	selectionFailure	synchronous

Name	Assign-Copy-Query		
Description	A process with a receive-reply pair with an intermediate assign that uses a query in a from element.		
Test case: Good-Case	input	expected	operation
	5	5	synchronous

Name	Assign-Copy-KeepSrcElementName		
Description	A receive-reply pair with an intermediate assign with a copy that has keepSrcElementName set to yes. This should trigger a fault.		
Test case: Good-Case	input	expected	operation
	1	mismatchedAssignmentFailure	synchronous

Name	Assign-Copy-IgnoreMissingFromData		
Description	A receive-reply pair with an intermediate assign with a copy that has ignoreMissingFromData set to yes and contains a from element with an erroneous xpath statement. Therefore, the assign should be ignored.		
Test case: Good-Case	input	expected	operation
	5	-1	synchronous

Name	Assign-Copy-GetVariableProperty		
Description	A receive-reply pair with an intermediate assign that uses the getVariableProperty function.		
Test case: Good-Case	input	expected	operation
	5	5	synchronous

Name	Assign-Copy-DoXslTransform		
Description	A receive-reply pair with an intermediate assign that uses the doXslTransform function.		
Test case: Good-Case	input	expected	operation
	5	5	synchronous

Name	Assign-Copy-DoXslTransform-InvalidSourceFault

Continued on next page

Table A.1 – *Continued from previous page*

Description	A receive-reply pair with an intermediate assign that uses the doXslTransform function without a proper source for the script.

Test case: Good-Case	input	expected	operation
	1	xsltInvalidSource	synchronous

Name	Assign-Copy-DoXslTransform-XsltStylesheetNotFound
Description	A receive-reply pair with an intermediate assign that uses the doXslTransform function, but where the stylesheet does not exist.

Test case: Good-Case	input	expected	operation
	1	xsltStylesheetNotFound	synchronous

Name	Assign-Copy-DoXslTransform-SubLanguageExecutionFault
Description	A receive-reply pair with an intermediate assign that uses the doXslTransform function, but where the actual stylesheet has errors.

Test case: Good-Case	input	expected	operation
	1	subLanguageExecutionFault	synchronous

Name	Assign-VariablesUnchangedInspiteOfFault
Description	A receive-reply pair with two intermediate assigns, the second of which produces a fault that is handled by the process-level faultHandler to send the response. Because of the fault, the second assign should have no impact on the response.

Test case: Good-Case	input	expected	operation
	1	-1	synchronous

Name	Invoke-Async
Description	A receive-reply pair with an intermediate asynchronous invoke.

Test case: Good-Case	input	expected	operation
	5	5	synchronous

Name	Invoke-Sync
Description	A receive-reply pair with an intermediate synchronous invoke.

Test case: Good-Case	input	expected	operation
	1	1	synchronous

Name	Invoke-Sync-Fault
Description	A receive-reply pair with an intermediate synchronous invoke that should trigger a fault.

Test case: Good-Case	input	expected	operation
	-5	CustomFault	synchronous

Name	Invoke-Empty
Description	A receive-reply pair with an intermediate invoke of an operation that has no message associated with it. No definition of inputVariable or outputVariable is required.

Continued on next page

Table A.1 – *Continued from previous page*

Test case: Good-Case	input	expected	operation
	5	5	synchronous

Name	Invoke-ToParts
Description	A receive-reply pair with an intermediate synchronous invoke that uses the toParts syntax.

Test case: Good-Case	input	expected	operation
	5	5	synchronous

Name	Invoke-FromParts
Description	A receive-reply pair with an intermediate synchronous invoke that uses the fromParts syntax.

Test case: Good-Case	input	expected	operation
	5	5	synchronous

Name	Invoke-Correlation-Pattern-InitAsync
Description	An asynchronous receive that initiates a correlationSet used by a subsequent invoke that also uses a request-response pattern and is thereafter followed by receive-reply pair that also uses the correlationSet.

Test case: Good-Case	input	expected	operation
	1		asynchronous
	1	1	synchronous

Name	Invoke-Correlation-Pattern-InitSync
Description	A synchronous receive that initiates a correlationSet used by a subsequent invoke that also uses a request-response pattern and is thereafter followed by receive-reply pair that also uses the correlationSet.

Test case: Good-Case	input	expected	operation
	1	0	synchronous
	1	1	synchronous

Name	Invoke-Catch
Description	A receive-reply pair with an intermediate invoke that results in a fault for certain input, but catches that fault and replies.

Test case: Good-Case	input	expected	operation
	-5	0	synchronous

Name	Invoke-Catch-ExplicitFault
Description	A receive-reply pair with an intermediate invoke that results in a fault for certain input, but catches that fault and replies. The fault is declared in the Web Service Definition of the partner service.

Test case: Good-Case	input	expected	operation
	-6	0	synchronous

Name	Invoke-CatchAll

Continued on next page

Table A.1 – *Continued from previous page*

Description	A receive-reply pair with an intermediate invoke that results in a fault for certain input, but catches all faults and replies.		
Test case: Enter-CatchAll	input	expected	operation
	-5	0	synchronous

Name	Invoke-CompensationHandler		
Description	A receive-reply pair combined with an invoke that has a compensation-Handler, followed by a throw. The fault is caught by the process-level faultHandler. That faultHandler triggers the compensationHandler of the invoke which contains the reply.		
Test case: Good-Case	input	expected	operation
	1	0	synchronous

Name	Receive		
Description	A single asynchronous receive.		
Test case: Good-Case	input	expected	operation
	1		asynchronous

Name	Receive-Correlation-InitAsync		
Description	Two asynchronous receives, followed by a receive-reply pair, and bound to a single correlationSet.		
Test case: Good-Case	input	expected	operation
	1		asynchronous
	1		asynchronous
	1	1	synchronous

Name	Receive-Correlation-InitSync		
Description	One synchronous receive, one asynchronous receive, followed by a receive-reply pair, and bound to a single correlationSet.		
Test case: Good-Case	input	expected	operation
	1	0	synchronous
	1		asynchronous
	1	1	synchronous

Name	ReceiveReply-MessageExchanges		
Description	A simple receive-reply pair that uses a messageExchange.		
Test case: Good-Case	input	expected	operation
	1	1	synchronous

Name	Receive-AmbiguousReceiveFault		
Description	An asynchronous receive that initiates two correlationSets, followed by a flow with two sequences that contain synchronous receive-reply pairs for the same operation but differnet correlationSets. Should trigger an ambiguousReceive fault.		

Continued on next page

Table A.1 – *Continued from previous page*

	input	expected	operation
Test case: Good-Case	1		asynchronous
	1	ambiguousReceive	synchronous

Name	Receive-ConflictingReceiveFault
Description	An asynchronous receive that iniates a correlationSet, followed by a flow with two sequences that contain synchronous receive-reply pair for the same operation and correlationSet. Should trigger a conflictingReceive fault.

	input	expected	operation
Test case: Good-Case	1		synchronous
	1	conflictingReceive	synchronous

Name	ReceiveReply-ConflictingRequestFault
Description	A synchronous interaction, followed by intermediate while that subsequently enables multiple receives that correspond to a single synchronous message exchange. Should trigger a conflictingRequest fault.

	input	expected	operation
Test case: Good-Case	1	1	synchronous
	1		synchronous
	1	conflictingRequest	synchronous

Name	ReceiveReply-CorrelationViolation-No
Description	A receive-reply pair that uses an uninitiated correlationSet and sets initiate to no. Should trigger a correlationViolation fault.

	input	expected	operation
Test case: Good-Case	1	correlationViolation	synchronous

Name	ReceiveReply-CorrelationViolation-Yes
Description	Two subsequent receive-reply pairs which share a correlationSet and where both receives have initiate set to yes.

	input	expected	operation
Test case: Good-Case	1	1	synchronous
	1	correlationViolation	synchronous

Name	ReceiveReply-CorrelationViolation-Join
Description	A receive-reply pair that initates a correlationSet with an intermediate invoke that tries to join the correlationSet. The join operation should only work if the correlationSet was initiate with a certain value.

	input	expected	operation
Test case: Good-Case-1	1	correlationViolation	synchronous

	input	expected	operation
Test case: Good-Case-2	2	2	synchronous

Name	ReceiveReply

Continued on next page

A. Conformance Test Suites

Table A.1 – *Continued from previous page*

Description	A simple receive-reply pair.		
Test case: Good-Case	input	expected	operation
	5	5	synchronous
Name	ReceiveReply-Correlation-InitAsync		
Description	An asynchronous receive that initiates a correlationSet followed by a receive-reply pair that uses this set.		
Test case: Good-Case	input	expected	operation
	5		asynchronous
	5	5	synchronous
Name	ReceiveReply-Correlation-InitSync		
Description	A synchronous recieve that initiates a correlationSet followed by a receive-reply pair that uses this set.		
Test case: Good-Case	input	expected	operation
	5	0	synchronous
	5	5	synchronous
Name	ReceiveReply-FromParts		
Description	A receive-reply pair that uses the fromPart syntax instead of a variable.		
Test case: Good-Case	input	expected	operation
	1	1	synchronous
Name	ReceiveReply-ToParts		
Description	A receive-reply pair that uses the toPart syntax instead of a variable.		
Test case: Good-Case	input	expected	operation
	1	1	synchronous
Name	ReceiveReply-Fault		
Description	A receive-reply pair replies with a fault instead of a variable.		
Test case: Good-Case	input	expected	operation
	1	syncFault	synchronous
Name	Throw		
Description	A receive-reply pair with an intermediate throw. The response should a soap fault containing the bpel fault.		
Test case: Good-Case	input	expected	operation
	1	completionConditionFailure	synchronous
Name	Throw-WithoutNamespace		
Description	A receive-reply pair with an intermediate throw that uses a bpel fault without explicitly using the bpel namespace. The respone should be a soap fault containing the bpel fault.		
Test case: Good-Case	input	expected	operation
	1	completionConditionFailure	synchronous

Continued on next page

Table A.1 – *Continued from previous page*

Name	Throw-FaultData		
Description	A receive-reply pair with an intermediate throw that also uses a faultVariable. The content of the faultVariable should be contained in the response.		
Test case: Good-Case	input	expected	operation
	1	1, completionConditionFailure	synchronous

Name	Throw-CustomFault		
Description	A receive-reply pair with an intermediate throw that throws a custom fault that undefined in the given namespace. The response should be a soap fault containing the custom fault.		
Test case: Good-Case	input	expected	operation
	1	testFault	synchronous

Name	Throw-CustomFaultInWsdl		
Description	A receive-reply pair with an intermediate throw that throws a custom fault defined in the myRole WSDL. The response should be a soap fault containing the custom fault.		
Test case: Good-Case	input	expected	operation
	1	syncFault	synchronous

Name	Rethrow		
Description	A receive activity with an intermediate throw and a fault handler with a catchAll. The fault handler rethrows the fault.		
Test case: Good-Case	input	expected	operation
	1	completionConditionFailure	synchronous

Name	Rethrow-FaultDataUnmodified		
Description	A receive activity with an intermediate throw that uses a faultVariable. A fault handler catches the fault, changes the data, and rethrows the fault. The fault should be the response with unchanged data.		
Test case: Good-Case	input	expected	operation
	1	1, completionConditionFailure	synchronous

Name	Rethrow-FaultData		
Description	A receive activity with an intermediate throw that uses a faultVariable. A fault handler catches and rethrows the fault. The fault should be the response along with the data.		
Test case: Good-Case	input	expected	operation
	1	1, completionConditionFailure	synchronous

Name	Wait-For		
Description	A receive-reply pair with an intermediate wait that pauses execution for five seconds.		

Continued on next page

Table A.1 – *Continued from previous page*

Test case: Good-Case	input	expected	operation
	5	5	synchronous

Name	Wait-For-InvalidExpressionValue
Description	A receive-reply pair with an intermediate wait. The for element is assigned a value of xs:int, but only xs:duration is allowed.

Test case: Good-Case	input	expected	operation
	5	invalidExpressionValue	synchronous

Name	Wait-Until
Description	A receive-reply pair with an intermediate wait that pauses the execution until a date in the past. Therefore, the wait should complete instantly.

Test case: Good-Case	input	expected	operation
	5	5	synchronous

Name	Empty
Description	A receive-reply pair with an intermediate empty.

Test case: Good-Case	input	expected	operation
	5	5	synchronous

Name	Exit
Description	A receive-reply pair with an intermediate exit. There should not be a normal response.

Test case: Good-Case	input	expected	operation
	1		synchronous

Name	Validate
Description	A receive-reply pair with an intermediate variable validation. The variable to be validated describes a month, so only values in the range of 1 and 12 should validate successfully.

Test case: Input Value 13 should return validation fault	input	expected	operation
	13	invalidVariables	synchronous

Name	Validate-InvalidVariables
Description	A receive-reply pair with an intermediate variable validation. The variable to be validated is of type xs:int and xs:boolean is copied into it.

Test case: Good-Case	input	expected	operation
	1	invalidVariables	synchronous

Name	Variables-UninitializedVariableFault-Reply
Description	A receive-reply pair where the variable of the reply is not initialized.

Continued on next page

Table A.1 – *Continued from previous page*

Test case: Good-Case	input	expected	operation
	1	uninitializedVariable	synchronous

Name	Variables-UninitializedVariableFault-Invoke
Description	A receive-reply pair with intermediate invoke. The inputVariable of the invoke is not initialized.

Test case: Good-Case	input	expected	operation
	1	uninitializedVariable	synchronous

Name	Variables-DefaultInitialization
Description	A receive-reply pair where the variable of the reply is assigned with a default value.

Test case: DefaultValue-10-Should-Be-Returned	input	expected	operation
	5	10	synchronous

Name	Sequence
Description	A receive-reply pair enclosed in a sequence.

Test case: Good-Case	input	expected	operation
	5	5	synchronous

Name	While
Description	A receive-reply pair with an intermediate while that loops for n times, where n is equal to the input.

Test case: Good-Case	input	expected	operation
	5	5	synchronous

Name	RepeatUntil
Description	A receive-reply pair with an intermediate while that loops for n+1 times, where n is equal to the input.

Test case: Good-Case	input	expected	operation
	2	3	synchronous

Name	RepeatUntilEquality
Description	A receive-reply pair with an intermediate while that loops for n times, where n is equal to the input.

Test case: Good-Case	input	expected	operation
	2	2	synchronous

Name	Flow
Description	A receive-reply pair with an intermediate flow that contains two assigns.

Test case: Good-Case	input	expected	operation
	5	7	synchronous

Continued on next page

Table A.1 – *Continued from previous page*

Name	Flow-Links
Description	A receive-reply pair with an intermediate flow that contains two assigns which have a precedence relationship between each other using links.

Test case: Good-Case	input	expected	operation
	1	2	synchronous

Name	Flow-BoundaryLinks
Description	A receive-reply pair with an intermediate flow that contains an assign and a sequence with an assign, as well as a link pointing from the former to the later assign. That way the links crosses the boundary of a structured activity, the sequence.

Test case: Good-Case	input	expected	operation
	1	2	synchronous

Name	Flow-Links-JoinCondition
Description	A receive-reply pair with an intermediate flow that contains three assigns, two of which point to the third using links. Both links have transitionConditions and their target a joinCondition defined upon them. A joinFailure should result, given not both of the links are activated.

Test case: Good-Case-1	input	expected	operation
	1	joinFailure	synchronous

Test case: Good-Case-2	input	expected	operation
	3	6	synchronous

Name	Flow-Links-JoinFailure
Description	A receive-reply pair with an intermediate flow that contains three assigns, two of which point to the third using links. Both links have transitionConditions and their target a joinCondition defined upon them. The transitionConditions do never evaluate to true, resulting in a joinFailure on each invocation.

Test case: Good-Case-1	input	expected	operation
	1	joinFailure	synchronous

Test case: Good-Case-2	input	expected	operation
	3	joinFailure	synchronous

Name	Flow-Links-SuppressJoinFailure
Description	A receive-reply pair with an intermediate flow that contains three assigns, two of which point to the third using links. Both links have transitionConditions and their target a joinCondition defined upon them. The transitionConditions do never evaluate to true, resulting in a joinFailure on each invocation. However, this joinFailure is suppressed.

Test case: Good-Case-1	input	expected	operation
	1	3	synchronous

Continued on next page

Table A.1 – *Continued from previous page*

Test case: Good-Case-2	input	expected	operation
	3	5	synchronous

Name	Flow-Links-TransitionCondition
Description	A receive-reply pair with an intermediate flow that contains three assigns, two of which point to the third using links. Both links have transitionConditions that do fire only if the input is greater than two.

Test case: Good-Case-1	input	expected	operation
	2	4	synchronous

Test case: Good-Case-2	input	expected	operation
	3	6	synchronous

Name	Flow-GraphExample
Description	An implementation of the flow graph process defined in Sec. 11.6.4.

Test case: Good-Case-1	input	expected	operation
	1	1	synchronous
	1	1	synchronous
	1		asynchronous
	1	1	synchronous
	1		asynchronous

Test case: Good-Case-2	input	expected	operation
	1	1	synchronous
	1		asynchronous
	1	1	synchronous
	1	1	synchronous
	1		asynchronous

Test case: Good-Case-3	input	expected	operation
	1	1	synchronous
	1	1	synchronous
	1		asynchronous
	1		asynchronous
	1	1	synchronous

Test case: Good-Case-4	input	expected	operation
	1	1	synchronous
	1		asynchronous
	1	1	synchronous
	1		asynchronous
	1	1	synchronous

Name	Flow-Links-ReceiveCreatingInstances
Description	A flow with a starting activity (receive with createInstance set to yes) and a non-starting activity (assign), where a precedence relationship is defined using links.

Continued on next page

Table A.1 – *Continued from previous page*

Test case: Good-Case	input	expected	operation
	5	6	synchronous

Name	If
Description	A receive-reply pair with an intermediate if that checks whether the input is even.

Test case: Not-If-Case	input	expected	operation
	1	0	synchronous

Test case: If-Case	input	expected	operation
	2	1	synchronous

Name	If-Else
Description	A receive-reply pair with an intermediate if-else that checks whether the input is even.

Test case: Else-Case	input	expected	operation
	1	0	synchronous

Test case: If-Case	input	expected	operation
	2	1	synchronous

Name	If-ElseIf
Description	A receive-reply pair with an intermediate if-elseif that checks whether the input is even or divisible by three.

Test case: Not-If-Or-ElseIf-Case	input	expected	operation
	1	0	synchronous

Test case: If-Case	input	expected	operation
	2	1	synchronous

Test case: ElseIf-Case	input	expected	operation
	3	2	synchronous

Name	If-ElseIf-Else
Description	A receive-reply pair with an intermediate if-elseif-else that checks whether the input is even or divisible by three.

Test case: Else-Case	input	expected	operation
	1	0	synchronous

Test case: If-Case	input	expected	operation
	2	1	synchronous

Test case: ElseIf-Case	input	expected	operation
	3	2	synchronous

Name	If-InvalidExpressionValue
Description	A receive-reply pair with an intermediate if that should throw an invalidExpressionValue fault because of an invalid condition.

Continued on next page

Table A.1 – *Continued from previous page*

Test case: Selection Failure	input	expected	operation
	1	invalidExpressionValue	synchronous

Name	ForEach
Description	A receive-reply pair with an intermediate forEach that loops for n times, where n is equal to the input. Each iteration the current loop number is added to the final result.

Test case: 0-equals-0	input	expected	operation
	0	0	synchronous

Test case: 0plus1-equals-0	input	expected	operation
	1	1	synchronous

Test case: 0plus1plus2-equals-3	input	expected	operation
	2	3	synchronous

Name	ForEach-NegativeStopCounter
Description	A receive-reply pair with an intermediate forEach that should always fail with an invalidExpressionValue fault as finalCounterValue is negative.

Test case: NegativeStopCounter	input	expected	operation
	1	invalidExpressionValue	synchronous

Name	ForEach-CompletionCondition
Description	A receive-reply pair with an intermediate forEach that should terminate given two of its children have terminated. N+1 children are scheduled for execution, where n is equal to the input. If N+1 is less than two, an invalidBranchConditionFault should be thrown.

Test case: Skipping the third iteration	input	expected	operation
	2	1	synchronous

Test case: Cannot meet completion condition	input	expected	operation
	0	invalidBranchCondition	synchronous

Name	ForEach-CompletionCondition-Parallel
Description	A receive-reply pair with an intermediate forEach that should terminate given two of its children have terminated. N+1 children are scheduled for execution in parallel, where n is equal to the input. If N+1 is less than two, an invalidBranchConditionFault should be thrown.

Test case: Skipping the third iteration	input	expected	operation
	2	1	synchronous

Continued on next page

A. Conformance Test Suites

Table A.1 – *Continued from previous page*

Test case: Cannot meet completion condition	input	expected	operation
	0	invalidBranchCondition	synchronous

Name	ForEach-CompletionCondition-SuccessfulBranchesOnly
Description	A receive-reply pair with an intermediate forEach that should terminate given two of its children have terminated successfully. Each child throws a fault, given the current counter value is even. N children are scheduled for execution, where n is equal to the input.

Test case: Good-Case-1	input	expected	operation
	5	6	synchronous

Test case: Good-Case-2	input	expected	operation
	10	6	synchronous

Name	ForEach-CompletionConditionFailure
Description	A receive-reply pair with an intermediate forEach that should terminate given two of its children have terminated. N+1 children are scheduled for execution in parallel, where n is equal to the input. If N+1 is less than two, an invalidBranchConditionFault should be thrown. This is a seperate test case that tests only for the failure.

Test case: Expect completionConditionFailure	input	expected	operation
	1	completionConditionFailure	synchronous

Name	ForEach-Parallel
Description	A receive-reply pair with an intermediate forEach that executes its children in parallel.

Test case: 0plus1plus2-equals-3	input	expected	operation
	2	3	synchronous

Name	ForEach-Parallel-Invoke
Description	A receive-reply pair with an intermediate forEach that executes its children in parallel.

Test case: 0plus1plus2-equals-3	input	expected	operation
	102		synchronous
	2	3	synchronous
	101	true	synchronous
	102	3	synchronous

Name	ForEach-NegativeStartCounter
Description	A receive-reply pair with an intermediate forEach that should always fail with an invalidExpressionValue fault as startCounterValue is negative.

Continued on next page

Table A.1 – Continued from previous page

Test case: Iterate-Twice	input	expected	operation
	2	invalidExpressionValue	synchronous

Name	ForEach-TooLargeStartCounter
Description	A receive-reply pair with an intermediate forEach that should always fail with an invalidExpressionValue fault as startCounterValue is initialized with a value that exceeds xs:unsignedInt.

Test case: invalid-ExpressionValue	input	expected	operation
	2	invalidExpressionValue	synchronous

Name	ForEach-CompletionCondition-NegativeBranches
Description	A receive-reply pair with an intermediate forEach that should always fail with an invalidExpressionValue fault as branches is initialized with a negative value.

Test case: invalid-ExpressionValue	input	expected	operation
	2	invalidExpressionValue	synchronous

Name	Pick-Correlations-InitAsync
Description	An asynchronous receive that initiates a correlationSet, followed by a pick with a synchronous onMessage that correlates on this set.

Test case: Good-Case	input	expected	operation
	1		asynchronous
	1	1	synchronous

Name	Pick-Correlations-InitSync
Description	A receive-reply pair that initiates a correlationSet, followed by a pick with a synchronous onMessage that correlates on this set.

Test case: Good-Case	input	expected	operation
	1	1	synchronous
	1	2	synchronous

Name	Pick-CreateInstance
Description	A pick with a synchronous onMessage that has createInstance set to yes.

Test case: Good-Case	input	expected	operation
	1	1	synchronous

Name	Pick-OnAlarm-For
Description	An onAlarm with for test case. The test contains a receive-reply pair that initiates a correlationSet and an intermediate pick that contains an onMessage and an onAlarm with an for element. The onAlarm should fire after two seconds and the process should reply with a default value.

Test case: Good-Case	input	expected	operation
	1	-1	synchronous

Continued on next page

Table A.1 – *Continued from previous page*

Name	Pick-OnAlarm-Until
Description	A receive-reply pair that initiates a correlationSet and an intermediate pick that contains an onMessage and an onAlarm with an until element. The onAlarm should fire immediately.

Test case: Good-Case	input	expected	operation
	1	-1	synchronous

Name	Scope-Compensate
Description	A scope with a receive-reply pair where the reply is located in a compensationHandler. The scope is followed by a throw and the compensationHandler is invoked from the process-level faultHandler that catches the fault using compensate.

Test case: Good-Case	input	expected	operation
	1	1	synchronous

Name	Scope-CompensateScope
Description	A scope with a receive-reply pair where the reply is located in a compensationHandler. The scope is followed by a throw and the compensationHandler is invoked from the process-level faultHandler that catches the fault using compensateScope.

Test case: Good-Case	input	expected	operation
	1	1	synchronous

Name	Scope-ComplexCompensation
Description	Complex scope compensation test case that implements the scenario described in Sec. 12.4.2.

Test case: Good-Case	input	expected	operation
	1	3	synchronous

Name	Scope-RepeatedCompensation
Description	A scope with a receive-reply pair where the reply is located in a compensationHandler. The scope is followed by a throw. The process-level faultHandler that catches the fault contains two subsequent compensates the second of which should be treated as empty.

Test case: Good-Case	input	expected	operation
	1	1	synchronous

Name	Scope-CorrelationSets-InitAsync
Description	A scope with an asynchronous receive which initiates the correlation set and a receive-reply pair, as well as a scope-level definition of a correlationSet that is used by the messaging activities.

Test case: Good-Case	input	expected	operation
	1		asynchronous
	1	2	synchronous

Name	Scope-CorrelationSets-InitSync

Continued on next page

Table A.1 – *Continued from previous page*

Description	A scope with two subsequent receive-reply pairs and a scope-level definition of a correlationSet that is used by the messaging activities.		
	input	expected	operation
Test case: Good-Case	1	1	synchronous
	1	2	synchronous
Name	Scope-EventHandlers-InitAsync		
Description	An asynchronous receive followed by a wait and a process-level onMessage eventHandler. The receive initiates a correlationSet on which the onMessage correlates with a synchronous operation.		
	input	expected	operation
Test case: Good-Case	5		asynchronous
	5	5	synchronous
Name	Scope-EventHandlers-InitSync		
Description	A receive-reply pair followed by a wait and a process-level onMessage eventHandler. The receive initiates a correlationSet on which the onMessage correlates with a synchronous operation.		
	input	expected	operation
Test case: Good-Case	1	1	synchronous
	1	2	synchronous
Name	Scope-EventHandlers-OnAlarm-For		
Description	A receive-reply pair and a process-level onAlarm eventHandler. The receive is followed by a wait that pauses execution for five seconds. The eventHandler waits for two seconds and replies to the receive.		
	input	expected	operation
Test case: Good-Case	5	5	synchronous
Name	Scope-EventHandlers-OnAlarm-RepeatEvery		
Description	A receive-reply pair with an intermediate wait and a process-level onAlarm eventHandler. The eventHandler repeats execution every second and adds one to the final result. The intermediate wait pauses execution for 2.2 seconds, after which the current result is replied.		
	input	expected	operation
Test case: Good-Case	5	true	synchronous
Name	Scope-EventHandlers-OnAlarm-RepeatEvery-For		
Description	A receive-reply pair with an intermediate wait and a process-level onAlarm eventHandler. The eventHandler repeats execution every second and adds one to the final result. The repetition takes place after one second, so the handler should repeat exactly once. The intermediate wait pauses execution for 2.2 seconds, after which the current result is replied.		
	input	expected	operation
Test case: Good-Case	5	true	synchronous

Continued on next page

Table A.1 – *Continued from previous page*

Name	Scope-EventHandlers-OnAlarm-RepeatEvery-Until
Description	A receive-reply pair with an intermediate wait and a process-level onAlarm eventHandler. The eventHandler repeats execution every second and adds one to the final result. The repetition takes place after a date in the past, so the handler should execute immediately. The intermediate wait pauses execution for 2.2 seconds, after which the current result is replied.

Test case: Good-Case	input	expected	operation
	5	true	synchronous

Name	Scope-EventHandlers-OnAlarm-Until
Description	A receive followed by a scope with an onAlarm eventHandler and a wait. The onAlarm waits until a date in the past and should therefore execute immediately. Its body contains the reply to the initial receive.

Test case: Good-Case	input	expected	operation
	5	5	synchronous

Name	Scope-EventHandlers-Parts
Description	An asynchronous receive followed by a wait and a process-level onMessage eventHandler. The receive initiates a correlationSet on which the onMessage correlates with a synchronous operation. Furthermore, the onMessage uses the fromPart syntax.

Test case: Good-Case	input	expected	operation
	5		asynchronous
	5	5	synchronous

Name	Scope-FaultHandlers
Description	A scope with a receive followed by a intermediate throw. The fault that is thrown is caught by the scope-level faultHandler by its faultName. Inside this faultHandler is the reply to the initial receive.

Test case: Good-Case	input	expected	operation
	5	5	synchronous

Name	Scope-FaultHandlers-CatchAll
Description	A scope with a receive followed by a intermediate throw. The fault that is thrown is caught by the scope-level catchAll faultHandler. Inside this faultHandler is the reply to the initial receive.

Test case: Good-Case	input	expected	operation
	5	5	synchronous

Name	Scope-FaultHandlers-FaultElement
Description	A scope with a receive followed by a intermediate throw. The fault that is thrown is caught by the scope-level faultHandler that uses a faultVariable and faultElement configuration. Inside this faultHandler is the reply to the initial receive.

Continued on next page

Test case: Good-Case	input	expected	operation
	5	5	synchronous

Name	Scope-FaultHandlers-FaultMessageType
Description	A scope with a receive followed by a intermediate throw. The fault that is thrown is caught by the scope-level faultHandler that uses a fault-Variable and faultMessageType configuration. Inside this faultHandler is the reply to the initial receive.

Test case: Good-Case	input	expected	operation
	5	5	synchronous

Name	Scope-ExitOnStandardFault
Description	A scope with receive-reply pair and an intermediate throw. There is no faultHandler, but the exitOnStandardFault attribute of the scope is set to yes.

Test case: Good-Case	input	expected	operation
	5		synchronous

Name	Scope-ExitOnStandardFault-JoinFailure
Description	A scope with a receive-reply pair and an intermediate throw that throws a joinFailure. There is no faultHandler, but the exitOnStandardFault attribute of the scope is set to yes. However, the exitOnStandardFault sematics do not apply to joinFailures.

Test case: Good-Case	input	expected	operation
	1	joinFailure	synchronous

Name	Scope-FaultHandlers-CatchOrder
Description	A scope with a receive followed by a intermediate throw. The scope is associated with mulitple faultHandlers. A specific one of these should catch the fault and only inside this faultHandler is the reply to the initial receive. The process is adapted from the example in Spec. 12.5.

Test case: Good-Case	input	expected	operation
	1	1	synchronous

Name	Scope-FaultHandlers-VariableData
Description	A scope with a receive followed by a intermediate throw. The fault that is thrown is caught by the scope-level faultHandler that uses a faultVariable and faultMessage configuration. Inside this faultHandler is the reply to the initial receive and the data replied is the content of the faultVariable.

Test case: Good-Case	input	expected	operation
	1	0	synchronous

Name	Scope-MessageExchanges
Description	A scope with a receive-reply pair and a scope-level definition of messageExchanges.

Continued on next page

Table A.1 – *Continued from previous page*

Test case: Good-Case	input	expected	operation
	1	1	synchronous

Name	Scope-PartnerLinks
Description	A scope with a receive-reply pair and an intermediate invoke. The partnerLink which is invoked is defined at scope-level.

Test case: Good-Case	input	expected	operation
	1	1	synchronous

Name	Scope-Variables
Description	A scope with a receive-reply pair and an intermediate invoke. The partnerLink which is invoked is defined at scope-level.

Test case: Good-Case	input	expected	operation
	1	1	synchronous

Name	Scope-Variables-Overwriting
Description	A scope with a receive-reply pair and another nested scope. The nested scope overwrites a variable of the parent scope. Child-level manipulation of this variable should not be visible at the parent scope.

Test case: Good-Case	input	expected	operation
	123	3	synchronous

Name	Scope-Isolated
Description	A receive-reply pair that encloses a flow with ten isolated scopes which all increment the result by one. As the scopes should not run in parallel, the outcome must be deterministic.

Test case: Good-Case	input	expected	operation
	1	11	synchronous
	4	14	synchronous
	123	133	synchronous

Name	Scope-TerminationHandlers
Description	A scope with a receive-reply pair and a nested scope in between. That scope in turn contains a flow with two parallel scopes. Both scopes pause execution for a short period. The scope that resumes execution first throws a fault caught by the faultHandler of its parent scope. The should trigger the execution of the terminationHandler of its sibling scope.

Test case: Good-Case	input	expected	operation
	5	-1	synchronous

Name	Scope-TerminationHandlers-FaultNotPropagating

Continued on next page

Description	A scope with a receive-reply pair and a nested scope in between. That scope in turn contains a flow with two parallel scopes. Both scopes pause execution for a short period. The scope that resumes execution first throws a fault caught by the faultHandler of its parent scope. The should trigger the execution of the terminationHandler of its sibling scope. That terminationHandler also throws a fault which should not be propagated.

Test case: Good-Case	input	expected	operation
	5	-1	synchronous

Name	Scope-RepeatableConstructCompensation
Description	A receive followed by a while that contains a scope with a compensationHandler. After the while comes a throw and its fault is caught by the process-level faultHandler. This faultHandler first invokes compensation of all scopes and the replies to the initial receive. The content of the reply depends on the execution of the compensationHandlers.

Test case: Good-Case	input	expected	operation
	3	3	synchronous

Name	MissingReply
Description	A receive for a synchronous operation with no associated reply.

Test case: Good-Case	input	expected	operation
	1	missingReply	synchronous

Name	MissingRequest
Description	A receive and a reply which belong to different messageExchanges. On the execution of the reply, a missingRequest fault should be thrown.

Test case: Good-Case	input	expected	operation
	1	missingRequest	synchronous

Table A.2.: WCP Test Cases

Property	Pattern Test
Name	**WCP01-SequencePattern**

Test case: Good-Case	input	expected	operation
	1	1AB	synchronous

Name	WCP02-ParallelSplitPattern

Test case: Good-Case	input	expected	operation
	1	1AB	synchronous

Name	WCP03-SynchronizationPattern

Continued on next page

Table A.2 – *Continued from previous page*

Test case: Good-Case	input	expected	operation
	1	1AB	synchronous

Name	WCP04-ExclusiveChoicePattern		
Test case: Good-Case-1	input	expected	operation
	1	1A	synchronous
Test case: Good-Case-2	input	expected	operation
	11	11B	synchronous

Name	WCP05-SimpleMergePattern		
Test case: Good-Case-1	input	expected	operation
	1	1A	synchronous
Test case: Good-Case-2	input	expected	operation
	11	11B	synchronous

Name	WCP06-MultiChoicePattern		
Test case: Good-Case-1	input	expected	operation
	1	AYZ	synchronous
Test case: Good-Case-2	input	expected	operation
	2	ABZ	synchronous
Test case: Good-Case-3	input	expected	operation
	3	ABC	synchronous

Name	WCP06-MultiChoicePattern-Partial		
Test case: Good-Case-1	input	expected	operation
	1	AYZ	synchronous
Test case: Good-Case-2	input	expected	operation
	2	ABZ	synchronous
Test case: Good-Case-3	input	expected	operation
	3	ABC	synchronous

Name	WCP07-SynchronizingMergePattern		
Test case: Good-Case-1	input	expected	operation
	1	AYZ	synchronous
Test case: Good-Case-2	input	expected	operation
	2	ABZ	synchronous
Test case: Good-Case-3	input	expected	operation
	3	ABC	synchronous

Name	WCP07-SynchronizingMergePattern-Partial

Continued on next page

Table A.2 – *Continued from previous page*

Test case: Good-Case-1	input	expected	operation
	1	AYZ	synchronous

Test case: Good-Case-2	input	expected	operation
	2	ABZ	synchronous

Test case: Good-Case-3	input	expected	operation
	3	ABC	synchronous

Name	WCP09-DiscriminatorPattern		

Test case: Good-Case	input	expected	operation
	1	1	synchronous

Name	WCP10-ArbitraryCyclesPattern		

Test case: Good-Case-1	input	expected	operation
	1	1ABC	synchronous

Test case: Good-Case-2	input	expected	operation
	2	2BC	synchronous

Test case: Good-Case-3	input	expected	operation
	3	3C	synchronous

Name	WCP11-ImplicitTerminationPattern		

Test case: Good-Case	input	expected	operation
	1	1	synchronous

Name	WCP16-DeferredChoicePattern		

Test case: Good-Case-1	input	expected	operation
	1	1	synchronous

Test case: Good-Case-2	input	expected	operation
	1	1	synchronous

Name	WCP12-MultipleInstancesWithoutSynchronizationPattern		

Test case: Good-Case-1	input	expected	operation
	102		synchronous
	1		synchronous
	101	true	synchronous
	102	2	synchronous

Test case: Good-Case-2	input	expected	operation
	102		synchronous
	2		synchronous
	101	true	synchronous
	102	3	synchronous

Continued on next page

Table A.2 – *Continued from previous page*

Name	WCP12-MultipleInstancesWithoutSynchronizationPattern-Partial		
	input	expected	operation
Test case: Good-Case	102		synchronous
	100		synchronous
	101	true	synchronous
	102	4	synchronous

Name	WCP12-MultipleInstancesWithoutSynchronizationPattern-While-Partial		
	input	expected	operation
Test case: Good-Case-1	1	1	synchronous
	input	expected	operation
Test case: Good-Case-2	2	2	synchronous

Name	WCP13-MultipleInstancesWithAPrioriDesignTimeKnowledgePattern		
	input	expected	operation
Test case: Good-Case-1	102		synchronous
	1		synchronous
	101	true	synchronous
	102	4	synchronous
	input	expected	operation
Test case: Good-Case-2	102		synchronous
	2		synchronous
	101	true	synchronous
	102	4	synchronous

Name	WCP13-MultipleInstancesWithAPrioriDesignTimeKnowledgePattern-Partial		
	input	expected	operation
Test case: Good-Case	102		synchronous
	100		synchronous
	101	true	synchronous
	102	4	synchronous

Name	WCP14-MultipleInstancesWithAPrioriRuntimeKnowledgePattern		
	input	expected	operation
Test case: Good-Case-1	102		synchronous
	1		synchronous
	101	true	synchronous
	102	2	synchronous

Continued on next page

Table A.2 – *Continued from previous page*

	input	expected	operation
Test case: Good-Case-2	102		synchronous
	2		synchronous
	101	true	synchronous
	102	3	synchronous

Name	WCP19-CancelActivityPattern		

Test case: Good-Case-1	input	expected	operation
	1	1A	synchronous

Test case: Good-Case-2	input	expected	operation
	0	0B	synchronous

Name	WCP20-CancelCasePattern		

Test case: Good-Case-1	input	expected	operation
	1	1	synchronous

Test case: Good-Case-2	input	expected	operation
	0		synchronous

Name	WCP18-MilestonePattern		

Test case: Pick-AsyncMessage	input	expected	operation
	1	1	synchronous
	1		asynchronous
	1	8	synchronous

Test case: Pick3sTimeout	input	expected	operation
	1	1	synchronous
	1	9	synchronous

Name	WCP17-InterleavedParallelRoutingPattern		

Test case: Good-Case	input	expected	operation
	1	AW1ABW2B	synchronous

A.2. BPMN Test Cases

In contrast to the BPEL tests, there is exactly one test step per test case for the BPMN test suite, since there is no additional interaction with a process instance during execution. Each test step is described by its *input* and the expected execution *trace*. The *input* corresponds to the value a certain process variable is initialized with and the *trace* corresponds to the tokens expected in the process log file for a passing test. Table A.3 lists the test cases for the BPMN conformance test suite described in Sect. 3.2.3.3.

Table A.3.: BPMN Conformance Test Cases

Property	Conformance Test
Name	CallActivity-GlobalTask
Description	Definitions contains a GlobalScriptTask which is called by a CallActivity.
Test case 1	input / trace task1, task2
Name	CallActivity-Process
Description	A collaboration with two participants. One process calls the other one through a callActivity.
Test case 1	input / trace task1, task2
Name	Cancel-Event
Description	A simple test for canceling a transaction. This test uses the two allowed cancel event types:CancelEndEvent (within the transaction) and CancelBoundaryEvent (interrupting, attached to the transaction).
Test case 1	input / trace task1, task2
Name	Conditional-BoundaryEvent-SubProcess-Interrupting
Description	A test for an conditional boundary event attached to asub process which is marked as interrupting.
Test case 1	input trace a task3
Test case 2	input trace b task1, task2
Name	Conditional-BoundaryEvent-SubProcess-NonInterrupting
Description	A test for an conditional boundary event attached to asub process which is marked as non interrupting.
Test case 1	input trace a task1, task2, task3
Test case 2	input trace b task1, task2
Name	Conditional-IntermediateEvent
Description	A test for an intermediate conditional event: ConditionIntermediate checks a condition set at process instantiation. If the condition is fulfilled the process completes, if not the process is locked at the event and should not complete.

Continued on next page

Table A.3 – *Continued from previous page*

Test case 1	input	trace
	a	task1

Test case 2	input	trace
	b	

Name	Conditional-StartEvent-EventSubProcess-Interrupting
Description	A test for an interrupting conditional start event in an event sub process

Test case 1	input	trace
	a	task1

Name	Conditional-StartEvent-EventSubProcess-NonInterrupting
Description	A test for an conditional start event in an event sub process which is marked as non interrupting.

Test case 1	input	trace
	a	task1, task2

Name	Compensation-BoundaryEvent-SubProcess
Description	Tests whether the compensation boundary event can be attached to asub process.

Test case 1	input	trace
		task1

Name	Compensation-EndEvent-SubProcess
Description	A test with a compensation end event placed in a sub process which should trigger the compensation of the task performed before.

Test case 1	input	trace
		task1

Name	Compensation-EndEvent-TopLevel
Description	A test with a top level compensation end event which should trigger the compensation of the task performed before.

Test case 1	input	trace
		task1

Name	Compensation-IntermediateEvent
Description	A test with a top level compensation intermediate event which should trigger the compensation of the task performed before.

Test case 1	input	trace
		task1

Name	Compensation-StartEvent-EventSubProcess
Description	A test with an event SubProcess, triggered by an Compensation StartEvent.The compensation is triggered by an Intermediate Throw Event placed outside the subprocess.

Continued on next page

Table A.3 – *Continued from previous page*

Test case 1	input	trace
		task1

Name	Compensation-TriggeredByCancel
Description	A test with a transaction which ends with a CancelEnd Event. In the course of canceling the transaction all successful executed tasks have to be compensated. Therefore, the compensational task Task1 has to be executed.

Test case 1	input	trace
		task1

Name	ComplexGateway
Description	A process with five scriptTasks and two complexGateways. Three of the tasks are enclosed by the complexGateways and each one is enabled based on input data. The activationCondition of the converging complexGate is set to 'activationCount >= 1', so the gateway should fire for any number of activated incoming branches.

Test case 1	input	trace
	a	task1, task4

Test case 2	input	trace
	b	task2, task4

Test case 3	input	trace
	c	task3, task4

Test case 4	input	trace
	ab	task1, task2, task4

Name	Error-BoundaryEvent-SubProcess-Interrupting
Description	A test for the error boundary event attached to a sub process.The task (task2) following the SequenceFlow originating from the boundary event should be executed. The Task (task3) following the normal outgoing sequence flow after the SubProcess must not be executed.

Test case 1	input	trace
		task1, task2

Name	Error-BoundaryEvent-Transaction-Interrupting
Description	A test for the error boundary event attached to a transaction.The task (task2) following the SequenceFlow originating from the boundary event should be executed. The Task (task3) following the normal outgoing sequence flow after the Transaction must not be executed.

Test case 1	input	trace
		task1, task2

Name	Error-EndEvent-TopLevel
Description	A simple test for the ErrorEndEvent in a top level process.

Continued on next page

Table A.3 – *Continued from previous page*

Test case 1	input	trace
	task1, ERROR-thrownErrorEvent	

Name	Error-StartEvent-EventSubProcess-Interrupting
Description	A test for the error start event in an event sub process. After the execution of the EventSubProcess the flow should continue normally.

Test case 1	input	trace
	task1, task2, task3	

Name	Escalation-BoundaryEvent-SubProcess-Interrupting
Description	A test for an escalation event interrupting a subprocess.The task (task2) following the Intermediate EscalationEvent and the Task (task4) following the normal outgoing sequence flow after the SubProcess must not be executed. The SequenceFlow originating from the boundary event is activated and therefore Task3 should be executed.

Test case 1	input	trace
	task1, task3	

Name	Escalation-BoundaryEvent-SubProcess-NonInterrupting
Description	A test for an escalation event NOT interrupting a subprocess.All tasks (Task1-4) should be executed.

Test case 1	input	trace
	task1, task2, task3, task4	

Name	Escalation-EndEvent-SubProcess
Description	A test for an escalation end event defined in a SubProcess.Only the task attached to the BoundaryEvent should be executed.

Test case 1	input	trace
	task1	

Name	Escalation-EndEvent-TopLevel
Description	A test for an escalation end event in a top level process.

Test case 1	input	trace
	task1, ERROR-thrownEscalationEvent	

Name	Escalation-IntermediateThrowEvent
Description	A test for an escalation intermediate throw event: Task1 can only be executed if the event has been thrown (and caught).

Test case 1	input	trace
	task1	

Name	Escalation-StartEvent-EventSubProcess-Interrupting
Description	A test for the interrupting escalation start event in an event SubProcess. Task1 within in the (normal) SubProcess should not be executed. Task 2 should be executed.

Continued on next page

Table A.3 – *Continued from previous page*

Test case 1	input	trace
	task2	

Name	Escalation-StartEvent-EventSubProcess-NonInterrupting
Description	A test for the escalation start event in an event sub process which is marked as "non interrupting". Task2 within in the (normal) SubProcess and Task3 which is defined after the SubProcess should be executed.

Test case 1	input	trace
		task1, task2, task3

Name	EventBasedGateway-Signals
Description	A process with five scriptTasks, a diverging parallelGateway, a diverging eventBasedGateway, an intermediate signal throw event and two intermediate signal catch events. The parallelGateway points to the eventBasedGateway in one branch and, in the other branch, throws the signal. This signal is caught by one of the branches following the eventBasedGateway.

Test case 1	input	trace
		task1, task2, task4

Name	EventBasedGateway-Timer
Description	A process with three scriptTasks, a diverging eventBasedGateway and two intermediate catch events. One of the catch events refers to a signal that is never thrown and the other one to a timer. Only the branch of the timer should ever be executed.

Test case 1	input	trace
	task2	

Name	ExclusiveDiverging-InclusiveConverging
Description	A process with four scriptTasks, a diverging exclusiveGateway and a converging inclusiveGateway. Two of the tasks are enclosed between the gateways and only one of them is triggered depending on input data. The inclusiveGateway should merge the incoming branches.

Test case 1	input	trace
	b	task2, task3

Test case 2	input	trace
	a	task1, task3

Test case 3	input	trace
	ab	task1, task3

Name	ExclusiveDiverging-ParallelConverging
Description	A process with four scriptTasks, a diverging exclusiveGateway and a converging parallelGateway. Two scriptTasks are enclosed by the gateways and the execution should deadlock, because only one incoming branch of the parallelGateway should ever be executed. Hence, the scriptTask following the parallelGateway should never be executed.

Continued on next page

Table A.3 – *Continued from previous page*

Test case 1	input	trace
	a	task1

Test case 2	input	trace
	b	task2

Test case 3	input	trace
	ab	task1

Name	ExclusiveGateway
Description	A process with four scriptTasks and exclusiveGateways. The execution of two of the tasks is controlled by the exclusiveGateways and only one of the tasks is actually executed.

Test case 1	input	trace
	b	task2, task3

Test case 2	input	trace
	a	task1, task3

Test case 3	input	trace
	ab	task1, task3

Test case 4	input	trace
	c	ERROR-runtime

Name	ExclusiveGateway-Default
Description	A process with five scriptTasks and exclusiveGateways. The execution of three of the tasks is controlled by the exclusiveGateways based on the input and only one of the tasks is actually executed.Two tasks are triggered through sequenceFlows with conditionExpressions and one is triggered through a sequenceFlow which is marked as default.

Test case 1	input	trace
	b	task2, task4

Test case 2	input	trace
	a	task1, task4

Test case 3	input	trace
	ab	task1, task4

Test case 4	input	trace
	c	task3, task4

Name	ExclusiveGatewayMixed
Description	A process with six scriptTasks and three exclusiveGateways.One of the gateways acts as a mixed gateway. Each pair of exclusiveGateways encapsulates two script tasks.The enabling of these scriptTasks depends on input data

Test case 1	input	trace
	a	task2, task4, task5

Continued on next page

Table A.3 – *Continued from previous page*

Test case 2	input	trace
	b	task1, task3, task5

Test case 3	input	trace
	ab	task1, task3, task5

Name	InclusiveDiverging-ExclusiveConverging
Description	A process with four scriptTasks, a diverging inclusiveGateway and a converging exclusiveGateway. Two of the tasks are encapsulated by the gateways. Either one, none, or both of the scriptTasks are enabled based on input data and as a result the exclusiveGateway should either fire once or twice.

Test case 1	input	trace
	ab	task1, task3, task2, task3

Test case 2	input	trace
	a	task1, task3

Test case 3	input	trace
	b	task2, task3

Name	InclusiveDiverging-ParallelConverging
Description	A process with four scriptTasks, a diverging inclusiveGateway and a converging parallelGateway. Two scriptTasks are enclosed by the gateways and the execution should deadlock if only one incoming branch of the parallelGateway is enabled. Hence, the scriptTask following the parallelGateway should only be executed in a single case.

Test case 1	input	trace
	a	task1

Test case 2	input	trace
	b	task2

Test case 3	input	trace
	ab	task1, task2, task3

Name	InclusiveGateway
Description	A process with four scriptTasks, two of which are encapsulated by inclusiveGateways. Either one, none, or both of the scriptTasks are enabled based on input data.

Test case 1	input	trace
	ab	task1, task2, task3

Test case 2	input	trace
	a	task1, task3

Test case 3	input	trace
	b	task2, task3

Continued on next page

Table A.3 – *Continued from previous page*

Test case 4	input	trace
	c	ERROR-runtime

Name	InclusiveGateway-Default
Description	A process with five scriptTasks, three of which are encapsulated by inclusiveGateways. One of the scriptTasks acts as a default task. Either one, both of the others or the default task are executed based on input data.

Test case 1	input	trace
	c	task3, task4

Name	MultiInstanceTask-AllBehavior
Description	A scriptTask that is marked as a sequential multiInstance task and is enabled three times and its behavior set to all.The task has a signal boundary event attached that points to another script task. The event should never be thrown.

Test case 1	input	trace
		task1, task1, task1, task2

Name	Lanes
Description	A collaboration with a single participant with two lanes. Lanes have no effect on the execution and should be ignored.

Test case 1	input	trace
		task1, task2, task3

Name	Link-Event
Description	A simple test for link events

Test case 1	input	trace
		task1

Name	LoopTask-LoopMaximum
Description	A scriptTask with standardLoopCharacteristics and a condition that always evaluates to true. Additionally a loopMaximum is set to three.

Test case 1	input	trace
		task1, task1, task1, task2

Name	LoopTask-NoIteration-TestBeforeFalse
Description	A scriptTask with standardLoopCharacteristics and a condition that always evaluates to false, but has testBefore set to false and, hence, should be executed once.

Test case 1	input	trace
		task1, task2

Name	LoopTask-NoIteration-TestBeforeTrue
Description	A scriptTask with standardLoopCharacteristics and a condition that always evaluates to false and has testBefore set to true. Hence, the task should never be executed.

Continued on next page

Table A.3 – *Continued from previous page*

Test case 1	input	trace
		task2

Name	MultiInstanceTask-NoneBehavior
Description	A scriptTask that is marked as a sequential multiInstance task and is enabled three times and its behavior set to none.The task has a signal boundary event attached that points to another script task. The event should be thrown for every task execution

Test case 1	input	trace
		task1, task3, task1, task3, task1, task3, task2

Name	MultiInstanceTask-OneBehavior
Description	A scriptTask that is marked as a sequential multiInstance task and is enabled three times and its behavior set to one.The task has a signal boundary event attached that points to another script task. The event should be thrown once.

Test case 1	input	trace
		task1, task3, task1, task1, task2

Name	MultiInstanceTask-Parallel
Description	A scriptTask that is marked as a parallel multiInstance task and is enabled three times

Test case 1	input	trace
		task1, task1, task1, task2

Name	MultiInstanceTask-Sequential
Description	A scriptTask that is marked as a sequential multiInstance task and is enabled three times

Test case 1	input	trace
		task1, task1, task1, task2

Name	ParallelDiverging-ExclusiveConverging
Description	A process with four tasks, a diverging parallelGateway and a converging exclusiveGateway. Two of the tasks are executed in parallel and then merged by the exclusiveGateway. As a result, the task following the exclusiveGateway should be followed twice.

Test case 1	input	trace
		task1, task3, task2, task3

Name	ParallelDiverging-InclusiveConverging
Description	A process with four tasks, a diverging parallelGateway and a converging inclusiveGateway. Two of the tasks are executed in parallel and merged by the inclusiveGateway.

Test case 1	input	trace
		task1, task2, task3

Name	ParallelGateway

Continued on next page

Description	A process with four scriptTasks and two parallelGateways. Two of the scriptTasks are surrounded by the parallelGateways.
Test case 1	input — trace
	task1, task2, task3

Name	ParallelGateway-Conditions
Description	A process with four scriptTasks and two parallelGateways. Two of the scriptTasks are surrounded by the parallelGateways and the sequenceFlows pointing to the mergine gateway have conditions. These conditions should be ignored by an engine.
Test case 1	input — trace
	a — task1, task2, task3
Test case 2	input — trace
	b — task1, task2, task3
Test case 3	input — trace
	ab — task1, task2, task3
Test case 4	input — trace
	c — task1, task2, task3

Name	Participant
Description	A collaboration with a single participant
Test case 1	input — trace
	task1

Name	SequenceFlow
Description	A process with two scriptTasks connected by a sequenceFlow
Test case 1	input — trace
	task1

Name	SequenceFlow-Conditional
Description	A process with three scriptTasks connected by sequenceFlows. The first scriptTask points to the other tasks with sequenceFlows. One of these sequenceFlows is associated with a conditionExpression
Test case 1	input — trace
	a — task1, task2
Test case 2	input — trace
	b — task2

Name	SequenceFlow-ConditionalDefault
Description	A process with three scriptTasks connected by sequenceFlows. The first scriptTask points to the other tasks with sequenceFlows. One of these sequenceFlows is associated with a conditionExpression, the other one is marked as default

Continued on next page

Table A.3 – *Continued from previous page*

Test case 1	input	trace
	a	task1

Test case 2	input	trace
	b	task2

Name	SequenceFlow-ConditionalDefault-Normal
Description	A process with four scriptTasks connected by sequenceFlows. The first scriptTask points to the other three tasks with sequenceFlows. The first of these sequenceFlows is associated with a conditionExpression, the second one is marked as default and the third has no condition associated. This is a special case document in Sec. 13.2.1, p. 427.

Test case 1	input	trace
	b	task2, task3

Name	Signal-EndEvent-SubProcess
Description	A test to test a signal end event placed in a SubProcess. The thrown signal is caught by an attached boundary event.

Test case 1	input	trace
		task1

Name	Signal-BoundaryEvent-SubProcess-NonInterrupting
Description	A test for a signal boundary event NOT interrupting a subprocess. All tasks (Task1-4) should be executed.

Test case 1	input	trace
		task1, task2, task3, task4

Name	Signal-BoundaryEvent-SubProcess-Interrupting
Description	A test for a signal boundary event interrupting a subprocess. The task (task2) following the Intermediate SignalEvent and the Task (task4) following the normal outgoing sequence flow after the SubProcess must not be executed. The SequenceFlow originating from the boundary event is activated and therefore Task3 should be executed.

Test case 1	input	trace
		task1, task3

Name	Signal-IntermediateEvent-ThrowAndCatch
Description	A test for signal intermediate events: After a parallel split onebranch of the process awaits a signal which is thrown by the other branch.

Test case 1	input	trace
		task1

Name	Signal-StartEvent-EventSubProcess-Interrupting
Description	A test for the interrupting signal start event in an event SubProcess. Task1 within in the (normal) SubProcess should not be executed. Task 2 should be executed.

Continued on next page

Test case 1	input	trace
		task2

Name	Signal-StartEvent-EventSubProcess-NonInterrupting
Description	A test for the signal start event in an event sub process which is marked as "non interrupting". Task2 within in the (normal) SubProcess and Task3 which is defined after the SubProcess should be executed.

Test case 1	input	trace
		task1, task2, task3

Name	SubProcess
Description	A process that contains a subProcess

Test case 1	input	trace
		task1, task2

Name	Transaction
Description	A process that contains a transaction

Test case 1	input	trace
		task1, task2

Name	Terminate-Event
Description	A test for a terminate end event

Test case 1	input	trace

Name	Timer-IntermediateEvent
Description	A process with two scriptTasks. There is a intermediateCatchEvent in between the tasks that delay the execution for a short period of time.

Test case 1	input	trace
		task1

Name	Timer-BoundaryEvent-SubProcess-Interrupting
Description	A process with multiple scriptTasks and a subProcess with timer events. The execution of the subProcess is delayed by an intermediate timer event for a short amount of time. In the meantime, a boundary timer event should fire and interrupt the subProcess.

Test case 1	input	trace
		task3

Name	Timer-BoundaryEvent-SubProcess-NonInterrupting
Description	A process with multiple scriptTasks and a subProcess with timer events. The execution of the subProcess is delayed by an intermediate timer event for a short amount of time. In the meantime, a boundary timer event should fire without interrupting the subProcess.

Test case 1	input	trace
		task1, task2, task3

Continued on next page

Table A.3 – *Continued from previous page*

Name	Timer-StartEvent-EventSubProcess-Interrupting
Description	A process with an ordinary subProcess and an event subProcess.The subProcess encloses the event subProcess and the latter is started by a timer startEvent. The event subProcess interrupts the activities of its parent subProcess.
Test case 1	input trace <hr> task2
Name	Timer-StartEvent-EventSubProcess-NonInterrupting
Description	A process with an ordinary subProcess and an event subProcess.The subProcess encloses the event subProcess and the latter is started by a timer startEvent. All activities should be executed without interruption.
Test case 1	input trace <hr> task1, task2, task3

B. Portability Test Assertions

In Table B.1, this section lists the test assertions encoded in the bpp tool that have been used to perform the practical evaluation of portability metrics presented in Sect. 4.4. As described in Sect. 4.4.2, they consist of a unique *ID*, a *description* of the process element they are targeted at, a *target* that corresponds to an XPath expression which is executed during their evaluation, and a *degree* which identifies their severity with respect to portability. The table has been generated automatically from the code of the bpp tool.

Table B.1.: Portability Test Assertions

Property	Test Assertion
ID	bpp-r1
Description	A process definition should not use the doXslTransform() extension function
Target	//*[local-name() = 'from' and contains(. , 'doXslTransform')] | //*[local-name() = 'to' and contains(. , 'doXslTransform')]
Degree	5
ID	bpp-r2
Description	A process definition should not rely on the semantics of keepSrcElementName in a \<copy\> construct
Target	//*[@keepSrcElementName='yes']
Degree	7
ID	bpp-r3-1
Description	A process definition must not use the empty variant in a from-spec in an assignment
Target	//*[local-name() = 'from' and not(text()) and not(node()) and empty(@variable) and empty(@part) and empty(@partnerLink) and empty(@endpointReference) and empty(@property) and empty(@expressionlanguage) and empty(@expression)]
Degree	9
ID	bpp-r3-2
Description	A process definition must not use the empty variant in a to-spec in an assignment
Target	//*[local-name() = 'to' and not(text()) and not(node()) and not(@variable) and not(@part) and not(@partnerLink) and not(@endpointReference) and not(@property) and not(@expressionlanguage) and not(@expression)]
Degree	9

Continued on next page

Table B.1 – *Continued from previous page*

ID	bpp-r3-3
Description	A process definition may directly assign an int-value in a from-spec in an assignment
Target	//*[local-name() = 'from' and (string(number(.)) != 'NaN') and not (./*[text()])]
Degree	1

ID	bpp-r3-4
Description	A process definition may assign a property in a from-spec in an assignment
Target	//*[local-name() = 'from' and exists(@property)]
Degree	1

ID	bpp-r4
Description	A process definition should not use dynamic invocation based on the re-assignment of a partnerLink
Target	//*[local-name() = 'to' and not(empty(@partnerLink))]
Degree	4

ID	bpp-r5
Description	A process definition may use a query in a copy operation
Target	//*[local-name() = 'from' or local-name() = 'to']/*[local-name() = 'query']
Degree	1

ID	bpp-r6
Description	A process definition should not use validation during an assignment
Target	//*[@validate='yes']
Degree	5

ID	bpp-r7
Description	A process definition should not use the shortcut syntax for catching a fault during a service invocation.
Target	//*[local-name() = 'invoke']/*[local-name() = 'catch']
Degree	7

ID	bpp-r8
Description	A process definition should not use the shortcut syntax for catching any fault during a service invocation
Target	//*[local-name() = 'invoke']/*[local-name() = 'catchAll']
Degree	3

ID	bpp-r9
Description	A process definition should not use the shortcut syntax for using compensation during a service invocation
Target	//*[local-name() = 'invoke']/*[local-name() = 'compensationHandler']
Degree	3

ID	bpp-r10
Description	A process definition should not use correlations in a service invocation

Continued on next page

Target	//*[local-name() = 'invoke' and exists(@outputVariable)]/*[local-name() = 'correlations']/*[local-name() = 'correlation' and exists(@pattern)]
Degree	4

ID	bpp-r11
Description	A process definition should not omit the variable when invoking a web service operation that does not expect an input message
Target	//*[local-name() = 'invoke' and empty(@inputVariable) and empty(@outputVariable) and not(child::fromParts) and not (child::toParts)]
Degree	5

ID	bpp-r12-1
Description	A process definition should not use the fromParts shortcut syntax during a service invocation
Target	//*[local-name() = 'invoke']/*[local-name() = 'fromParts']
Degree	4

ID	bpp-r12-2
Description	A process definition should not use the toParts shortcut syntax during a service invocation
Target	//*[local-name() = 'invoke']/*[local-name() = 'toParts']
Degree	5

ID	bpp-r13
Description	A process definition should not use correlations during the receipt of a message
Target	//*[local-name() = 'receive']/*[local-name() = 'correlations']
Degree	3

ID	bpp-r14-1
Description	A process definition should not use the fromParts shortcut syntax during the receipt of a message
Target	//*[local-name() = 'receive']/*[local-name() = 'fromParts']
Degree	4

ID	bpp-r14-2
Description	A process definition should not use the toParts shortcut syntax when replying to an invocation
Target	//*[local-name() = 'reply']/*[local-name() = 'toParts']
Degree	5

ID	bpp-r14-3
Description	A process definition should not explicitly reply a fault in a <reply> activity
Target	//*[local-name() = 'reply' and exists(@faultName)]
Degree	2

ID	bpp-r14-4
Description	A process definition may use messageExchanges in a <reply> or a <receive> activity
Target	//*[(local-name() = 'reply' or local-name() = 'receive') and exists(@messageExchange)]

Continued on next page

Table B.1 – *Continued from previous page*

Degree	1
ID	bpp-r15
Description	A process definition should not use the rethrow activity.
Target	//*[local-name() = 'rethrow']
Degree	3
ID	bpp-r16
Description	A process definition should not use a faultVariable when rethrowing a fault
Target	//*[local-name() = 'catch' and exists(@faultVariable)]//*[local-name() = 'rethrow']
Degree	6
ID	bpp-r17
Description	A process definition should not use the throw activity to propagate faults out of the scope of the process
Target	//*[local-name() = 'throw' and not(ancestor::*[(local-name() = 'scope' or local-name() = 'process') and (child::*[local-name() = 'faultHandlers'])])]
Degree	3
ID	bpp-r18
Description	A process definition should not use the throw activity with a faultVariable to signal faults
Target	//*[local-name() = 'throw' and exists(@faultVariable)]
Degree	5
ID	bpp-r19
Description	A process definition should not use the validate activity
Target	//*[local-name() = 'validate']
Degree	5
ID	bpp-r20
Description	A process definition should not initialize a variable with a default value
Target	//*[local-name() = 'variable']/*[local-name() = 'from']
Degree	3
ID	bpp-r21
Description	A process definition may use the <wait> activity
Target	//*[local-name() = 'wait']
Degree	1
ID	bpp-r22-1
Description	A process definition should not use the getVariableProperty() extension function in a <from> statement
Target	//*[(local-name() = 'from') and contains(. , 'getVariableProperty')]
Degree	2
ID	bpp-r22-2
Description	A process definition should not use the getVariableProperty() extension function in a <condition> statement

Continued on next page

Target	//*[(local-name() = 'condition') and contains(. , 'getVariableProperty')]
Degree	2
ID	bpp-r23
Description	A process definition should not use the <compensateScope> activity to signal compensation
Target	//*[local-name() = 'compensateScope']
Degree	2
ID	bpp-r24
Description	A process definition should not use message-based eventHandlers
Target	//*[local-name() = 'eventHandlers']/*[local-name() = 'onEvent']
Degree	5
ID	bpp-r25
Description	A process definition may use timeout-based eventHandlers
Target	//*[local-name() = 'eventHandlers']/*[local-name() = 'onAlarm']
Degree	1
ID	bpp-r26
Description	A process definition should not use isolated scopes
Target	//*[local-name() = 'scope' and @isolated='yes']
Degree	3
ID	bpp-r27-1
Description	A process definition should not define correlationSets on scope-level
Target	//*[local-name() = 'scope' and child::*[local-name()='correlationSets']]
Degree	4
ID	bpp-r27-2
Description	A process definition may define messageExchanges on scope-level
Target	//*[local-name() = 'scope' and child::*[local-name()='messageExchanges']]
Degree	1
ID	bpp-r27-3
Description	A process definition should not define partnerLinks on scope-level
Target	//*[local-name() = 'scope' and child::*[local-name()='partnerLinks']]
Degree	2
ID	bpp-r27-4
Description	A process definition may define variables on scope-level
Target	//*[local-name() = 'scope' and child::*[local-name()='variables']]
Degree	1
ID	bpp-r28
Description	A process definition should not use the <compensate> activity to signal compensation
Target	//*[local-name() = 'compensate']
Degree	2

Continued on next page

Table B.1 – *Continued from previous page*

ID	bpp-r29
Description	A process definition should not use the fromParts shortcut syntax in a message-based eventHandler
Target	//*[local-name() = 'eventHandlers']/*[local-name() = 'onEvent']/*[local-name() = 'fromParts']
Degree	6

ID	bpp-r31-1
Description	A process definition should not catch a fault based on the faultVariable. Catching faults by name only is recommended
Target	//*[local-name() = 'faultHandlers']/*[local-name() = 'catch' and exists(@faultVariable)]
Degree	2

ID	bpp-r32
Description	A process definition may use a compensationHandler within a <while>, <forEach> or <repeatUntil> activity
Target	//*[local-name() = 'while' or local-name() = 'forEach' or local-name() = 'repeatUntil']//*[local-name() = 'compensationHandler']
Degree	1

ID	bpp-r33
Description	A process definition should not use terminationHandlers
Target	//*[local-name() = 'terminationHandler']
Degree	4

ID	bpp-r34-1
Description	A process definition may use the flow activity
Target	//*[local-name() = 'flow']
Degree	1

ID	bpp-r34-2
Description	A process definition should not use links
Target	//*[local-name() = 'links']
Degree	2

ID	bpp-r34-3
Description	A process definition should not use a joinCondition to merge links
Target	//*[local-name() = 'joinCondition']
Degree	5

ID	bpp-r34-4
Description	A process definition should not use a transitionCondition to merge links
Target	//*[local-name() = 'source' and child::*[local-name() = 'transitionCondition']]
Degree	2

ID	bpp-r35
Description	A process definition may use the forEach activity
Target	//*[local-name() = 'forEach']

Continued on next page

Degree	1
ID	bpp-r36
Description	A process definition should not use the forEach activity with a completion-Condition
Target	//*[local-name() = 'forEach']/*[local-name() = 'completionCondition']
Degree	4
ID	bpp-r37
Description	A process definition should not use correlations in an onMessage eventHandler in a pick activity
Target	//*[local-name() = 'pick']/*[local-name() = 'onMessage']//*[local-name() = 'correlations']
Degree	2
ID	bpp-r38
Description	A process definition may use a timeout-based eventHandler in a pick activity
Target	//*[local-name() = 'pick']/*[local-name() = 'onAlarm']
Degree	1
ID	bpp-r41
Description	A process definition may use the repeatUntil activity
Target	//*[local-name() = 'repeatUntil']
Degree	1
ID	bpp-r42
Description	A process definition should not use the repeatUntil activity with a condition that uses '='
Target	//*[local-name() = 'repeatUntil']/*[local-name()='condition' and contains(., '=')]
Degree	2
ID	bpp-r43
Description	A process definition may use the forEach activity with the parallel attribute set to 'yes'
Target	//*[local-name() = 'forEach' and (@parallel = 'yes')]
Degree	1
ID	bpp-r44
Description	A process definition should not use the forEach activity with a completion-Condition and parallel attribute set to 'yes'
Target	//*[local-name() = 'forEach' and (@parallel = 'yes')]/*[local-name() = 'completionCondition']
Degree	6
ID	bpp-r45
Description	A process definition should not use the forEach activity with a completion-Condition and a negative number of branches

Continued on next page

Table B.1 – *Continued from previous page*

Target	//*[local-name() = 'forEach']/*[local-name() = 'completionCondition']/*[local-name() = 'branches' and starts-with(text(),'-')]
Degree	6
ID	bpp-r46
Description	A process definition should not use the forEach activity with a negative startCounterValue or finalCounterValue
Target	//*[local-name() = 'forEach']/*[(local-name() = 'startCounterValue' and starts-with(text(),'-')) or (local-name() = 'finalCounterValue' and starts-with(text(),'-'))]
Degree	4
ID	bpp-r47
Description	A process definition should not use the forEach activity with a too large startCounterValue
Target	//*[local-name() = 'forEach']/*[(local-name() = 'startCounterValue' and (number(text()) >= 4294967295))]
Degree	4
ID	bpp-r48
Description	A process definition should not use the forEach activity with a completion-Condition and the successfulBranchesOnly attribute set to 'yes'
Target	//*[local-name() = 'forEach']/*[local-name() = 'completionCondition']/*[local-name() = 'branches' and (@successful-BranchesOnly = 'yes')]
Degree	4
ID	bpp-r39
Description	A process definition must not have a namespace different from http://docs.oasis-open.org/wsbpel/2.0/process/executable namespace
Target	//*[local-name() = 'process' and not(namespace-uri() = 'http://docs.oasis-open.org/wsbpel/2.0/process/executable')]
Degree	8
ID	bpp-r40
Description	A process definition must not contain non-BPEL elements

Continued on next page

Target	//*[not(ancestor::*[local-name() = 'literal']) and not(local-name() ='process') and not(local-name() = 'import') and not(local-name() = 'partnerLinks') and not(local-name() = 'partnerLink') and not(local-name() = 'variables') and not(local-name() = 'variable') and not(local-name() = 'correlationSets') and not(local-name() = 'correlationSet') and not(local-name() = 'sequence') and not(local-name() = 'if') and not(local-name() = 'condition') and not(local-name() = 'elseif') and not(local-name() = 'else') and not(local-name() = 'while') and not(local-name() = 'repeatUntil') and not(local-name() = 'pick') and not(local-name() = 'onMessage') and not(local-name() = 'correlations') and not(local-name() = 'correlation') and not(local-name() = 'fromParts') and not(local-name() = 'fromPart') and not(local-name() = 'toParts') and not(local-name() = 'toPart') and not(local-name() = 'onAlarm') and not(local-name() = 'for') and not(local-name() = 'until') and not(local-name() = 'flow') and not(local-name() = 'links') and not(local-name() = 'link') and not(local-name() = 'targets') and not(local-name() = 'joinCondition') and not(local-name() = 'target') and not(local-name() = 'sources') and not(local-name() = 'source') and not(local-name() = 'transitionCondition') and not(local-name() = 'forEach') and not(local-name() = 'startCounterValue') and not(local-name() = 'finalCounterValue') and not(local-name() = 'completionCondition') and not(local-name() = 'branches') and not(local-name() = 'receive') and not(local-name() = 'assign') and not(local-name() = 'copy') and not(local-name() = 'from') and not(local-name() = 'to') and not(local-name() = 'empty') and not(local-name() = 'reply') and not(local-name() = 'scope') and not(local-name() = 'messageExchanges') and not(local-name() = 'messageExchange') and not(local-name() = 'eventHandlers') and not(local-name() = 'faultHandlers') and not(local-name() = 'compensationHandler') and not(local-name() = 'terminationHandlers') and not(local-name() = 'compensate') and not(local-name() = 'compensateScope') and not(local-name() = 'catch') and not(local-name() = 'catchAll') and not(local-name() = 'rethrow') and not(local-name() = 'repeatEvery') and not(local-name() = 'throw') and not(local-name() = 'invoke') and not(local-name() = 'wait') and not(local-name() = 'exit') and not(local-name() = 'query') and not(local-name() = 'literal') and not(local-name() = 'serviceref') and not(local-name() = 'EndpointReference') and not(local-name() = 'exit') and not(local-name() = 'Address') and not(local-name() = 'onEvent')]
Degree	8

ID	bpp-r30
Description	A process definition should not rely on the semantics of exitOnStandardFault
Target	//*[@exitOnStandardFault='yes']
Degree	3

ID	bpp-r31-1
Description	A process definition must not rely on the correct triggering of xsltInvalidSource fault
Target	//*[local-name() = 'faultHandlers']/*[local-name() = 'catch' and contains(@faultName,'xsltInvalidSource')]
Degree	8

ID	bpp-r31-3
Description	A process definition must not rely on the correct triggering of subLanguageExecutionFault

Continued on next page

281

B. Portability Test Assertions

Target	//*[local-name() = 'faultHandlers']/*[local-name() = 'catch' and contains(@faultName, 'subLanguageExecutionFault')]
Degree	9

ID	bpp-r31-4
Description	A process definition should not rely on the correct triggering of xsltStyleSheetNotFound
Target	//*[local-name() = 'faultHandlers']/*[local-name() = 'catch' and contains(@faultName,'xsltStyleSheetNotFound')]
Degree	6

ID	bpp-r31-5
Description	A process definition must not rely on the correct triggering of unsupportedReference fault
Target	//*[local-name() = 'faultHandlers']/*[local-name() = 'catch' and contains(@faultName,'unsupportedReference')]
Degree	8

ID	bpp-r31-6
Description	A process definition should not rely on the correct triggering of selectionFailure
Target	//*[local-name() = 'faultHandlers']/*[local-name() = 'catch' and contains(@faultName,'selectionFailure')]
Degree	3

ID	bpp-r31-7
Description	A process definition should not rely on the correct triggering of ambiguousReceive
Target	//*[local-name() = 'faultHandlers']/*[local-name() = 'catch' and contains(@faultName,'ambiguousReceive')]
Degree	7

ID	bpp-r31-8
Description	A process definition must not rely on the correct triggering of conflictingReceive
Target	//*[local-name() = 'faultHandlers']/*[local-name() = 'catch' and contains(@faultName,'conflictingReceive')]
Degree	9

ID	bpp-r31-9
Description	A process definition must not rely on the correct triggering of conflictingRequest
Target	//*[local-name() = 'faultHandlers']/*[local-name() = 'catch' and contains(@faultName,'conflictingRequest')]
Degree	9

ID	bpp-r31-10
Description	A process definition should not rely on the correct triggering of correlationViolation
Target	//*[local-name() = 'faultHandlers']/*[local-name() = 'catch' and contains(@faultName,'correlationViolation')]

Continued on next page

Degree	7

ID	bpp-r31-11
Description	A process definition should not rely on the correct triggering of uninitialized-Variable
Target	//*[local-name() = 'faultHandlers']/*[local-name() = 'catch' and contains(@faultName,'uninitializedVariable')]
Degree	4

ID	bpp-r31-12
Description	A process definition should not rely on the correct triggering of invalidExpressionValue
Target	//*[local-name() = 'faultHandlers']/*[local-name() = 'catch' and contains(@faultName,'invalidExpressionValue')]
Degree	3

ID	bpp-r31-13
Description	A process definition should not rely on the correct triggering of missingReply
Target	//*[local-name() = 'faultHandlers']/*[local-name() = 'catch' and contains(@faultName,'missingReply')]
Degree	7

ID	bpp-r31-14
Description	A process definition should not rely on the correct triggering of missingRequest
Target	//*[local-name() = 'faultHandlers']/*[local-name() = 'catch' and contains(@faultName,'missingRequest')]
Degree	7

ID	bpp-r31-15
Description	A process definition should not rely on the correct triggering of joinFailure
Target	//*[local-name() = 'faultHandlers']/*[local-name() = 'catch' and contains(@faultName,'joinFailure')]
Degree	4

ID	bpp-r31-16
Description	A process definition should not rely on the correct triggering of invalidVariables
Target	//*[local-name() = 'faultHandlers']/*[local-name() = 'catch' and contains(@faultName,'invalidVariables')]
Degree	5

ID	bpp-r31-17
Description	A process definition should not rely on the correct triggering of completionConditionFailure
Target	//*[local-name() = 'faultHandlers']/*[local-name() = 'catch' and contains(@faultName, 'completionConditionFailure')]
Degree	6

ID	bpp-r31-18

Continued on next page

Table B.1 – *Continued from previous page*

Description	A process definition should not rely on the correct triggering of suppressJoin-Failure
Target	//*[local-name() = 'faultHandlers']/*[local-name() = 'catch' and contains(@faultName,'suppressJoinFailure')]
Degree	2

ID	bpp-r31-19
Description	A process definition should not rely on the correct triggering of mismatchedAssignmentFailure
Target	//*[local-name() = 'faultHandlers']/*[local-name() = 'catch' and contains(@faultName, 'mismatchedAssignmentFailure')]
Degree	6

C. Adaptability Scores

In Table C.1, this section lists all adaptable elements used in the evaluation of adaptability discussed in Chap. 6. Every element is described by its *name* and a *documentation* that outlines design decisions. Moreover, we list the XPath *expression* that can be used to select the element in a BPMN file. Finally, the *adaptions* correspond to the alternatives that exist for a particular element. The size of the list of adaptions is also shown in the first column. The table has been generated automatically from the code of the metrics suite.

Table C.1.: Adaptability Scores

Property	Element
Element name	adHocSubProcess
Documentation	Due to its unstructured nature, no general advice can be given on how to adapt an adHocSubProcess
Expression	//*[local-name() = 'definitions']//*[local-name() = 'adHocSubProcess']
Adaptions (0)	[]
Element name	businessRuleTask
Documentation	A businessRuleTask can be adapted by another task that can be used to trigger (programmatically or manually) the execution of a business rule through another program and return the result
Expression	//*[local-name() = 'definitions']//*[local-name() = 'businessRuleTask']
Adaptions (7)	[serviceTask, userTask, scriptTask, sendAndReceiveTask, globalScriptTask, globalUserTask, globalBusinessRuleTask]
Element name	callActivity
Documentation	A callActivity can be adapted by replacing it with a replica of the called globalActivity or process embedded into the calling process
Expression	//*[local-name() = 'definitions']//*[local-name() = 'callActivity']
Adaptions (1)	[embedIntoProcess]
Element name	cancelEndEvent
Documentation	Since there is no alternative endEvent with transactional sematics, this event cannot be adapted
Expression	//*[local-name() = 'definitions']//*[local-name() = 'endEvent' and (child::*[local-name() = 'cancelEventDefinition'] or child::*[local-name() = 'eventDefinitionRef' and text() = //*[local-name() = 'cancelEventDefinition']/@id]) and (count(child::*[contains(local-name(),'ventDefinition')]) = 1)]
Adaptions (0)	[]

Continued on next page

Table C.1 – *Continued from previous page*

Element name	compensationEndEvent
Documentation	Since there is no alternative endEvent with compensation sematics, this event cannot be adapted
Expression	//*[local-name() = 'definitions']//*[local-name() = 'endEvent' and (child::*[local-name() = 'compensationEventDefinition'] or child::*[local-name() = 'eventDefinitionRef' and text() = //*[local-name() = 'compensationEventDefinition']/@id]) and (count(child::*[contains(local-name(),'ventDefinition')]) = 1)]
Adaptions (0)	[]
Element name	compensationStartEvent
Documentation	A compensationStartEvent cannot be adapted since there is no alternative start event with compensational semantics
Expression	//*[local-name() = 'definitions']//*[local-name() = 'subProcess' and @triggeredByEvent = 'true']/*[local-name() = 'startEvent' and @isInterrupting = 'true' and (child::*[local-name() = 'compensationEventDefinition'] or child::*[local-name() = 'eventDefinitionRef' and text() = //*[local-name() = 'compensationEventDefinition']/@id]) and (count(child::*[contains(local-name(),'ventDefinition')]) = 1)]
Adaptions (0)	[]
Element name	complexGateway
Documentation	The general behavior of the complexGateway cannot be emulated by any other construct
Expression	//*[local-name() = 'definitions']//*[local-name() = 'complexGateway']
Adaptions (0)	[]
Element name	conditionalStartEvent
Documentation	A conditionalStartEvent can be adapted to another startEvent that represents normal control-flow and is fired through a trigger
Expression	//*[local-name() = 'definitions']//*[local-name() = 'startEvent' and (child::*[local-name() = 'conditionalEventDefinition'] or child::*[local-name() = 'eventDefinitionRef' and text() = //*[local-name() = 'conditionalEventDefinition']/@id]) and (count(child::*[contains(local-name(),'ventDefinition')]) = 1)]
Adaptions (4)	[messageStartEvent, signalStartEvent, multipleStartEvent, parallelMultipleStartEvent]
Element name	errorEndEvent
Documentation	There is no equivalent for this end event, since it terminates all active threads and signals a fault
Expression	//*[local-name() = 'definitions']//*[local-name() = 'endEvent' and (child::*[local-name() = 'errorEventDefinition'] or child::*[local-name() = 'eventDefinitionRef' and text() = //*[local-name() = 'errorEventDefinition']/@id]) and (count(child::*[contains(local-name(),'ventDefinition')]) = 1)]
Adaptions (0)	[]
Element name	escalationEndEvent

Continued on next page

Table C.1 – *Continued from previous page*

Documentation	There is no equivalent for this end event, since it does not terminate all active threads and, at the same time, signals a problem
Expression	//*[local-name() = 'definitions']//*[local-name() = 'endEvent' and (child::*[local-name() = 'escalationEventDefinition'] or child::*[local-name() = 'eventDefinitionRef' and text() = //*[local-name() = 'escalationEventDefinition']/@id]) and (count(child::*[contains(local-name(),'ventDefinition')]) = 1)]
Adaptions (0)	[]
Element name	eventBasedGateway
Documentation	An eventBasedGateway can be adapted to a solution where an intermediate multipleCatchEvent waits for the occurence of one among a set of events and a different control-flow path is taken by a following gateway, depending on the type of event
Expression	//*[local-name() = 'definitions']//*[local-name() = 'eventBasedGateway' and not (@eventGatewayType = 'parallel') and not (@instantiate = 'true')]
Adaptions (3)	[intermediateMultipleCatchEventFollowedByExclusiveGateway, intermediateMultipleCatchEventFollowedByInclusiveGateway, intermediateMultipleCatchEventFollowedByComplexGateway]
Element name	eventSubProcess
Documentation	EventSubProcesses can be adapted to a different form of subProcess that is executed through a callActivity. In case of an interrupting startEvent, the subProcess can be embedded into the normal flow of control (thus halting the parent process). In case of a noninterrupting startEvent the subProcess must be called in parallel to the normal flow using a parallelGateway.
Expression	//*[local-name() = 'definitions']//*[local-name() = 'subProcess' and @triggeredByEvent = 'true']
Adaptions (3)	[callActivityAndTransactionSubProcess, callActiviyAndAdHocSubProcess, callActivityAndOrdinarySubProcess]
Element name	exclusiveGateway
Documentation	An exclusiveGateway can be adapted to any other gateway that allows for the triggering of one among a set of branches
Expression	//*[local-name() = 'definitions']//*[local-name() = 'exclusiveGateway']
Adaptions (3)	[eventBasedGateway, complexGateway, inclusiveGateway]
Element name	globalBusinessRuleTask
Documentation	A globalBusinessRuleTask can be adapted through another task that triggers (programmatically or manually) the execution of a business rule through another program and returns the result
Expression	//*[local-name() = 'definitions']//*[local-name() = 'globalBusinessRuleTask']
Adaptions (7)	[serviceTask, userTask, scriptTask, businessRuleTask, sendAndReceiveTask, globalScriptTask, globalUserTask]
Element name	globalManualTask
Documentation	A globalManualTask can be embedded into a process as an ordinary manual task. Apart from this, there is no alternative way to represent an arbitrary external action in general

Continued on next page

Table C.1 – *Continued from previous page*

Expression	//*[local-name() = 'definitions']//*[local-name() = 'globalManualTask']
Adaptions (1)	[manualTask]
Element name	globalScriptTask
Documentation	A globalScriptTask can be the adaptions can be embedded into the process as an ordinary scriptTask or be adapted to another task that triggers the execution of a script at another entity (programmatically or manually). A receiveTask is not suitable as it passively waits without performing an action and a businessRuleTask is too specific
Expression	//*[local-name() = 'definitions']//*[local-name() = 'globalScriptTask']
Adaptions (5)	[serviceTask, sendTask, userTask, scriptTask, globalUserTask]
Element name	globalUserTask
Documentation	A globalUserTask can be embedded into the process as an ordinary userTask or be adapted through another task that is programmed to ask for user input
Expression	//*[local-name() = 'definitions']/*[local-name() = 'globalUserTask']
Adaptions (5)	[scriptTask, serviceTask, sendTask, globalScriptTask, userTask]
Element name	inclusiveGateway
Documentation	An inclusiveGateway can only be adapted to a complexGateway which is strictly more expressive
Expression	//*[local-name() = 'definitions']//*[local-name() = 'inclusiveGateway']
Adaptions (1)	[complexGateway]
Element name	instantiatingEventBasedGateway
Documentation	An instantiatingEventBasedGateway can be adapted to a solution where the multiple startEvents are merged by an exclusiveGateway
Expression	//*[local-name() = 'definitions']//*[local-name() = 'eventBasedGateway' and not (@eventGatewayType = 'parallel') and (@instantiate = 'true')]
Adaptions (1)	[startEventsFollowedByExclusiveGateway]
Element name	instantiatingParallelEventBasedGateway
Documentation	An instantiatingParallelEventBasedGateway cannot be adapted since there is no alternative way to avoid the instantiation of the process until multiple events have been received
Expression	//*[local-name() = 'definitions']//*[local-name() = 'eventBasedGateway' and (@eventGatewayType = 'parallel') and (@instantiate = 'true')]
Adaptions (0)	[]
Element name	intermediateCompensationThrowEvent
Documentation	An intermediateCompensationThrowEvent cannot be adapted since there is no other intermediate throw event with compensation semantics
Expression	//*[local-name() = 'definitions']//*[local-name() = 'intermediateThrow-Event' and (child::*[local-name() = 'compensationEventDefinition'] or child::*[local-name() = 'eventDefinitionRef' and text() = //*[local-name() = 'compensationEventDefinition']/@id]) and (count(child::*[contains(local-name(),'ventDefinition')]) = 1)]
Adaptions (0)	[]

Continued on next page

Table C.1 – *Continued from previous page*

Element name	intermediateConditionalCatchEvent
Documentation	An intermediateConditionalCatchEvent can be adapted to another intermediate catch event that triggers normal control-flow continuation
Expression	//*[local-name() = 'definitions']//*[local-name() = 'intermediateCatchEvent' and (child::*[local-name() = 'conditionalEventDefinition'] or child::*[local-name() = 'eventDefinitionRef' and text() = //*[local-name() = 'conditionalEventDefinition']/@id]) and (count(child::*[contains(local-name(),'ventDefinition')]) = 1)]
Adaptions (4)	[intermediateSignalCatchEvent, intermediateMessageCatchEvent, intermediateMultipleCatchEvent, intermediateMultipleParallelCatchEvent]
Element name	intermediateEscalationThrowEvent
Documentation	An intermediateEscalationThrowEvent can be adapted to another intermediate throw event that leads to exceptional control-flow continuation and is fired by a trigger
Expression	//*[local-name() = 'definitions']//*[local-name() = 'intermediateThrowEvent' and (child::*[local-name() = 'escalationEventDefinition'] or child::*[local-name() = 'eventDefinitionRef' and text() = //*[local-name() = 'escalationEventDefinition']/@id]) and (count(child::*[contains(local-name(),'ventDefinition')]) = 1)]
Adaptions (4)	[intermediateMessageThrowEvent, intermediateSignalThrowEvent, intermediateMultipleThrowEvent, intermediateMultipleParallelThrowEvent]
Element name	intermediateMessageCatchEvent
Documentation	An intermediateMessageCatchEvent can be adapted to another intermediateCatchEvent used in normal control-flow that consumes a trigger
Expression	//*[local-name() = 'definitions']//*[local-name() = 'intermediateCatchEvent' and (child::*[local-name() = 'messageEventDefinition'] or child::*[local-name() = 'eventDefinitionRef' and text() = //*[local-name() = 'messageEventDefinition']/@id]) and (count(child::*[contains(local-name(),'ventDefinition')]) = 1)]
Adaptions (4)	[intermediateSignalCatchEvent, receiveTask, intermediateMultipleCatchEvent, intermediateParallelMultipleCatchEvent]
Element name	intermediateMessageThrowEvent
Documentation	This event can be adapted to a sendTask or another intermediateThrowEvent used in normal control-flow that provides a signal
Expression	//*[local-name() = 'definitions']//*[local-name() = 'intermediateThrowEvent' and (child::*[local-name() = 'messageEventDefinition'] or child::*[local-name() = 'eventDefinitionRef' and text() = //*[local-name() = 'messageEventDefinition']/@id]) and (count(child::*[contains(local-name(),'ventDefinition')]) = 1)]
Adaptions (4)	[intermediateSignalThrowEvent, sendTask, intermediateMultipleThrowEvent, intermediateParallelMultipleThrowEvent]
Element name	intermediateMultipleCatchEvent
Documentation	An intermediateMultipleCatchEvent can be reduced to the available alternative catch events surrounded by gateways that allow for the selection of one among a set of branches

Continued on next page

289

Table C.1 – *Continued from previous page*

Expression	//*[local-name() = 'definitions']//*[local-name() = 'intermediateCatchEvent' and not(@parallelMultiple = 'true') and (count(child::*[contains(local-name(),'ventDefinition')]) > 1)]
Adaptions (3)	[intermediateCatchEventsAndExclusiveGateway, intermediateCatchEventsAndInclusiveGateway, intermediateCatchEventsAndComplexGateway]
Element name	intermediateMultipleParallelCatchEvent
Documentation	An intermediateMultipleParallelCatchEvent can be reduced to the available alternative catch events surrounded by a gateway that triggers multiple parallel branches
Expression	//*[local-name() = 'definitions']//*[local-name() = 'intermediateCatchEvent' and (@parallelMultiple = 'true') and (count(child::*[contains(local-name(),'ventDefinition')]) > 1)]
Adaptions (3)	[intermediateCatchEventsAndParallelGateway, intermediateCatchEventsAndInclusiveGateway, intermediateCatchEventsAndComplexGateway]
Element name	intermediateMultipleThrowEvent
Documentation	An intermediateMultipleThrowEvent can be reduced to the available alternative throw events surrounded by a gateways that allow for the selection of one branch
Expression	//*[local-name() = 'definitions']//*[local-name() = 'intermediateThrowEvent' and not(@parallelMultiple = 'true') and (count(child::*[contains(local-name(),'ventDefinition')]) > 1)]
Adaptions (3)	[intermediateThrowEventsAndExclusiveGateway, intermediateThrowEventsAndInclusiveGateway, intermediateThrowEventsAndComplexGateway]
Element name	intermediateNoneThrowEvent
Documentation	An intermediateNoneThrowEvent can be adapted to another intermediateThrowEvent that leads to normal control-flow continuation. Lacking a specific signal that can be caught, the event can also be ignored
Expression	//*[local-name() = 'definitions']//*[local-name() = 'intermediateThrowEvent' and not(child::*[contains(local-name(),'ventDefinition')])]
Adaptions (5)	[deleteEvent, intermediateMessageThrowEvent, intermediateSignalThrowEvent, intermediateMultipleThrowEvent, intermediateParallelMultipleThrowEvent]
Element name	intermediateSignalCatchEvent
Documentation	A intermediateSignalCatchEvent can be adapted to another intermediateCatchEvent that is used in normal control-flow and catches a trigger
Expression	//*[local-name() = 'definitions']//*[local-name() = 'intermediateThrowEvent' and (child::*[local-name() = 'catchEventDefinition'] or child::*[local-name() = 'eventDefinitionRef' and text() = //*[local-name() = 'catchEventDefinition']/@id]) and (count(child::*[contains(local-name(),'ventDefinition')]) = 1)]
Adaptions (4)	[intermediateMessageCatchEvent, intermediateConditionalCatchEvent, intermediateMultipleCatchEvent, intermediateParallelMultipleCatchEvent]
Element name	intermediateSignalThrowEvent

Continued on next page

Table C.1 – *Continued from previous page*

Documentation	A intermediateSignalThrowEvent can be adapted to another intermediate throw event that leads to normal control-flow continuation and fires a trigger
Expression	//*[local-name() = 'definitions']//*[local-name() = 'intermediateThrow-Event' and (child::*[local-name() = 'signalEventDefinition'] or child::*[local-name() = 'eventDefinitionRef' and text() = //*[local-name() = 'signalEventDefinition']/@id]) and (count(child::*[contains(local-name(),'ventDefinition')]) = 1)]
Adaptions (4)	[intermediateMessageThrowEvent, intermediateConditionalThrowEvent, intermediateMultipleThrowEvent, intermediateParallelMultipleThrowEvent]
Element name	intermediateTimerCatchEvent
Documentation	An intermediateTimerCatchEvent can be adapted to another intermediate catchEvent that has a trigger and leads to normal control-flow continuation, as it is possible to calculate the expiration of the time and trigger the event when it occurs
Expression	//*[local-name() = 'definitions']//*[local-name() = 'intermediate-CatchEvent' and (child::*[local-name() = 'timerEventDefinition'] or child::*[local-name() = 'eventDefinitionRef' and text() = //*[local-name() = 'timerEventDefinition']/@id]) and (count(child::*[contains(local-name(),'ventDefinition')]) = 1)]
Adaptions (5)	[intermediateConditionalCatchEvent, intermediateMessageCatchEvent, intermediateSignalCatchEvent, intermediateMultipleCatchEvent, intermediateParallelMultipleCatchEvent]
Element name	interruptingCancelBoundaryEvent
Documentation	An interruptingCancelBoundaryEvent cannot be adapted since its semantics with respect to transaction cancelation are unique
Expression	//*[local-name() = 'definitions']//*[local-name() = 'boundaryEvent' and @isInterrupting = 'true' and (child::*[local-name() = 'cancelEventDefinition'] or child::*[local-name() = 'eventDefinitionRef' and text() = //*[local-name() = 'cancelEventDefinition']/@id]) and (count(child::*[contains(local-name(),'ventDefinition')]) = 1)]
Adaptions (0)	[]
Element name	interruptingCompensationBoundaryEvent
Documentation	An interruptingCompensationBoundaryEvent cannot be adapted since its semantics with respect to compensation are unique
Expression	//*[local-name() = 'definitions']//*[local-name() = 'boundaryEvent' and @isInterrupting = 'true' and (child::*[local-name() = 'cancelEventDefinition'] or child::*[local-name() = 'eventDefinitionRef' and text() = //*[local-name() = 'cancelEventDefinition']/@id]) and (count(child::*[contains(local-name(),'ventDefinition')]) = 1)]
Adaptions (0)	[]
Element name	interruptingConditionalBoundaryEvent
Documentation	An interruptingConditionalBoundaryEvent can be adapted to another interrupting boundary event that represents normal control-flow continuation

Continued on next page

Table C.1 – *Continued from previous page*

Expression	//*[local-name() = 'definitions']//*[local-name() = 'boundaryEvent' and @isInterrupting = 'true' and (child::*[local-name() = 'conditionalEventDefinition'] or child::*[local-name() = 'eventDefinitionRef' and text() = //*[local-name() = 'conditionalEventDefinition']/@id]) and (count(child::*[contains(local-name(),'ventDefinition')]) = 1)]
Adaptions (4)	[interruptingSignalBoundaryEvent, interruptingMessageBoundaryEvent, interruptingMultipleBoundaryEvent, interruptingMultipleParallelBoundaryEvent]
Element name	interruptingConditionalStartEvent
Documentation	An interruptingConditionalStartEvent can be adapted to another interrupting start event that represents normal control-flow
Expression	//*[local-name() = 'definitions']//*[local-name() = 'subProcess' and @triggeredByEvent = 'true']/*[local-name() = 'startEvent' and @isInterrupting = 'true' and (child::*[local-name() = 'conditionalEventDefinition'] or child::*[local-name() = 'eventDefinitionRef' and text() = //*[local-name() = 'conditionalEventDefinition']/@id]) and (count(child::*[contains(local-name(),'ventDefinition')]) = 1)]
Adaptions (4)	[signalStartEvent, messageStartEvent, multipleStartEvent, multipleParallelStartEvent]
Element name	interruptingErrorBoundaryEvent
Documentation	An interruptingErrorBoundaryEvent can be adapted to another interrupting boundary event that leads to exceptional control-flow continuation
Expression	//*[local-name() = 'definitions']//*[local-name() = 'boundaryEvent' and @isInterrupting = 'true' and (child::*[local-name() = 'errorEventDefinition'] or child::*[local-name() = 'eventDefinitionRef' and text() = //*[local-name() = 'errorEventDefinition']/@id]) and (count(child::*[contains(local-name(),'ventDefinition')]) = 1)]
Adaptions (3)	[interruptingEscalationBoundaryEvent, interruptingMultipleBoundaryEvent, interruptingMultipleParallelBoundaryEvent]
Element name	interruptingErrorStartEvent
Documentation	An interruptingErrorStartEvent can be adapted to another interrupting start event that leads to exceptional control-flow continuation
Expression	//*[local-name() = 'definitions']//*[local-name() = 'subProcess' and @triggeredByEvent = 'true']/*[local-name() = 'startEvent' and @isInterrupting = 'true' and (child::*[local-name() = 'errorEventDefinition'] or child::*[local-name() = 'eventDefinitionRef' and text() = //*[local-name() = 'errorEventDefinition']/@id]) and (count(child::*[contains(local-name(),'ventDefinition')]) = 1)]
Adaptions (3)	[escalationStartEvent, multipleStartEvent, multipleParallelStartEvent]
Element name	interruptingEscalationBoundaryEvent
Documentation	An interruptingEscalationBoundaryEvent can be adapted to another interrupting boundary event that leads to exceptional control-flow continuation
Expression	//*[local-name() = 'definitions']//*[local-name() = 'boundaryEvent' and @isInterrupting = 'true' and (child::*[local-name() = 'escalationEventDefinition'] or child::*[local-name() = 'eventDefinitionRef' and text() = //*[local-name() = 'escalationEventDefinition']/@id]) and (count(child::*[contains(local-name(),'ventDefinition')]) = 1)]

Continued on next page

Table C.1 – *Continued from previous page*

Adaptions (3)	[interruptingErrorBoundaryEvent, interruptingMultipleBoundaryEvent, interruptingMultipleParallelBoundaryEvent]
Element name	interruptingEscalationStartEvent
Documentation	An interruptingEscalationStartEvent can be adapted to another interrupting start event that leads to exceptional control-flow continuation
Expression	//*[local-name() = 'definitions']//*[local-name() = 'subProcess' and @triggeredByEvent = 'true']/*[local-name() = 'startEvent' and @isInterrupting = 'true' and (child::*[local-name() = 'escalationEventDefinition'] or child::*[local-name() = 'eventDefinitionRef' and text() = //*[local-name() = 'escalationEventDefinition']/@id]) and (count(child::*[contains(local-name(),'ventDefinition')]) = 1)]
Adaptions (3)	[errorStartEvent, multipleStartEvent, multipleParallelStartEvent]
Element name	interruptingMessageBoundaryEvent
Documentation	An interruptingMessageBoundaryEvent can be adapted to another interrupting boundary event that fires a signal and leads to normal control-flow continuation
Expression	//*[local-name() = 'definitions']//*[local-name() = 'boundaryEvent' and @isInterrupting = 'true' and (child::*[local-name() = 'messageEventDefinition'] or child::*[local-name() = 'eventDefinitionRef' and text() = //*[local-name() = 'messageEventDefinition']/@id]) and (count(child::*[contains(local-name(),'ventDefinition')]) = 1)]
Adaptions (4)	[interruptingSignalBoundaryEvent, interruptingConditionalBoundaryEvent, interruptingMultipleBoundaryEvent, interruptingMultipleParallelBoundaryEvent]
Element name	interruptingMessageStartEvent
Documentation	An interruptingMessageStart event can be adapted to another interrupting start event that leads to normal control-flow continuation
Expression	//*[local-name() = 'definitions']//*[local-name() = 'subProcess' and @triggeredByEvent = 'true']/*[local-name() = 'startEvent' and @isInterrupting = 'true' and (child::*[local-name() = 'messageEventDefinition'] or child::*[local-name() = 'eventDefinitionRef' and text() = //*[local-name() = 'messageEventDefinition']/@id]) and (count(child::*[contains(local-name(),'ventDefinition')]) = 1)]
Adaptions (4)	[signalStartEvent, conditionalStartEvent, multipleStartEvent, multipleParallelStartEvent]
Element name	interruptingMultipleBoundaryEvent
Documentation	An interruptingMultipleBoundaryEvent can be adapted by multiple interrupting boundary events that link to a merging gateway
Expression	//*[local-name() = 'definitions']//*[local-name() = 'boundaryEvent' and (@isInterrupting = 'true') and not(@parallelMultiple = 'true') and (count(child::*[contains(local-name(),'ventDefinition')]) > 1)]
Adaptions (3)	[multipleInterruptingBoundaryEventsFollowedByExclusiveGateway, multipleInterruptingBoundaryEventsFollowedByInclusiveGateway, multipleInterruptingBoundaryEventsFollowedByComplexGateway]
Element name	interruptingMultipleStartEvent

Continued on next page

C. Adaptability Scores

Table C.1 – *Continued from previous page*

Documentation	An interruptingMultipleStartEvent can be adapted to multiple different eventSubProcesses with one start event each
Expression	//*[local-name() = 'definitions']//*[local-name() = 'subProcess' and @triggeredByEvent = 'true']/*[local-name() = 'startEvent' and (@isInterrupting = 'true') and not(@parallelMultiple = 'true') and (count(child::*[contains(local-name(),'ventDefinition')]) > 1)]
Adaptions (1)	[multipleEventSubProcessesWithSingleStartEvents]
Element name	interruptingParallelMultipleBoundaryEvent
Documentation	A multipleParallelBoundaryEvent cannot be adapted since there is no other way to ensure that multiple events are thrown in parallel in the context of a single activity
Expression	//*[local-name() = 'definitions']//*[local-name() = 'boundaryEvent' and (@isInterrupting = 'true') and (@parallelMultiple = 'true') and (count(child::*[contains(local-name(),'ventDefinition')]) > 1)]
Adaptions (0)	[]
Element name	interruptingParallelMultipleStartEvent
Documentation	A multipleParallelStartEvent cannot be adapted since there is no other way to avoid the instantiation of a process unless multiple conditions are satisfied
Expression	//*[local-name() = 'definitions']//*[local-name() = 'subProcess' and @triggeredByEvent = 'true']/*[local-name() = 'startEvent' and (@isInterrupting = 'true') and (@parallelMultiple = 'true') and (count(child::*[contains(local-name(),'ventDefinition')]) > 1)]
Adaptions (0)	[]
Element name	interruptingSignalBoundaryEvent
Documentation	An interrupting signal boundary event can be adapted to another interrupting boundary event that represents normal control-flow continuation
Expression	//*[local-name() = 'definitions']//*[local-name() = 'boundaryEvent' and @isInterrupting = 'true' and (child::*[local-name() = 'signalEventDefinition'] or child::*[local-name() = 'eventDefinitionRef' and text() = //*[local-name() = 'signalEventDefinition']/@id]) and (count(child::*[contains(local-name(),'ventDefinition')]) = 1)]
Adaptions (4)	[interruptingMessageBoundaryEvent, interruptingConditionalBoundaryEvent, interruptingMultipleBoundaryEvent, interruptingMultipleParallelBoundaryEvent]
Element name	interruptingSignalStartEvent
Documentation	An interruptingSignalStartEvent can be adapted to another interrupting start event that represents normal process instantiation
Expression	//*[local-name() = 'definitions']//*[local-name() = 'subProcess' and @triggeredByEvent = 'true']/*[local-name() = 'startEvent' and @isInterrupting = 'true' and (child::*[local-name() = 'signalEventDefinition'] or child::*[local-name() = 'eventDefinitionRef' and text() = //*[local-name() = 'signalEventDefinition']/@id]) and (count(child::*[contains(local-name(),'ventDefinition')]) = 1)]
Adaptions (4)	[messageStartEvent, conditionalStartEvent, multipleStartEvent, multipleParallelStartEvent]

Continued on next page

Table C.1 – *Continued from previous page*

Element name	interruptingTimerBoundaryEvent
Documentation	An interruptingTimerBoundaryEvent can be adapted to another interruptingBoundaryEvent that leads to normal control-flow continuation and fires a trigger, as it is possible to calculate the expiration of the temporal condition and trigger the event when it occurs
Expression	//*[local-name() = 'definitions']//*[local-name() = 'boundaryEvent' and @isInterrupting = 'true' and (child::*[local-name() = 'timerEventDefinition'] or child::*[local-name() = 'eventDefinitionRef' and text() = //*[local-name() = 'timerEventDefinition']/@id]) and (count(child::*[contains(local-name(),'ventDefinition')]) = 1)]
Adaptions (6)	[interruptingSignalBoundaryEvent, interruptingConditionalBoundaryEvent, interruptingMessageBoundaryEvent, interruptingSignalBoundaryEvent, interruptingMultipleBoundaryEvent, interruptingParallelMultipleBoundaryEvent]

Element name	interruptingTimerStartEvent
Documentation	An interruptingTimerStartEvent can be adapted to another startEvent that leads to normal control-flow continuation and requires a trigger, as it is possible to calculate the expiration of the temporal condition and trigger the event when it occurs
Expression	//*[local-name() = 'definitions']//*[local-name() = 'subProcess' and @triggeredByEvent = 'true']/*[local-name() = 'startEvent' and @isInterrupting = 'true' and (child::*[local-name() = 'timerEventDefinition'] or child::*[local-name() = 'eventDefinitionRef' and text() = //*[local-name() = 'timerEventDefinition']/@id]) and (count(child::*[contains(local-name(),'ventDefinition')]) = 1)]
Adaptions (5)	[messageStartEvent, signalStartEvent, conditionalStartEvent, multipleStartEvent, multipleParallelStartEvent]

Element name	linkCatchEvent
Documentation	Link events are only relevant to visualization and therefore not relevant for adaptation
Expression	//*[local-name() = 'definitions']//*[local-name() = 'intermediateCatchEventEvent' and (child::*[local-name() = 'linkEventDefinition'] or child::*[local-name() = 'eventDefinitionRef' and text() = //*[local-name() = 'linkEventDefinition']/@id]) and (count(child::*[contains(local-name(),'ventDefinition')]) = 1)]
Adaptions (0)	[]

Element name	linkThrowEvent
Documentation	Link events are only relevant to visualization and therefore not relevant for adaptation
Expression	//*[local-name() = 'definitions']//*[local-name() = 'intermediateThrowEventEvent' and (child::*[local-name() = 'linkEventDefinition'] or child::*[local-name() = 'eventDefinitionRef' and text() = //*[local-name() = 'linkEventDefinition']/@id]) and (count(child::*[contains(local-name(),'ventDefinition')]) = 1)]
Adaptions (0)	[]

Element name	loopSubProcess

Continued on next page

Table C.1 – *Continued from previous page*

Documentation	Looping subProcesses can be embedded in code and surrounded by ordinary looping mechanisms or adapted to different types of subProcesses.
Expression	//*[local-name() = 'definitions']//*[(local-name() = 'subProcess') and (child::*[local-name() = 'standardLoopCharacteristics'])]
Adaptions (5)	[embeddedfragmentWithExclusiveGateways, embeddedfragmentWithInclusiveGateways, embeddedfragmentWithComplexGateways, eventSubProcessAndLoopThatTriggersEvents, adHocSubprocess]
Element name	loopTask
Documentation	A loopTask can be adapted by loop or ad hoc subProcesses or by a combination of the task with different gateway types
Expression	//*[local-name() = 'definitions']//*[(local-name() = 'receiveTask' or local-name() = 'serviceTask' or local-name() = 'manualTask' or local-name() = 'businessRuleTask' or local-name() = 'userTask' or local-name() = 'sendTask'or local-name() = 'scriptTask' or local-name() = 'globalUserTask' or local-name() = 'globalManualTask' or local-name() = ' globalScriptTask' or local-name() = 'globalBusinessRuleTask') and (child::*[local-name() = 'standardLoopCharacteristics'])]
Adaptions (6)	[exclusiveGatewaysAndSequenceFlows, inclusiveGatewaysAndSequenceFlows, complexGatewaysAndSequenceFlows, loopSubProcess, adHocSubProcess, eventSubProcess]
Element name	manualTask
Documentation	There is no alternative and generally applicable way to represent an arbitrary external action
Expression	//*[local-name() = 'definitions']//*[local-name() = 'manualTask']
Adaptions (1)	[globalManualTask]
Element name	messageEndEvent
Documentation	A messageEndEvent can be adapted to another type of endEvent that refers to ordered termination and produces a trigger
Expression	//*[local-name() = 'definitions']//*[local-name() = 'endEvent' and (child::*[local-name() = 'messageEventDefinition'] or child::*[local-name() = 'eventDefinitionRef' and text() = //*[local-name() = 'messageEventDefinition']/@id]) and (count(child::*[contains(local-name(),'ventDefinition')]) = 1)]
Adaptions (2)	[signalEndEvent, multipleEndEvent]
Element name	messageStartEvent
Documentation	A messageStartEvent can be adapted to another startEvent that represents ordered process instantiation and is triggered in some fashion.
Expression	//*[local-name() = 'definitions']//*[local-name() = 'startEvent' and (child::*[local-name() = 'messageEventDefinition'] or child::*[local-name() = 'eventDefinitionRef' and text() = //*[local-name() = 'messageEventDefinition']/@id]) and (count(child::*[contains(local-name(),'ventDefinition')]) = 1)]
Adaptions (4)	[conditionalStartEvent, signalStartEvent, multipleStartEvent, parallelMultipleStartEvent]
Element name	multipleEndEvent

Continued on next page

Table C.1 – *Continued from previous page*

Documentation	A multipleEndEvent can be adapted to multiple alternative events followed by a noneEndEvent
Expression	//*[local-name() = 'definitions']//*[local-name() = 'endEvent' and not(@parallelMultiple = 'true') and (count(child::*[contains(local-name(),'ventDefinition')]) > 1)]
Adaptions (1)	[multipleIntermediateEventsFollowedbyNoneEndEvent]
Element name	multipleParallelStartEvent
Documentation	A multipleParallelStartEvent cannot be adapted since there is no other way to avoid the instantiation of a process unless multiple conditions are satisfied
Expression	//*[local-name() = 'definitions']//*[local-name() = 'startEvent' and @parallelMultiple = 'true' and (count(child::*[contains(local-name(),'ventDefinition')]) > 1)]
Adaptions (0)	[]
Element name	multipleStartEvent
Documentation	A multipleStartEvent can be reduced to one of the available alternative start events
Expression	//*[local-name() = 'definitions']//*[local-name() = 'startEvent' and not(@parallelMultiple = 'true') and (count(child::*[contains(local-name(),'ventDefinition')]) > 1)]
Adaptions (3)	[multipleStartEventsWithExclusiveGateway, multipleStartEventsWithInclusiveGateway, multipleStartEventsWithComplexGateway]
Element name	noneEndEvent
Documentation	A noneEndEvent can be adapted to any other endEvent that represents ordered termination
Expression	//*[local-name() = 'definitions']//*[local-name() = 'endEvent' and not(child::*[contains(local-name(),'ventDefinition')])]
Adaptions (3)	[messageEndEvent, signalEndEvent, multipleEndEvent]
Element name	noneStartEvent
Documentation	A noneStartEvent can be adapted to another start event that represents normal process instantiation
Expression	//*[local-name() = 'definitions']/*[local-name() = 'process']/*[local-name() = 'startEvent' and not(/*[contains(local-name(),'ventDefinition')])]
Adaptions (5)	[messageStartEvent, conditionalStartEvent, signalStartEvent, multipleStartEvent, parallelMultipleStartEvent]
Element name	nonInterruptingConditionalBoundaryEvent
Documentation	A nonInterruptingConditionalBoundaryEvent can be adapted to another non-interrupting boundary event that leads to normal control-flow continuation
Expression	//*[local-name() = 'definitions']//*[local-name() = 'boundaryEvent' and not(@isInterrupting = 'true') and (child::*[local-name() = 'conditionalEventDefinition'] or child::*[local-name() = 'eventDefinitionRef' and text() = //*[local-name() = 'conditionalEventDefinition']/@id]) and (count(child::*[contains(local-name(),'ventDefinition')]) = 1)]

Continued on next page

Table C.1 – *Continued from previous page*

Adaptions (4)	[nonInterruptingSignalBoundaryEvent, nonInterruptingMessageBoundaryEvent, nonInterruptingMultipleBoundaryEvent, nonInterruptingMultipleParallelBoundaryEvent]
Element name	nonInterruptingConditionalStartEvent
Documentation	A nonInterruptingConditionalStartEvent can be adapted to another non-interrupting start event that represents normal control-flow continuation
Expression	//*[local-name() = 'definitions']//*[local-name() = 'subProcess' and @triggeredByEvent = 'true']/*[local-name() = 'startEvent' and not(@isInterrupting = 'true') and (child::*[local-name() = 'conditionalEventDefinition'] or child::*[local-name() = 'eventDefinitionRef' and text() = //*[local-name() = 'conditionalEventDefinition']/@id]) and (count(child::*[contains(local-name(),'ventDefinition')]) = 1)]
Adaptions (4)	[signalStartEvent, messageStartEvent, multipleStartEvent, multipleParallelStartEvent]
Element name	nonInterruptingEscalationBoundaryEvent
Documentation	A nonInterruptingEscalationBoundaryEvent cannot be adapted since there is no other non-interrupting boundary event that leads to exceptional control-flow continuation. Error events are only interrupting
Expression	//*[local-name() = 'definitions']//*[local-name() = 'boundaryEvent' and not(@isInterrupting = 'true') and (child::*[local-name() = 'escalationEventDefinition'] or child::*[local-name() = 'eventDefinitionRef' and text() = //*[local-name() = 'escalationEventDefinition']/@id]) and (count(child::*[contains(local-name(),'ventDefinition')]) = 1)]
Adaptions (0)	[]
Element name	nonInterruptingEscalationStartEvent
Documentation	A nonInterruptingEscalationStartEvent cannot be adapted since there is no other non-interrupting start event that represents exceptional control-flow continuation
Expression	//*[local-name() = 'definitions']//*[local-name() = 'subProcess' and @triggeredByEvent = 'true']/*[local-name() = 'startEvent' and not(@isInterrupting = 'true') and (child::*[local-name() = 'escalationEventDefinition'] or child::*[local-name() = 'eventDefinitionRef' and text() = //*[local-name() = 'escalationEventDefinition']/@id]) and (count(child::*[contains(local-name(),'ventDefinition')]) = 1)]
Adaptions (0)	[]
Element name	nonInterruptingMessageBoundaryEvent
Documentation	A nonInterruptingMessageBoundaryEvent can be adapted to another non-interrupting boundary event that transmits a signal and represents normal control-flow continuation
Expression	//*[local-name() = 'definitions']//*[local-name() = 'boundaryEvent' and not(@isInterrupting = 'true') and (child::*[local-name() = 'messageEventDefinition'] or child::*[local-name() = 'eventDefinitionRef' and text() = //*[local-name() = 'messageEventDefinition']/@id]) and (count(child::*[contains(local-name(),'ventDefinition')]) = 1)]
Adaptions (4)	[nonInterruptingSignalBoundaryEvent, nonInterruptingConditionalBoundaryEvent, nonInterruptingMultipleBoundaryEvent, nonInterruptingMultipleParallelBoundaryEvent]

Continued on next page

Table C.1 – *Continued from previous page*

Element name	nonInterruptingMessageStartEvent
Documentation	A nonInterruptingMessageStartEvent can be adapted to another non-interrupting start event that leads to normal control-flow continuation
Expression	//*[local-name() = 'definitions']//*[local-name() = 'subProcess' and @triggeredByEvent = 'true']/*[local-name() = 'startEvent' and not(@isInterrupting = 'true') and (child::*[local-name() = 'messageEventDefinition'] or child::*[local-name() = 'eventDefinitionRef' and text() = //*[local-name() = 'messageEventDefinition']/@id]) and (count(child::*[contains(local-name(),'ventDefinition')]) = 1)]
Adaptions (4)	[signalStartEvent, conditionalStartEvent, multipleStartEvent, multipleParallelStartEvent]

Element name	nonInterruptingMultipleBoundaryEvent
Documentation	A nonInterruptingMultipleBoundaryEvent can be adapted by multiple non-interrupting boundary events that link to a merging gateway
Expression	//*[local-name() = 'definitions']//*[local-name() = 'boundaryEvent' and not (@isInterrupting = 'true') and not(@parallelMultiple = 'true') and (count(child::*[contains(local-name(),'ventDefinition')]) > 1)]
Adaptions (3)	[multipleNonInterruptingBoundaryEventsFollowedByExclusiveGateway, multipleNonInterruptingBoundaryEventsFollowedByInclusiveGateway, multipleNonInterruptingBoundaryEventsFollowedByComplexGateway]

Element name	nonInterruptingMultipleStartEvent
Documentation	A nonInterruptingMultipleStartEvent can be adapted to multiple different eventSubProcesses with one startEvent each
Expression	//*[local-name() = 'definitions']//*[local-name() = 'subProcess' and @triggeredByEvent = 'true']/*[local-name() = 'startEvent' and not (@isInterrupting = 'true') and not(@parallelMultiple = 'true') and (count(child::*[contains(local-name(),'ventDefinition')]) > 1)]
Adaptions (1)	[multipleEventSubProcessesWithSingleStartEvents]

Element name	nonInterruptingParallelMultipleBoundaryEvent
Documentation	A multipleParallelBoundaryEvent cannot be adapted since there is no other way to ensure that multiple events are thrown in parallel in the context of a single activity
Expression	//*[local-name() = 'definitions']//*[local-name() = 'boundaryEvent' and not (@isInterrupting = 'true') and (@parallelMultiple = 'true') and (count(child::*[contains(local-name(),'ventDefinition')]) > 1)]
Adaptions (0)	[]

Element name	nonInterruptingParallelMultipleStartEvent
Documentation	A multipleParallelStartEvent cannot be adapted since there is no other way to avoid the instantiation of a process unless multiple conditions are satisfied
Expression	//*[local-name() = 'definitions']//*[local-name() = 'subProcess' and @triggeredByEvent = 'true']/*[local-name() = 'startEvent' and not (@isInterrupting = 'true') and (@parallelMultiple = 'true') and (count(child::*[contains(local-name(),'ventDefinition')]) > 1)]
Adaptions (0)	[]

Continued on next page

C. Adaptability Scores

Table C.1 – *Continued from previous page*

Element name	nonInterruptingSignalBoundaryEvent
Documentation	A nonInterruptingSignalBoundaryEvent can be adapted to another non-interrupting boundary event that leads to normal control-flow continuation
Expression	//*[local-name() = 'definitions']//*[local-name() = 'boundaryEvent' and not(@isInterrupting = 'true') and (child::*[local-name() = 'signalEventDefinition'] or child::*[local-name() = 'eventDefinitionRef' and text() = //*[local-name() = 'signalEventDefinition']/@id]) and (count(child::*[contains(local-name(),'ventDefinition')]) = 1)]
Adaptions (4)	[nonInterruptingMessageBoundaryEvent, nonInterruptingConditionalBoundaryEvent, nonInterruptingMultipleBoundaryEvent, nonInterruptingMultipleParallelBoundaryEvent]
Element name	nonInterruptingSignalStartEvent
Documentation	A nonInterruptingSignalStartEvent can be adapted to another non-interrupting start event that represents normal process instantiation
Expression	//*[local-name() = 'definitions']//*[local-name() = 'subProcess' and @triggeredByEvent = 'true']/*[local-name() = 'startEvent' and not(@isInterrupting = 'true') and (child::*[local-name() = 'signalEventDefinition'] or child::*[local-name() = 'eventDefinitionRef' and text() = //*[local-name() = 'signalEventDefinition']/@id]) and (count(child::*[contains(local-name(),'ventDefinition')]) = 1)]
Adaptions (4)	[messageStartEvent, conditionalStartEvent, multipleStartEvent, multipleParallelStartEvent]
Element name	nonInterruptingTimerBoundaryEvent
Documentation	A nonInterruptingTimerBoundaryEvent can be adapted to another non-interrupting boundary event that represents normal control-flow continuation and is fired by a trigger, as it is possible to calculate the expiration of the temporal condition and trigger the event when it occurs
Expression	//*[local-name() = 'definitions']//*[local-name() = 'boundaryEvent' and not(@isInterrupting = 'true') and (child::*[local-name() = 'timerEventDefinition'] or child::*[local-name() = 'eventDefinitionRef' and text() = //*[local-name() = 'timerEventDefinition']/@id]) and (count(child::*[contains(local-name(),'ventDefinition')]) = 1)]
Adaptions (5)	[noninterruptingSignalBoundaryEvent, noninterruptingConditionalBoundaryEvent, noninterruptingMessageBoundaryEvent, noninterruptingMultipleBoundaryEvent, noninterruptingParallelMultipleBoundaryEvent]
Element name	nonInterruptingTimerStartEvent
Documentation	A nonInterruptingTimerStartEvent can be adapted to another startEvent that represents normal control-flow and is fired through a trigger, as it is possible to calculate the expiration of the temporal condition and fire the trigger the event when it occurs
Expression	//*[local-name() = 'definitions']//*[local-name() = 'subProcess' and @triggeredByEvent = 'true']/*[local-name() = 'startEvent' and not(@isInterrupting = 'true') and (child::*[local-name() = 'timerEventDefinition'] or child::*[local-name() = 'eventDefinitionRef' and text() = //*[local-name() = 'timerEventDefinition']/@id]) and (count(child::*[contains(local-name(),'ventDefinition')]) = 1)]
Adaptions (5)	[signalStartEvent, conditionalStartEvent, messageStartEvent, multipleStartEvent, parallelMultipleStartEvent]

Continued on next page

Table C.1 – *Continued from previous page*

Element name	parallelEventBasedGateway
Documentation	A parallel eventBasedGateway can be adapted to a solution where the events are processed through catch events before a gateway that merges parallel branches
Expression	//*[local-name() = 'definitions']//*[local-name() = 'eventBasedGateway' and (@eventGatewayType = 'parallel') and not (@instantiate = 'true')]
Adaptions (2)	[inclusiveGateway, complexGateway]

Element name	parallelGateway
Documentation	A parallelGateway can be replaced by other gateways that allow for parallelism, given the conditions of these gateways are set to trigger all branches
Expression	//*[local-name() = 'definitions']//*[local-name() = 'parallelGateway']
Adaptions (2)	[inclusiveGateway, complexGateway]

Element name	parallelMultiInstanceSubProcess
Documentation	ParallelMultiInstanceSubProcesses can be embedded in the parent process and surrounded by a complexGateway to trigger the same branch multiple times or they can be adapted to an adHocSubProcess
Expression	//*[local-name() = 'definitions']//*[(local-name() = 'subProcess') and (child::*[local-name() = 'multiInstanceLoopCharacteristics' and @isSequential='false'])]
Adaptions (2)	[embeddedfragmentWithComplexGateways, adHocSubprocess]

Element name	parallelMultiInstanceTask
Documentation	A parallelMultiInstanceTask can be be adapted to a subProcess that allows for the execution of multiple instances in parallel
Expression	//*[local-name() = 'definitions']//*[(local-name() = 'receiveTask' or local-name() = 'serviceTask' or local-name() = 'manualTask' or local-name() = 'businessRuleTask' or local-name() = 'userTask' or local-name() = 'sendTask' or local-name() = 'scriptTask' or local-name() = 'globalUserTask' or local-name() = 'globalManualTask' or local-name() = ' globalScriptTask' or local-name() = 'globalBusinessRuleTask') and (child::*[local-name() = 'multiInstanceLoopCharacteristics' and @isSequential='false'])]
Adaptions (2)	[multiInstanceSubProcess, adHocSubProcess]

Element name	receiveTask
Documentation	A receiveTask can be adapted to another task that can be used to wait for a message (programmatically or manually)
Expression	//*[local-name() = 'definitions']//*[local-name() = 'receiveTask']
Adaptions (7)	[serviceTask, userTask, scriptTask, globalScriptTask, globalUserTask, intermediateMessageCatchEvent, eventSubprocessWithMessageStartEvent]

Element name	scriptTask
Documentation	A scriptTask can be adapted by another task that triggers (programmatically or manually) the execution of a script. A receiveTask is not suitable, as it is passively waits without performing an action and a businessRuleTask is too specific
Expression	//*[local-name() = 'definitions']//*[local-name() = 'scriptTask']
Adaptions (5)	[serviceTask, sendATask, userTask, globalUserTask, globalScriptTask]

Continued on next page

Table C.1 – *Continued from previous page*

Element name	sendTask
Documentation	A sendTask can be adapted to another task that, programmatically or manually, triggers the sending of a message. A receiveTask is not suitable as it passively waits without performing an action and a businessRuleTask is too specific. Also intermediate message throw events can serve as alternative
Expression	//*[local-name() = 'definitions']//*[local-name() = 'sendTask']
Adaptions (6)	[serviceTask, scriptTask, userTask, globalScriptTask, globalUserTask, intermediateMessageThrowEvent]
Element name	sequenceFlow
Documentation	A sequenceFlow is a basic language element that cannot be adapted
Expression	//*[local-name() = 'definitions']//*[local-name() = 'sequenceFlow']
Adaptions (0)	[]
Element name	sequentialMultiInstanceSubProcess
Documentation	SequentialMultiInstanceSubProcesses can be embedded into the parent processes and be surrounded by ordinary looping mechanisms or adapted to different types of subprocesses
Expression	//*[local-name() = 'definitions']//*[(local-name() = 'subProcess') and (child::*[local-name() = 'multiInstanceLoopCharacteristics' and @isSequential='true'])]
Adaptions (5)	[embeddedfragmentWithExclusiveGateways, embeddedfragmentWithComplexGateways, eventSubProcessAndLoopThatTriggersEvents, adHocSubprocess, loopSubProcess]
Element name	sequentialMultiInstanceTask
Documentation	A sequentialMultiInstanceTask can be adapted to an ordinary sequential loop or a different represenation thereof, as well as to different subProcesses.
Expression	//*[local-name() = 'definitions']//*[(local-name() = 'receiveTask' or local-name() = 'serviceTask' or local-name() = 'manualTask' or local-name() = 'businessRuleTask' or local-name() = 'userTask' or local-name() = 'sendTask' or local-name() = 'scriptTask' or local-name() = 'globalUserTask' or local-name() = 'globalManualTask' or local-name() = ' globalScriptTask' or local-name() = 'globalBusinessRuleTask') and (child::*[local-name() = 'multiInstanceLoopCharacteristics' and @isSequential='true'])]
Adaptions (6)	[exclusiveGatewaysAndSequenceFlows, complexGatewaysAndSequenceFlows, loopTask, loopSubProcess, multiInstanceSubProcess, adHocSubProcess]
Element name	serviceTask
Documentation	the adaptions of a serviceTask can be used to programatically or manually trigger service execution, possibly combined with a receive task in case of synchronous communication. A receiveTask alone is not suitable as it is passively waits without performing an action and a businessRuleTask is too specific. Also intermediate throwing and catching message events can be used.
Expression	//*[local-name() = 'definitions']//*[local-name() = 'serviceTask']
Adaptions (6)	[scriptTask, userTask, sendTask, globalScriptTask, globalUserTask, intermediateMessageThrowAndCatchEvents]

Continued on next page

Table C.1 – *Continued from previous page*

Element name	signalEndEvent
Documentation	A signalEndEvent can be adapted to another type of endEvent that represents ordered termination and produces a trigger
Expression	//*[local-name() = 'definitions']//*[local-name() = 'endEvent' and (child::*[local-name() = 'signalEventDefinition'] or child::*[local-name() = 'eventDefinitionRef' and text() = //*[local-name() = 'signalEventDefinition']/@id]) and (count(child::*[contains(local-name(),'ventDefinition')]) = 1)]
Adaptions (2)	[messageEndEvent, multipleEndEvent]

Element name	signalStartEvent
Documentation	A signalStartEvent can be adapted to another startEvent that represents normal process instantiation and provides a trigger
Expression	//*[local-name() = 'definitions']//*[local-name() = 'startEvent' and (child::*[local-name() = 'signalEventDefinition'] or child::*[local-name() = 'eventDefinitionRef' and text() = //*[local-name() = 'signalEventDefinition']/@id]) and (count(child::*[contains(local-name(),'ventDefinition')]) = 1)]
Adaptions (4)	[messageStartEvent, conditionalStartEvent, multipleStartEvent, parallelMultipleStartEvent]

Element name	subProcess
Documentation	An ordinary subProcess can be embedded into the process or replaced by a more specific type of subProcess
Expression	//*[local-name() = 'definitions']//*[local-name() = 'subProcess' and not (@triggeredByEvent = 'true' or child::*[local-name() = 'multiInstanceLoopCharacteristics'] or child::*[local-name() = 'standardLoopCharacteristics'])]
Adaptions (4)	[embeddIntoProcess, transactionSubProcess, eventSubProcess, adHocSubProcess]

Element name	subProcessStartEvent
Documentation	A startEvent of an ordinary subProcess cannot be adapted since it is the only way of starting non-eventSubProcesses
Expression	//*[local-name() = 'definitions']//*[local-name() = 'subProcess' and not(@triggeredByEvent = 'true')]/*[local-name() = 'startEvent']
Adaptions (0)	[]

Element name	task
Documentation	A plain task is a kind of wildcard element for an unspecified task and irrelevant to process execution
Expression	//*[local-name() = 'definitions']//*[local-name() = 'task' or local-name() = 'globalTask']
Adaptions (0)	[]

Element name	terminateEndEvent
Documentation	Since there is no alternative endEvent that results in immediate termination without compensation or event handling, this event cannot be adapted

Continued on next page

C. Adaptability Scores

Table C.1 – *Continued from previous page*

Expression	//*[local-name() = 'definitions']//*[local-name() = 'endEvent' and (child::*[local-name() = 'terminateEventDefinition'] or child::*[local-name() = 'eventDefinitionRef' and text() = //*[local-name() = 'terminateEventDefinition']/@id]) and (count(child::*[contains(local-name(),'ventDefinition')]) = 1)]
Adaptions (0)	[]
Element name	timerStartEvent
Documentation	A timerStartEvent can be adapted to another startEvent that represents normal flow and is triggered in some fashion, as it is possible to calculate the expiration of the time and trigger the event when it does
Expression	//*[local-name() = 'definitions']//*[local-name() = 'startEvent' and (child::*[local-name() = 'timerEventDefinition'] or child::*[local-name() = 'eventDefinitionRef' and text() = //*[local-name() = 'timerEventDefinition']/@id]) and (count(child::*[contains(local-name(),'ventDefinition')]) = 1)]
Adaptions (5)	[conditionalStartEvent, messageStartEvent, signalStartEvent, multipleStartEvent, parallelMultipleStartEvent]
Element name	transactionSubProcess
Documentation	A transactional context cannot be emulated with any other element in BPMN
Expression	//*[local-name() = 'definitions']//*[local-name() = 'transaction']
Adaptions (0)	[]
Element name	userTask
Documentation	A userTask can be adapted through another task that is programmed to ask for user input
Expression	//*[local-name() = 'definitions']//*[local-name() = 'userTask']
Adaptions (5)	[scriptTask, serviceTask, sendAndReceiveTask, globalScriptTask, globalUserTask]